SPALDING GRAY'S AMERICA

Spalding Gray's America

William W. Demastes

An Imprint of Hal Leonard Corporation
New York

Published in 2008 by Limelight Editions
An Imprint of Hal Leonard Corporation
7777 West Bluemound Road
Milwaukee, WI 53213

Trade Book Division Editorial Offices
19 West 21st Street, New York, NY 10010

Printed in the United States of America

Book design by Mark Lerner

Text credits can be found on pages 271–272, which constitute an extension of this copyright page.

Library of Congress Cataloging-in-Publication Data
Demastes, William W.
  Spalding Gray's America / William W. Demastes.
     p. cm.
  Includes bibliographical references and index.
  ISBN 978-0-87910-360-6
  1. Gray, Spalding, 1941-2004. 2. Dramatists, American—20th century.
  3. Storytelling in literature. 4. American drama—20th century—History and criticism. I. Title.
  PS3557.R333Z64 2008
  812'.54—dc22

                              2008039960

ISBN 978-0-87910-360-6

www.limelighteditions.com

Find your bliss.
—Joseph Campbell

Contents

Foreword

Spalding

1

January 1970, the Performing Garage, SoHo, New York City. The Performance Group (TPG), under my direction, is showing *Makbeth*, a version of Shakespeare's Scottish play. On Sunday after the last performance of the week, the actor playing Malcolm tells me he is quitting to play Mr. Peanut on a national promotional tour. Feeling betrayed, I decide that *Makbeth* will not miss a beat. Rifling through glossy photos and resumes, I come on a face with extraordinarily wide-set eyes staring at me with a look between astonishment and innocence.

Spalding Gray.

A strange name, Spalding. A tennis ball. I phone him. "Can you come in tomorrow morning?" "Yes." After an audition in the unheated Performing Garage (we ran the space heater only just before performances), I offer Spalding the role on the condition that he will be ready to go by Thursday. We begin rehearsing Monday night. By Thursday, *Makbeth* goes on without a hitch. No matter that the play was a box office flop, or that the Group was torn by infighting and would deconstruct in a few weeks. I had my revenge against Mr. Peanut. And Spalding Gray began his fifteen-year run with The

Performance Group/Wooster Group. Spalding alludes to his experience in *Makbeth* in his *A Personal History of the American Theatre*.

Spalding didn't come unattached. In 1970, he was living with Elizabeth LeCompte, who, with her sister Ellen, was operating a bookstore in Saratoga Springs, New York. Soon after Spalding began working with the Performance Group, Liz became my assistant. She first did graphic design, then took over the direction of *Commune* when in 1971 Joan MacIntosh and I left for a long journey (our first) to Asia. Later she acted in plays I directed: *The Tooth of Crime, The Marilyn Project, Mother Courage,* and *Cops.* Finally, in 1980, LeCompte took over the artistic leadership of what became the Wooster Group. This is not the place to tell the story of the emergence of the Wooster Group from the Performance Group—except as that history illuminates the relationship between Spalding and me.

After *Makbeth* closed in January 1970, TPG disintegrated. Not only was the failure of *Makbeth* intolerable after the success of *Dionysus in 69* but also, more importantly, I no longer wanted to work with untrained actors. When the smoke cleared, no one but Joan MacIntosh was left who had been in *D69* and only Steven Borst, MacIntosh, and Spalding remained from *Makbeth*. TPG was TPG in name, but in practice, it was a new Group. As I wrote in *Environmental Theater*:

> After the breakup of TPG in 1970, I was extremely confused. When Joan MacIntosh, Stephen Borst, and I decided to go on, I didn't know how to go on. I felt like the end of Samuel Beckett's *The Unnamable*: . . . "you must go on, I can't go on, I'll go on." We invited Spalding Gray to go on with us. . . . Joan, Steve, Spalding, and I ran workshops, talked about "new people," started to get the Group together. At the same time we began work on *Commune*. New people came into the Group: James Griffiths, Patric Epstein, Bruce White, Patricia Bower, Mik Cribben, Jayme Daniel, and a little later Elizabeth LeCompte.

Over time, some people left and others came aboard, but there were no more explosions. During the 1970s, the core TPG included Gray, MacIntosh, LeCompte, Borst, Griffiths, James Clayburgh, Timothy Shelton, Bruce Rayvid, Ron Vawter, and me.

In *Commune*, I continued the experiment of mixing the "real lives" of the performers with the personae they performed. This was a technique I'd explored in *Dionysus in 69* but with roots going much further back in the visual arts, surrealism, and other kinds of what would become known as performance art. The idea of "self-portrait" was firmly established in the visual arts starting with the paintings of Jean Fouquet and Albrecht Durer in the fifteenth century. Rembrandt, of course, painted many self-portraits—and the line continued through to Van Gogh, Kahlo, and a host of others. Photography brought self-portraiture into popular culture in a big way. But strangely, the "real theater" had been exempt. I decided to change that in *Commune*. I asked each performer to introduce her- or himself to the audience by singing a "song of first encounter," an autobiographical item that opened the show. Spalding sang:

> Oh the entrances from the wings
> The sniffing on the brandy
> From the Rhode Island shore I wandered back
> Squat little man in a yoga position.
> Oh more like a congenial chat
> Into a production of *Makbeth*
> Saying my words very well.
> What was behind all that?
> A roaring lion of a man
> Or a little black spider?

When I asked each performer to select a name for their characters, only Spalding decided to use his own, "Spalding."

The way I assembled *Commune*'s text was by knitting together various source materials gleaned from literature, books on communes, newspapers, TV, and group improvisations. Each performer brought in favorite items. We strove to tell a story—loosely—of how "American history," with a special emphasis on the Vietnam War, might be narrated by Charles Manson and his "family" on August 9, 1969, the night after they murdered Sharon Tate and four others. Spalding had a particular love for Herman Melville's *Moby-Dick*. Spalding was brought up in Rhode Island, near the sea, and he had a deep affinity for New England sea lore. He chose these lines from *Moby-Dick* to narrate the murder of Tate: "At last gush after gush of clotted red gore as if it had been the purple lees of red wine shot into the frighted air and falling back again ran dripping down her motionless flanks. Her heart had burst."

Commune ends with Spalding being interviewed:

> CLEMENTINE: What would you describe as the role of the artist in today's society?
> SPALDING: The role of the artist?
> CLEMENTINE: Yes.
> SPALDING: Yes, yes, of course.
> *A long freeze. Then* SPALDING . . . *sits, takes out a penny whistle and blows. Like a factory whistle ending the work day. He plays a tune. The others go to the tub and wash, return clothing to spectators, relax. Performance rhythms subside into everyday rhythms.*

I go on about *Commune* at length because his work on that production set Spalding on the road he was to follow: looking to himself, his memories, his fascinations and obsessions, his way of speaking and self-presentation—the "I" and the "me" of his life—for both his material and his style; telling stories by himself, of himself. In *Commune* I gave Spalding permission to be himself in front of an audience—to not "hide" in "character" or "impersonation," but to find and display his own way to "be" in the theater. As Spalding himself commented in 2002:

In *Commune* I played "Spalding," the role Spalding. That was my first move toward autobiography, but I didn't realize it at the time. My character Spalding was very much how Richard perceived me, how he saw me from the outside as a kind of watcher. He would watch and comment on the action.

It's not that *Commune* was already what the *Rhode Island Trilogy* plus *Point Judith* or the monologues became, but that Spalding's experience in *Commune* opened onto the path that led directly to those later works.

2

People remember Spalding as the centerpiece of *Three Places in Rhode Island* and/or as a great autobiographical monologist. They tend to forget how excellent an actor he was. After *Commune*, Spalding got TPG roles aplenty. He was Hoss in our rendition of Sam Shepard's *The Tooth of Crime* (1972–73), Swiss Cheese and the Farmer in Brecht's *Mother Courage and Her Children* (1974–76), a Cop in Terry Curtis Fox's *Cops* (1978), and the Bishop in Jean Genet's *The Balcony* (1979)—all directed by me. You can see the kind of quality character acting he was capable of by viewing James McCarthy and Kenneth Kobland's film of *The Tooth of Crime*. But *Tooth* also gave Spalding the next rung on his ladder up to the monologues. As Spalding, again in 2002, recalls it:

> [In *Tooth*] I do a very long soliloquy about a fight that I'd been in. Richard said, "I want you at the end of this—" (while the drums were going full blast) "—to drop your character. Drop all this character you've built up of Hoss, and just stand there"—in the middle of this circle, surrounded by the audience. Richard said, "Go neutral," as the saying was then. I remember standing there in my green cape, trying to be neutral with a shaved head, and a jock strap, and feeling this onion of the character peeling away, peel after peel, and then standing there like this, looking at the audience's faces. . . . And then Richard said, "Just take the

time, as long as you want to stand there, and when you feel ready to move, then go to the other side of the room and begin your next scene." And that was a really important space for me to go into every night, I really looked forward to that. It was a very powerful, beautiful meditation. It began to occur to me, What if I didn't rebuild my character? If I continued to stand here, looking at the audience. What might I say? And I think that's where the first curiosity and temptation came in that I might be able to publicly be Spalding Gray. At that time it was just a fantasy, nothing I thought of really doing.

It was not that Spalding, after *Commune*, suddenly gave up "regular" acting. But as he got very good at it he also was able to step away from his role and confront the audience directly.

When Spalding worked "in character" he always found something unique, strange, and right simultaneously. He was a great Brechtian actor, and *Mother Courage* showed why. Playing Swiss Cheese as an overgrown perplexed innocent (those eyes again), garbed in an olive green Boy Scout uniform, Swiss Cheese "did his best" (as the Scout Oath instructs) with such a chilling simplicity—speaking his words one syllable at a time—that he became a simpleton Christ literally hanging above the audience awaiting his execution. As Swiss Cheese slowly rotated in the air, the other performers sat directly below him, musical instruments in hand, singing the "Song of the Hours," comparing Swiss Cheese's situation to the Passion of Christ. Later in the run, Spalding did a stint as the Cook, but Swiss Cheese was his signature role.

Further from Jesus you cannot get than *Cops*, a hyper-real production set in George's, an all-night diner. The environment was "hyper-real," like a photorealist painting. Jim Clayburgh built the environment in TPG's second theater, the Envelope (next door to the Performing Garage), using the furnishings we had purchased from a defunct diner. George's was equipped with a working grill, refrigerator, sink, glass-door cabinets for the food, counter, stools, tables, chairs, fluorescent overhead lights, and a working public telephone.

George cooked eggs, while Mickey the waitress (LeCompte) served donuts, toast, and coffee. A rain machine was set up outside the front door and all entrances were made from Wooster Street. George's was so real that people came in off the street hoping to grab a bite, only to be disappointed when they found out they were in a theater. The cast were future Wooster Group mainstays: Spalding, LeCompte, Vawter, and Willem Dafoe. Also Steve Borst, who died young in the mid-1980s. Spalding brought to *Cops* Czerwicki, a uniformed cop, a well-honed character who spent the larger part of the performance splayed bloody and dead next to Mickey-LeCompte on George's floor.

By my last production with TPG, *The Balcony* in the late fall and winter of 1979, Spalding was no longer interested in character work, not even for me. He camped his way through his role of the Bishop. By 1979, Spalding had already done all of the *Rhode Island Trilogy*, was working on *Point Judith*, and was pointing ahead to his career as a monologist. In April 1979, just as we were starting work on *The Balcony*, Spalding showed the first version of his first monologue, *Sex and Death to the Age 14*. He continued to work on *Sex and Death* that summer during TPG's residency at Connecticut College in New London, where we also rehearsed *The Balcony*. Close by in Rhode Island, LeCompte shot the ocean scenes for *Point Judith*. That summer Spalding focused on himself as the material and medium of his art. He tested further versions of *Sex and Death* with Conn College students in dorm performance spaces. Spalding and I discussed his style of delivery and the students' reactions to the stories he told. This work went back not only to *Commune* but also to a two-week residency we had shared at the University of California in Santa Cruz in the mid-1970s, where Spalding got students to tell "real stories" from their lives.

3

In the spring of 1976, TPG brought *Mother Courage* to India. We performed in New Delhi, Kolkata (Calcutta), Mumbai (Bombay), Bhopal, Lucknow, and Singjole, a village near Kolkata. What went on during the production was one thing, what happened around the production was something else. After performing in Kolkata, TPG held meetings on March 16 and 17. There were tensions in the Group. I didn't want another explosion like what had followed *Makbeth*. In my notebook from 1976, I wrote:

> These meetings are good because they open the possibility for change—even total liberation. For me the liberation can come in two ways: Control over TPG so it is an instrument of mine; or freedom from the Group so I can pursue these experiments on my own. In either case I can get free of the ego struggles. I no longer think the Group must reflect what I hope the coming society should be. I now think the instrument must be sharp and held in strong hands—and when it cuts it ought not to cut into itself but into the world around it. Otherwise people will mostly subjectivize their lives, turn on or into each other, fail to do anything more than "express" themselves—while not relating either to the society or to theoretical problems of performance theory, the art. It's the intersection of these two that interests me—not "holding together" a group (whatever its reputation). Reputations come and go, even art passes. But certain theories and social systems abide, if not for all time, for a long time. I want to teach, change the order of society, and have-make fun.

Reading this notebook entry now, thirty-one years later, I both blush at and admire my own agenda. More to the point here, the Kolkata meetings—indeed the whole *Courage* in India tour—marked a break at the end of a process. The period of TPG history that started with *Commune* ended with *Courage*. From 1973 on, I encouraged others to direct under the aegis of TPG. Steve Borst directed Michael McClure's *The Beard* and Leeny Sack worked on *The Survivor and the Translator*, which she opened in 1980 after leaving TPG. In 1975, Spalding and LeCompte showed *Sakonnet Point*, the first of the *Rhode Island Trilogy*, in the *Courage* environment. From the 1976

Kolkata meetings onward, centrifugal energy prevailed. Ron Vawter and Libby Howes, and soon after Willem Dafoe, joined with LeCompte and Spalding. Although we all would work together on *Cops* and all but LeCompte would work on *The Balcony*, the process was in motion that would lead to my departure and the emergence of the Wooster Group. From *Sakonnet Point* onward, Spalding focused on performances whose material was his own life. In re-reading my notebook entries of 1975 and 1976, I see that his intensely personal expression and my stated goals were incompatible. From *Courage* onward—aside from the discussions we had at Connecticut College in 1979—I became more of a spectator than a director of Spalding's own pieces. Spalding's enablers and artistic advisors were first LeCompte, then Renée Shafransky, and finally Kathie Russo.

After TPG's final performance of *Courage* in Mumbai on April 6, most people went back to the United States. Joan MacIntosh, Spalding, and I stayed in India. Over the next ten months I traveled—alone and with MacIntosh—in India, southeast Asia, Hong Kong, Japan, and then back to India before returning to America in February 1977. After Mumbai, Spalding headed for the Pune ashram of Bhagwan Shree Rajneesh, later known as Osho, with LeCompte. She told me that Spalding participated in some of the ashram's activities, she to a lesser degree. Rajneesh already had a reputation as a "sex guru," and Spalding was very excited about participating in "tantric meditations." He was drawn to spiritual leaders—something he got from his Christian Science mother—and when they were also sexual leaders, they were irresistible. Before leaving for the ashram, Spalding looked forward to a spiritual awakening ignited by sex. Throughout the India tour, he was fascinated by Indian sex practices as he experienced and fantasized them. Once he told me how after he'd gotten a rubdown, the young boy masseur gave him a blowjob. "I didn't ask, he just went down on me," Spalding said, amazed. "We weren't even alone, we were in a room with plenty of other people." Spalding believed Rajneesh offered this kind of experience, framed in tantric practice. He was not alone. Thousands of Westerners flocked to Rajneesh's ashram. But there is more to it.

I cannot say what happened to Spalding in Pune. But after leaving the ashram, he and LeCompte traveled to Kashmir and some of the Tibetan settlements in the foothills of the Himalayas. When they were about to leave India in June, Spalding couldn't decide whether to return to New York or go on to Bali. His indecision escalated into a crisis. He left India in a state of confusion that intensified when he got back to America. He was profoundly disturbed and disoriented. In early October while I was still in India, I got a letter from LeCompte describing the situation. I don't have the letter itself, but I do have my notebook entry about it, Spalding, and our work:

> Liz's letter concerning Spald is really frightening: He is having a psychotic break. What is our work worth from the individual, human side if it cannot prevent, channel, or deal with this? If he is so far gone, clearly the work is not "whole-making," at least the way we (he) have (has) been doing it. And what of him? And his future? Can he work on *Sakonnet Point*, on his new piece? What of *Mother Courage*? Somehow I think his crisis is about identity: at his age what has he to "show" for his life? Or is that the crisis I'd have if I were him? Probably. His symptoms were indecision concerning whether to go to New York or to Bali [after India]. New York=work, Bali=adventure, especially sexual adventure. But what caused the breakdown? . . . Where does this leave the future? The illusion that the work is a therapy either must be abandoned—or the work must be made actually therapeutic. Or is it Spalding's failure to do the work—that is, to really follow through on his impulses and to examine himself? I don't know—though I think both are true, each in its own way.

Once back in the United States, Spalding went into therapy and slowly recovered. But whatever took place in India exposed a fault line that, when he was under stress, could and did rupture. Spalding tells his version of his India sojourn in his *India and After (America)*.

4

Spalding's last years were very hard on him. After his catastrophic 2001 auto accident in Ireland, he never returned to "normal" (in quotation marks because Spalding's normal was not everyone else's normal). He was physically and emotionally blasted. In an effort to restore himself, he accepted, or had forced on him, skull surgery, electric shock treatments, and drug therapies. He was no longer the master of his own doings. And every slip down the slope toward inself-sufficency led only to worse. The times I saw him during his last years, he could not focus. He was both too inside himself and too distant. He was obsessed with his Sag Harbor home, which he sold to buy another and then wanted to repurchase but could not. This failure to recuperate an item he had lost or abandoned or sold (as he told it, against his will) became the trope of his final months. Guided by Kathie Russo, his wife, Spalding tried to exorcise his demons and restore his viability by performing *Life Interrupted*, his piece about the automobile accident in Ireland and his subsequent attempts at recovery.

I last saw him perform at P.S. 122 in the fall of 2003. For me especially, because I knew him so well from "before," watching and listening to Spalding in the half-empty, dingy black box theater was excruciating and embarrassing. He paused not because he was deploying a gifted performer's inherent skill of withholding, but because he did not know where he was in his act. When he walked to show how his shortened leg gave him a jerky limp, the exhibition was awkward and made me queasy. Sometimes spectators laughed. But at what? This man performing was not the highly reflexive genius of the double and triple entendre. He was not laughing at himself. Was I supposed to laugh at my friend's obvious physical pain and mental difficulties? The apt ironies of his earlier monologues, products of his great ability to both identify with himself and then offer a Brechtian remark, were gone. He was on a journey toward some unknown place without his reflecting mirror showing him where he had been so that he could sardonically comment on his situation. He was working very hard just to remember what to say even though he was reading his own prepared text. He couldn't connect to his text or find the humor in it, or use it as a springboard for improvisational riffs of inspired language and gesture. There was nothing funny about the story, no light at the end of the tunnel. The electric flow of his performing switched on and off, like a bad electrical connection. His body hurt. He seemed terribly afraid. Afterward, backstage, Spalding introduced me to Oliver Sacks. "Oliver is . . . my . . . my . . . advisor," Spalding said. Sacks said something about how performing in public was good therapy.

Once, during the spring before he committed suicide, I visited Spalding in the mental ward of an uptown Manhattan hospital. I remember passing through locked doors—the patients were thought to be a danger to themselves and maybe to others. Spalding was in a private room. He was gaunt. I no longer saw innocence in his eyes. When open, they were seeking a focus but not finding it. For long periods of time, he kept his eyes closed. He wasn't dozing, but he wasn't present either. Heavily drugged, he could hardly talk. He was suspended between his injuries, his fears of illness, his hatred of the medical establishment, and his need for help. His memory—the great gift and weapon of his creativity—was broken. And what's worse, he knew his memory was broken. He was all too aware of what he was not aware of. He told me about the dent in his forehead, the metal plate over a part of his brain. He knew, but he could not focus. It was so sad to see him living this contradiction. He was agitated; his whole body seemed to sputter.

I opened a book and began reading to him from *Sex and Death*. He calmed. Hearing his own words quoted back to him seemed to please him. He enjoyed the flow of his words, even if they came from my mouth. Later that year I visited him in his loft on Wooster Street. I tried to have a conversation, but he was not really able to take up the threads of talk. I recalled how sublimely conversational Spalding was, or rather, had been. Again I read to him. When in January 2004 I read that Spalding had vanished from the Staten Island Ferry, I knew what had happened before forensics confirmed it.

He was (already) dead.

—Richard Schechner

Acknowledgments

Anyone who met Spalding Gray knows what a genuinely kind and almost obsessively curious man he was. On more than a few occasions, he took the time with me to wander through all kinds of topics, jumping from ideas suited for a college seminar to discussions best reserved for the locker room. And he liked to see and do things that other people often ignore or overlook. Even anonymously dropping in on the Jimmy Swaggart televangelist ministry on a Sunday morning in my Louisiana hometown of Baton Rouge was something that Spalding just couldn't pass up. Or taking a detour to see the Vicksburg Civil War battlefield and looking for the Rhode Island monument. Whoever knew Spalding has stories to tell of the unexpected and unusual; mine no doubt pale in comparison. The point here is that everything seemed to interest him; nothing seemed to bore him. If this book captures anything of Spalding's hunger for experiencing life at its fullest, then it's done its job. Thanks, Spalding, for doing what you did.

Even a labor of love sometimes needs financial support, and this book has been generously supported by the Department of English and the College of Arts and Sciences at Louisiana State University, Baton Rouge. The book also needed time in order to come into being, and I was lucky enough to have that too with the generous support of the state of Louisiana, which extended an ATLAS (Award to Louisiana Artists And Scholars) Grant that allowed me to take a full year to finish this project without interruption. Thanks in particular to Anna Nardo and Guillermo Ferreyra, who cheered me on from their high administrative perches. They certainly didn't have to, and that's what makes them special among "bosses."

A very big thank you goes to Richard Schechner, who spent a good deal of his valuable time talking with me about his relationship with Spalding, from the heady 1960s right up to Gray's last days. And an even bigger thank you goes out to Kathie Russo, who was also very generous with her time and patient with my queries. Spalding was lucky to have a friend like Richard and a wife like Kathie. I was lucky too, because without them I'm not sure what this book would have looked like. Thank you, Richard and Kathie.

I'm pretty fortunate in my own friends and need to thank three of them for helping me work through my ideas. Mike Vanden Heuvel was literally there when I first met Spalding several years ago (we were all in line waiting to see a Sam Shepard play starring John Malkovich). Mike and I have talked a lot about theater in general and the Wooster Group (Mike's specialty) and Spalding Gray (my passion) in particular. Chris Wheatley was there—again literally (along with Mike)—the last time I saw Spalding (in a bar near Washington Square waiting to go to a play), and we've all three spent countless hours talking about theater, performance, and other topics of mind-altering import. Thanks, guys. Bob Vorlicky (along with his genius of a son, Sasha) also has been loads of help, being a man with the great good fortune of living in New York City and holding down a job that pays him to go to just about every out-of-the-way venue for performance that the city has to offer. He's been indispensable in putting so much into perspective for me.

Thanks of a different order go out to my agent, June Clark. She did what needed to be done to get this book into print. That included providing a good deal of hard-nosed editorial advice to a fairly know-it-all author. Dogged persistence barely begins to describe

June's efforts. Thanks for sticking it out with me. And thanks too for introducing me to Michael Messina of Applause Theatre Books. He's a great publisher to work for and with. I'd also like to thank Dave Olson and Jamie Askin for helping me with the book's photos. Clay Hapaz, archivist of the Wooster Group, was also incredibly accommodating. And a big thanks goes out to several very special photographers who helped me in many small and not so small ways. Thanks especially to Paula Court, Nigel Dickson, and Noah Greenberg.

Finally, thanks to my wife, Jean, whose idea it was to write this book. What a great idea!

SPALDING GRAY'S AMERICA

Spalding Gray at the Statue of Liberty. (Photo courtesy of Kathie Russo.)

Introduction

Living in the U.S.A., 1941–2004

Forget history books. Anyone interested in getting to understand contemporary life in the United States should rent a video or check out a book by Spalding Gray. Maybe do both. This master storyteller and dynamic stage presence had the dubious good fortune to live through and think about some of the most exciting, challenging, and frustrating times in U.S. history. Growing up during the "idyllic" postwar Truman and Eisenhower years, expanding his consciousness during the cultural revolution of the 1960s, finding his way through the confusing 1970s and 1980s, and finally discovering the joys of domesticity in the 1990s, Spalding Gray took his experiences and brought that thing we call "America" to life onstage with piercing insight, disarmingly ironic humor, and a personal touch that won't soon be duplicated.

It's his monologues, of course, that capture our imaginations, though he was involved in all sorts of different ventures, including experimental theater, Broadway theater, films, television, and even novel writing. In the monologues, Gray captured the spirit of the times by using himself as a sort of lightning rod, a strange attractor toward which everything seems to gather. Early monologues like *Sex and Death to the Age 14*; *Booze, Cars, and College Girls*; and *47*

Beds draw on Gray's early life, from his recollections of experiencing V-J Day as a preschooler to his lost but not unproductive ramblings during the heady, chaotic 1960s. Even the titles of these pieces hint at tales familiar to anyone who grew up in America during the baby boomer years: sex, alcohol, cars, and, well, more sex. There is joy and enthusiasm in all of these works, but there's a brooding discomfort too, a sense that all is not quite right in the land of plenty. *Nobody Wanted to Sit Behind a Desk* and *Terrors of Pleasure: The House* take us through the frightening processes of growing up while trying to avoid slipping into a tedious life of middle-class conformity. His signature *Swimming to Cambodia* speaks of a growing awareness that America has not had an altogether positive influence on the world at large. *Monster in a Box* describes standing on the doorstep of success, being on the verge of realizing the American Dream while sensing a certain hollowness that lurks in the shadows alongside that dream. *Gray's Anatomy* continues where *Monster in a Box* leaves off, tackling the spiritual and emotional emptiness of our current popular visions of the American Dream. The next monologue, *It's a Slippery Slope*, shows what happens when we buy into that American Dream without thinking deeply about its worthiness. What Gray reminded us, and what we often forget, is that this "American Dream" thing really only works when we have the courage to forge our own dreams. Sadly, we too often buy into the dreams manufactured in Hollywood or on Madison Avenue, and realize the errors of our ways too late to recover onto a healthy and happy path.

Gray stumbled often, and he sometimes stumbled pretty badly. But he persisted in seeing, feeling, and sensing that life is worth living and happiness is worth pursuing. It took a while, but after all his run-ins with the rich and glamorous and wise and powerful, he finally did find contentment in a home by a hearth that bears the stamp of the kind of authentic life he failed to find as he ran his decades-long gauntlet through all that glitters in American culture. Fifty years into his life—by most standards pretty late in the day—Gray found the home he was looking for, as he reported in *Morning, Noon and Night*.

This monologue is as touching—though as quirky—a love song as you'll find from the twentieth century.

The idea that Gray discovered contentment rather late in the day is actually something that distinguishes Spalding as an artist. In fact, many things came late for Gray, but that tardiness actually served him well. He graduated from college later than usual and was just old enough to see things that most tunnel-visioned college kids often miss. He likewise came to the 1960s with the eyes and ears of a far more "grown-up" twenty-something observer. So while he was swept along by the radical 1960s tides of change, he also *saw* the world around him and could reflect upon rather than just indulge himself in that world.

When Gray achieved professional success with *Swimming to Cambodia*, it happened when he was already in his forties, after years of paying his dues. Though he indulged himself during those rather heady times, he wasn't some spoiled child star incapable of knowing or appreciating what was happening. It was something special and Gray knew it. Then, miracle of miracles, in his fifties he became a father and eventually a family man.

All of these delayed events helped make Gray the artist he was. He experienced things as the most mindless child would, fully immersed in the moment, because he remained forever young at heart. But he came to those life events with the older eyes of an observer and critic. Take parenthood, for example. In their teens or twenties, most of us don't have the capacity fully to appreciate the experience of having children, trapped as we are in the day-to-day struggle just to muddle through. Though there really isn't any way *not* to muddle through such things, having children later in life allows for a level of self-awareness and even occasional detachment that permits reflection and use of gathered wisdom. That applies to child rearing for sure. The same can be said of success: the earlier we experience it, the less we appreciate it. And so it went with Gray's life. He did what we all have done, but he did it with a little more verve and he gave it a lot more scrutiny.

What we discover when we are in Gray's presence is that while the details of his life curiously meandered in ways that make him a true American original, the larger portrait he created of himself bears a surprising resemblance to our own. He was a unique and quirky man who somehow captured the essence that drifts through the lives of virtually all Americans. That surprising synchronicity drew us all close to this very funny storyteller, giving us the feeling we had somehow known him all our lives. In the process he encouraged many of us to crash through the locked doors and suburban fences that so effectively isolate us all from our neighbors.

Through his work onstage, in film, and in print, he gave us a fellow-feeling companion with whom virtually everyone could identify. Together, we winced when Gray described souring relationships, knowing what it feels like to experience loss. We cheered when success came his way, knowing the special nature of such occasions. We glowered with him at the incompetence of our leadership and felt the sting of failure when good intentions went awry. We found that we all long for the "perfect moment" that was Gray's Holy Grail. And we basked with him in warmth he discovered when he finally unlocked the joys of becoming a family man. He reminded us that the pursuit of happiness is a full-time job, that the American dream is a journey rather than a destination. And his final days sadly reminded us that the happiness we pursue will not be permanent.

Gray shared almost everything with us, but he did far more than offer up personal confessions. Somehow, by sharing his life experiences, he did the far more important thing of telling us about ourselves as a culture and a nation, with a directness and appeal that simply can't be found in history books, political science texts, or the *Congressional Record*. Gray the consummate storyteller offered honest, usually hilarious, and often poignant confessions that bear witness to a world that has generated ever more frequent moments of isolation, self-doubt, and despair. These are feelings that wash over us all with increasingly greater frequency than any of us cares to admit. Gray was willing to deal with such moments. But in a spirit that is almost uniquely American, he never allowed us to wallow in the misery that often accompanies those times of doubt, desperation, and panic. Optimism pervaded his performances, even as he recounted dark times when a positive attitude seemed more like foolhardiness. But, then, isn't that what America is all about?

Gray's perspective on life in our world always took on an absurdly funny luster that penetrated his audience and offered us all a sense that, whatever our particular woes, we're all in it together. And that is a good thing. Like many of the baby boomer generation—and like many before and since—Gray survived America's many cycles of crisis and crisis management, finally settling into a life of well-deserved domestic contentment, tormented only by the day-to-day demands placed on a husband and father.

It looked like Gray's lust for life had prevailed once and for all, even over his frequent and sometimes macabre attraction to death. If anything marks America as truly American, it's the resilient optimism that Gray exhibited through all but that final excruciating chapter in his life when death finally got the upper hand. Sadly, through all the turmoil that was his life—and that inspired his art—Gray would be subjected to one last major and protracted crisis. On June 22, 2001, while in Ireland on vacation with his family, celebrating his sixtieth birthday, he fell victim to a senseless automobile accident. It left him struggling for two and a half years with a painful trauma that seemed unlikely ever to relent. On Saturday, January 10, 2004, Spalding Gray went missing from his New York City loft. He was last seen early Sunday morning, January 11, riding the Staten Island Ferry. On March 8, 2004, Gray's body was pulled from New York's East River.

What is truly extraordinary about Spalding Gray is not how (or why) he died, but *how he lived*. He was a genuinely funny man. He could make us laugh at the most mundane and seemingly unfunny things. He could befriend a stranger on a train or a plane just as easily as he could charm an audience of hundreds—or thousands. And he could make us think.

In many ways seemingly ordinary, Gray generated a body of au-
tobiographically inspired work in the theater that attracted waves of
support even though he didn't seem to have the credentials to pull
it off. He wasn't a war hero, political leader, sports legend, rock star,
famous actor, or corporate dynamo deserving particular admiration.
He hadn't survived some horrendous ordeal from which admirers
should draw personal strength. He wasn't one of the embodiments
of youth that today so superficially dominate pop culture. He was a
man whose celebrity derived primarily from his being himself, and
being not all that different from the rest of us. After all, what is
unique about being a white, heterosexual, Anglo-Saxon, Protestant
male of middle-class origins? It seems that Gray's public exception-
ality may very well have been his personal unexceptionality. What
separated Gray from the rest of us was his overwhelming curiosity,
his willingness to try things that most of us would fear to attempt.
But Gray's uniqueness surfaced most fully when he told his stories.
He had "it," that thing that captivates friends and strangers alike,
draws them in with a sort of gravitational attraction difficult to break
away from. In short, he was natively talented "middle America" at its
energized, dynamic, curious, instinctive best.

What Gray did with his rather unexpected celebrity more than
anything else was to expose our selves to ourselves through himself.
He "volunteered" as a patient for us all to study, becoming the thing
on the dissecting table for us to observe and analyze. We could study
him as he went from the simmering 1950s to the turbulent 1960s
and on into the twenty-first century, seeing in his experiences the
effects of those times on this "typical" middle American. But we got
more than just some clinically "academic" view of American life and
living. Gray provided an exhilarating and personal touch by articu-
lately and humorously reporting the effects of his exposure to this
often strange and frequently inscrutable American culture. How did
he do it? First by haunting and observing those two "center stages"
of American culture, New York City and Los Angeles, and then by
taking to the stage himself to report his findings. He chose to dive

in and to experience what it was to be a sentient being in the many worlds he discovered. Then, as a reporter onstage, he presented the raw material of his observations, enveloping audiences in the sensory overload of his life to the point that they shared in the experiences, resulting in the type of bonding often longed for but rarely actually experienced in the theater. And he did all this *just by talking*.

Of course, Gray was doing far more than just talking. He worked hard at his craft, elevating his talent as a storyteller to an art form rarely (if at all) recuperable by the most ambitious of imitators. He seemed to have been sitting on the sidelines of every significant cultural movement or event of the last five decades, watching with an eye for the unusual and sharing his often quirky experiences by talking to us in his signature deskside manner. One felt that there was something intense and very significant going on when we were in Spalding's presence, despite his disarming affability.

The theater in which Spalding worked was every bit as exciting as the world he experienced outside. His career spanned five of the most dynamic decades that American theater had yet experienced. He was trained in traditional forms, then moved to Richard Schechner's Performance Group, and later cofounded and worked with the Wooster Group. Then he famously went solo. At his peak, he was a regular Lincoln Center attraction, and he took his shows on the road to cities and towns throughout the United States and Europe, all with great success. Videos and films of his performances soon followed, as did printed collections of his monologues. He even wrote a novel. This pretty average guy with an above-average eye for the unusual and a great gift for storytelling had basically made a career of being "American."

If there was a formula to Gray's success, it's one that very few have been able to duplicate. He was a disarmingly astute cultural critic who went into his own skin to understand himself, and by understanding himself he came to understand the ebb and flow of life in that dominant cultural phenomenon known as "America." As a white, middle-class, heterosexual male of Northern European descent able to trace his ancestry all the way back to America's Founding Fathers, Gray had a reasonably privileged seat at the movable American feast of the past forty to fifty years. But he was always aware that the privilege was unearned and always felt a certain guilt that his good fortune didn't extend to everyone. In other words, amid all the indulgence that was Spalding Gray's life, he also scrutinized *why* he was so privileged.

And when he did scrutinize his privilege, he went a big step toward criticizing America's one great flaw: its willingness to perpetuate a world unequally divided between haves and have-nots even while propagandizing a doctrine of equal opportunity. Gray could never be considered a political animal—at least not in the way so many left-leaning artists are political—but he offered political insights perhaps even more profound than what is offered by banner-waving activism. Except for *Swimming to Cambodia*—his breakthrough monologue about America's Vietnam-era missteps in Southeast Asia—most of his works seem distinctly apolitical. But, again like much of the politics of middle America itself, Gray's politics might run silent, but they ran deep. His core values extended farther than simply looking out for number one. Even in his most self-absorbed moments, Gray never abandoned his heartfelt belief that other people are what makes life worth living. This may not be sexy enough for banner-waving activism, but it's a pretty important cornerstone upon which to build a way of looking at and living in the world. The theater helped Gray make his point. It served him well.

Spalding Gray's career in the theater takes us through incredibly dynamic times in American culture and on the American stage. It's well worth following his adjustments and transformations in reaction to the changeable world we all have struggled to survive and understand. Working his way through life and sharing his experiences with his public, Gray was always invigorating, invariably thought-provoking, and frequently troubling. But he was never less than fully entertaining in a way that can only be described as resiliently American.

1

Taking Middle America to SoHo

Middle America is more a state of mind than a geographical locale. It has something to do with pursuing the American Dream, which has something to do with the pursuit of happiness. What is so attractive about the idea of America is that it allows each of us to devise our own goals and choose our own ways to reach them. This almost infinite flexibility is ingenious. But this means that we all have to devise our own American Dream, staying wary of tempting con artists determined to sweep us up into theirs. So much of American popular culture offers up glittering dreams that rarely, if ever, really live up to their billing. But the optimism of youth and much-publicized examples of success encourage us as we make our way. There are no guarantees, but the fact that everyone can try and some will succeed is what makes middle America such a vibrant place to be.

Spalding Gray's life in the theater pretty easily qualifies as an example of the American Dream come true, though not in any formulaic or expected way. His monologues capture Gray's meandering story of the pursuit of that American Dream, revealing that the journey is sometimes more interesting than the destination.

Spalding Grows Up

The Gray family found middle America in Rhode Island. In fact, Spalding's childhood could very easily have made him the poster child for mid-century, white bread, mainstream America. It appeared as "normal" and unexceptional as could be, and, despite his later successes, it would be almost impossible for anyone to look back on Spalding Gray's childhood and say they could see greatness on the rise.

Spalding Gray was born Thursday, June 5, 1941, in Barrington, Rhode Island. His father, Rockwell, was a good provider, and his mother, Bette, was his emotional comfort. He had two brothers who seem to have been pretty decent kids. He was healthy and had a good gang of friends always ready to play. He spent summers at the beach with his family, and the rest of the year he was an indifferent student striving mightily to avoid the tests and homework that would cut into his free time. He wasn't a troublemaker. He just wasn't any good in the classroom. And he really didn't care.

Spalding's lack of childhood drive and discipline wasn't such a problem in those simpler times before the regimented heyday of today's soccer mom. Spalding's mom and dad didn't seem overly concerned with his life of carefree abandon. And Grandma even enabled little "Spud" in his pursuit of fun by doing his math homework for him. The times were good, and there was no real concern for the future. Nothing in Spalding's childhood suggested he had any intentions of going anywhere special. At least on the surface, there weren't any signs of specialness. He was as normal as normal could be.

As childhood gave way to adolescence, Spalding, more interested in preserving his childhood than thinking about his future, never did actually buckle down and study. Nor did he develop any particularly unique or unusual interests. He wasn't really interested in sports. He certainly wasn't putting on plays in the basement or anything like that. Cars caught his attention for a time, and so did girls. But generally life just moved forward in a string of lazy days at play. Finally, his parents grew concerned and took the drastic measure of sending

Spalding to boarding school, hoping a new setting and greater discipline would get him on track. But the problem was never exactly a matter of discipline: it seems Spalding suffered from undiagnosed dyslexia, which likely would have prevented him from ever succeeding in the classroom without the special help and attention that didn't exist in the 1950s.

At boarding school, however, things did take a lucky turn. For the first time, a teacher took a personal interest in Spalding. The school's drama teacher noticed that he had a photographic memory and encouraged him to memorize a role for a play. He took the teacher's advice, and he won a part in the school's production of *The Curious Savage*. Audiences laughed at his antics onstage, and for he first time he felt official approval in a "grown-up" setting. He got more involved in theater, and his enthusiasm for the stage helped him to hang on in school. At twenty he finally graduated from Fichton Academy, eligible for college and hungry to become an actor. When Boston University refused to admit him into its theater program, he matriculated at the more accommodating Emerson College down the road. By accident more than anything else, Gray's career was on its way.

By 1965, nearly twenty-four years old, Gray had earned his degree from Emerson College, but his real education had only just begun. Degree in hand and acting career in mind, he was about to enter a world where almost everything he had been taught to that point would be challenged. Never a very good schoolroom student, Gray would prove to be a far better student of the "real world."

Gray's Early Life in the Theater

A little good luck at Fichton Academy got Spalding started, but his decision to pursue theater as a career was more than casual. No one may have been able to see it at the time, but Spalding was the kind of kid who lived an unorthodox inner life. He tells us in one of his earliest monologues that when he was as young as four years old, he was already thinking about *why* things were the way they were. That natural curiosity never abandoned him. He needed to find a way to take advantage of it, and he eventually found that the "make-believe" world of the theater was just the place.

His curiosity had an unusual accomplice: the dyslexia that made him such a poor student. As it turns out, dyslexia probably wasn't a bad thing. Imagine what he would have been like had he somehow become a good student swept along by a solid but solidly conventional education. Being a hopeless case on school-related projects allowed him to drift through his childhood as a sort of untutored suburban Huck Finn. Huck-like, he had the free time to think things through on his own without falling into any conventional schoolbook ways of thinking. During those early years, Spalding looked at everything with open eyes and could use his imagination to pull it all together, sometimes in strange and original ways. Ultimately, he must have felt the theater would allow him to share his world with others.

Gray made his way into the theater world just prior to a particularly revolutionary period in American history, culture, and art. The theater world, like the rest of the world, was about to break out of its 1950s-era status-quo self-contentment and into a whirlwind of experimentation and change. But not yet. What that meant for Spalding in his early years as an actor was that he was destined to meet with initial disappointment, to the point that he almost gave up on the profession. He took his traditional actor's training and set out to make a living in regional theater. He served as a resident actor at Smith College and did stock theater work at the Champlain Shakespeare Festival, Tufts Arena Theatre, and Orleans Arena (Cape Cod). His regional credits included stints at the Image Theatre (Boston), The Gallery Theatre (Saratoga, NY), Theatre by the Sea (Portsmouth, NH), Theatre Company of Boston, and the Williamstown Theatre. Many of his roles were in standard fare like *Much Ado About Nothing*, *Candida*, *The Master Builder*, *The Way of the World*, *We Bombed in New Haven*, and *Under Milk Wood*. Some productions were more contemporary, like Beckett's *Krapp's Last Tape*, Brendan Behan's *The Quare Fellow*, and Ann Jellicoe's *The*

Knack. And he did secure the role of Edmund in O'Neill's *Long Day's Journey into Night*, one of several plays he'd return to later in his career. So his early time in theater seemed promising, if a bit conventional. It was that conventionality that left him disappointed. The *business* of acting had overwhelmed the appeal, leaving him, like so many young artists of the early 1960s, looking for more. But he wasn't quite sure what he was looking for, or exactly what he was missing.

Gray's biggest theater break and most eye-opening disappointment at the time occurred when he signed on with Houston's Alley Theatre, where he would earn his Actor's Equity card. As a junior member of the ensemble, he was forced into minor roles and was even on occasion required to do the offstage sound effects. Clearly, this wasn't the kind of career he was looking for. However, he likely would've been willing to serve his apprenticeship if he thought he'd finally get his chance at self-expressive self-fulfillment. But the theater world he'd entered seemed to provide *no one* with self-expressive opportunities. And that left him pretty disillusioned.

In fact, the most memorable event of his Houston stay had nothing to do with developing his craft in any obvious way. While cast in the unchallenging role of Lead Angel in *The World of Sholom Aleichem*, Gray decided to try a change in diet. But living mostly on beans and tofu didn't suit his meat-and-potato stomach, and he soon began having to cope with the effects. During one performance, he recalls in one of his later monologues, he built up enough gas to fill his floor-length angel's gown. When he and the host of angels walked onstage, he released his silent-but-deadlies and, he claims, almost asphyxiated his fellow angels. Adolescent stuff to be sure, the kind of thing that mature professionals don't do, or at least that grown-ups don't talk about. But there's a point here. This curious, mischievous, and self-experimenting kid refused to grow up. But getting the mischievous kid in Spalding onstage and having him do more than just sabotage his colleagues would require going beyond the traditional stage.

Gray's overall experience in the regional theater world left him disillusioned. The business of the theater, he discovered, led to conservative productions of "marketable" plays performed before audiences looking more for simple entertainment than for anything of real substance. What Gray was experiencing, of course, was exactly the discontent that others of his generation were feeling, exactly the discontent that was generating revolutions in New York City.

Mr. Gray Goes to New York

After duly earning his Equity card in Houston, Gray made his move to New York, hearing about the new energies and new opportunities percolating throughout the city. He went with high hopes, but at first what he found wasn't much better than what he'd experienced in Houston. Gray's early high points included off-Broadway roles in Tom O'Horgan's *Tom Paine* (in March 1968) and Robert Lowell's adaptation of a Nathaniel Hawthorne short story, *Endecott and the Red Cross* (in May 1968). But as luck would have it, he stumbled onto the pioneering avant-garde work of Julian Beck and Judith Malina, Charles Ludlum, Robert Wilson, Richard Foreman, and Joseph Chaikin. And Gray's world would never be the same again.

The new directions these people were taking theater excited and energized Gray. While still working to make a living on the more traditional stage, he entered a workshop run by Joyce Aaron, a member of Chaikin's Open Theatre who was influenced by the teachings of experimentalists like Antonin Artaud and Jerzy Grotowski. Chaikin's Theatre was part of a growing movement in American theater that concentrated on individual self-awareness and personal control. It was a very personal and physical theater that steered away from traditional plays, that is, away from "stories" with handy, crafted rising climaxes, plot devices, and endings with messages. Instead, the movement was toward self-expression without self-conscious control. It was self-aware but not self-conscious, meaning that it pursued truth "uncorrupted" by the ordering devices of the mind and consciousness.

It was raw, and it was alive. It was certainly opposed to the well-made play genre that dominated most traditional theater, and it definitely stood opposed to the Broadway system, dominated by producers, directors, playwrights, and marketers rather than by actors.

In this new theater, the actor or, better yet, the performer was encouraged to reach into him- or herself and to discover the buried "voice" of personal identity. Stanislavskian method acting, which Gray knew from his college and regional theater days, encouraged actors to find their inner selves too. But all too often that self-discovery was rerouted to serve the purposes of a text, playwright, or director. Giving center-stage attention to the performer was the beginning of something new and something big for Spalding. This sort of self-expressive theater seems to have been exactly what he'd longed for since his days at Fichton Academy, and earlier.

Although Gray was formally trained in the Stanislavskian tradition, he realized through his regional theater experiences that he wasn't the kind of person suited to pretend to be someone else. He had learned all the tricks of the acting trade, and he knew how to use them. But he wanted to perform *himself* rather than to disappear into the skin of some unfamiliar character created by an unfamiliar playwright. This growing awareness led him to Aaron's workshop, and he quickly learned that he wasn't alone in his feelings about theater and performance. He had just been in the wrong place, out in the regional hinterlands where this new movement hadn't yet arrived. He learned in New York that he had arrived at the same conclusions that many of the revolutionary practitioners and teachers had reached. And because he arrived at these same conclusions on his own, these New York practitioners didn't have to teach Gray how to think differently about theater. He was already there. What they needed to do was supply the encouragement and supporting advice for him to act on the ideas he'd already begun developing. The time was ripe for Gray to come along and to transform himself into the kind of theater person he always wanted to be.

This new theater emphasized presenting performers generating their own ways of finding and performing "truth and authenticity." "Know thyself" became the performer's *artistic* mantra, replacing the actor's *craft* of "getting into character" and doing what the script, playwright, and director want. Among the exercises Gray remembers in Aaron's workshop was the one requiring students to stand and tell stories solely based on personal events of the day. A storyteller from as far back as he could remember, Gray was a master of the exercise from the beginning. He tells us that on that first day when his turn came, he "experienced a memory film" in front of his small workshop audience and had "no trouble editing or selecting which material to use as I spoke." This sort of tuning in to personal experience, so difficult for many of the workshop members, was practically second nature for Gray. Perhaps he heard the term for the first time when Aaron asked Gray, "Very interesting. Who wrote that *monologue* for you?" It would be a full decade before Gray seriously returned to this thought, but the idea that there might be value in telling his life story onstage stayed with him.

What happened before Gray moved onto the storytelling stage by himself was a decade of self-discovery and artistic development that transformed a gaseous rebel without a cause into an artist with a story to tell and a means to get it out. Gray's growing interest in alternative theater led him to discover and later join the Performance Garage, under Richard Schechner's guidance, in 1970. He joined as an emergency replacement for the role of Malcolm in the Group's *Makbeth* (based on Shakespeare's *Macbeth*). He was the first of a new series of performers to eventually replace the Performance Group's original membership, which had just completed the sensational *Dionysus in 69* (opened in 1968), one of the great signature pieces of the 1960s alternative theater movement. Gray saw *Dionysus in 69* and "can remember sitting up on the highest platform with my heart in my mouth." *Dionysus in 69* was a free-wheeling and exhilarating experience, packed with love, dance, song, liberated libidos, and glorious nudity.

Dionysus in 69 had the added feature of allowing the actors literally to be themselves even as they were performing certain roles within the piece. This was where Gray wanted to be. Joining the Group and meeting Richard Schechner were profoundly important events in Gray's career, and in his life. Schechner was a young intellectual dynamo, a Ph.D. from Tulane University with a faculty appointment at NYU and a passion for the streets. And here was Gray, an intuitively talented actor with more training than most and a willingness to take his skills to a new and utterly unorthodox level. He and Schechner hit it off from the start, and the relationship blossomed into a lifelong professional and personal friendship. It was clear that Gray had found his place, far from his traditionalist experiences and far from traditionalist disappointment.

It can't be overemphasized just how fortunate Spalding Gray was when it came to being in the right place at the right time on numerous occasions in his life. By good fortune, someone had encouraged him as a teenager to try acting. By good fortune, he was given the chance to try out traditional theater and to build up a sense of what was missing. And now, by good fortune, he found Schechner. Here he was, in New York City, stumbling from one stroke of good luck to another. As a last-minute replacement, he was sucked into one of the most dynamic theater groups of the period. Through Richard Schechner and his band of performers, Gray would evolve and absorb a variety of experiences that would reappear later in different ways.

Alongside this new theater, a new political activism was also being forged. Gray entered this dynamic avant-garde performance environment at a time when political activism couldn't be avoided, disregarded, or overlooked. As a result, a certain rising political consciousness would be unavoidable. And Gray's exposure to this activist world was a good thing, especially given that politics was not something he would have been drawn to on his own. It ultimately sharpened his vision and gave bite to his perspective on the world around him.

However, Gray didn't become a political activist for any specific cause per se. The highly politicized "acting-up" brand of 1960s protest wasn't his style. But Gray would internalize these dawning sensibilities and eventually develop his own manner of confrontation as the 1960s gave way to the 1970s and 1980s. Perhaps because he hadn't fully experienced the 1960s revolution from its very beginning, or perhaps because he was a bit older than the other bright-eyed activists of the period, Gray was less resolutely committed to the period's radicalism. But this may have made him more ready for what was to come when the ecstasy of the 1960s gave way to more sober political activism and less spectacular forms of performance expression.

We see here another interesting pattern in Gray's life and career. Trained in the traditional form but never fully committed to it, he moved to revolutionary alternatives but never fully bought into their underlying politics. That meant he would be ready to move in new directions when the times warranted, carrying with him only baggage from the past that was of more permanent value and dropping what had become dated. It was his ability to harness the winds of cultural change in his own art that would prevent him from becoming a museum piece, cultural artifact, or historical curiosity. He seemed always to be part of what was happening at the *present* moment, never trapped by living in the past or even by trying to resurrect it. So he was committed to the cultural counterrevolution of the 1960s and early 1970s, but when the time came to move on, he did what most Americans who lived through the 1960s did. He moved on, too. In fact, movement to the future is something of an American hallmark that Spalding seemed more than happy to embrace. Moving out of the 1960s may have been difficult for many people bitterly disappointed by the sober realization that the hoped-for utopia would not arrive. The bitterness affected Spalding too, but rather than dwell on the matter, he moved on.

It's important, however, to understand the influence that Richard Schechner and his 1960s-era band of performers had on Gray. Through them he would evolve and absorb a variety of experiences that would reappear in different ways when in the 1980s he began doing monologues in front of ever-growing audiences.

Gray and the Performance Group

For the moment, Gray would learn what he could from Schechner. Following *Makbeth*, the group prepared for *Commune* (opened in December 1970), a project that Schechner generated with the help of his performers, all collaboratively interacting and developing a piece during hours and hours of unstructured group improvisation. The inspiration for *Commune* was the infamous Manson family, whose sensational ritual murder of Sharon Tate and others represented a "commune" gone bad. The piece also touched upon the equally infamous My Lai massacre in Vietnam. And it included what amounted to a collage of scenes, images, and actions of America, ranging from the Pilgrims sailing to the New World and happening upon the Statue of Liberty to life unfolding on a contemporary commune in Death Valley. All the scenes were inspired to critique the American cultural obsession with property, private ownership in general, and a willingness among the privileged classes to turn to violence in order to preserve their dubious entitlements.

The improvisations for *Commune* were emotive and full of free associations among the performers, designed in part to reflect how the Manson commune may have behaved on the evenings before and after their notorious murder rampages. The Group avoided simply "telling a story" in straight narrative form, preferring a free and unordered flow of images and vignettes to generate more basic emotions and feelings. It was part of a radical practice that Schechner called Environmental Theater, based on the assumption that seeing, feeling, and thinking differently about the world is a necessary first step to actually changing it. Schechner argued that theater could best bring that change about. His ideas opened a world of new possibilities for Gray and his fellow performers, sprung in opposition to the old ways of thinking about the theater process. Schechner schematized the differences between the old and new theaters in the following way:

TRADITIONAL	NEW
plot	images/events
action	activity
resolution	open-ended
roles	tasks
themes/thesis	no pre-set meaning
stage distinct from house	one area for all
script	scenario or free form
flow	compartments
single focus	multifocus
audience watches	audience participates, sometimes does not exist
product	process

These new ideas, so clearly laid out, mesmerized Gray. He enjoyed the theater for what seemed to be the first time in a long time. Swept into the swirl of energy and the smell of revolution, Gray couldn't be happier. Something big was happening, and there he was in the middle.

Commune began with an event—the Manson family Sharon Tate murder—out of which the performance piece organically grew into something more than a helter-skelter tale of murder and mayhem. Next, Schechner would direct his performers' energies to feed off of and respond to actual plays. He asked them to respond not just as actors in the play but as actors who were aware that they were performing the roles of actors. So rather than perform the play as it "was meant to be performed," they used the scripts as catalysts to generate spin-off ideas and emotions that weren't technically "in the play." The result was a sort of "all the world's a stage" event where performers were clearly *acting* as actors. Calling attention to the make-believe quality of acting encouraged everyone involved—audiences as well as performers—to consider the degree to which we all behave in less-than-authentic ways. To what degree, they seemed to be asking, do we all take on roles and behave like actors in the world beyond the theater?

This seems to have been exactly the kind of experimentation that Gray was looking for. He found a place where he would be able to reflect on real life without it really being real life. The result was an "art" form that came close to and often even blurred the lines between itself and real life, which gave more vitality to real life as it was "acted out." Fun stuff, but there was a decided seriousness behind all of this play. And it intrigued Gray.

Of Schechner's several Performance Group experiments with actual plays, one work stands out as particularly important in Gray's development as a performer and thinker: Sam Shepard's *The Tooth of Crime* (Performance Garage production, 1972). Shepard is of course a master observer in his own right of that thing called "America." Though the two men saw the world in notably different ways, this early contact with another "middle American" was important for Gray, and the effects would become pretty apparent later in his monologues.

In *The Tooth of Crime*, Gray played Hoss. Hoss is not an easy character to describe, being rock star, gangster, cowboy, and cultural icon all wrapped into a single "American" character. As the play opens, he is at the peak of his power. That means Hoss can go nowhere from there but down, which is exactly what happens as he is challenged by his more youthful arch-nemesis, Crow. They eventually engage in a duel of style that amounts to a verbal face-off to the death. Language is their weapon of choice, and the confrontation is truly explosive.

Hoss is a dynamic mix of all the clichés of rugged individualism that have captured the American imagination for generations. He is confident, sexually potent, fearless, a born leader. And he has "earned" his perch at the top of the heap through grim determination, talent, and a cold-hearted killer's instinct to prevail. Crow, on the other hand, has found a shortcut to the top of the heap. Instead of hard work, talent, and guts, he has discovered (to draw upon the old advertising jingle) that image is everything. Hoss understands the power of the image and masters it in his own way, but Crow has

Spalding Gray as Hoss in Sam Shepard's *The Tooth of Crime*. (Photo courtesy of Kathie Russo.)

come to realize that image doesn't have to be earned by sweat and hard work. Smoke and mirrors will do just as well and work far more quickly. Celebrity, for example, once meant someone was famous for having done something, but Crow understands that celebrity can be earned simply by manufacturing an image of it. This point doesn't sound so new today, but Shepard was among the first to grasp the direction America was headed back in the early 1970s. Posturing has to be dazzling, and if the right chord is struck, fame follows. In this new world, Shepard sees our culture won over by empty glitz and glamour rather than by the old American virtues of hard work and real talent.

In this world of power mongering, language has become the tool of force and control, and (recall that this is the early 1970s) the language of rock 'n' roll has become the most powerful cultural weapon of all, the perfect accumulation of all the basic instinctual urges found in aggressive masculinity. It's the same masculinity that "owns," manipulates, and controls the world, and the same masculinity that is mixed up with the idea of what it means to be "American." The sounds and rhythms that Shepard captures in the play embody the spirit of braggart and bold America at its most confident, or at least at its most audacious. Riveting stuff, to be sure.

Among the several changes Schechner made to *The Tooth of Crime* was to have his performers invest themselves personally in the play by giving them the freedom to adapt the roles to fit their own personalities. Schechner intentionally muddied the distinction between having performers represent the characters of the play and having them present themselves onstage more as the flesh-and-bone human beings they actually were. It's almost as if the actors walked on as themselves and then donned the masks of the character roles they were playing. Their own personalities stood side by side with and frequently melted into their characters in the play.

The freedom Schechner gave his performers to personally embellish the roles they were playing really appealed to Gray. Schechner summarized the free-wheeling process of putting together his production:

> First we sang the play as if it were an opera. Every line was sung, sometimes as recitative, sometimes as aria, sometimes solo, and sometimes in chorus. Then we sang the play as a kind of Jagger-like talking jazz. . . . Then we read the play "naturalistically," as if every scene were taken directly from life. In none of the explorations were we trying to figure out the dialogue from the point of view of characterization. The performers were feeling the language

out, weighing it, discovering how it moved, what its possibilities were. The text was treated concretely—not simply as sound nor simply as denotation, but as something conditioned by sound.

Schechner infected his performers with the realization that language communicates in many ways and at levels sometimes far more influential than the stated, factual or denotative levels we generally listen for. Picking the right word makes all the difference between sounding like an outlaw and sounding like a bureaucrat. Picking the right tone and rhythm can put a person in control; the wrong tone or a halting rhythm turns the tide to defensiveness. These are only a few of several complex ideas Gray would take away from *The Tooth of Crime*.

The play provided the perfect opportunity to demonstrate how the world of rock music had risen out of and then helped further to mold what we call reality. Even today (well past the heyday of the mega-rock bands), we are still affected by lyrics, music, and images of the great rock stars. Given the overwhelming power of that "art form," it only makes sense that we all behave to one degree or another as rock stars do, bluffing our way through life as best we can with upturned lips and gloved hands, wearing leather pants and underwear as outerwear. More to the point as far as Shepard and Schechner (and Gray) are concerned is how we use language to declare our aggressive tendencies and to mark off our territory from the rest of the world.

What intrigued Schechner and inspired Gray was how that sort of highly theatrical behavior and "regular" human day-to-day behavior coexist side by side in the real world. In the end, lifestyle role-playing is not just what rock stars, actors, and other performers do. We all adopt the same kinds of role-playing in our own lives, to the point that one of the biggest problems for modern humans is the near impossibility of being able to tell who we really are.

Schechner's strategy with this play paralleled his larger agenda of studying image and authenticity in American culture and how they have come to dominate our increasingly confused sense of "who we are" in this world. We witness how glitz and show have become easily worn and then just as easily discarded as new styles of "authenticity" rise and fade. Is it possible to find anything genuine in a world so dominated by "style"? And, maybe even more unsettling, is such authenticity any longer even of worth in our world? What are the alternatives? In the case of the nearly universal allure of rock culture, its icons are less an elitist clique of artists than a sampling of trends and fashions influencing virtually all of us in one way or another. To some degree, we have all become inauthentic and superficial, pursuing glitz and glamour rather than substance and authenticity. This perspective makes for a pretty grim vision of American culture.

Through his experiences with Shepard and Schechner, Gray came to understand how fragile the notion of "being real" in the contemporary world actually is. Hoss's more authentic brand of American originality is overwhelmed and abandoned in favor of the naïve experiments of empty self-indulgence in the "gloriously liberating" 1960s. Gray too seems to have felt this sense of emptiness. Through his connection with Schechner, Gray was encouraged to work toward more a substantive understanding and presentation of his *self.* This general point about personal authenticity very likely additionally highlighted exactly why he disliked traditional theater, since its focus is the craft of pretending to be someone else, the height of inauthenticity and an intentional sham.

Schechner provided Gray the perfect opportunity to weigh the pros and cons of stealing away from traditional theater altogether and becoming an authentic original. It's tough enough for the average middle American to stay the course of personal authenticity, having seen the quick rise to wealth and power certain audacious "celebrities" achieved by being ostentatiously inauthentic. Being in the acting profession, where inauthentic "show" is a condition of success, must have made the issue for Gray even more complex. Trying to maintain personal authenticity on the stage is a tricky business indeed, but one that he felt was worth pursuing.

While performing in *The Tooth of Crime*, Gray was exposed to the play's aggressively masculine world of power and control. It was an almost perfect capsule of the kind of competitive and violent behavior that is valorized in American culture as "right" for males. A sort of Darwinian survival-of-the-fittest mentality encourages "manly" domination over the many weak and "unmanly" others in the world as the manly few reap benefits at the expense of the "unmanly" many. This mentality can be seen as the root of all kinds of cultural ills, including sexism and racism. One could reasonably argue that this type of accepted aggression and oppression was precisely the kind of thing that spawned a Manson commune or a My Lai massacre, the central subjects that Schechner and Gray confronted in *Commune*.

Sam Shepard himself seems to personify our culture's preferred brand of masculinity, with his rugged cowboy behavior that seems to make him truly a man's man, a flesh-and-bone Marlboro Man called "Sam Shepard." Of course, this "Sam Shepard" image is in large part a media creation. Who knows if the real Sam Shepard is like the persona we learn about in *People* magazine? True to the "message" of *The Tooth of Crime*, the image may be more powerful than the man, and it epitomizes the rugged individualism traditionally admired and troublingly aspired to by male youths of many American generations.

The Tooth of Crime as a whole can be seen as an endorsement of this unfortunate sort of American male machismo, since the only real choice males seem to have in the play is to *really* be a man's man, as Hoss is, or to *pretend* to be one, as Crow does. It's not much of a choice, of course, and it's a criticism some people have of Shepard's highly masculinized vision of America. However, it would also be fair to say that Shepard is actually criticizing the limited, myopic vision of America that offers too few choices of how to be a male American, and a white male at that. And almost nothing is said about other types of Americans.

Whatever the case, this sort of competitive machismo was not in Gray's nature. He was not suited to be either Hoss *or* Crow. But then, a cursory review of all the kinds of people who make up "manhood" in America (and abroad) should reveal that only a very few men in the world actually conform to either brand of masculinity. And that's not necessarily a bad thing, though cultural pressures often seem to suggest otherwise. There must be other options, an issue with which Gray struggled for much of his life. Curiously, though, his growing sense of not being fully successful as a man's man was among the several qualities that made Gray and his art so sympathetically intriguing to that rather large group of men and women who don't match or endorse the outsized version of masculinity that *The Tooth of Crime* seems to present and that mainstream American culture celebrates.

Determining how to be a man on his own terms was a significant part of Gray's larger process of finding his own substantial self. It's reasonable to suggest that this idea of developing a comfortable masculinity obsessed Gray his entire life, much as it obsesses America in general.

Gray may have learned another very troubling lesson working on *The Tooth of Crime*. Hoss loses his fight with Crow, but rather than live defeated in a world that celebrates empty show, he chooses to maintain his hard-earned masculine authenticity by making a dramatic exit—committing suicide onstage. Gray perhaps saw this as an act of affirmation in a world void of meaning and value. Suicide attracted and intrigued Gray for most of his adult life. The attraction began in earnest when his mother committed suicide, and it followed him even to his last living days. But that point deserves discussion elsewhere.

2

Incubating "Spalding Gray"

The Wooster Group

Richard Schechner's Performance Group had its Performing Garage home in a small converted warehouse on SoHo's Wooster Street. For Spalding and his colleagues, the Garage was a place to get away from the debilitating demands of commercial theater. It was a haven that allowed them to experiment at their own pace with performance styles and ideas that weren't going to succeed under the glaring light of Broadway-style corporate-theater prime time. But then, that was never their target audience, and filling producers' pockets with cash wasn't their goal. The Group had a different clientele, a small but dedicated following that welcomed their experimentation and an activist local press—headed by the *Village Voice*—that reported and publicized with a sharp but sympathetic critical eye. And that really was good enough for Spalding, at least for the time being.

Had Gray chosen to remain with the Performance Group, he would likely be remembered today as one of the great experimentalists of the period, having created a valuable body of work during this free-flowing, dynamic period of theater experimentation. As it turned out, he didn't stay on. But this time was crucial in Gray's eventual development as a stand-alone monologist, because it was then and there that he developed his craft, found his voice, and built up the needed confidence to move forward.

Part of what Spalding would come to understand while working with the Group was that the times were changing very quickly, and not necessarily for the better. To keep up with America in general, he would need to learn to change with it, or at least to know it well enough to comment on and critique it. The later 1970s in America (and abroad) evolved into something clearly different in tone and feel from what was experienced in the 1960s and early 1970s. The almost giddy optimism that a new day would soon be dawning was replaced by a growing realization that that much hoped-for day would never come, at least not anytime soon. The Vietnam War's end rattled rather than strengthened America's confidence in itself. The Great Society that President Johnson had envisioned in the 1960s was swallowed up by a stinging economic recession. And conservative political retrenchment was the inevitable result. It's as if the great carnival celebration of youthful optimism that was the 1960s cultural revolution had awakened to the sober light of a gloomy, overcast, hung over reality. Everyone seemed to have decided that the best thing to do was to dust themselves off, go their separate ways, and find jobs. Or, given the recession, try to find jobs.

A look at the Performance Group's work reveals that Gray and his colleagues anticipated this shift to private resignation and sober introspection well before the mid-1970s. As early as Gray's first participation in the Group in the late 1960s, many of the offerings prophetically reflected the darker vision that seemed to be making cultural headway. Gone were the liberating conceits of *Dionysus in 69*, replaced by more pensive broodings on Charles Manson and My Lai. It became increasingly apparent to these artists that if hope and optimism were to survive into the 1970s and beyond, they would have to include a much more toned-down vision of change, far less spectacular, more cautious, far less naïvely utopian.

Despite this more pensive mood, however, the 1960s did have a positive and even lasting effect. People did go back to work for

Spalding Gray, circa 1973. (Photo courtesy of Kathie Russo.)

corporate America, but it was not entirely with the tunnel-visioned goal of personal advancement that seemed to have pervaded the 1950s. Rather, there was a lingering discontentment with what seemed to be a return to "normal." Despite appearances, at least for some of us, going our separate ways was no longer good enough.

In the theater, a decided turn toward introspection reflected this larger return to and obsession with individualized self-preservation and self-improvement. On the surface, it appeared that even avant-garde experimental theater was throwing in the towel and accepting a return to worlds of fragmented isolationism disconnected from the social consciousness that the "new" theater of the 1960s nurtured. But even in this less flamboyant version of experimental theater, something hinted that general discontentment and a desire for change were still alive. No one seemed terribly satisfied with the idea of returning to the 1950s, and in its own way the experimental theater became the place where the flame of the 1960s would still burn, though perhaps not as brightly as in the early days of unbounded optimism.

Reflecting dissatisfaction at the resignation that at least appeared to pervade American culture, Gray's own evolution during this period reveals something of a refusal merely to abdicate to the way things were. Rather, he seems to have begun to understand the value of taking a step back and learning how to operate in this confusing and increasingly oppressive culture, increasingly buried under an illusive façade of empty glamour and glitz.

Gray's Wooster Agenda: *Three Places in Rhode Island*

In his 1986 preface to the published text of his early monologues collectively entitled *Sex and Death to the Age 14*, Gray acknowledges his great debt to Schechner and the Performance Group, crediting Schechner with being the first person to encourage him "to be myself first, before I thought of acting a role or taking on a character." Schechner's encouragement was the spark that eventually led Gray to enter into a spin-off collaboration with Elizabeth LeCompte and others from the Performing Group, which eventually became the Wooster Group, cofounded by Gray and LeCompte.

The creative experimental work that became *Three Places in Rhode Island* led to the creation of the Wooster Group, though the transition was almost imperceptible, given that the original parts of *Three Places* were first presented under the auspices of the Performance Group. This is an important point, because it returns us to that trend in Gray's career. Rather than making clean breaks with the past as he moved forward, he simply folded the past into the present—and the future. Almost seamlessly, Gray's Performance Group days became his Wooster Group days.

And in this case in particular, the past shaped the present (and future) in yet another way. What became the Wooster Group's signature early work was all inspired in one way or another by Gray's childhood and adolescence. What is really amazing is that, somehow, Gray was able to draw so many other people into his world, including Performance Group members of genuine talent (and eventual fame) like Ron Vawter, Libby Howes, and Willem Dafoe. Gray's enigmatic appeal had already begun to draw others to cast their lot with this talented storyteller.

But while Gray's raw material was the thing around which the Group would now orbit, this material would be transformed into experimental theater as a result of what they had all learned from Schechner. Schechner had always insisted that his actors needed to know who they were before they could be effective performers in the type of alternative theater he was advocating. Gray frequently highlighted the point himself: "Richard Schechner . . . was a liberator from assembly line acting techniques. The way that I interpreted Schechner's theories was that I was free to do what I wanted, be who I was." The result was a band of performers who took Schechner's teachings to heart and did what he most wanted them to do: declare their independence from the constricting shackles of theatrical tradition, including its ways of acting but also—and more importantly—its ways of thinking.

This group of performers created a series of improvisations generated in creative collaboration and creatively choreographed by Elizabeth Lecompte. Everything was based on the life memories of Gray, but the memories were altered, transformed, and remolded by the active input of all the other group members, whose own recollections spun off of Gray's. His childhood vacations, sibling rivalries, meaningful friendships, and family crises led others to recall their own similar experiences and to share them with the Group.

The results, however, were anything but collages of life stories told like fairy tales. Instead, productions were non-narrative, emotively free-wheeling, and very physical, often silent but filled with dance, pantomimes, literary allusions, and games. The result of this rather chaotic, more or less decentralized collaborative process was more a collective cultural history than a singular self-reflection upon Gray's own life. Gray confirms as much when he observes, "The source of the work was myself, but the final product was a result of the collective conceptual actions of all involved. Thus, in the end, it is a group autobiography."

With the help of the Wooster Group, Gray came to understand that the idea of "me" had built into it the idea of "everyone else" as well. Or at least of "almost everyone else." If he could present something of himself onstage, he would also effectively be presenting something of other people as well.

The Wooster Group's 1975 first effort, *Sakonnet Point*, evolved into a meditation on childhood, what Gray described as "a silent mood piece which represented the child before speech." The second

Spalding Gray in *Sakonnet Point*. (Photo copyright Ken Kobland, courtesy of The Wooster Group.)

piece, *Rumstick Road* (1977), "was about the child learning to speak by listening and imitating." Gray adds: "It was based on a series of audio tapes I'd made of my family. The work evolved as a docudrama in which we improvised a series of actions using the family audio tapes as background text. Eventually these improvisations were set and scored." In this second piece, clearly a new light was dawning for Gray. He began to sense that his own personal experiences had larger resonance by themselves, and *Rumstick Road* showed his growing confidence that his own memories reached out to other people without being filtered through the experiences of his colleagues. As a result, in *Rumstick Road*, Gray became much more comfortable actually "playing" himself, calling himself "Spalding Gray," and he "took on no outside character." Ultimately, Gray's transformation into an "auto-performer" began in the third piece, *Nayatt School* (1978).

In *Nayatt School*, Gray reports, "the monologue form I'd been developing found its full expression." He adds:

> Much of *Nayatt School* was based on a deconstruction of T. S. Eliot's *The Cocktail Party*, and at the beginning of the piece I performed a short monologue about my relationship to that play while sitting at a long wooden table. The other members of The Wooster Group were my first audience. Each day when I'd come in for rehearsal they would ask me to tell it again, and I did, while Liz taped it. Each day it was embellished and edited and grew as a text until at last we transcribed it.

This short opening monologue converted Gray the actor into Gray the person or personality for the first time. The rest of the performance would leave his audiences with the dilemma of deciding to see Gray as the flesh-and-blood person they'd just met or as the actor who was supposed to disappear into his role when the "real" performance began. It was sort of like watching a friend onstage who never really dissolves into the role she's playing. This is exactly what Gray was looking for, a blurring of reality and fiction, and what attracted him to Schechner and the Performance Group several years earlier. *Nayatt School*'s introduction of Gray the monologist to the theater made it increasingly apparent that he was on the verge of going it on his own.

In 1979, the Wooster Group and Gray put together an epilogue to the trilogy, *Point Judith*. It was a piece that responded in large part to Eugene O'Neill's landmark work *Long Day's Journey into Night*. By 1979, Gray had fully discovered how much he enjoyed being an autoperformer, and this epilogue in fact was something of a farewell for him. The Performance Group/Wooster Group experience helped Gray to develop a fresh and confident way of looking at the world. And he would carry those insights with him throughout his breakaway career, often in harmony with the Wooster Group's own evolving agenda, which would go on without him even into the twenty-first century and win avant-garde acclaim on its own. But while the Wooster Group remained rather esoteric in its performance agenda, Gray's newfound approach to communicating with his audience took him away from his experimental, "highbrow" roots and into the "middlebrow" world of ever-larger audiences and venues.

It can't be highlighted enough, however, that this turn would probably never have occurred without the Group's heavy influence on Gray's understanding of and attitudes toward art and culture. He would have to come to terms, for example, with the fact that his early efforts were more narcissistically confessional than culturally relevant. What he began to learn through the Wooster Group, however, was that this narcissism wasn't necessarily a bad thing. He needed to develop his skills of observation into something that audiences could relate to. Eventually he discovered the trick: while he was introspectively observing "Spalding Gray," he was also observing "America" in miniature. Narcissistic, yes, but with the right sorts of tweaking, culturally relevant. If this weren't true, Gray's agenda would have had an extremely short shelf life.

The first important step was to blend self-awareness with self-distancing and objective analysis. This was evident in the first of the

Sakonnet Point. Pictured (l–r) Spalding Gray, Libby Howes. (Photo copyright Ken Kobland, courtesy of The Wooster Group.)

Rhode Island trilogy pieces, *Sakonnet Point*, which Gray describes "as a series of simple actions . . . that created a series of images like personal, living Rorschachs. These images were not unlike the blank, white wall in Zen meditations, nor were they unlike the mirror reflection of a good therapist." This sort of highly personal bent and highly personal therapeutic appearance became something of a hallmark of much of the Wooster Group's work. *Sakonnet Point* was the kind of "highbrow" production that has frequently been criticized as shrinking theater from a public to a private art form, reflecting rather than challenging the general 1970s cultural tendency toward privacy and isolation. It was a theater that appeared to endorse isolation over community.

Gray, however, disagreed that this highly personal work had abandoned a sense of community. While it definitely was nothing like the bonding in the effusive and fully physical happenings of the 1960s, he argued that "what the audience saw was the reflection of their own minds, their own projections." In other words, Gray's private art reached the public domain of his audience, though in subtler ways than Schechner's fully participatory environmental theater of the 1960s advocated. The free-love, free-expression, openly physical touch of the 1960s became more of a cerebral connection by the late 1970s.

The artfulness of art was a new focus for Gray and his collaborators. And once again Gray became vulnerable to charges of private self-indulgence, this time in the form of subscribing to "mere aestheticism." His "art-for-art's sake" appearance had self-expressive charm, but it seemed to have abandoned any real community or "communal" relevance. This too, however, was more a case of toning down the exuberance rather than abandoning the spirit of the 1960s. This new performance continued the "tradition" of community-engaging art by advocating anti-status quo perspectives much as Schechner's art strove to do. But Gray did so in a much more "open-nerved" manner, starting from the personal and then moving outward. Gray says of his "new" brand of art:

> It became not the art of pretending I was someone else but an art that began to approach the idea that I was someone else. I wanted to give up the names, to close the gaps. It was no longer to be the "Stanley Kowalski self" or the "Hamlet self," but now it was a play of moods, energies, aspects of self. It became the many-in-the-one that had its source in the archetype of the performer, not in the text.

The "many-in-the-one" was Gray's aesthetic refrain. So the truer he was in "dissecting" himself, the truer he would be in revealing human nature in general.

While the archetypes of the Western world (like Hamlet and Stanley) had come from the pen of the playwright, Gray embraced the performance paradigm as the more immediate, more pure source of "archetypal" humanity. He had become interested in the connection between performance in life and performance in art, extending the concept well beyond his own isolated self and moving in a direction found in his and Schechner's earlier work with plays like Shepard's *The Tooth of Crime*. Gray's new style did allow him rather selfishly to discover his "self," but in this presentation and discovery, he discovered other selves as well:

> By chance, I might suddenly find myself performing an action that was an aspect of me, and, upon reflection see it as an action belonging to Orpheus. Then, for that moment, I would be both Spalding and Orpheus. I was never one or the other and could be someone or something completely different for each audience member because they also live with their "names" and associations. It is their story as well as mine.

This process of interidentity yielded a sense of community that penetrated far deeper than the superficial contacts of the 1960s had ever reached, uniting performer and audience by a growing awareness of common experience. At least that was the theory. If the Rhode Island trilogy succeeded, it should build foundations for community by encouraging audiences to enact their own self-completions, which would pave the way for them to find common ground on which to communicate with "other selves," beyond and after connecting with Spalding Gray.

Another aspect of Gray's trilogy is at first glance problematic. Gray notes that "all of *Sakonnet Point* was built from free associations within the performing space. There were no 'ideas' about how it should be, nor was there any attempt to tell a meaningful story." Two commentators in the influential journal *The Drama Review* built on this: James Bierman notes that the piece "is more evocative in style than expositional," and Arnold Aronson concludes that the work's "value lay not in any informational structure but in their capacity for evoking further images and moods. The creators did not intend to provoke thought but rather an inward contemplation." This performance piece relied upon hard-to-define images and moods. The problem is that audiences generally look for "author's messages" in traditional art—in theater as well as other forms—and this type of art distinctly avoids offering messages. It doesn't even offer story lines to follow, at least not in any traditional sense. This new approach could have one of two general effects: it could alienate and frustrate audiences or it could catalyze them to make up their own stories from the raw material placed in front of them, making them active participants in the performance event. The intention, of course, is to generate the latter response. And Gray seemed to think it worked, especially with that smaller, non-Broadway kind of audience that had adopted the Performance and Wooster Group: "Often, what the audience saw was the reflection of their own minds, their own projections." The process requires an active desire on the part of the audience, and Gray was aware of this. These sorts of works might lose their audiences. But Gray was willing to take that chance, for at this point in his career he strongly identified with a growing avant-garde tradition concerned with such involvement:

> I think *Sakonnet Point* was like the work of Robert Wilson and Meredith Monk. I had found that while watching their work my mind was left free to associate and my eye was grounded in watching the execution of their chosen actions. It was this grounding of my eye that gave my mind a quality of freedom I'd not experienced in theatre before. For me, the work of Wilson and Monk was dealing with the use of, and investigation into the nature of, mind projections. This seemed to be getting to the roots of what theatre and life are about. It is a kind of therapeutic lesson about how we create our own world through our projections.

Gray firmly believed that his own *Sakonnet Point* "was very involving and seemed therapeutic for the audience as well as the performer." Schechner's advocacy of some sort of literal, physical involvement of

Rumstick Road. Pictured (l–r): Spalding Gray, Libby Howes, Bruce Porter. (Photo copyright Ken Kobland, courtesy of The Wooster Group.)

the audience had been replaced by perceptual, conceptual, emotional, and mental involvement. Whether or not Gray's efforts succeeded as thoroughly and completely as he desired, it was clear at this point in his career that he was attracting a relatively small but dedicated audience of converts.

For the moment, Gray would continue on this highbrow (and fairly humorless) tack. When the Group moved on to *Rumstick Road*, they focused on Gray's mother's suicide, a central traumatic event in his life to which he would later return in many of his monologues. Again, though, autobiographical presentation was a catalyst for inspiration rather than an end in itself. Gray notes, "Although the basis of the piece was the voices and pictures of my family, the other performers were free to take off from this material and develop their own scores." He admits that the piece is "confessional" but asserts that it "was also an act of distancing" since the performances were critical commentaries on certain events rather than actual reenactments of them. Gray observes, "Finally, if it is therapeutic, it is not so much so in the fact that it is confessional but in the fact that it is ART. The historic event of my mother's suicide is only a part of the fabric of that ART. Finally, the piece is not about suicide; it is about making ART."

By the time the Group got to the trilogy's third piece, *Nayatt School*, they were ready to use their evocative style to full effect, presenting and expressing feelings and ideas that had been growing in the two earlier pieces. Basically, *Nayatt School* concentrated on the effects of being introduced to Freudian psychology, which had been seeping into the collective consciousness as a tool to explain the onslaught of neuroses and psychoses in America (and elsewhere). Gray argues that despite its frankly distorted perspective on the world in general and its often confusing jargon in particular, Freudian psychology is nevertheless quite "real." Gray observes, "I felt and believed this at the time and wanted to make a theatre piece that was not only a reflection of that strange world, but the world itself." Years later, in 2002, Gray would acknowledge reading the work of British psychiatrist D. W. Winnicott, whose studies of mother-child relationships led to the phrase, "the good-enough mother." Perhaps hungry for more than Freudian psychology could offer, Gray was actually looking for ways to understand that his very disturbed mother, though by no means perfect, was the sort of "good-enough" mother that is part of the upbringing of all "normal" children. Winnicott describes what this means:

> There is no possibility whatever for an infant to proceed from the pleasure principle to the reality principle or towards or beyond primary identification . . . , unless there is a good-enough mother. The good-enough "mother" (not necessarily the infant's own mother) is one who makes active adaptation to the infant's needs, an active adaptation that gradually lessens, according to the infant's growing ability to account for failure of adaptation and to tolerate the results of frustration.

This "good-enough mother" idea would obsess Gray for virtually his whole adult life, given his own mother's bouts with insanity and eventual suicide, and even more because he really believed that he'd had "a pretty normal childhood." If nothing else, *Nayatt School* was Gray's first attempt to come to psychological terms—in his art—with his relationship with his mother, offering by extension opportunities for his audience to do the same with their own relationships.

In fact, Gray states that he moved beyond therapy in the trilogy to reflect upon more universal "themes of loss." The various parts of the trilogy, he says, "are not just about the loss of my mother but about the feeling of loss itself. I have had this feeling for as long as I can remember. It is the feeling that the 'I' that I call 'me' is only a visitor here. No, not even a visitor because a visitor goes elsewhere after he visits. I have no word for it, and the work is the attempt at giving expression to that absent word." If Gray began with personal experience, he wanted to move that experience to a plane that reflected more than just his own condition. Gray admits, "I fantasize that if I am true to art it will be the graceful vehicle which will return me to life." But in this process something more than personal therapy occurs, for "the very act of communication takes it into a 'larger vein' and brings it back to community."

Coming to Terms with Cultural Oppression

On the surface, at least, the trilogy is entirely apolitical. There's not even a hint of political commentary or current events, which seems almost unfathomable given that these performers were all basically activist children of the 1960s. In fact, this trend in the Wooster Group likewise occurred in much of the theater of the mid-1970s and later, and was something of a cultural reflection in general. The failure of the 1960s cultural revolution stung activist and idealistic America, and at first glance it seems that people simply gave up on the pursuit of love, hope, charity, and change.

Gray and the Wooster Group, however, are evidence that what actually happened was less a matter of giving up than of changing strategies. As noted above, the group took one giant step backward and turned in upon itself, hoping that getting in touch with "self" would be a first step toward getting in touch with "others." But getting in touch with themselves was either caused by or the cause of a very important revelation. The 1960s pitted the youthful cultural revolution against the tyrannical "establishment," famously labeled the military-industrial complex. It was an us-against-them vision that believed change would only come about by destroying dastardly capitalism and its supporting institutions of oppression. Gray and the Wooster Group, among several other perceptive cultural observers and critics, seem to have settled upon a different revelation after the collapse of that revolutionary fervor, which seemed to have imploded under its own idealism. Could it be that even the advocates of change—hippies and yippies included—were as guilty as their establishmentarian opponents of having made the world the detestable place it had become? Could it be that to change the world, we need to begin by first changing ourselves? After all, aren't we all part of the world that we claim to be so oppressive and unjust? And if we're part of that unjust world, doesn't that mean that we are in some way part of the problem?

This rising sense of universal complicity, this realization that "the enemy is us," seems to have infected even American antiestablishment culture as the 1960s receded into history, leaving a numbness that was and continues to be difficult to overcome. Cultural critics generally identify this feeling to be "the postmodern condition." And many Americans turned to getting on with the business of lining their pockets in a world whose mantra was fast becoming "greed is good." But there remained a determined core of 1960s-style hangers-on who saw a need for gainful self-reflection to discover the "enemy within." By finding that inner source of all our troubles, they clung to the hope that change could once again be advocated. This is one way of looking at the introspective turn that occurred in the mid-1970s. It helps to explain the sometimes vague defenses against critics' charges of isolationism that Gray and others made.

Saying things like "I see others in myself" was perhaps accurate. But there was a bigger point to be made: "I see even my enemy in myself."

The battle lines that seemed so clear in the 1960s melted away by the mid-1970s, leaving many Americans considering more precisely what they were fighting against. If it was American imperialism, wasn't it the very military-industrial complex that ensured that the inflow of goods and materials from around the world was sufficient to keep us warm and comfortable? Was it better to give up my car to reduce dependence on foreign oil, or should we keep pipelines flowing even at the expense of equity and justice? If we're opposed to taking advantage of the uneducated and unskilled, shouldn't we first face the fact that the goods and services we can so comfortably afford to purchase are the result of oppressing this labor force? Do we really want to help third-world countries if that means our standard of living might suffer?

To deal with these matters of personal complicity in a culture that seems to thrive on oppression and injustice, more subtle post-1960s avant-garde art—the brand of which Gray and the Wooster Group were part—converted to a guerrilla-style strategy that required taking positions "on the inside," working behind the lines and undercover, and revealing the flawed self-assurances within each of us upon which our culture is constructed. Clearly less sensationally robust and certainly less appealing than the anticultural, us-against-them, throw-up-the-barricades assaults of the 1960s, this new alternative theater was also far less naïve about what it could and could not do. Such theater of complicity was less obviously antiestablishment, and at times it could even be seen as the oppressor's compliant stooge. Accepting that we're all part of the problem made it less obvious that we're not in some way actually *endorsing* the system. How can the well-intended pull themselves out of this apparent hopeless, downward spiral?

As noted earlier, LeCompte, Gray, and others worked on *The Rhode Island Trilogy* in 1975, which included *Sakonnet Point* (1975),

Rumstick Road (1977), *Nayatt School* (1978), and an epilogue entitled *Point Judith* (1979). The titles all identify geographical sites that are in some way related to Gray's life. But while all the pieces by title connect Gray's life to geographical America, they unfold as art in ways that seemingly have very little to do with America per se. What audiences receive from the stage is a series of responsive exercises, autobiographical flashbacks, any number of sights, sounds, and actions that began as group member responses to Gray's life. The result is a multiplicity of possible audience reactions. But because audiences are given so much "freedom" to respond as they choose to these decentered events, the seemingly apolitical performance in a subtle way became fundamentally political. Consider that as a culture, we have almost completely permitted big government and Big Brother media to act and think on our behalf, so it's ironic that we consider ourselves a democracy. What if someone tells us to wake up and think on our own? On one level, that was exactly what the group was doing.

Sakonnet Point began as a set of dance improvisations spinning off of Gray's work with Robert Wilson's Byrd Hoffman School of Byrds, generating a sort of preverbal activity to capture the innocence of childhood. The improvisations were allowed to develop in their own organic manner; only later did LeCompte add taped recordings of various reminiscences by Gray of his family life. The movement of the piece reflects a childlike mentality that has yet to be molded by cultural expectations of "proper" life-in-step behavior. The movement in the piece was freed from the concern that *expression* had to be an expression *of* something. Other than an expression of the experience of being alive, there was no "author's message."

David Savran, whose book *Breaking the Rules* documents the Wooster Group's early years, calls attention to how this process evolves in the piece and the openness it encourages. He highlights a point in the piece where "Boy" playfully pretends to strangle himself. He collapses and plays dead, and then "Spalding" enters, tests to see if "Boy" is alive, and eventually hands "Boy" off to "Man," who carries "Boy" away. Gray described the scene as "an action that seemed intuitively right, that Liz liked as a director, and that agreed with me. There was no discussion of it. I was like a dancer at the time, in the sense that I was only concerned with executing the movement and doing it with full concentration in my body." LeCompte adds: "It was just a nice move. I liked it. I saw Erik [as "Boy"] liked to play with his wrists. So we asked him to do things with his hands. And always, with kids, the fun thing to do is to pretend something's strangling you. So he did it as an improv. He liked to do it. Kids like to pretend they're dying." Here we see a characteristic dimension of the Wooster Group agenda, a willingness to bypass or override that culturally inculcated urge to get meaning out of everything and instead allow the untrained or instinctive urges of the body to take over. Moving away from a rationalist urge to make sense of everything, to know facts, Gray and LeCompte look instead for a language of the body, and through the body they are looking for a level of consciousness unobstructed by what we are trained by our cultural upbringing to look for. The body has its own memory and, when given the opportunity, it constructs its own story. But the process is not really explainable through traditional means, and therefore it runs the risk of being appreciated merely for its playful but meaningless, purely "aesthetic" value. It *looks* like we're just playing around, so it surely can't be important. At least that's what the grown-up in us says.

And if we're just playing around, when will we get to the serious business at hand? Gray's description of a process in *Rumstick Road* should help. The piece centers around Gray's reminiscences of the suicide of his mother, Bette. As the group did its warm-up exercises, they would listen to the various taped interviews of surviving family members that Gray had compiled. Gray recalls one tape-recollected instance of his mother claiming to be visited by Christ and being healed of her then-current ailment:

> We worked on the situation of [Ron] Vawter being a Christ figure
> and [Libby] Howes the mother figure. We read from Acts in the

Bible and one image, the image of Christ healing a sick person by spitting in his ear, captured our imaginations. This led to Vawter becoming more directly physical with Howes and expressing a desire to tickle her stomach. Vawter slowly dropped out of the role of Christ and began to improvise a kind of Esalen-type of doctor-healer who both healed and tickled his patient to the point of very real uncontrollable laughter on the part of Howes, the mother-patient.

The problem is not that this is no longer anything close to Gray's autobiography, but that the little scene seems to have no relevance whatsoever to *anything*, autobiographical or otherwise. The transformation of Gray's recollection of Christ's visitation upon Bette into Vawter tickling Howes seems little more than a meaningless movement away from a factual story to a presentation of performers just goofing off.

However, it's possible to derive a very real political point to the action presented. Anyone who saw the piece would likely agree that *Rumstick Road* at least obliquely felt like a critique of medical and psychiatric professionals. The recorded tapes revealed that as these professionals treated Gray's mother for depression, they basically reduced her to a nonhuman object of "scientific" analysis, blind to the fact that she was a human being worthy of respect as an equal, even among highly trained specialists. Anyone who has gone to a medical specialist may have themselves experienced that feeling of being a scientific specimen, or at least of being a series of parts (an eye, ear, nose, liver) rather than a fully formed, fully conscious human being. Almost without giving it a second thought, we allow health care to dehumanize the patient/specimen it is supposed to "make whole." So we see in *Rumstick Road* that Bette suffered a dehumanizing process familiar to us all.

But rather than exhibiting any sort of outrage at this, *Rumstick Road*, rather humorously at this point, suggests that the medical process rather benignly manipulates living human beings in much the

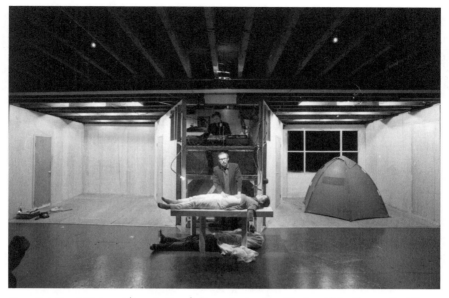

Rumstick Road. Pictured (top–bottom): Bruce Porter, Ron Vawter, Libby Howes, Spalding Gray. (Photo copyright Ken Kobland, courtesy of The Wooster Group.)

same way Vawter's tickling controls Libby Howes. Holding her down and tickling the breath out of her surely looks harmless enough, and we've all likely done it to someone once or twice in our lives. But is this benign? Or is it one simple example of what we and our culture "innocently" do to those we find we can control and manipulate? The scene seemed to tap into sexist oppression to boot: the male Vawter actually manipulates Howes's feminine body, presumably against her wishes. Subtle, and far from the more confrontational feminist political agenda found in the more aggressive art of the 1960s, the work is shadowed by an aesthetic-seeming appearance of play, but it is also a full presentation of the masculine domination that exists in even the most innocent-seeming activities. Are we part of a spirit of oppression when we tickle people into paroxysms of laughter? Could be.

Misinterpretation or even noninterpretation is entirely possible. It is more than likely that some audience members will see this tickling episode on a table as nothing more than "fun." It's also possible to see the scene as endorsing, with humorous approval, the current cultural position that the male does and should control the bodies of "flighty" females. It takes a different sort of audience eye to see that this performance may be designed to make us uncomfortable with this sort of masculine control, especially when that feminine is vulnerably "exposed," laid out as she is on an examination table, as Gray's mother presumably was on many occasions before her suicide. The Wooster Group, however, seems to have been willing to risk misinterpretation in the effort to expose audiences to other ways of seeing and to encourage active analysis rather than passive reception of what was placed before them. Being told in a traditional way (say, by way of "authors' messages") that dehumanizing oppression is wrong is one thing, but directly witnessing that dehumanization and actually identifying it on our own as inhuman is an entirely different level of awareness. Torture is clearly inhuman, but where does it all begin? Could it be that torture begins with the little tickling games we all played as kids? It's a point worth considering.

Here we see additional evidence of exactly how the Wooster Group escapes (or should escape) the charge of being merely self-involved and narcissistic. In its very subtle way, the Group actually involves the audience in the oppression presented onstage since as the audience watches this episode, it very likely laughs along, seeing this "minor" abuse of the woman as entirely natural, part of how men and women interact. The occasion still seems to be nothing more than harmless play. But is the helplessness of the woman really harmless, or does it reveal some level of generally accepted subordination of women in our culture? Consider, for example, whether the scene would be as funny if the woman were standing over a helpless male and "playfully" tickling him.

The subtlety of what the Group was attempting could easily be missed, but those laughing along may need to consider the point that we are to some small degree all "collaboratively" involved in the sort of abuse that ultimately led to Bette's dehumanization by the scientific community. And we may need to consider that we are all at least in part responsible for her suicide. Or we might simply see these things as good clean fun. And we might think that the medical community is doing its best when it deals with suffering human beings as patients or subjects—remaining oblivious to the group's point. So be it, at least for the moment.

The third part of the trilogy, *Nayatt School* (1978), marked Gray's transition from a Group participant to more of a solo artist—a transition that he would complete by the time the Group performed the epilogue, *Point Judith* (1979), which marked the end of Gray's formal involvement with the Wooster Group. *Nayatt School* opens with an actual Gray monologue where he describes his experiences working on a production of T. S. Eliot's *The Cocktail Party* and summarizes his recollection of the play's high points. Moving from the monologue opening, *Nayatt School* then critically analyzes *The Cocktail Party* through the same kind of subtle performance style perfected in *Rumstick Road*. That is to say, it doesn't directly editorialize as much as simply focus on matters of suicide and martyrdom that are romantically portrayed in *The Cocktail Party* as heroic or noble. It's a perspective that the Wooster Group wanted to challenge.

In *Nayatt School*, Gray himself becomes more centrally the object of study. Though the piece doesn't literally place him on the dissecting table as *Rumstick Road* did with Libby Howes, the process is similar. But in this case, it's not a matter of dissecting a victim so much as one of dissecting the oppressor in Gray and, by extension, the oppressor in us all. So Gray begins the piece as "Spalding Gray," relating directly to his audience his personal involvement as an actor who once performed in a production of *The Cocktail Party*. He then assumes numerous roles within the piece, alternating between being himself and performing roles of various characters, which each reveals some different dimension about "Spalding Gray."

Gray performs segments of the character Sir Henry Harcourt-Reilly, the mysterious psychologist of *The Cocktail Party* who actually encourages the soon-to-be-martyred Celia Copplestone to see the world in a way that romantically leads her to her doom. Moving

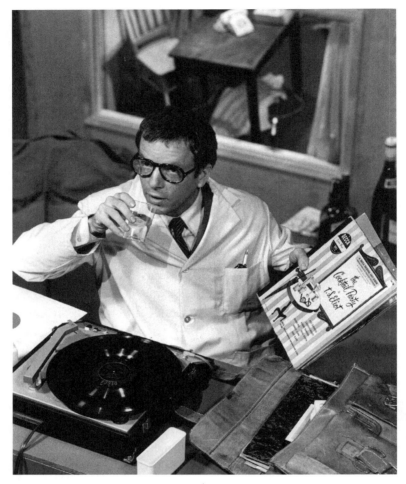

Nayatt School. Pictured: Spalding Gray. (Photo copyright Clem Fiori, courtesy of The Wooster Group.)

beyond that role and away from *The Cocktail Party* proper, Gray also plays a doctor, a lecturer, even a mad scientist, and finally a victimized son. The result is a rather troubling portrait of Gray, made by adding up the collage of roles that he has assumed. The engaging charm Gray exuded in his opening monologue actually hides pathological characteristics that are anything but charming or benign. Who really is "Spalding Gray"? Is he the nice guy who charms us in the opening monologue, or more like the arrogant analyst Harcourt-Reilly, a deceptive mad scientist bent on transforming the world for his own selfish ends? Or is he more like the long-suffering, helpless, and victimized son of a deranged, Celia-like mother? The answer, it seems, is that he is in part all of these people yet really none of them. Gray's identity shifts, compounds, and falls into suspicion altogether throughout the piece, leaving us to ask, who is this person in front of us?

In *Nayatt School,* the Wooster Group has presented a disarming charmer whose warm, engaging surface hides a monstrous soul. A discerning audience will likely recognize that Gray's alluring performance style is utilizing the very same strategies that deceptive politicians and captains of industry use to promote and disseminate disinformation, prejudice, and oppression for personal gain. Charm disarms, and Gray's charm, in the final analysis, is the same as that of the real-life oppressors who control world events. The difference is in degree, not in type. *Nayatt School* is a cautionary tale against falling under the spell of charismatic "performers" because by doing so we give up our right to think and act for ourselves. Audiences should remain perpetually suspicious of "charm," even or especially when the agenda seems charmingly benign.

In a world where so much 1960s promise led to so much 1970s disappointment, LeCompte, Gray, and their Group collaborators seem to have been determined to point out the root causes that led to such disappointment, implicating even themselves. Their early 1960s-style intentions of leading a revolution were as fundamentally flawed as the opposition they challenged. Winning people over through charismatic "coercion," through charming messages of revolution, could only have bred more of the same subordination and subservience that they so earnestly struggled to eliminate. The real problem, it seems, was less a matter of who was leading the people than that people were willing to be led. So the difference, if a revolution had actually occurred, would have been only a matter of who the new leader would be. Finally, the reformers who were trying to lead the revolution were as much an enemy as those they targeted in their politics, protests, and art. *Nayatt School* brings this important revelation home in a fully focused performative manner. Gray's disarming charm could be a weapon of oppression if it is used in a Pied Piper way to (mis)lead his audiences to ill-considered actions; he and others had to be wary.

Nayatt School, however, wasn't Gray's first—or only—confrontation with this notion of personal complicity. When the Group was performing the earlier piece *Rumstick Road*, a very curious string of events unfolded. In *Rumstick Road* they used confidential tape recordings from his grandmother and father as well as taped material of a confidential phone call with his late mother's psychiatrist. The result overflowed beyond the stage in a manner that likely thrilled the Group, even as they were apparently being misinterpreted. *Village Voice* critic Michael Feingold took particular issue with what he called the dishonorable brutality of using those tapes:

> I'd like to register a vehement protest about the morality of using private documents and tapes in this kind of public performance. I don't mean the legal rights involved, but the ethics of one's dealings with the audience. Prefacing one tape with the announcement that his grandmother has specifically asked him not to use it in the performance, Gray obviously thinks he's found a terrific way to rivet an audience's attention. So, obviously, he has. But I feel cheapened by having been made to participate in this violation of a stranger's privacy.

Feingold further observes that "to make a point of including dishonorable transactions like this . . . is to brutalize the audience, implicating them in the artist's pain instead of offering them a share in its transcendence."

Feingold accurately points out that Gray made his audiences accomplices in this breach of privacy by having them eavesdrop on the confidential recordings. It is a troubling point to consider. But

Feingold misses larger issues that can be drawn from the point. First of all, this publicly staged invasion of privacy is not significantly different from more conventional and accepted art forms that also probe the private affairs of others, relying on generally unauthorized eavesdropping to gather material and inspiration. Consider also the media and its apparent "right" to invade people's privacy, presumably in deference to some public need to know. There seems to be a fine line between private rights and public demand. And it's a fine line that requires considered analysis rather than knee-jerk responses, whether it comes from conservative or liberal quarters.

Gray himself responded to Feingold's complaint in a letter to the *Village Voice*, conceding that it was a "brutal act perhaps" to force audience involvement in this action, "but at the time we made *Rumstick*, we saw theatre as a place to make the personal public. O'Neill quoted his family in *Long Day's Journey into Night* and locked the play in a vault for 25 years. We live in a brutal time that demands immediate expression." Gray offers no apology because, quite simply, Feingold's complaint seems to have been exactly the kind of reaction the Group intended, though they likely had hoped that this reaction would be more understandably digested and internalized for what it was: a raw experience revealing that virtually all matters of real import involving two or more people require a certain degree of confrontational brutality. But Feingold's ensuing response to Gray's response shows that Feingold opposes the Group's implicating methods: "I don't like being made to participate in a morally dubious act like the unauthorized playing of a phone call." Feingold clearly missed the point, namely that within contemporary culture such forced participation is an unavoidable fact of life. We all benefit from such infringements on privacy, almost on a daily basis. In the ideal, it may be "wrong," but are there cases where the ends perhaps justify the means? For Gray, the psychiatrist is a perfect case study. How far is too far? That is a question with no easy answer. Unfortunately, Feingold's answer is to take a righteous position on the matter and ignore the realities of what he doesn't like. He's apparently even willing to deny that, like us all, he is the guilty beneficiary of this very sort of infringement on a daily basis simply by being a citizen of a culture that has overexposed its private parts to public scrutiny.

What Gray learned first and foremost in the heady days with the Wooster Group was that he would never fully be able to stand outside of his culture and offer cool, calculated critiques. That was what so many had attempted in the 1960s and early 1970s. Taking that sort of moral high ground was an invigorating agenda, but it was, in the final analysis, fundamentally and naïvely inauthentic. For Gray, it became apparent that the best way to critique flaws in our culture was to accept that we are part of that culture, and then to confront and resist it from within. And what better object of study than himself to get at the roots of culture's woes?

As a white heterosexual male of Western European extraction, Gray was *not* in a good position to stand outside of his own complicity when it came to the privileges he enjoyed simply by birth into a categorical position. And that was the heart of Gray's dilemma: how to actually challenge the very privileges he enjoyed as a straight white male.

Here is the second lesson that Gray took away from his Wooster Group experience. The Wooster Group admirably highlighted the notion that we are all inescapably complicit in the brutalizing enterprises of Western culture. But Gray seemed to want to go a step further by learning not just how to take personal responsibility for his complicity but also how to act on that revelation and perhaps to change the world in the bargain. The Wooster Group offered a first step toward breaking through the many cycles of oppression that benefit people like him. But he increasingly realized that he would have to move beyond the Wooster Group's singular agenda of critically *deconstructing* a culture. Challenging and deconstructing the cultural status quo was an important first step, but he felt that he had to go farther.

There were strong hints throughout his Wooster days that Gray sensed a potential for change well before he actually went out on his own. For example, Elizabeth LeCompte makes a simple and telling observation in describing Gray's departure from the Group following *Point Judith*. She describes the professional separation as a good and healthy mutual choice, explaining that in the works she was creating for Wooster, "Spalding was too sympathetic a character. He couldn't inhabit my anger. He came closest in *Nayatt* but it was uncomfortable for him. Ron [Vawter] is [now] the personification of that for me. Willem [Dafoe] also. . . . Spalding's persona was very dominant, very needy." This passage contains some curiously contradictory points on the matter of masculinity. The idea of Gray being a "dominant" presence is, of course, no surprise: guys are supposed to dominate. But the idea that he was "needy" and couldn't "inhabit anger" in ways that the other men could mark him as something of a masculine aberration. LeCompte adds, "Spalding's a very wonderfully needy performer. He needs his audience to love him very much. And he performs wonderfully under that, he blooms. But for me, because of my particular political bent and because of . . . my anger . . . I don't like to play with that stuff too much, it's like playing with fire." Gray needed the attention and even love of his audiences, whereas traditional definitions of masculinity seem more to demand that men need, if anything, conquests, possessions, and territory, not nurture. As noted of Gray's experiences with Shepard's *The Tooth of Crime*, his masculinity was again other than what is prescribed. And this early observation signals where Gray needed to head in order to move beyond what seem to be paralyzing confessions of personal guilt and complicity.

Confronting masculinity is central in *Point Judith* (1979), the Wooster Group's send-off of Spalding Gray. Part I, entitled "Rig," places Gray in the exclusive company of a group of male oil-rig workers. It's a macho-bravado piece, filled with aggression bound up in a portrayal of utter male contempt for the opposite sex. For the band of men onstage, women are little more than objects to be abused and "consumed" for personal pleasure. The second part of *Point Judith* seems almost a response to Feingold's complaint about

Point Judith (an epilog). Pictured (l–r): Willem Dafoe, Spalding Gray, Matthew Hansell, Ron Vawter. (Photo copyright Nancy Campbell, courtesy of The Wooster Group.)

the Group's invasion of privacy in *Rumstick Road*. It distills Eugene O'Neill's highly personal *Long Day's Journey into Night* and its invasion of his family's privacy, "brutally" focusing on the misogyny that is the family's undoing. The third part fantasizes about the source of O'Neill's family's brutality by imagining Mary Tyrone's youthful life in a convent, as reported in *Long Day's Journey*. This third part, life in a convent, is played mainly by the male members of the Group, to highlight that the cloistered life this woman led before marriage is itself a masculine fantasy of keeping a woman "pure" until she is to be handed over and "used" in a male-controlled world of marriage and family. It's a romantically misogynistic contrast to the more overt, brutal, and raucous misogyny performed by the boys in the opening piece. The point in both cases remains the same: women in our culture are subservient to men, their playthings and their trophies.

The expression and execution of patriarchal oppression marking LeCompte's epilogue is a curious sort of thing to do for a man who so uncomfortably wore his patriarchal mantle, being needy, hungry for love, and slow to anger. But perhaps LeCompte sensed that this might be her last professional opportunity to immerse Gray in a performance designed to expose him to the full culture of masculinized tyranny. Gray would deal with this matter in his own way in his future monologues. But it would take a long, circuitous path to get where he wanted to go.

Finding His American Voice

Gray's Early Monologues

Gray's interest in doing monologues (or autoperformances—some even call it stand-up comedy) seems a natural extension of his Wooster Group work, but his interest in standing before an audience as himself had begun even before he joined the Performance Group. Recall that he was something of a natural in the workshops he stumbled upon in his early days in New York. Pulling together events of the day and organizing the details of even a humdrum day seemed to be second nature for Gray, and people were always flocking around to hear his stories, from scullery co-workers to pretty discriminating theater colleagues. But why?

Clearly telling stories was a handy way to pass the time, but was this talent something Gray could craft into a career? Would people be interested enough actually to pay to hear him? Only a few stand-up comics had been successful doing anything like this up to that point. Will Rogers had made a career of storytelling, but that was more than a generation earlier. There was the Las Vegas brand of stand-up comic, but that wasn't what Gray was all about. And then there was Lenny Bruce. But Gray wasn't really like any of those stand-alone performers. And those folks weren't actors, which was a crucial part of who Gray was. If he were to go it alone, he had no ready-made formula and no role model to follow. In many ways, he had no idea at all where to go next. But his talents, and a bundle of pretty good fortune, seemed to know even if Spalding himself wasn't so sure.

As noted earlier, Gray's work in the 1973 Performance Group production of Shepard's *The Tooth of Crime* provided him the first big opportunity to be *himself* on stage. Gray recalls Schechner telling him that at a certain point in the play he should "'Drop your character. Drop all this character you've built up of Hoss, and just stand there'—in the middle of this circle, surrounded by the audience." After taking his time in this circle, Gray was then supposed to resume his role. He took Schechner's advice, and every night when the time to step out arrived,

> I really looked forward to it. It was a very powerful, beautiful meditation. It began to occur to me, What if I didn't rebuild my character? If I continued to stand here, looking at the audience. What might I say? And I think that's where the first curiosity and temptation came in that I might be able to publicly be Spalding Gray. At that time it was just a fantasy, nothing I thought of really doing.

By the time he was ready to leave the Wooster Group behind, he was ready to fulfill his fantasy.

Gray's Autoperformance Agenda

On the surface, at least, Gray's monologues bear little, if any resemblance to either the Performance or the Wooster Group's work, since Gray relied almost completely on his single "presence," seated at a table and talking to audiences without stage action and virtually without any props. *Village Voice* critic Don Shewey rather admiringly observed of Gray's early independent work that "unlike his colleagues in the Wooster Group . . . , whose experimentation took them further into high-tech performance, Gray reclaimed the ancient art of storytelling, simply sitting at a desk and addressing an attentive audience in the intimacy of the Performance Garage." And *New York Times* critic Vincent Canby noted that Gray's reliance on simply talking eliminated almost every standard tool of the theater trade, body language included: "It would be a coup de theatre if he just stood up." Of course, Gray did manage to use his craft to great advantage even if it was a bit minimalist; he just stripped things down to avoid distracting fluff.

Shewey is right. In the 1970s, the Wooster Group and other experimental theater groups had turned more and more to technology and high theatricality, while Gray increasingly eliminated the various bells and whistles at his disposal, getting down to the basics. The difference, however, is more superficial than real because Gray brought with him the heart of the Wooster tradition. He just utilized a different approach to achieve the same end. We've noted already Gray's WASP background and upbringing, and Gray himself openly acknowledges in his monologues his comfortably privileged middle-class, New England heritage. In order to critique that world, he could turn radical, revolutionary bohemian and reject his roots, declaring independence from and opposition to the world he was born into, barricading himself in some free-loving commune or other enclave of American counterculture. Or he could accept that he had been "to the middle-class manor born" and find ways to critique that world of privilege by "working from within." As noted earlier, this second option seems hardly a position for an avant-garde performer to embrace. But Gray chose it. He learned its value during his time with the Wooster Group, and now he was going to build on that agenda and make it his own.

As he undertook this second option, Gray put several "Spalding Grays" to work. First, "Spalding the observer of events" went out into the world to experience as much of contemporary American life as possible, gathering anecdotes and stories from the world he daily confronted. From these daily details he worked to uncover cultural shortcomings from the vantage point of a privileged middle-class male for whom virtually all doors were opened. The results of this countercultural espionage were then handed over to "Gray the artist" to use in creating a work that would offer a critical perspective on the flaws and shortcomings Spalding the observer had unearthed. Gray the artist then would hand over the material, in monologue form, to "Gray the performer." But this performer was not some 1960s-style mouthpiece of revolution or Lenny Bruce voice of assault and confrontation. Rather, Gray the artist manufactured Gray the performer as a naïve stage presence who appeared fully incorporated into "the American system," a man taking full advantage of "the land of opportunity" and actually unaware of the ironies introduced into his onstage performance by Gray the artist. Who is the actual Spalding Gray? While this may be a *People* magazine kind of question, as far as Gray's Wooster-rooted agenda is concerned, it's irrelevant. This complex arrangement leads to onstage work that presents material, seemingly without comment, in a manner that might at first glance appear supportive of the status quo. A more savvy or perceptive audience, however, would see that Gray has created a persona who ironically utilizes an empowered but naïve and self-indulgent "Spalding Gray" character to unearth and then undermine the WASPish culture he indulges, feeds off, supports, and even emulates.

Gray's ironic approach clearly owes much to his association with the Wooster Group, which had warned that a certain guilt rubs off on everyone who lives and breathes within contemporary culture. Gray seemed to put himself in even greater jeopardy than the average citizen by risking the temptations of self-indulgence that go with taking the stage as an autoperformance center-of-attention "star." And many critics, reviewers, and audience members typically were unable to see beyond that, charging Gray with betraying his experimental roots and selling out to the status quo. He was willing to take this sort of criticism as he pursued his own brand of activist theater and art.

In order to confront the status quo with effect, Gray would need the same kind of active audience that he'd found in his Performance and Wooster Group days. That would be the only way for his more subtle art to challenge rather than seem to support the status quo.

How audiences "read" Gray's performances would determine his ultimate success, and what he was doing was by no means hammer-on-the-head obvious. Gray's language basically undermines Gray the performer's self-indulgent, charming, seemingly harmless presence. In other words, what he tells us in his monologues is alluringly entertaining, but the words themselves begin to sound somehow unreliable or incomplete. This disconnect between Gray the charmer and the words Gray the charmer speaks leaves it up to the audience to generate its own conclusions about what is "right" or "good."

For the audience, there is the undisputed "pleasure in the text" that we all enjoy as we get caught up in the twisted tales that Gray presents. And on the face of it, the experience is all empty self-indulgence. There is hardly ever anything *really* culturally critical in what Gray says. We learn nothing, for example, about the great world events that unfold around us and around Gray—no politics, no world catastrophes of either human or natural origin. And we rarely hear Gray step forward (metaphorically speaking) and accuse the Western world of injustice and oppression. Gray the performer is simply not a confrontational or judgmental person.

The result is that it could be relatively easy to dismiss this gadfly performer as a self-indulgent buffoon, a clownish dupe of cultural authority. But this disarmingly charming process is exactly what Gray intends. Having put us at intellectual ease, he can then take us, off guard, into unexpected realms of self-revelation. In many ways the process is parallel to plays and movies where a police inspector pretends to be a fool (or actually is a fool) in order to ensnare a suspect in a fatal error or unwitting confession. As Gray bumbles through his inspection of the world, we as audience need to step in and organize the evidence on our own, coming to our own conclusions about guilt and complicity. Being encouraged to go beneath the surface of the stories that this bumbling but charming Gray presents, the audience can begin to see that Gray's work is actually a well-orchestrated presentation, provided the audience is prepared to look for the critique buried under the bumbling, that is.

For Gray, keeping open the possibility that audiences might confuse his intentions and see him as a mere self-indulgent egoist is deliberate. And it had a secondary, positive effect. Without at least a hint of that sort of confusion, it would have been far less likely that Gray could have entered the mainstream of popular culture as successfully as he did. Consider that mainstream America is generally uncomfortable with radical assaults on itself and tends to exclude those types of artists from its parties. Thankfully, Gray's "hidden" agenda has been misread by enough of the world's rich and powerful that they were drawn in by his charming and disarming surfaces. And this misperception of Gray's designs, in turn, kept certain doors open to him that had long since been closed to his more radical, activist colleagues.

Gray himself realized that the Spalding Gray we see on stage is really several Spalding Grays. *Rivkala's Ring* (1986) is a monologue that Gray adapted from a Chekhov story, commissioned for the collection of short dramatic works entitled *Orchards*. It's a monologue designed to be performed by someone other than Gray himself, so as a complement to the piece, Gray offers advice on how to perform it that sums up his view of his own persona on stage: "I see the character [in *Rivkala's Ring*] as a manic-y paranoid person who's spinning off these kind of paranoid delusions, trying to make order out of a very frightening and chaotic existence. So I see it fashioned after my character, the character of Spalding Gray that I do in the monologues." The passage acknowledges his awareness of at least two Spalding Grays and outlines the personality of the entertainer as a manic-y, paranoid charmer. So although it might at times be difficult to distinguish Gray the private citizen and observer of life from Gray the performer, Gray himself insists that there is a difference, and that we be aware of it whenever he's onstage.

Gray's "manic-y" paranoia is a deliberately manufactured characteristic (though it seems also to have been a characteristic of Gray the private citizen). Onstage, it renders the performer authoritatively harmless and disarming, enabling him to draw the audience into the monologue, overriding the defenses with which the audience might resist, say, a political manifesto. Only infrequently does the man who has charmed the audience get sucked into the processes of any sort of self-realization—political or otherwise—and when it does happen, it's invariably to his own great surprise. Even when a self-realization washes over Gray the performer, it is always belated and rather cryptic, giving audience members the chance to arrive at their own conclusions first. Gray the performer is totally immersed in his narrative, obsessed with himself, and that is all we literally see. And since the performer onstage is so guileless, it is generally left to the audience to deduce the ironies built into the piece by Gray the behind-the-scenes artist, who is ironically detached from and subtly contemptuous of the performer behind the desk.

Learning to Trust Himself: *India and After (America)*, *Interviewing an Audience*, and *In Search of the Monkey Girl*

Although Gray did perform brief monologues in *Three Places in Rhode Island*, *India and After (America)*, first performed in 1979, is his first stand-alone performance. It is based on his experiences in India in 1976, when he was with the Performance Group touring their version of Berthold Brecht's play *Mother Courage*. While in India, Gray suffered a nervous breakdown, returned to the United States, and began to deal with what became an intensely manic-depressive response to his mother's 1967 suicide, the event that was part of the initiating inspiration for *Three Places in Rhode Island*.

But *India and After (America)* is more than a simple retelling of Gray's recollections during these trying times. He wasn't working to create an autobiographical, chronological memoir designed to somehow archive his memory. Gray realized early in his career that memory plays tricks with the raw material of reality. In the process, memory and its tricks become part of reality as it tinkers with "facts" and reorganizes itself and the "outside world" in sometimes seemingly impossible ways. These sometimes unreliable but always uncanny twists and turns intrigued Gray far more than point-by-point recollections of simple facts. He obviously understood that humans can and often do reconstruct memories into storylike patterns that conform to a chronological beginning, middle, and end. It's a pattern that we often expect, but also one that Gray thought rather tedious and uninteresting, little more than mere journalism. He found that when we leave memory to its own devices, we discover how consciousness interacts with the world around it and contributes its own bits of truth to the story, expanding on what holds its interest. Memory that's allowed to play with the facts of life and living unfolds into something far more complex and interesting, revealing things about the mind that simply don't surface when we generate mere chronology. So while Gray does generate a sort of history in his work, his sort of history is always a product of the present moment in which a memory of the past is generated. And it typically bears little resemblance to the chronologized version of events typically found in history books.

The period between 1976 and 1977—Gray's focus in *India and After (America)*—is what Gray called "a very intense period for me. It was very . . . very chaotic and just one of those . . . big change periods, a metamorphosis." He would have done a disservice to this chaotic time by simply reducing it to a conventional history that would not have revealed anything about the curious nature of his *memory* of that hectic past. Factual details might be important, but exactly how Gray's mind dealt with the past is of at least equal importance. So what he does in *India and After (America)* is similar to what he did with his Performance and Wooster colleagues. But instead of reusing their strategies of having the consciousnesses of other performers alter, redirect, and refocus his life material, Gray chose to go with the flow of totally uncontrolled and unmodified randomness, reflecting what he actually experienced during that troubling period.

What he did in performance was ingenious. He had a colleague, Meghan Ellenberger, sit behind a desk with a dictionary and stopwatch, and she randomly selected a word from the dictionary, read the definition, then arbitrarily announced a time limit from one to seven minutes. She started her stopwatch, and Gray would respond to the word by constructing an anecdote, allusion, or association that had to be completed within the allotted time (or he would be cut off). On occasion, Gray remained completely silent, staring quietly out into the audience. But usually he would have something to say. And generally he would complete his anecdote just as the announced time was running out. The element of surprise built into the process—for him and the audience—gave each performance a sort of high-wire-act-without-a-net quality that reflected the tenuous control over life that Gray had experienced during that period. It duplicated on stage what was going on in Gray's head during his breakdown in India and after.

In the videotaped performance held by the New York Public Library (dated November 14, 1982, part of the Billy Rose Collection in Lincoln Center), Gray is given thirty-eight words in the span of ninety minutes. They range from common words like "friend," "drown," and "setting" to arcane terms like "descrescendo," "triangulate," and "dragonade." Not all words generated memories of India. For example, "porridge" sparked a memory of a walk in Kashmir that ended with Gray surrounded by a band of ragged schoolboys. But "lucrative" stirred up memories of Gray's post-India trip across the United States in a hippie bus called "American Gypsy." The stories are all in a chronological jumble. But they somehow add up to a complete, though hardly logical—at least not in any conventional or rational sense—performance. It is anything but a well-crafted, traditionally structured story.

This process is an ingenious revision of the interplay between the performers that had been the Performance Group and Wooster Group agenda. Rather than working with the presence of the multiple consciousnesses of other performers playing off of Gray's life, Gray decided to focus on random adaptations of his own single consciousness. The words inspired discrete memories and subdued any urge on Gray's part to string things together. And they completely eliminated any possibility of reducing his memories to something resembling a travelogue documentary. The results came closer to capturing the truth of what was going on in his mind, which had cut loose from the kinds of organizing strategies that we've all been taught to use when we deal with memory. There was no attempt to generate a cause-and-effect explanation of things, and no interest in making sure events followed in chronological sequence. Truth existed in freshly recollected fragments.

It became increasingly apparent that the present moment was what really mattered. While we as audience members might have been interested in the events that Gray recounts, what really intrigues and captivates the audience is watching what he is doing *now*. We're all caught up in the event of the moment, how Gray's here-and-now will work with and capitalize on memories of the past. Audiences got an experience that Gray would emphasize in later performances: that everything in one way or another is *now*, even the past. Furthermore, the random word associations in the piece come closer, in the final analysis, to presenting an experience *right now* of the fragmented events Gray suffered through during that chaotic past. This onstage strategy made the past more real and *present* for audiences than any conventional story would have. In a way, audiences witnessed actual madness onstage at the very moment of performance, seeing fragments of mind and memory spin off with no central control trying to organize them into oneness.

In an extreme way, Gray is sharing an extreme version of what needs to occur in all of us on a daily basis in order to remain "sane." He is indirectly pointing out that we actually have to go a long way to get to the organized and orderly style of memory that we often mistakenly consider to be natural. Life is not orderly or logical by itself; rather, our minds mold experience into intriguing but finally artificial order. Without our mind's active organizing input, we come closer to seeing the random flow and flux that is the thing called reality. Or at very least, we see that without the active input of our minds, the "real" world is a very different place than we think it is.

What is particularly engaging about the performance is what begins to happen in the audience. As viewers grow increasingly aware of the rules of the game, they begin to accumulate the fragmented episodes that Gray presents for each word, and the first instinct is to try to organize the pieces into a complete story. But soon we begin to appreciate Gray's untamed mental state. Rather than trying to reconstruct some sort of narrative chronology, we turn to experiencing something about how memory works.

India and After (America) closes with a sort of summary "experiment" for the audience to consider. As Gray completes his last word recollection, the assistant repeats all the words used in the evening, in their own chronological order. What winds up happening is that the dictionary meanings of the words take a back seat and are replaced by our own memories of what those words inspired Gray to say. David Savran, an early follower of Gray's career, offers a pretty solid recollection of this sort of experience:

> When, for example, the spectator hears *termite* in the final roll call, he may remember less the insect than the description of Gray suspended in a banyan tree. The recapitulation thereby provides a retrospective index of how meanings change through personal associations, of how a private trauma has been transformed into a structured public event, and of how pain has been translated into memory.

Here are several levels of memory at work: the audience's fresh memories of a recently completed performance, which are memories of Gray's memories of a more distant past, and the whole string affected by a random use of dictionary terms. That random beginning, we eventually realize, encourages the audience to experience the extent to which our minds actually contribute to the manufacture of memory and ultimately to the manufacture of reality as we know it.

In *India and After (America)*, the past is brought to life each evening in significantly different manifestations, initiated by the rudimentary building block of dictionary meanings, but those dry definitions are given life through Gray's immediate responses *and* by the audience's own varied and unique recollections. If the 1960s celebrated liberation from constraints of the past, and if, for example, Sam Shepard (in *The Tooth of Crime*) let out a nostalgic sigh for that past, Gray was fast coming to realize that past and present are parts of the same fabric of consciousness, indivisible and inseparable.

Interviewing an Audience (first performed in 1980) turned the spotlight directly on the audience. Like *India and After (America)*, it is an exercise that changed each night. And though it was less ingenious in conception than *India and After (America)*, it did emphasize Gray's keen interest in audience contact and was so popular that he continued to perform it over a span of several years. He describes the process:

> I hang out with the audience in the lobby. I come up to anyone and say, "Look, if I call your name tonight would you be willing to talk about any topic that comes up?" And if the person says yes, I'll take down the name and ask a few questions. "What is your occupation? How old are you?" That will be the extent, that's all I will know about them. Then they come up onstage and sit with me and I begin with, "How'd you get here today? What were you driving? What were you thinking? How much did you have to drink?" And if a person goes with the questions it turns into a wonderful dialogue. We begin to hear a story about what it is to live in the world. It's a sharing. The theatre becomes a community.

Having dispensed with the "total theater" idea of the 1960s, which was so dedicated to breaking down barriers between performers and audiences, Gray generated an alternative strategy by empowering audience members with their own stage presence and relinquishing (or at least minimizing) his own stage power in the process. The goal of community so prevalent in Schechner's Performance Group agenda was realized in Gray's theater of talking.

In a 1982 interview Gray acknowledges the debt to his Group roots that led to *Interviewing an Audience*: the piece "brings me back to one of my sources. . . . Just as I learned to take responsibility for myself and share control with others from working with the Performance Group and the Wooster Group, I'm now sharing some of the control I have as a monologist with members of an audience." Shared control, however, is more than a trick to win over an audience. In a 2002 interview Gray saw the communal dimension that unfolded during each performance of *Interviewing an Audience* as a sort of *political* event "that says, 'What's going on in this room has the potential to be much more interesting than Jay Leno or David Letterman or Jerry Springer.' . . . I tell people: 'Your stories are absolutely important. Let's not live through Hollywood stars'." With *Interviewing an Audience* Gray engages in a politics of shared, communal empowerment among "normal" people, allowing individuals basically the same privileges of recounting their lives that he had assumed for himself in *India and After (America)* and would claim more completely in his succeeding monologues.

What Gray does that's so different from a Leno or Letterman interview is encourage his fellow participants to reveal more about themselves than simple factual details. He's looking for something true to the heart rather than journalistically accurate or compelling. *That*'s the glue that binds humans to one another, and it's something rarely acknowledged in the modern world. Gray wanted his theater to be a refuge for such truth-revealing events.

Mere factuality is, of course, an American cultural compulsion. We're always hungry to get to the facts of a situation. But this isn't a compulsion for Gray. His work actually works to show the wasted energy we expend in the pursuit of facts rather than the more tenuous strands of truth buried in emotions and feeling. Too often, our culture hungers for empirical evidence, turning a blind eye or deaf ear to deeper truths that exist alongside, beneath, or beyond empiricism. Even as a child, Gray seemed to have been far less interested in material factuality than with the memories that coexisted alongside it.

In his preface to *Sex and Death to the Age 14*, Gray reports going to the University of Santa Cruz in 1978, where he met Amelie Rorty, who was teaching a class called "The Philosophy of Emotions." He confided to her that he had artistically hit a dead end. (He was getting near what would be the end of his Wooster Group phase.) And because his work had dead-ended, he tells her he had "a feeling that the world was also coming to an end." He continues:

> I told her I thought we had come to the end of the white middle-class world as we knew it. She took me at my word and said, "Well, Spalding, during the collapse of Rome, the last artists were the chroniclers." And all the bells went off inside me. Of course, I thought, I'll chronicle my life. . . . Each performance was to be a personal epitaph. Each night my personal history would disappear on a breath.

Hardly a description of mere history, Gray's idea of a chronicle seemed almost folklorish, interested more in the daily *rhythms* of life than in the *events* that made it into the evening news. His personal chronicle, freshly and newly recounted each night, would document Gray's own experiences as felt *at the moment*, tempered by his nightly moods and even by things like his encounters on the way to the theater. He would become a personal witness to truths beyond facts, not a living newspaper but an embodied voice speaking as a sort of *Zeitgeist* in the flesh, responding to what he experienced and reporting its emotional and psychological effects upon him. In the bargain, he presented us with an American Everyman.

Ideally for Gray, the material world both inspires and corroborates that which emotively and feelingly exists alongside it. Ideally, the two worlds would interact and coexist. And they best interweave and interrelate in the performance space that Gray would later identify as his "transitional object" or "transitional phenomenon," using phrases he discovered in the works of the British psychologist D. W. Winnicott. It's the space in which, according to Winnicott, "inner reality and external life both contribute" and allow for "the perpetual human task of keeping inner and outer reality separate yet interrelated." In this regard, Gray's agenda has always run somewhat contrary to our dominant cultural predisposition for "just the facts," just the empirically verifiable trinkets and baubles of existence.

But Gray doesn't side with the nonmaterialist or spiritual world, as some people do following a rejection of the material world. That's the kind of radical turn that happened, for example, with his mother. Gray, however, never fully turns his back on the material. He doesn't opt for some spiritually ecstatic, immaterial and otherworldly existence, though at times that was what Gray the performer tried to pursue. Gray had come to realize that "to be" in this world requires actively being a part of the world, which includes full interaction with other human beings. To be a human individual is to be involved and engaged, which in turn requires being recognized and appreciated by the others who populate the world. Interaction is key, and what better place to bring this about than in the theater?

Gray's 1981 piece, *In Search of the Monkey Girl*, is a big step in his career up to this point. First of all, it dispenses with "tricks" like using a dictionary or calling an audience member onstage, falling more in line with the self-created, memory-drifting storytelling style that Gray would perfect in his later, more fully autobiographical monologues. In this monologue, for the moment at least, Gray is willing to concentrate more on "others" than on himself. (Later he'd be able to balance the two a bit better.) His subject is a group of carnival workers at a fair outside of Nashville, Tennessee. Gray is commissioned to write the text of a photo essay on carnival workers (which became the 1982 book *In Search of the Monkey Girl*), and he travels with photographer Randy (Randal Levenson) to visit the fair, both of them going undercover as "carnies."

Gray is drawn in by the free-spirited, "entrepreneurial" side-show "freaks" and does much to humanize them for his audiences. He meets and befriends various of these midway curiosities, circus-tent performers, and their families, including (but only briefly) Priscilla, "the monkey girl." Quirky and independent, these people are in their own ways pursuing the American Dream, returning to homes during the off-season, raising families, and saving up for retirement. What Gray shows us is that these carnival hucksters aren't much different than everyone else, except for the fact that they more sensationally do what we all rather more respectably do: "sell" our unique skills to whoever will take notice and pay, in order to make a living.

Gray basically normalizes these fringe people, neither vilifying nor romanticizing their lives. Instead, he presents them with all their human strengths and weaknesses and therefore indirectly makes them appear to be nothing more than exotic versions of ourselves. In fact, Gray himself appears to be more like these carnival entertainers than Gray the performer ever actually admits. In front of his own audience, he too is something of a sideshow freak, though that actual point is never made. But that, again, is Gray the artist's agenda: to leave conclusions like that open for his audiences to arrive at more or less on their own.

What is particularly interesting about this monologue is that toward the end Gray reveals that the resulting illustrated book—the reason he and Randy went down to Nashville—upsets one of the families whose sideshow secrets are revealed in the book. The complaint generates a spiral of complicity in the monologue where, first, the showmen are shown to "rip off" their customers with illusion for profit and then Gray is shown to have ripped off the showmen by creating the book about them for his own profit. Though everyone does finally settle the dispute, the point lingers for the audience to mull over. Drawn into the strange goings-on of a carnival, the audience witnesses a cycle of manipulation reminiscent of Gray's *Rumstick Road* controversy with Michael Feingold. *In Search of the Monkey Girl* reveals how our culture is set up in a way that has people manipulating others and working always for the upper hand to turn a profit. At the far end of this manipulative spiral, Gray's own audience is technically gulled by Gray into participating in this hucksterism by paying him to talk to them about these other people's lives.

To be blunt, Gray has exposed his own stock in trade for what it is: a profit-making sideshow that capitalizes on the private lives of these human carnie "objects of study." Audiences are led, finally, to consider that what we all do in daily life is not so different from what either the carnies or Gray are up to.

4

Rediscovering America
Gray's Early "Autobiographical" Monologues

When Aristotle famously observed that humans are political animals, he was observing that humans are by nature social creatures. We aren't programmed to live or work in isolation but rather need to live together in a community. The Greeks called that community the *polis*, and it required its citizenry to do far more than give a neighborly nod on a sidewalk or take an occasional turn in the voting booth. Everyone was supposed to strive publicly for the general good of every individual in the group. If Aristotle was right, then the city or the community is where we belong, and the more entwined we are with our fellow citizens, the better it will be for the health of everyone. We *need* each other, and in that sense of the term, we are all *political* animals. Seeing ourselves as autonomous subjects independently vying for comfort, control, and personal security is really not a healthy or even sane way to go. Unfortunately, this is exactly what our modern culture endorses, encouraging us all to stand "free," unencumbered, and on our own two feet. If the Greeks were right, this pursuit of independent living explains exactly why we find ourselves so discontented in this modern world of plenty. Simply put, we're applying all our energy and resources to pursuing the wrong thing: independence.

How do we get back to a world in which it's not a sign of weakness to want to mix with and even depend upon other people? Why not look at "us" instead of "me" as the most important unit of measure? The question ties in nicely with Gray's growing concern that there was more to do in the theater than simply criticize the failings of the world. He and his Wooster Group colleagues recognized that they needed to critique cultural oppression by showing how our pursuit of "me" was harmful to others. And the very fact that they (and we) are part of this culture means we all need to come to terms with our roles in that culture of oppression. We're all guilty to some degree of the sorts of oppression that the 1960s counterculture had identified. That meant that Gray and the Wooster Group had to do more than merely repudiate our culture's cruelties. After all, repudiation of our culture amounted to little more than repudiating ourselves!

The members of the Wooster Group realized that they needed to turn to confessional processes that testified to our own transgressions in the world. They could no longer sit smugly among their equally smug audience supporters and rail against the machine—because like it or not, they were *part* of the machine. Their work would need to bear witness to the oppression for which we are all personally responsible. We learn to oppress on the playground, in the classroom, at the office. Even keeping up with rent or mortgage payments, even buying produce at the neighborhood grocery store, involves us in an economic and social structure that thrives on unfair practices of all sorts. Everything we do, and everything we don't do, really boils down to a political gesture that confirms we're part of the system. And if the system is rotten, each of us shares in the blame.

But confessing guilt and complicity is not enough. The personal confessional sort of thing occurred with some frequency throughout the 1970s, and Gray went through that phase as he worked with the Wooster Group, but he clearly wanted to do more. He wanted to move beyond mere guilt and to find ways to build or rebuild communities that weren't founded on competition and aggression.

Mutual respect and understanding of the ways of others—that's the way out of our culture's many cycles of oppression.

Exactly how to accomplish this, however, was harder than it looked; good intentions alone aren't enough. As the Wooster Group pointed out in *Nayatt School*, even Gray's storytelling talents and charismatic allure had to be looked at with a certain degree of suspicion. They were exactly the sorts of tools that less scrupulous power mongers in our culture have masterfully used with tyrannical and oppressive effect. International corporations and political machines have told their "stories" with the help of Madison Avenue and Hollywood, and the results are often devastating for those who fall under their spell. The twentieth century was full of almost unimaginable examples of how the cult of personality can be used by megalomaniacs to breed greed, sow hatred, and foment mass destruction.

To be seen as more than an imitator of these kinds of self-empowerment, Gray would need to create a stage presence that saw the world as something not for the taking but for the giving. He would need to accept responsibility for what he was doing with his powers over his audience. If Gray could become an honest *witness* to what occurs in the world around us, and if his audiences could themselves bear witness to his experiences, then we all would begin to achieve something like a political unity in the theater. Gray would somehow have to generate a way to help us recognize that we are all in some way responsible *for* one another. That is what Spalding Gray was coming to realize as he developed his autobiographical monologues.

In those monologues, Gray tells his life, complete with personally humiliating blemishes, to a collection of strangers. But as he does this, he's also doing something more: "When I sit down to talk, the fact that I haven't memorized the lines makes my re-collecting immediate, in the present, actual . . . . I am doing public memory, and that's a very active and present thing." He might have notes in front of him, but each performance is fresh, slightly different, a response to the day and to his current audience. And that's no small thing, since he's making real contact with people in a world where even something as trivial as eye contact is often considered invasion of privacy. Then there's the matter of telling a "stranger" your personal thoughts and feelings. "Doing public memory" is not something Americans are supposed to do. And it's not something we're good at, unless it's done through memoirs and television interviews that have been scrubbed so clean as to confess almost nothing of real value or interest.

But Gray is different. He confesses all sorts of embarrassing and humbling actions, thoughts, and feelings. And that willingness to make himself vulnerable makes Gray guilty of breaking one of the central cultural codes of American masculinity. Real "men" (and, more and more, women, too) are supposed to stand alone, be strong and silent as they betray no doubt, no need, and confess no short-comings, failings, or insecurities. Put another way, Gray's very choice of art form, the confessional monologue, is an act of resistance against what our culture expects. Gray basically "feminizes" himself by pub-licly revealing his inner feelings. And that confessional mode goes a long way toward putting his audiences in control of the situation. We have something on him, and therefore we're safe with him.

In fact, part of Gray's humor stems from the fact he's so "out of character" as a man, as he confesses his inner feelings to all the world. Our culture insists that men don't, or shouldn't, speak about the things Gray speaks of, and sees that sort of behavior as "funny." Bragging has its unique set of culturally prescribed rules, and when those rules are followed it's acceptable male behavior. But there aren't any rules about how men are supposed to go about expressing inner feelings of doubt and uncertainty, mainly because *real* men don't suf-fer from doubt and uncertainty in the first place. Gray's monologues move instantly into self-doubt, panic, and worry, crashing up against what we're taught to expect from a "man." But then, as Gray demon-strates, this is not a bad thing.

Going Autobiographical

Between 1979 and 1985, Gray created a number of monologues that chronicled his life to that point: *Sex and Death to the Age 14*; *Booze,*

Cars, and College Girls; *47 Beds*; *Nobody Wanted to Sit Behind a Desk*; *Travels Through New England*; *Terrors of Pleasure: The House*; *A Personal History of the American Theatre*; *Seven Scenes from a Family Album*. These are the monologues where Spalding first famously converted that dissecting table in *Rumstick Road* to a simple desk. He sat behind it with a glass of water, a notebook, and a microphone, and he eventually began costuming himself in his hallmark L.L. Bean flannel shirt. And he talked.

In 1981, Gray reported the reason behind this career choice, moving from the Performance Group to the Wooster Group and finally out on his own:

> For me there is nothing larger than the personal when it is communicated well. The very act of communication takes it into a "larger vein" and brings it back to the community. The personal confessional, stripped of its grand theatrical metaphors, is what matters to me now. . . . This personal exploration has made me more politically aware because now that I've come to myself as authority I have found that I still feel repressed and because of this feeling of repression I am forced to look further into the outside world for its source.

It's a curious thing to have a white male full of the "power" that comes with being a successful performer still feel repressed. But it's a genuine sentiment, and most likely one many of us feel, even those of us labeled "successful" by our culture's standards.

For some people at least, that may sound a bit confusing—which returns us, again, to the point that not everyone "gets" Spalding Gray's art. His storytelling style is unique, often very subtle, and oftentimes even very sincere people misunderstand exactly what he's doing. Consider David Guy's 1986 *New York Times* book review of Gray's first published collection of monologues, entitled *Sex and Death to the Age 14*. Guy observes, "Unfortunately, I simply don't find these stories interesting. They seem disjointed and incomplete;

they wander aimlessly; they make no point." He then concludes: "I have no doubt that Mr. Gray has a love of the banal and boring that borders on the mystical. But as long as people have been telling stories they have been embellishing them, not because they want to be untruthful, but because they believe a higher truth can be found in an artful lie. Also, of course, because when they did not embellish, they noticed their listeners starting to nod off."

Guy has clearly read the monologues closely. And he's a smart guy, so his criticism can't be written off. But like Michael Feingold in his misviewing of *Rumstick Road*, Guy failed to see the deeper purpose behind Gray's strategy of writing in that "disjointed and incomplete" manner. The breaches in the traditional storytelling craft are strategies echoing Gray's Wooster Group work. Gray is basically asking his audiences to recognize the holes in his stories and to complete them on their own. If we really get into what Gray is saying, we'll see something of ourselves in those stories and can join Gray in the overall experience. Feingold and Guy accurately find the key points in Gray's work, but they both miss that these strategies are actually strengths rather than flaws in Gray's craft.

Another curiosity in the review is that Guy presumes to know that what Gray is reporting is merely unembellished fact, a summary of the banalities of Gray's life. Again, he misses a key point because Gray is doing more than just spewing out a bundle of personal recollections of self-doubt and personal uncertainty. According to Guy, Gray has failed to glue his stories together with the "manly" stamp of bold self-understanding and simple self-assurance. So Guy is possibly correct in noting that the well-made stories with built-in messages that he advocates would likely attract a larger audience or readership. But that would very likely have been a different audience than Gray actually wanted to attract. Writing more dynamically self-assured and less mundane stories would actually have damaged the very thing Gray was trying to accomplish. If you're trying to generate male doubt in a world where only masculine self-confidence is culturally permitted, then you'll need to tell different kinds of stories.

How does all of this work? *Sex and Death to the Age 14* (1980), Gray's first stand-alone autobiographical monologue, opens with a memory from when he was four years old: "I can remember riding beside the Barrington River on the back of my mother's bicycle and she was shouting out and celebrating because we had just dropped the bomb on the Japs in Hiroshima, and that meant that her two brothers were coming home. A lot of people died in World War II. I didn't know any."

Gray's opening lines highlight that his monologue will concentrate on *memory*. But it's not a "first" memory, as we might presume it should be, given that this monologue basically begins at the beginning. This memory is actually a celebration of an *end*, and a massive geopolitical end at that, placed curiously at the beginning of Gray's story. Then too, it can be seen as introducing the new beginning of postwar life in America, which seems also to be a good starting point for Gray's own life's odyssey. Beginning or end, whatever the feeling is, Gray also introduces us listeners right up front to death, the thing that would obsess Gray his whole life, though here he acknowledges having no personal experience with it. To this point at least, the young Spalding Gray in the monologue has been isolated from all but a happy conclusion to a massive global conflict where America came out as undisputed champion of freedom and democracy. The Bomb may have cruelly punctuated the end of a long, bloody world war and paved the way for the global atomic age, but the suffering from that war and the anxiety for the future are nowhere to be felt.

The end of World War II is clearly a momentous event worth chronicling. Cheering with hope for returning troops is also worth recording. It's even possible that this event on the back of his mom's bike is actually Gray's first memory, and even more likely that this is Gray's first memory of the bigger world beyond his own childhood neighborhood. All of which seems to make the event worthy of some sort of grand comment from Gray, like "It was a great day," or at least "It was my first memory." This is probably what Guy would have expected. But Gray sidesteps this opportunity, picks up on the word "death," and moves away from World War II and Hiroshima.

Gray slips into his own personal world. He recalls "the first death which occurred in *our* family," of all things, the relatively trivial death of a pet. Then, picking up on the idea of a "pet," he tells us that that pet once bit him. Recalling the physical pain of that bite helps him to drum up a memory that moves him forward to age fourteen, when he and friends tried to "knock ourselves out" by holding their breaths, which never worked until one day he tried it alone in the bathtub, passing out and burning his arm on a nearby hot radiator. But being the son of a Christian Scientist mother, he didn't get it medically treated and went to school the next day, where he mortified the school nurse with his open wound. The monologue then returns to the dog's death, as Gray recalls he was wearing a T-shirt with a red heart on it, "and after the dog died I remember seeing the heart—my heart, the dog's heart, a heart—float up against a very clear blue sky." The sky in Barrington, Rhode Island, in 1946 was pollution-free. He then tells us that his mother told him that following the death of the dog, he stopped speaking for a period of time: "She said they were thinking of taking me to a psychiatrist." No wonder Guy was confused!

As early as 1967, Gray had strong interest in the behavior of children, especially those on the asphalt playgrounds of New York City: "Their play seemed random: like molecular energy patterns, too fast for me to frame or put together in my eye. It was all color, mixed with the sound of voices and traffic." His memories of his own childhood in *Sex and Death to the Age 14* suggest that Gray was interested in trying to remember what it was like to *think* like a kid, in the random way that kids think, as if he were somehow less corrupted by the organizing principles of the mind that we develop as adults. Gray seems to have been searching for pure recollections of the experiences that children have. Thinking or being like a kid is something that Gray and the Wooster Group celebrated in *Sakonnet Point* when they performed without "adult" commentary and response in favor of prelinguistic, childlike play. But in this monologue Gray isn't try-ing to slip into the make-believe world of a child. He's not trying to represent what it would be like to think like a child. He's not doing, for example, what Lily Tomlin did with her Edith Ann character (sitting in an oversized rocking chair and punctuating her childish insights with "And that's the truth."); Gray's aim is to *be* childlike while *remaining* the adult that he is. And in a nutshell, that's Spald-ing Gray, at least the Spalding Gray we're going to see onstage for the rest of his career: innocence struggling against corruption.

Death, thoughts of death, more dead pets, semidangerous compe-titions with friends, owning and selling a shotgun, learning to dance, kissing contests, alien encounters with girls and sexuality, sexual confusion, masturbation. Associations and brief anecdotes are what make up *Sex and Death to the Age 14*, capturing a sense of what it was like to grow up in that place called "middle America," carefree, in need of nothing. But toward the end of the monologue, Gray reports a comment he made at that age, while being interviewed by the headmaster for admission into Fichton Academy: "Out of no-where, I said, 'Well, since *they* invented the hydrogen bomb, there is no future. Not only does it negate my consciousness, it negates that of Beethoven's." The comment returns us to the monologue's begin-ning, and it's an adult, *reflective* comment, one of the only ones in the monologue. Fittingly, it popped out of Gray's fourteen-year-old mouth in a grown-up setting, within the "serious" institutional con-fines of the headmaster's office.

On the verge of being forced to "grow up," Spalding finally blurts out something that seems to have occupied his childhood memory since war's end. Through a decade of what seemed to be an idle and carefree childhood, the unspoken bombs of Hiroshima and Nagasaki have been specters haunting Gray for some time. It's now up to us to consider how these specters likely affected Gray's behavior during that decade of his life. How idyllic it must have been to roam unchecked by care or worry. He was in the land of plenty, and lacked nothing. But the memory of the Bomb, subdued throughout the monologue, apparently has lurked in young Spalding's consciousness. Just under the surface of Gray's carefree behavior, it might have been the thing that leaned him toward those curiously inserted thoughts of death and all the seemingly unfounded childhood fears, insecurity, and concern for tomorrow that increasingly occupy his imagination. The Bomb seems to have infected Gray's otherwise harmless, aimless, and disconnected monologue with an uneasy sense that all is not right with the world even though everything appears to be just fine.

"The Bomb" is the elephant in the room that no one talks about, but Gray sets things up in the monologue so that we're invited to see it for what it is, a debilitating thing that could very well have inspired a whole generation of adolescent fear and phobia, which then transformed into defensiveness, isolation, and aggression. Gray's monologue tells of a childhood that appears to have been a string of little power plays that Spalding never quite mastered. For example, he couldn't bring himself to hunt ducks. And though his aggressive tendencies toward his "girlfriend" never actually harmed the girl, they certainly hint at low self-esteem on Gray's part. How, exactly, should a child deal with the fact that no place, really, is safe from annihilation? While annihilation was never really immanent throughout Gray's childhood, it was clearly an ominous possibility, at least in the minds of Gray and his generation. With such a specter hovering over daily life, what path could lead to happiness?

Basking in the postatomic, 1950s glow of America at its political and cultural peak, living life as a young, middle-class, presumably heterosexual white male of Anglo-Saxon origin, the young Spalding is the beneficiary of all American culture can offer. The monologue certainly doesn't paint a portrait of a child in any obvious despair, though the image is not quite that of a glorious summer of normal boyish discoveries. Then again, what exactly is it to be normal in America, or anywhere else in the world for that matter? That's the kind of thing that Gray's monologue seems to be tinkering with. Consider the point in the monologue when, at about the time Gray started taking dance lessons (not really a normal boy's pastime), he tells us about keeping two "erotic" pictures nearby, to be pulled out in time of need:

> One was of Prince Charles jumping over hurdles as a young boy, which I kept under the bed and used to look at every time I was anxious. The other was the collapse of Rome, with everyone crawling around in the streets half naked. Maybe they had the plague. I thought, this is really sexy: Anything goes now because there are no more rules. Everyone can just do what they want sexually.

Whatever icons young boys held dear in America during the Truman and Eisenhower years, Prince Charles and the Fall of Rome are not typically on the list. But how much of the growing great silent majority known as the baby boomer generation was in fact holding John Wayne or some other bit of Americana in their imaginations rather than something that wasn't exactly culturally prescribed as "wholesome"?

Was there more than just an occasional lurking uncertainty behind the great 1950s-era American cultural myth of confidence and progress? Could there have been a general but quiet contemplation on the suffering that attended the military, scientific, and technological triumphs that led to the destruction of Hiroshima and Nagasaki? Gray doesn't ask these questions straight out, preferring to share his unreflected-upon experiences with his audiences. And by sharing his childhood with us through the eyes of an adult, he reminds us that history is never just in the past but shadows us in the present. To say, as Guy does, that these are "banal and boring" is a vast understatement. But while not nearly as sensational or as horrific as the stories told by the generation who fought World War II, Gray's postwar witness is perhaps even more crucial to the matter of seeing our way through the world we now occupy, a world without any clear sanctuaries from senseless violence. There really is no place to hide.

Booze, Cars, and College Girls follows *Sex and Death to the Age 14*. It's a three-part piece with each part focusing on one of the trinity of cool that Spalding lists in the title. Booze, cars, and college girls are almost mythic ingredients of a normal boy's movement into adulthood. But his encounters with each of these three ingredients are less than normal, at least when compared to stereotyped expectations.

The *Booze* section doesn't dive into anything like the glory days of Gray's youth. Strangely enough, it opens with a summary of Gray's roots on his maternal side:

> My mother was a Christian Scientist, so she didn't drink. But she drank a lot before she became one. She used to date Jed Hanley, whose father owned the Narragansett Brewery and whose grandfather owned the Mount Hope Bridge. My mother, Jed, and the whole gang would go down to Prudence Island for Keg Parties. . . . Mom told me that she remembered lying under the dripping spigot to catch the last drops, and then she'd stagger home.

The rest of the monologue focuses on Spalding's almost obsessive and even lurid determination to get drunk under any circumstances. Virtually all of the attempts occurred while he was underage, mainly while he attended Fichton Academy in New Hampshire. The second section, *Cars*, begins a little more hopefully: "My father owned a '54 two-tone gray and royal blue Ford. . . . I didn't have my driver's license, but I loved to drive and would often ask my mother if I could go park the car in the garage. I would go out and sit in the car, put on my sunglasses and just rev the engine until I felt like James Dean in *Giant*." Though this is a hopeful beginning, things take something other than an All-American turn in this section too. *College Girls* doesn't wait to let us know that things won't go well, opening on something of a humiliating note:

> I was a virgin when I entered college. Freshman year I was at a party, and my friend Stubbs came up to me and said, "You see that girl? Her name's Sandy, and she goes down. . . . " We spent the night together. I began by licking her breasts. She said, "Who

do you think I am, your mother?" Then we had intercourse and I came in about 30 seconds.

This is less than an innocent, *Happy Days* type of adolescence. And the monologue is far different than a good moralistic tale of lessons learned from scrapes survived because befuddlement continues even after each lesson-learning event.

The tidiness of our collective recollections about the 1950s doesn't quite fit Gray's life, and the monologue hints that the various rites of passage that represent growing up in America might be at least a bit misleading. Booze, cars, and sex were parts of the "real" or typical American path to adulthood, and for most of us they were far different from the romanticized experiences in books or film. If we romanticize our experiences at all, it's usually well after they occur, with imagined nostalgia that ignores the less romantic realities of that march into adulthood. Gray chooses to be more real, and by his example, he asks that we do the same.

Booze ends with a road trip that requires his dad to come and retrieve him and his friends—no tale of bacchanalian joy, only embarrassing excess and humiliating dissipation. *Cars* relates how Gray's adventures led to accidents, near-death experiences, and at best only a temporary feeling of James Dean-like power and control. It ends with Spalding burning out the brakes on his father's new Austin-Healey (driving with the parking brakes on) in front of a crowd of onlookers, an event that leads him to conclude, "I knew my racing career was over." And Spalding's freshman-year sexual entry into manhood may have been normal enough in its sweaty simplicity, but it's far from any of the typical fantasies of youthful experience. And from that dubious beginning we are told of a whole succession of disappointments. *College Girls* ends with Spalding desperately running after his college sweetheart in an act of utter, humiliating futility. Then he "nobly" chooses to go asexual and dedicate himself to his art, only to be "disgusted" by the macho gusto and manly success of his roommate, whose conquest's underwear winds up floating down from upstairs onto Spalding's impotent head. The monologue finally ends, "And shortly after that I was drafted," reminding us that Spalding was now a man, complete with all his culture's rights, privileges, and obligations, including being called on to go to war.

We later learn that he avoids the draft and misses the formal exercise of army boot camp. But we've already seen Gray go through the boot camp of growing up during the 1950s and early 1960s, nostalgically remembered as the time that was dreamy innocence, when all was right with America, especially if you were a middle-class white male. To be black or to be a woman, or to be other than a "he-man" white male, was to be among the less fortunate. Witnesses to black life in the American South, for example, could offer horrific examples of cruelty. And women to that point had few options to pursue as adults, trapped in roles mainly designed to serve their masculine masters. By contrast, Spalding's life was enviably comfortable and secure, so the minor bumps and bruises that he experienced along the way don't seem to rank as anything he should've complained about. In fact, if Gray had actually *complained* about his life during his monologues, a reasonable audience would probably have seen him as a whining, spoiled malcontent.

But Gray doesn't complain. He surely knows better than to rail against his bad fortune when so many others are far less fortunate. However, in their own ways, his accounts subtly reveal that there was something not quite complete even for those living the good life of the privileged class claiming to be "true" Americans and therefore rightful heirs to the American Dream. That there was discontent among disenfranchised women, blacks, and other minorities is not surprising. That there was discontent among the privileged and rising middle class *is* a surprise, though it would've been terribly bad form if Gray had openly complained about his life. So for Gray the problem was how to register discontent without sounding like a malcontent.

Here we come to Gray's implicit compact with his audience. Gray the artist provides Gray the performer with experiences from

Gray the American citizen. Gray the artist inserts a creeping tone of discomfort into the monologues, which helps him gauge whether or not his audiences—who are usually white and middle class—may feel similarly about their lot in life. The hope was that this squirming sense of discomfort would strike a common chord and reveal that it was part of a larger sense of discomfort that perhaps an entire class of people were feeling. He was trying to reach out to a group of people who were too materially well-off to openly and in good conscience publicly complain, but who nevertheless felt discomfort with their lives and even felt trapped by their more or less enforced silence. Could it be that the hollowness of this successful America was felt by more than Gray alone? In matters of creature comfort, all was well, but that clearly wasn't enough. And if Gray was right, discontentment was being felt by the fully enfranchised, the folks who were actually living what was billed as the American Dream. It was enough to lead one to wonder about the level of discomfort among those who were excluded from that dream.

Gray's third anthologized monologue is *47 Beds*. This quirky sexual travelogue begins with Gray telling us about waking up early after a particularly restless night on a futon in his brother's living room: "In order to calm myself down, instead of counting sheep, which I thought might put me back to sleep and I didn't want to do that, I started counting beds and realized that I'd slept in about 47 since the first of March." But the bed count isn't so much a boast as it is a hidden wish that the number had been far fewer. He's a drifter without his own bedpost on which to hang his hat. And that's not a good thing for a man intent on finding happiness and security.

Not quite convinced that the traditional path would lead him to happiness, and not quite sure what alternate routes he should try, Spalding seems uncertain about doing anything with gusto, basically preferring to let the wind determine where he goes. Even trying to settle in with his brother Channing and developing some sort of a normal sibling relationship seems a bit off:

Usually, when I go to visit my brother in Providence, we talk about music, Buddhism, gurus, and the quickest way to enlightenment. We were always practicing the I-am-one-who-is-doing-this method. No matter what you're doing, you say, "I am one who is picking this up, I am one who is. . . . " And eventually, the book says, you get something of a liberating distance, whatever that might be, rather than aesthetic distance.

Things are unusual from the start, but even this unusual family contact has additional strains: Channing has now become a landlord, and apparently his own search for peace in selfhood has been replaced by the daily struggle of managing property and tenants, which at the moment is going poorly. Spalding, of course, is not part of this adult scene. Even though he doesn't want to remain a drifter, he's still not quite ready to grow up. This, in fact, is one of the basic tensions one feels in all of Gray's monologues, a sense that Spalding is physically aging but emotionally and psychologically stagnant, still looking for childlike (some would say childish) "liberating distance." Should he accept that "growing up" is a good thing, or should he cling to his innocence?

Not entirely sure which path to take, Gray gives us a long list of errant attempts to make connections in all the wrong places and all the wrong ways. He tells us, for example, that while in India with the Performance Group, he "became sexually obsessed" and visited an ashram run by Bhagwan Shree Rajneesh, hoping to find fulfillment through guilt-free sexual contact. Disappointment follows, of course, and "the following day I decided to give up on liberation for a while and see India instead." However, inevitably returning to his longing for liberation, he "ends up in a Zendo in the Catskills," misinterprets one of the rituals, and is mortified to find out "that all this time I'd been eating the offerings to Buddha": "When I realized this I had two strong reactions. One was very familiar: guilt. The other was that I might be enlightened before anyone else as a result of my eating. It gave me great courage to go and meditate, which was done by sitting on a cushion, staring at a white wall, counting your breath from 1 to 10."

The meditation is interrupted as usual, and enlightenment doesn't occur. As always, Gray's efforts to find mystical, alternative, and/or Eastern cures to his undiagnosed Western spiritual malaise are all failures. These are curious and even entertaining experiences, but they're always failures when it comes to the enlightenment he seeks.

Amid Gray's almost obsessive spiritual hunger, the monologues always reveal that he's equally interested in the physical side of life. Looking for "guilt-free" sex in *religious* retreats is a good example. Then there's the time in Paris when Gray reads an interview with renowned spiritualist Elisabeth Kübler-Ross in *Playboy* magazine:

> She . . . said that after we die, before we go to the Godhead, we pass through a nonphysical state called the ethereal body. After we leave the ethereal body, it's determined whether or not we have completed our destinies. If we haven't, and in most cases we haven't, there's a reincarnation process in which we, as the ethereal spirit, have the choice to come back. That was the exciting part, to me, because I'd never been aware of choice in my life, and I thought, well at least I'll have the chance to come back and work out my destiny in the best of all possible conditions, in the right family.

Gray's passage here is a loaded one, outlining a pattern that Gray would master in his later monologues. He's attracted to the idea that the spirit can only improve its otherworldly status through what it does while it is part of a worldly body. The spirit and the body need to work together for salvation, whatever that might be. We see here that Gray is never really willing to abandon the world of the physical even when he's focusing on spirituality. Though he'll eventually find a fusion of the two, at this point the most he can do is dream that somehow, somewhere in the future, he will find that elusive common ground where body and soul melt into a harmonious, singular existence. Meanwhile, however, the search continues.

In addition to this longing for a spiritual/physical fusion, Gray seems to have a sense that he's going in the wrong direction by looking to the East for answers to his questions about life and happiness. *Playboy* may not be the optimal place to find spiritual salvation, but at the time it was by far the "hippest" place in the West to look. Although Gray takes advantage of several Eastern-influenced spiritual opportunities, it seems that his heart really is committed to discovering Western, and even more precisely, "American" means to peace and happiness. They are clearly going to be unorthodox, but it seems that the West is home and it is finally there that he'll need to find his place. As we've seen, in the earlier monologues, especially in *Sex and Death to the Age 14*, Gray has grown up in and is bound to a Western way of looking at things. And he appears to have been loyal to the Western ways even as he experiences ongoing disappointments that encourage him to look to the East. Finally, though, if enlightenment is to occur, it will need to be by Western means.

Gray notes also that getting to "better conditions" in life includes somehow belonging to the "right family." This buried bit of feeling stands out as one of the few critical statements that Gray allows himself to make in all of his early monologues: his family was not quite "right." But Gray quickly moves on to other matters after uttering the point. Nothing more is said. Most audience members by this point would have known that Gray's mother had committed suicide in 1967 after suffering numerous bouts of mental illness, serious blows to any hope for family normalcy. Mental illness was certainly not covered in the popular television situation comedies. Usually, unorthodox matters like this were swept under the carpet or rolled into the closet. But Spalding is willing to tell all.

Generally speaking, Spalding's tales of his "slightly" aberrant behavior as an adolescent cast shadows over the notion that he was a normal, archetypal, or prototypical baby boomer kid born into a typical family. But it's also possible—and this is important—to suggest that such a thing as a normal or typical family didn't exist in the 1950s or 1960s, or even today. The ideal presented through myth and media could be mere fantasy. And it's also possible that the many aberrant realities swept out of public sight were more the norm than the aberration. Therefore, our aspirations to live the American Dream of success and normalcy may be doomed to disappointment by the very fact that the dream simply is unattainable. It is what it is: a dream.

People in Gray's audience might have been able to conclude that their family was "better" or "worse" than his, but it's unlikely any (or many) of us would have been able to announce that our own families fit the profile of the "right family" that Gray was looking for. Gray leaves it open for us all to consider the possibility that we all survive some degree of family dysfunction. And if we all have experienced dysfunction of one sort or another, then we need to recognize a curious point, namely that dysfunction may be the American norm. This basically normalizes Gray's unique experiences as well as our own, since though all of our life experiences are different in detail, they are generally parallel in type. We all are curiously aberrant in our own quirky—and sometimes tragic—ways. With any luck, confessing this will lead to some sort of personal liberation.

Family is of course a central obsession for Gray. Given that he had problems finding a place within the family structure, he was forced to try even harder within one of the other often bizarre relationships with which he experimented. This search folds into Gray's larger search for what he calls an "authentic experience" as he wanders through life. It's what will later become the search for a "perfect moment" in *Swimming to Cambodia*, but the quest surfaces even before that important work. Presumably for Gray, having an authentic moment will be something like a religious experience that will get him to a place where he can finally feel he "belongs," even if for only a brief, fleeting moment.

Reporting in *47 Beds* his travels through Greece and all the inauthentic and touristy things that country offers its visitors, Gray gets

to share with us an early authentic experience. It happens after a
long string of touristy encounters on beaches and at bars, when he's
given the chance to experience ancient Greece by holding an actual
two-thousand-year-old human skull. At that moment, he is literally
connected to the beginnings of the Western world. But true to Gray's
insecurities, instead of finding some sense of cool connection, he
panics, fearing that having had this authentic moment means his
life will come to an end. It's a logical conclusion for Gray to make if
it were true that life is like some sort of storybook, complete with a
moralistic beginning, middle, and end. For better or for worse, however, life's not so tidy, and Gray does survive his authentic moment
without succumbing to a dramatic end. And that becomes a story of
its own.

On his return home, after having that "authentic experience,"
Gray generates a bizarre but not entirely unusual plan:

> So I started making up little prayers—not exactly prayers, more
> like conditions, little promises. I was thinking: All right, all right,
> all right. . . . if this plane doesn't crash, I promise, I promise, I
> promise I will make Art out of this experience. No entertainment.
> No more entertainment! I didn't know who I was making con-
> ditions *to*, maybe the *Village Voice*, maybe the *New York Times*,
> maybe God.

Negotiating with his god of bargains, however, reduces this authen-
tic/religious experience to something hardly religious at all. In fact,
Gray shows still another level of dysfunctionality in his understanding of life and the religious explanations that are supposed to make
sense of it. His foolhardy negotiation involves a "naughty or nice"
ethic of reward and punishment, a reduction of religious mystery
to a system of economics. Be good and be rewarded; be bad and
be punished. Remember how Santa jingles instill this sentiment in
us even as children, drawing initially from religious sentiments that
have little to do with reward and punishment. Moving between the

material and the spiritual takes Gray back to that way of looking at the world, reducing the spiritual to what our culture would call an economy of equitable exchange. It's a logical and pretty widespread way to come to terms with the world, but it does little more than return us to the simple materialism that Gray was trying to escape. Later in his career, Gray will reverse this idea that all the world's a market and everything has a retail value, and that will get him closer to the happiness he's looking for. It's a reversal that will undermine the Western cultural materialism that has such a hold on Gray and that seems to screw up most of his efforts to find freedom. But at the time of *47 Beds*, he is still utterly confused about how to find the happiness he's looking for.

Gray does reveal a hint of what it will take to become a normal and maybe even a happy human toward the end of *47 Beds*. Returning home to a New York he calls "Hell City," he immediately escapes to Rhode Island to visit his father and stepmother, whose existence is nothing short of the middle-American suburban ideal, complete with "an automatic ice machine, a trash compactor, an electric bread maker, a cordless telephone." Seeing this leads Gray to announce, "then I realized that a big part of living is conformity." Fortunately, this point is immediately adjusted when Gray decides to visit an old friend in Delaware. At age forty, Ryan has just become a grandfather, and his life since high school has been occupied by raising a family. Sitting around and talking to his old buddy, Gray talks about his troubles and tells Ryan that he copes as everyone in New York City copes, by getting therapy. When Gray describes his sessions as "a chance to reflect and go over everything that happened [at the end of a week] in front of a witness," Ryan responds with, "Reflect? I haven't had time to do that in twenty years and everything's going fine down here!" Gray seems shocked that an unreflected-upon life could actually be a good thing. But maybe, in some cases, it is.

Up to this point, Gray has had the opportunity to live a life into near middle age fretting about himself and egocentrically searching for personal self-fulfillment as he embraces the right to the pursuit of happiness. In contrast, his friend seems to have found all the contentment that Spalding lacks and hungers for by having chosen a more traditional, homegrown, Western alternative. Ryan's life has clearly been more than accumulating the material possessions of suburbia that seems the hallmark of modern American conformity. And this contentment doesn't require all the fashionable psychological soul-searching that Gray has been engaged in his whole life. The traditional family option, freed from all the contemporary upgrades, never strikes Gray as an option to try. At least not for the moment.

What follows in *47 Beds*, however, does signal a first step toward considering that option, though it's a first step that Gray will need to take several times before he's ready for a second step. Following the visit with Ryan, Gray returns to New York City to find an acquaintance he'd met in Greece, Arjuna Aziz, who needs Gray to help him settle into the city. Gray tells us that Arjuna is actually afflicted with more phobias than he's ever had himself. Arjuna especially fears the destruction of his skin by daily exposure to the world, revealing a literal sense of superficiality personified. Disgusted by Arjuna's display of extreme egocentrism, Spalding reports: "For the first time, I heard this adult voice coming out of me and I realized that at last I had gotten the narcissistic child outside myself. I had that child right there in front of me in the form of Arjuna." He ends the piece, "I wonder if I'll ever get in touch with any normal people." This momentary "mature" moment does not hold, however, poorly equipped as Gray is to maintain it. He'll shortly return to looking in all the wrong places for adult sustenance because he continues to wonder when he will ever meet "normal" people and settle into a "normal" life. Here he's revealing to us that he's still trying to find that spot in the world that conforms to the cultural ideal he's been brought up to believe exists. But he continues to miss a point that travels with him wherever he goes, that it seems more and more that "normal" actually doesn't exist. Sometime, Gray is going to have to begin looking for something else.

Maybe Gray's pursuit of the normal is so obsessive because his life was so abnormal. But then, as suggested above, most of our lives are abnormal to some degree. Gray, of course, goes one step beyond most of us by choosing the career that he did, since acting is clearly an unusual choice for anyone looking for "reality." But then again, Gray's career was in the theater, and the *teatrum mundi* (all the world's a stage) theme was central both to his perception of the world and to how our culture in general sees the world. We're all actors playing some role on a stage that we call real life.

Gray's monologue *A Personal History of the American Theatre* summarizes his professional career as an actor before he turned to his monologues. It's a monologue full of "memories, stories, and associations around and about forty-nine plays which I acted in between 1960 and 1970." Wanting to highlight the unpredictability of living and the disorderliness of memory, Gray returns to a strategy that parallels *India and After (America)*: "The names of all these plays were printed on 5 X 8 cards and the cards were placed in a box with a clear plastic front. During the course of the monologue, I turn each card by hand to reveal a new play title to the audience and then proceed to tell stories out of my experiences with each play." Like life, live theater thrives on the unexpected, and Gray added one more randomizing element as he worked to defy any urge to organize his life experiences into mere chronology.

But the experience of this monologue was more than a game. Gray explains the apparently inadvertent seriousness of play when he discusses his first acting experience, doing *The Curious Savage* in boarding school. When he gets to this play in the monologue, he reports:

> I think that certain people decide to become professional actors, just like certain people decide to become doctors and dentists. . . . And they study it and become an actor. It's an act of will. . . .
>
> But with other people it's an ontological condition. There's no way out. They're born into it. They find that they are "acting out"

all the time, and they don't know what to do about it. They have
these inappropriate responses to reality, and they are trying to find
a nice place to "act out" other than in an insane asylum.

Now for me, I think it was the ontological condition. I was
bored with life, actually. I know I shouldn't have been. I know I
should have been thankful. But it was all so flat. It was just a flat
thing. And I would keep hyping it up with this kind of "acting
out."

Gray's life in the theater engages an "ontological condition" that
he claims is unique to himself. What he doesn't realize—or at least
doesn't say—is that it's a condition we all experience, even if we
choose to become doctors or dentists. We're all actors involved in
self-creation. It's a game with serious consequences.

How to master this game of self-creation remains a problem for
Gray the actor as it does for all of us. *Nobody Wanted to Sit Behind a
Desk*, as the title implies, captures Gray's and our culture's perpetual
restlessness stemming from a general unwillingness to assume a role
that is out there for all of us to fall into. Nobody grows up dreaming
of working a nine-to-five job, but many of us will settle for that kind
of work as we "grow up." Gray's father, we find out at the end of the
monologue, is the source of the title. It's his summary of "how he felt
about the fact that none of his sons had chosen to go into business
like he had." It seems that the entire baby boomer generation is restless, searching for it frankly knows not what.

Of, course, ironically, Gray's career did involve sitting behind a
desk, but not one in a cubicle or private office. His brand of success
behind the desk first requires an existence beyond the desk. So Gray's
monologue opens with his return from Amsterdam to New York,
where his girlfriend Renée is waiting with a car to travel cross-country to San Francisco. It's July 4, 1976, the American bicentennial. But
the car never makes it out of New York City, breaking down even before the journey begins. As they walk home, "people were throwing
firecrackers at us out of their windows. It felt like a war zone."

From this broken-down bicentennial reentry into America after months abroad, Gray and Renée do eventually depart on their cross-country trip. They spend the first night at his brother Rocky's house in Pennsylvania, where Rocky had just found a job at a boys' school: "Rocky is a specialist in the history of thought, so he'd had trouble finding work in the United States." After a brief stay, Spalding and Renée get to a polluted Lake Michigan. Renée points out rather glumly, "This looks like Gerald Ford country." Despite the industrial debris along the shore and in the water, Spalding refuses to be deterred from his pleasures and jumps in for a swim. In Minnesota they get a motel room and watch parts of the Republican Convention: "I drank can after can of 3.2 beer while wild-eyed reporters hyped the whole thing up like cheap theater. 'Bush is going to do it! Look out for Bush!' Bush this, Bush that, until completely bushed, we fell asleep." In the Black Hills of South Dakota, Spalding meets up with a friend of a friend whose father was an Irish immigrant who married a Native American. Gray tells us that during the father's first days in America, hunger drove him nearly to steal a chicken, but "at the last minute a voice said in his ear, 'You haven't stolen anything yet,' and he put the chicken back and went to bed hungry." It's a nice story of the hardships of early immigrant life, met with an overriding sense of ethical behavior found less and less often in today's amoral world of instant gratification.

Spalding and Renée get to sleep in a teepee, work to overcome their fear of rattlesnakes by creating "a magic protective circle of rocks around the bed," and choose to visit a "true Western town that looked like a set for 'Gunsmoke'" rather than attend a protest against uranium mining or watch a 400-acre forest fire. The myth of the Old West, it appears, has greater allure than the more problematic realities that currently occupy its inhabitants. They next visit Yellowstone, which Gray had learned about when he was eight years old by reading *Mickey Mouse Sees the USA*. His conclusion, after not seeing a single bear, is that Yellowstone "was nothing like *Mickey Mouse Sees the USA*." Traveling through Bozeman, Montana, Renée tells Gray an anecdote about the stormy personal lives of Dashiell Hammett and Lillian Hellman, which leaves Gray wondering if he and Renée are doomed to a similar violent end. In Missoula he meets an old friend who teaches theater at the university: "Then some local friends of his who worked at Anaconda came over for beers. They told stories about how they'd get real drunk in the winter and go for moonlight hikes in Yellowstone. Listening to them talk I thought these men could be my native gurus. I dreamed of the day I'd have the time to return to Yellowstone some winter to hike with them."

In Oregon he searches for "the perfect lake," finds it, swims in it, and then has sex with Renée, hoping maybe to please her since she's become frustrated with Spalding's control of the trip. They finally reach Santa Cruz, California, and stay with Jim Bierman, whose peaceful 100 acres overlooking the Pacific Ocean is nearly paradise except for the fact that Santa Cruz happened to be the murder capital of the United States. They immerse themselves in the liberation culture until Renée finally flies back to New York and Spalding drives up to San Francisco, "the city of encounter groups, the city of therapy, still."

Gray's cross-country adventure is a highly selective survey of Americana plotted out by a self-professed sensualist looking for good times. In the final analysis, it's not so much what Gray encounters as it is a matter of seeing that almost *anything* can be found in the wide expanses of the American West. America, it seems, can be all things to all people, anything each of us wants it to be. Ironically, of course, this vast vision of America that Gray experiences reveals one thing that America can't be or refuses to be, and that is a community. The vastness of America minimizes or even eliminates any need for people to make compromises in the name of building community, allowing "rugged" individuals the space to be themselves and live without interference from others. When space and resources are virtually unlimited, there's no need to think about doing anything for "the good of a majority." If you don't like what's happening where you are, you can simply do the Huck Finn thing and "light out" for less populated territory.

This is an incredibly tantalizing vision of the American West. And if it were ever actually true that people were absolutely free from having to deal with troublesome neighbors, it is fast becoming a vastly inaccurate perception. In the monologue, Gray reminds us of Santa Cruz's crime rate, suggesting that even the vast wild West is closing in on its population and making it ever more important for people to think about their neighbors. But the ideal of a land that encourages individual self-determination remains the myth that we've generally been brought up to dream about, and the vastness of the West, even today, seems to be a natural argument in favor of the myth.

Gray's American West experience, however, is curiously solidified when he meets Sam Shepard in San Francisco. This *Tooth of Crime* playwright, icon of Western masculinity (though Shepard was born in Illinois), is a man of rugged authenticity and substance who personifies the West that Spalding has just pioneered across:

> He asked me out to see Lou Reed. I was real nervous, kind of like on a first date. I had been involved for two years in his *The Tooth of Crime*, which is about a styles match between Hoss and Crow—two styles meeting and having a stand-off, a word battle, a styles match. Suddenly, it was like the play had come to real life, which was much more exciting for me than the play itself, because here was Sam Shepard himself, who had a very different style from mine. He was very West Coast.

But the encounter is more than a match of more or less equal "styles." Caught up in the allure of the West, Gray wants to capture some of Shepard's style: "Most of the time I was in San Francisco I couldn't figure out how to get shoes to make me feel more like a man." His failure to be able to walk in something like Shepard's shoes makes Spalding feel less like a man in Shepard's presence, an uncomfortable and unsatisfying feeling that he wants to overcome: "I'd been feeling more and more light, light, light on my feet—too light for my age. . . . The point was that I was feeling very light that particular night and Sam was very heavy, in his cowboy boots, and we were going to see Lou Reed." He clearly admires Shepard's "true" American manifestation of masculinity: "Sam picked me up in his Ford Bronco, which smelled of wild horses. In fact, he had his saddle in the back seat. He was smoking Old Golds and going through the gears, saying to me, 'You guys in the East are too pessimistic. You should see what it takes to get a *horse* down'."

The admiration clearly rising from this encounter with Shepard draws Spalding almost back to his days in *Booze, Cars, and College Girls* or earlier, those formative years when he tried without much success to mold himself into someone cool and manly, a genuine copy of a true American original. In Shepard, Gray found a man who appeared to have succeeded. In contrast, there is Spalding, who takes on Shepard in a manly game of pool and "made this total freak shot. I hit one ball, it jumped over another ball, and hit *another* ball, which went in." Spalding looks up. And he tells us, "Sam took a long pause, looked down at it [the table] and said, 'That must be what you call a New England shot.' Then he put every ball in *bing, bing, bing. Bing. Bing.*" Gray can't compete in this "man's" world, and trying only depresses him.

Gray eventually goes to liberally sensitive, socially conscious, and decidedly non-"Western" Berkeley—across the bay from San Francisco—and in this non-cowboy boot world, he announces with relief, "I felt like a good guy, a nice guy, because people looked like me. I was feeling good." Then he returns to Santa Cruz, where he runs into another masculine nemesis, an old acquaintance whom Spalding believed he had outgrown; Gray "didn't want to compare male chauvinist notes anymore with him." He avoids an uncomfortable guy competition that would have involved listing female conquests, and eventually he finds his way back to New York City.

But despite returning to "the sanctuary" of Renée's New York loft, the city now strangely repels him even while he's still oddly attracted to it. The catalogue of activities he dives into even on his first day's return is full, ending with meeting a street person singing the praises of Las Vegas, which Spalding reminds us was where he'd once "been locked up for six days." Then he goes to Rhode Island, where he meets his dad and takes in Dad's simple assessment of the unusual career and life choices Spalding and his brothers have made: "I figured nobody wanted to sit behind a desk."

Though he never exactly says it, New York has allowed Spalding to take on a number of experimental life roles and try them on as he works to find out who he is and where he belongs. Clearly he was never meant to be a nine-to-five professional. And he was never meant to be a rugged Marlboro man, either. Running all the way back to his roots, Gray finds at least a bit of self-assurance through his father's sparse but telling comment, implying that his children had been given the freedom in their middle-American New England upbringing to become what they chose rather than what seemed culturally mandatory.

This monologue offers something of a visual gag throughout. For most of the performance, Gray sits in his chair *beside* his desk. A little off, a little unusual, but the audience grows accustomed to the new seating arrangement, just as with any behavior that's not quite symmetrical or normal. This point is confirmed when at the end of the monologue, Gray tells three short stories about his dad, all pointing to tolerance, if not old-fashioned displays of love on his father's part, imparting a sense of freedom to do as one chooses. It's not exactly the feeling of home that Gray wants to find, but it may be the next best thing.

Back on Familiar Territory

It's a pretty natural step for Gray's next monologue to focus on actually trying to go home again. In *Travels to New England* Spalding tells us of his return to his roots as he took his *Interviewing an Audience* success on the road. The plan was to go to New England for two months, "interviewing the audience in non-performance spaces, including golden age drop-in centers, paper mills, clothing mills, historical societies, and Grange halls." This return home includes seeing a local production of *Death of a Salesman*, that classic treatise on masculine conformity in a coldly dehumanizing capitalist world. Gray reports, "At first I saw it as a good omen for the tour because Willy Loman was talking about the New England route." It does seem like a good omen at first because at intermission Gray meets an old friend who is working on a film script. The writer offers Spalding the lead, saying, "I'm thinking you're perfect for the role." But the film is about a character who uses art (photography) to deceive and ultimately rape his victims. The point seems to be that maybe even Gray's innocent-seeming *Interviewing an Audience* has hidden ulterior motives behind it. Though again Gray leaves the connection for his audiences to make on their own, the encounter with his old friend leaves him disheartened as he returns to the equally disheartening conclusion to *Death of a Salesman*: "The rest of the play was kind of down for me. I kept seeing Willy as this outsider trying to get in, all the time wandering around the neighborhood going, 'What's the answer? What's the answer Bernard? What's the *answer*?'" Something of a low man/everyman himself, Gray seems doubly captivated by the events of the evening, first the one that implicates him as a possible perpetrator of oppression and second the one that implies his alienation from the New England world he so confidently believes to be his own. The rest of the monologue recounts Gray's own salesman route, selling himself much as *Death of a Salesman* argues that we all sell ourselves one way or another in whatever business we take on in this world.

Travels to New England does something most of his monologues don't do. It unfolds in clear chronological order, but the tale just doesn't add up to the complete portrait of his roots that Gray seems to have hoped for. Spalding's first stop in *Travels to New England* is Hartford, Connecticut, site of personal inspiration "because my favorite American poet Wallace Stevens had lived there." But when he looks up Stevens's home in semisuburbia, the experience "made me feel like I didn't belong there, like I was a weird kind of killer, like Joe Kallinger." Gray tells us that Joe Kallinger was a demented, delusional madman and suburban murderer, not unlike the rapist that Gray's friend wanted him to portray. After finding Stevens's house—currently occupied by "strangers" and complete with snarling dogs—he leaves. From Hartford he goes to Providence, Rhode Island, then to Boston. From there he goes to Provincetown, "Land's End, place of desire," which stirs up memories of three previous visits. This time, however, Gray leaves deflated rather than invigorated. He tells us that a person in the audience that night complained that Spalding needed to get rid of his tie and jacket: "Loosen up your tie and go out on the dunes—then you'll be able to talk to us. You're acting like some sort of a therapist." Even though Gray explains that he's "wearing a tie and jacket as a costume," he finally faces up to the fact that "they couldn't understand this concept . . . that I was trying to dress as *though* I had grown up in New England and had stayed and not gone to New York City."

From Provincetown, he goes to Acton, Massachusetts. Wondering why "I couldn't get in touch with history" throughout his odyssey, Gray goes to Walden Pond and "as I saw the pond in the distance through the bare spring trees, I thought of that other time, with Nora." These recollections lead Gray to have "visions of witchcraft because we were so close to Salem and also of Samson and Delilah," momentarily conflating American and biblical history into the personal experiences that were his life. Almost immediately Gray has erotic visions. He rushes to the site of Thoreau's cabin and tells us that he "stuck my cock deep in and shot into earth. I lay there, exhausted, completely fulfilled, thinking: what a fantastic union with mother earth." Following this bizarrely literal enactment of the generally metaphorical union between man and nature found in *On Walden Pond*, Gray asks, "I wonder how many times Thoreau did this? Maybe in this very spot even." There are, of course, no records to answer that question.

Groton, Massachusetts follows, and the performance at the Shirley Golden Age Drop-in Center turns into a reactionary revolt against even the most innocuous points this "New Yorker" tries to make. Thankfully, at the Golden Age Drop-in Center in Pepperell, Massachusetts, he's better received. But in Lawrence, Massachusetts, he's forced into an inadvertent class sensitivity lesson. Escorted by well-off Andover residents to his performance at the neighboring textile mill, he finds the millworkers suspicious of this man with upper-class connections. Then in Portsmouth, New Hampshire, Spalding stays with a host whose "wife's grandparents had been among the original members of the Oneida Colony, that free-love, polygamous experimental group of the 1800s. She was very interested in Elisabeth Kübler-Ross and transcendental thinking. She was a great Amazon of a woman, a sort of contemporary New England Transcendentalist."

The last stop on the tour is Willy Loman's own last stop, Portland, Maine, and a memorable *Interview* occurs, after which he is left completely alone: "They thought I was this famous busy person, some world-renowned talk-show host who needed to be left alone." He goes out for drinks with two theater employees, and "the next day I got on People Express and flew back to Manhattan, that island off the coast of America." The audience is welcomed to conclude that Gray is himself an island, pretty much against his wish. At least that's the impression left by his summary of this *home* tour, not to mention his cross-country experience in *Nobody Wanted to Sit Behind a Desk*.

Such a feeling of alienation is pervasive in mobile, transient, expansive America; it certainly isn't felt by Gray alone. Even if travels are restricted to turf familiar from childhood, chances are pretty good that loneliness will be at least part of the experience. The solution, it appears, is to put down new roots, which is what Gray stumbles into doing in *Terrors of Pleasure: The House*. He falls in love with a cabin in Krummville, New York, in the Catskills, but when he takes the plunge and buys a house, the results are anything but real satisfaction:

> Moving in was no big deal. I drove up, walked into the house, plopped down on the coffee-stained, gold-flecked Castro

Terrors of Pleasure: The House. (Photo by Nancy Campbell, courtesy of Kathie Russo.)

convertible surrounded by Ethan Allen furniture and just sat there waiting for the feeling of ownership to wash over me. Nothing came. . . . And I realized that I *had* no sense of ownership. Someone had lived there before me. Someone would live there after me. I was just passing through. Now I had to worry about making a will.

Not at all what he expected or hoped for. Gray returns to his New York loft with a sense of defeat. But in his New York neighborhood, unexpectedly, he experiences moments of place. When a friend visits from Berkeley, Gray proudly shows *his* city to this outsider. But the description is not exactly of "home." They walk past cars with burglar alarms going off, which everyone ignores, and join a circle of strangers looking at a stash of cash mysteriously dropped in the street and swirling in a small vortex of breeze.

Amid these experiences of trying to find or to make a home for himself, Gray read the 1980 book *Entropy*, which he says "states that matter and energy can only be changed in one direction, from usable to unusable, from order to chaos." But the book also notes that "the spiritual plane is not governed by the iron-clad dictates of the entropy law," meaning that the spiritual world can reverse entropy and generate order out of chaos. Gray concludes, "it might be possible to shift my attention to a more metaphysical state." So instead of fretting that he should have invested his money in something other than a dilapidated house, he once again briefly looks East and turns to thoughts of becoming a Buddhist monk, following the teachings of Bhagwan Rajneesh. But abandoning the material world is not for Gray, and when he finds the term "spiritual materialism," he concludes that "maybe instead of going to Rancho Rajneesh, I should go to Hollywood and do a few sitcoms and make enough money to restore the house to perfection." Then he'd have a material place to develop spiritual contentment, a perfect combination in Gray's mind.

Most people realize rather quickly that Hollywood is no place to discover one's place in the world, certainly not one's spiritual place. Being a realm of illusion and fantasy, and of countless dashed dreams to boot, Hollywood would be a foolish choice for anyone really to believe in. Gray is apparently savvy enough to know that fame won't save him, and his plans are not to find happiness by becoming a star. Rather, by succeeding in Hollywood he believes he'll be able to afford a "perfect home" in the Catskills. So off he goes with ambition in hand.

He returns from Hollywood after numerous auditions, fully hopeful of getting a call and landing a contract. The date is July 4, 1984, which, like the return date in *Nobody Wanted to Sit Behind a Desk*, suggests something of American mythic potential. The role he'd hoped for, however, goes to someone else, and in his money-hole cabin in the Catskills he has to deal with dilapidation without the resources to renovate: "Well, I was disappointed, but not surprised. I decided to go out on the porch and recount my blessings. After all, I had a fantastic girlfriend, a porch with a good view of state land, and some pure, wonderful well water."

But all is not well even now. The "pure, wonderful well water" turns out to be polluted by rotting corpses of animals in the pipes, and Gray fears he's contracted rabies after having swallowed half a glass of the stuff before realizing its toxicity. A wise local plumber talks him down from his panic: "Mr. Gray, life is really too short to be worrying about catching rabies from a well." And Gray concludes: "And a light bulb went on in my head and I thought, Wow, he's right. He's really right. Now, where do I go from here?"

What Gray achieves here is nothing that settles his life in any permanent way. More setbacks will inevitably ensue, which an altered state of mind might help him better survive, but his search for home, self-security, and contentment is far from complete.

5

Paradise Lost and Found

The Road to Cambodia

Although *Terrors of Pleasure: The House* chronicles Gray's early frustrations in Hollywood, his career is in fact dotted with minor successes in film and television, but none succeeded at propelling him into personal wealth or cinematic stardom. One minor role, however, as the U.S. consul in the 1984 film *The Killing Fields*, directed by Roland Joffe, took on a life of its own beyond the silver screen. It provided Gray with material that would vault him onto the center stage of American theater and into the cultural imagination as none of his previous works onstage or in film had. It also began a symbiotic relationship that he had only imagined possible, working his performance pieces into filmed events that expanded his audiences well beyond what the stage alone could generate. This perfect storm of experience, humor, insight, performance, and good fortune arrived in the form of Gray's landmark piece, *Swimming to Cambodia* (1985).

Swimming to Cambodia, the staged monologue as well as the eventual filmed version directed by Jonathan Demme, is without doubt Gray's most popular and successful enterprise. Gray's monologue is built upon his experiences in Thailand as part of the supporting cast of *The Killing Fields*. The film covers the 1970 genocidal events in

Cambodia involving the Khmer Rouge, indirectly initiated by CIA involvement in that country during the Vietnam War. *Swimming to Cambodia* combines that particular history lesson with Gray's more personal experiences in Thailand during his extended periods of downtime between filming sessions. Gray reports the evolution of *Swimming to Cambodia* in his introduction to the printed version: "It was almost six months after the filming of *The Killing Fields* that I began my first reports, and more than two years passed before I made my last adjustments. Over that time, *Swimming to Cambodia* evolved into a very personal work in which I made the experience my own. Life made a theme of itself and finally transformed itself into a work of fiction."

Created by internalizing his experience and then reflecting it in performances against two years' worth of audience feedback as a monologue, *Swimming to Cambodia* stands out, even today, as Gray's signature work.

Reflecting in 1999 on what at that point (following *Morning, Noon and Night*) he considered a completed career as a monologist searching for self and place, Gray observes rather fondly:

> I thought [at the time] that *Swimming to Cambodia* was political because it was a reenactment of the time when there was a secret bombing of Cambodia by the United States. I took a kind of left-ist stance—which was the position of the people who were doing the film *The Killing Fields*. I guess that was the first time that I took a stand on an issue. I know that the Performance Group once went to Washington to protest the bombing of Cambodia. I remember we were at a distance and I saw hardcore people who were doing a sitdown. I saw the horses ride over them and that's when I knew that I wasn't going to get any further involved.

In that regard, and true to his Wooster Group experience, in which political activism was seen as a naïve response to more deep-rooted cultural ills, *Swimming to Cambodia* is in fact *not* political in any

Swimming to Cambodia. (Photo copyright Paula Court, courtesy of Paula Court.)

traditional sense. But in another regard, the piece *is* political: it digs beneath superficial machinations to unearth the roots of our culture's pervasive, though often unintended oppression, the first step in a more substantial move toward hoped-for change.

However, what is most memorable about the piece is Gray's desperate search for "the perfect moment" in his Thai paradise. His self-serving pleasure seeking and totally nonresponsible experiences are almost mesmerizing. But what evolves is a subtle indictment of Gray's narcissistic urges as well as the cultural roots that uphold and even endorse such behavior, generally to the detriment of those who are recruited to stand by and serve those indulgences. Like when we watch a movie based on a Jane Austen novel, we are caught up by the luxury and forget the servants whose sweat and toil made it all possible. The pleasure, admiration, and even envy that *Swimming to Cambodia* generates in Gray's audience reveals our own longing for the pleasures that he seeks, and through that audience attraction the general indictment of all of us is virtually complete. Without ever directly saying so, Gray admits guilt at taking advantage of the less-fortunate Asian serving class, but he also draws his audiences into that guilt by exposing our implicit desires to be just like him, indulging our every whim and passion. His charm ensnares us all.

This is not to say that *Swimming to Cambodia* is in any notable sense any different than Gray's earlier works, except in that his cinematic experiences allow him to bring attention to one of the most dominant mechanisms used to draw us all into cultural complicity: the tantalizing allure of the Hollywood film industry. For though *The Killing Fields* "nobly" documents American-inspired atrocities of the recent past, the creation of the film itself unintentionally reveals the root causes of those atrocities even while rather naïvely working to condemn them in a manner not unlike the activism of the 1960s. It's not what we think or want to think about our world that matters so much as how we behave in that world. And when it comes to how we behave toward others, we behave rather badly, even when we think we're helping.

Swimming to Cambodia does move toward a sort of political agenda in a manner more obvious than Gray's earlier autobiographical works had. He had clearly moved beyond simply searching for narcissistic indulgence, if ever he were merely narcissistic in his art. He even reports about *Swimming to Cambodia* that he'd found an objective situation that broke any narcissistic spell he might previously have been under: "People writing reviews have called me a narcissist, and I would certainly admit to that. . . . But with 'Swimming to Cambodia' I found a larger issue outside of my personal neuroses." So even though the piece focused on Gray's pursuit of "the perfect moment," for a perceptive audience, his portrayal of the pursuit itself is entry into his critique. But then, if we look back on the earlier pieces, we see that *Swimming to Cambodia* isn't really so revolutionary, given that in each of the monologues we can find Gray playing with "larger issues" outside of his "personal neuroses."

In his introduction to the published version of *Swimming to Cambodia*, James Leverett confirms this point: "All of the monologues have had an added, often hidden dimension. If you stare at them long enough, you find that what has happened to Gray reflects in a startlingly illuminating way what has happened to the world, or at least a significant section of it, you and I certainly included." To this sense of Gray as everyman, Leverett adds the additional point that we've also witnessed in Gray's work: "But such allegorical relationships are never explicit, or even apparently deliberate." In fact, Gray deliberately undermines any idea that he is either becoming politicized or attempting to awaken his audience to anything like such an awareness. And the same really holds for *Swimming to Cambodia*.

For example, in Part Two, Gray tells us that he watched a tape called *Going Back*, about U.S. veterans returning to Vietnam after the war. But instead of focusing on what that film described as a campaign of senseless loss and destruction, Gray innocently marches forward with a shallow personal response: "Now, I was really taken by the tape, not so much by the Amerasian children in the streets [of

Hanoi], although they were beautiful, or the people who were suffering in the hospitals from the effects of Agent Orange, but I was taken
by the fact that Hanoi was filled with bicycles. . . . And I thought,
now there's where I'd like to go for my vacation."

Unconcerned with the suffering imposed upon the Vietnamese
by U.S. foreign policy, Gray sees the film as more of a travelogue
advertising Vietnam's beauty. Instead of the damage inflicted upon
this world, he sees what could or should become a vacation spot for
Americans. Then, just a step beyond such a callous train of thought,
Gray reports that he was "beginning to feel more and more like . . .
I really wanted to be a *real* foreign correspondent, not someone *playing* one." His eyes, however, are too ill-trained to see the suffering
placed before him. His reports home would likely be anything but
eye opening. What we see here is a man playing an empty-headed
American tourist who had just pretended to be a foreign correspondent and romantically deciding he really wants to be one. "What a
jerk," might be our first response.

But returning to the distinction between Gray the performer and
Gray the artist, an audience can see buried in the monologue something of a genuine correspondent's commentary on U.S. complicity
in generating so much past and present misery in a part of the world
long forgotten by postwar America. And that complicity includes
Gray himself. His ironic method of presentation has finally found
the perfect material to allow him to exhibit the full ironic potential
of his monologic style. Having mastered the art of infinite digression
and free association, Gray presents multiple levels of understanding in *Swimming to Cambodia* that demonstrate the results of his
Wooster and Performance Group exercises that were present but less
obvious in his earlier monologues. He pursues a surface and narcissistic goal of finding a "perfect moment" while a deeper, underlying
"moment of understanding" rises to just beneath the surface. It takes
the critical instincts of the audience to see beneath the surface and to
draw out the revelations that Gray the artist plants beneath the naïve
presentation of Gray the performer.

One of many strategies that Gray masters is repetition, introducing an event or a key phrase and then repeating what has become familiar at a slightly later point, making the tale something that the audience feels it owns. It's almost like a popular song refrain that a rock star uses to get his audience cranked up during a concert. We're led to anticipate certain things as the monologue unfolds, and by generating this sense of expectation, Gray effectively draws us into the plots and ploys of the life he retells. If we've followed Gray's career, we're already familiar with certain things that always pop up, like the dynamics of his relationship with his girlfriend. We know of his mother's suicide and other such events that Gray repeats, and to a degree we look forward to hearing about them all over again. Familiarity by repetition is a valuable trick to win an audience over.

But Gray adds even more subtle tricks within the monologue to draw us in. Jumping from Part One to Part Two of *Swimming to Cambodia*, Gray builds on several images and ideas, creating a shorthand of familiar ideas that draws the audience into his way of looking at the world. Consider, for example, Gray's announcement late in the performance that while in L.A. he successfully negotiated a complex highway grid and made all his appointments on time. "I felt a kind of Triumph of the Will," he says. Early in the monologue, Gray sets this point up by talking about how he uses his "Will"—he calls it "the Little King"—to coerce good fortune into getting him the job in *The Killing Fields*. Gray proclaims that if he could master his Will, "this act of will, willing Will, would have more power toward getting me the role in the film," which, of course, he gets. We grow comfortable seeing Gray manipulate the world through "Will" and start to look forward to seeing it pop up at other places. We're now equipped to anticipate Gray's thought processes. But is it really "Will" at work? Or is Gray just using that word to create an illusion of control over what was just a string of good fortune? The more he repeats this ploy, the more his audience can begin to suspect that maybe it's nothing more than an egotistical misconception of how or why something happens. Other examples abound throughout the monologue, resulting in Gray the artist empowering his audience to look fondly but critically at Gray the performer, in the hope the audience might develop a familiarity that will reach beyond or through the character's conclusions to its own level of understanding.

Of course, it's entirely possible for an audience member to miss Gray's ironic stance and see him as uncritically upholding or actually endorsing a "Will"-fully egotistical pursuit of personal gratification and material gain. Like us all, Gray is not above organizing his life story into self-serving plots. We're all guilty of self-importance and of seeking personal pleasure at other people's expense. And it would be the height of hypocrisy for us to claim that we can escape the gravitational attraction of controlling and feeding off of the world that surrounds us. Gray captures this condition as he moves back and forth between the unironic performer's pursuit of "the perfect moment" and his artist's veiled, ironic commentary on the foolhardiness of that pursuit.

Culture's ills and culture's potential for a growing self-awareness inhere in this single entity, Spalding Gray, even as both illness and cure inhere in each of us. In fact, that Gray's film version of *Swimming to Cambodia* has been so successful—and that his subsequent staged monologues were so well attended—may actually be in part a result of his having won over an audience unself-critically drawn to his tantalizing tales of mass consumption, dissipation, and unconsidered oppression. A good portion of his audience might have been there to hear about the "fun" he had. But this might not be a bad thing, because perhaps the only way to address this reactionary attraction is to draw that uncritical audience into the theater through disarming charm and humor and then to hit them with Gray's unrelenting but padded counterpunches. The strategy sucks in unwitting audiences and not only contributes to the piece's attractive humor but also draws the viewers who need to see these challenges to the consumerist status quo, without smelling of didacticism or sanctimony. He only points fingers at others by first pointing at himself.

So Gray opens *Swimming to Cambodia* by noting, "It was the first day off in a long time." He begins the monologue by highlighting his determination to enjoy himself in the hotel he calls "the pleasure prison." He innocently tells us how the Thai waiters actually enjoy manically serving their Western guests, seeming to believe what he says. He admiringly reports how many of his non-Asian film co-workers had bought Thai women to keep them company while they were in Thailand, without ever considering the women's feelings. Pampered with Western-style accommodations and luxuries daily flown in from the United States, these Westerners have everything they can imagine in order to enjoy their "day off" from work. And Gray offers the rationalization that because of *sanug*—the Thai practice of not doing anything that wasn't fun—he and everyone else feel comfortable treating the locals as willing objects of their pleasure.

This Westernized rationalization justifies easy oppression of the locals by accepting their seemingly willing submission. It's entirely possible to proclaim innocence in participating in this master-servant system, given that the servants curiously claim to *desire* their subservient positions. But it also doesn't take much thought to realize that such willing service exists because the only alternative for the locals would be to reject the advantages gained by serving these Western masters, and that would lead to even greater want and greater suffering. Gray the naïve performer is at this point unaware that there is a need to consider behaving differently, having fallen as he does into accepting the privileges presented to him as a Western birthright.

The extent to which Gray is naïvely part of the oppression unfolds throughout the monologue. After initially commenting on the practice of the film crew taking up Thai wives to pass the time, Gray later observes that he thought it was "a class thing" in that the Sparks—"the British electricians"—were the ones who openly engaged in the practice. But he then notes that "the actors didn't buy women out front. They were more secretive about it and would sneak around doing it at night." Being secretive is of course implicitly a confession that the practice is not entirely "proper." Otherwise, why sneak around? But then, rather surprisingly, Gray moves from commenting on these two groups to conceding that "you could very easily fall in love with a Thai whore" and later to admitting his own involvement in the practice, though he describes it using the ultimate euphemism: "Joy was my Pat Phong friend" (Pat Phong being Bangkok's red light district). He also notes that despite her "joyful" performance as his "girlfriend," Gray's Pat Phong Joy would often enter "a slightly drained and more reflective melancholy" that left Gray without words to explain.

While seeing the self-gratifying attraction of these mutually profitable experiences, Gray also confesses, after his return from Thailand, "I've heard the other side of it and know it exists the way the darker side of everything exists. Just recently, while driving in L.A., I heard a very angry woman talking on KPFK radio about an investigation she made of child prostitution in Thailand." The point is interesting in that Gray reports a report, not having himself actually sensed "the darker side" while happily participating in it. Gray here gives his audience the opportunity to reflect upon the fact that Western indulgence dehumanizes the non-Western pleasure objects. He even offers a glimpse of the differences between the non-Western victims and their Western counterparts, who have apparently freely made prostitution their profession. The New York and Amsterdam prostitutes with whom he's trafficked had been "cool, business-as-usual," presumably having chosen prostitution from among several business options. Gray seems to know deep down that his Pat Phong friend had no such options. And, most likely, neither had his New York and Amsterdam contacts.

If oppressing the other for personal pleasure and gain is detrimental to the oppressed, it also takes its toll on the humanity of the oppressor. Tellingly, among the things Gray imports to America from his experience in Southeast Asia is a renewed sense of dominant male entitlement, to the point that he confesses, "I treated Renée like a Thai whore and I refused to go food shopping and I didn't want to cook and I was a wha-wha-wha little two-year-old. Just wha-wha-wha all over the place." The tantalizing experience of being the central master of one's domain can be a transformative experience, though not in any noble, humane, or attractive way.

This dehumanization of the other is further relayed as Gray reports yet another experience, again offering an analytic point generated by someone other than himself. In this case it's a comment he'd heard while working on the film, made by Neevy Pal, "a Cambodian who was related to Prince Sihanouk and a student [in the United States] at Whittier College." Gray tells us, almost with amusement, that she was "trying to organize all of the Cambodians in the bus because she felt *The Killing Fields* was a neocolonialist film, that the British were looking right through the Cambodians." Not bothering to reflect upon this observation, Gray the performer fails to internalize the point, choosing neither to agree nor to disagree with it. But it seems to have at least begun to hit home for Gray in a less-than-conscious fashion, for, later on, when trying to conceal his money prior to going out into the surf in search of his perfect moment, he worries that the Thais on the beach would find his stash: "And God knows they needed it more than I did. So, at last, I just took it and left it, fully exposed, on the beach." And then a little later, he's also told that everyone in the movie "was making the same salary except Sam Waterston, who was making a little more, and the Cambodians, who were making a lot less." That conversation reveals that Gray himself is making less than the American/British average, which spins him into a competitive frenzy that concludes with him deciding to get an agent so as to avoid future injustice. He says nothing, however, about the injustice to the Cambodians and Thais. We as audience, however, have been given material to draw our own conclusions.

The urge to control and even dominate our world is generally a Western one. But it's also more specifically a *masculine* Western urge. And throughout the monologue Gray does everything he can to emulate the masculine ideal, from taking on his own Thai prostitute to treating his American girlfriend like a whore and otherwise behaving like a "man" even when it appears to be against his character. For example, when he believes his friend Ivan has drowned in the surf of the Indian Ocean, his first instinct is to "find the most responsible man that you can," little thinking that at least on the surface, *he* is a man, though far from responsible. This first instinct of course reveals that Gray doesn't quite fit the standard Western definition of masculinity, and other events verify this. He marvels at the masculine behavior of the correspondents he meets in the local bars, "Real People" who cavalierly tell stories about risking their lives as they masterfully control their own destinies. And then Gray notes:

> And then there was me, who was looking at this incredible bee that looked like a cartoon of a bee because it was so big and fluffy, and its stripes were so wide, and I was saying, "Wow! Look at that bee."
> And everyone said, "It's just a bee, Spalding."

His less-than-masculine predisposition being what it is, when Gray finally decides to leave Thailand, he decides, "I wanted to say goodbye like a man, and if I couldn't be one, I was going to imitate one." He does the determined, stoic, manly thing, shaking hands and offering masculine embraces. But his acting out this manly role betrays him in the end:

> And when I got to Athol Fugard, he turned to me and said, "So, Spalding. You're leaving Paradise?"
> "Athol (oh!) Athol (oh!) uh, Athol (uh!), I—I was thinking that maybe I should (oh!), eh, uh, wait a minute, Athol, you really think I, uh. . . . "

Fugard finally forces Gray to stand behind his decision: "Go back, Spalding! Take what you've learned here and go back."

Prior to this departure announcement, obsessing on John Malkovich as a "man," Gray observes: "The film was a 'buddy' movie, it was about *male bonding*. I'd never been with men in a situation like this in my life. . . . We'd all get together for lunch, or cocktails at six, and we'd all just sit around and *bond*, talking about what happened that day." The bonding, of course, involves idle male competition, in this case taking the form of telling jokes, and Gray decides to tell two because "I wanted to be one of the guys." His jokes are scatological and only incidentally sexual, but they do draw laughter from the crowd. Then Malkovich tells his joke (confirming for Gray, jealously, that he's "a good storyteller"), about a mouse trying to have sex with an elephant. A mischievous monkey drops a coconut on the elephant's head, staggering her as the mouse tries to mount her. As the elephant falls to her knees, the mouse cries out, "Yeah! Suffer, bitch!" Gray's childish scatology suffers in comparison to Malkovich's hilariously masculine misogyny.

But Gray's failure to really be one of the guys marks him—against his "Will"—as potentially possessing an empathic consciousness awaiting an awakening. It's his one really redeeming quality, though he certainly doesn't seem to realize it. When he travels to Los Angeles and makes his round of interviews for new roles, sitting in a casting director's office and being evaluated, he observes: "I suddenly and clearly realized what it feels like to be a woman scrutinized by a man. I've hardly ever had that feeling before. Only in Morocco." It's a vulnerability that, quite likely, John Malkovich never experienced. And it suggests a sensitivity that might transform into something other than a desire for masculine, Western dominion.

In fact, once Gray returns to America, something of a pathetic liberal response to all he's experienced ignites Gray into thoughts of action. Having returned from this apparently life-altering experience on the set of *The Killing Fields*, Gray declares: "I would be a changed man. I'd adopt a Cambodian family, I'd have my teeth taken care of, pay my taxes, clean my loft . . . wash the windows, get out all the old sweaters I never wear and take them to the Cambodian refugees in Far Rockaway. . . . At last I would do something for them. At last I'd be of service."

But placing his service to Cambodian refugees into a run-on list that includes personal domestic chores hardly sounds like the determined commitment of a changed man. And this incapacity to commit knocks up against a growing sense of guilt and contributes to Gray's next crisis, a psychological meltdown while vacationing with friends in the Hamptons: "I fled from the table with my hand across my forehead like I had a bad case of Dostoyevskian brain fever, like Konstantin Gavrilovich in *The Seagull*." Crying out, "I'm supposed to be in Thailand! Nothing is ever going to go right in my life again," Gray's consciousness seems to rebel against his self-indulgent, endlessly vacationing behavior. The panic, however, subsides, and Gray eventually turns not to helping others but to finding an agent in Hollywood for his own material advancement.

Ever separated from either the means or even the real will to help the Cambodians or Thais—his conflation of the two nationalities is itself telling—Gray in the above passage hints that he might never be able to help them, at least not in his current condition. The use of a simile "like a bad case of Dostoyevskian brain fever" reminds us how language works to make sense of the world. Gray's familiar center is in the Western world. Despite all his interest in Eastern cultures and religions, his life most comfortably connects with Western art and literature, a reminder that his sense of reality invariably derives from something other than reality itself. For example, when Gray first sees the Indian Ocean, he says, "It was like an oriental Hudson River School painting." When he sees "water buffalo posing like statues in the midst," he says, "they looked like the Thai entry in the Robert Wilson Olympic Arts event." Gray, in short, is trapped, filled with embedded Western images and thoughts, unable ultimately to grasp or comprehend the Eastern world he is experiencing without making it *like* something from his familiar Western world. When he meets two tourists on an isolated Thai beach, they ask him to "tell us of your travels of the world," to which he replies, "It was all like a big Hemingway novel," reinforcing the notion that he will always be a stranger in these foreign lands.

Gray even appears to have missed the irony of his evolved appreciation of journalists as real people. First, traveling on the nonactors' bus (hitching a free ride on the bus after his work had been completed), he longs to be on the "better bus . . . gliding over a smooth macadam highway, filled with every kind of artist." But then at a later brunch, he notices, "I was with these real foreign correspondents. Up until then I'd been hanging out with actors—they're no one. They're conduits." These journalists, however, "can just get on a plane and go with no sense of loss. One minute they're in Beirut, the next they're in a nuclear submarine off the coast of southern France, now they're here, eating and talking about their experiences. They see the whole world as their stage." What Gray is observing and admiring, however, is not so much that the journalists are free of Western prejudices as that everywhere has become an outpost and even playground of Western civilization. These people have passports to all ports of call because they are of the privileged class. They're ultimately not much different than Gray himself, except that Gray doesn't have the guts to go out there on his own. He's only excluded from this world-swallowing lifestyle as a result of his own "unmanly" indecision. Of the two tourists, the one named Jack becomes something of Gray's idol, "the kind of guy who could climb Mount Everest for the weekend just to ski down it and videotape himself doing it." The lives of these bold and beautiful Westerners seem to be a perpetual string of perfect moments. If only Gray had the manly guts.

Gray's own dream of a string of perpetual perfect moments leads to an "epiphany," but it's one that remains in line with conventional American wisdom. He comes to realize that the pursuit of "Cosmic Consciousness belongs to the independently wealthy in this day and age. . . . Go directly to Hollywood and get an agent. . . . Get a house in the Hamptons where you can have your *own* perfect moments in your *own* backyard." Controlled, mastered sublimity. But Gray is slapped out of his Hamptons reverie when, while on the beach in Thailand, he hears shouts of "Boat People! Boatpeopleboatpeopleboatpeople *Boat People*!" He looks out and then, as if in denial of the real world, asks: "But was it the real thing? I couldn't believe it—just when I was beginning to forget about Vietnam and dream of the Hamptons, these wretched sea gypsies came into view." Reality forces itself into Gray's consciousness at virtually every crucial point where he is about to spin off into fantasy and Westernized escapism. Sadly, the significance of these force-fed returns to reality invariably escapes him.

But then again, if Gray has problems fitting in in the exotic but alien East, he doesn't seem precisely comfortable in his Western world either. Even in America, he seems at times lost. He relates an incident in New York in which he couldn't communicate with his rowdy, disorderly neighbors. Sheepishly backing down from their aggressive verbal taunts, Gray observes: "I don't know the language. I knew the language when I was with my people in Boston in 1962, in white-bread homogeneous Boston, brick-wall Boston." Maybe so, but now he's without a sense of home even in his own America. Lost in a world that his birth would have once empowered him to possess, Gray takes on a certain abject otherness that is surprising for someone with such a background. Gray the performer seems to be growing up, sadder but wiser, and becoming more aware of the all-devouring nature of the world around him.

But the moments when he actually pronounces judgment on the world remain relatively rare, and even those are regularly undermined by his continual return to his narcissistic search for the "perfect moment." Amid the anxiety of his general condition, Gray the performer loves that search, hungers for it. Before leaving Thailand, he does experience his "perfect moment," swimming in the Indian Ocean beyond sight of shore. It begins in true Spalding fashion with Ivan telling him that they'll soon go scuba diving, to which Gray says, "Oh my God, at last. It's like an initiation. I'll become a man." Today, however, they both swim out into "the big stuff," and Gray finds that his courage takes him out even beyond where Ivan is swimming, unafraid of losing his money on the beach or even of being eaten by sharks: "Suddenly, there was no time and there was no fear and there was no body to bite. There were no longer any outlines. It was just one big ocean. My body had blended with the ocean. And there was just this round, smiling-ear-to-ear, pumpkin-head perceiver on top, bobbing up and down."

The description—a summary of the monologue's advertising poster and book cover—converts Gray to a mindless sensory organism who "was all very out of time until it was brought back into time by Ivan's voice calling, 'Spalding! Spalding, come back, man! I haven't tested those waters yet!'." The moment is lost: "I fell back into time and back into my body and I swam in to Ivan." Ivan claims to have almost drowned out there, leading Gray the imitator to think, "Now I'm going to have to go out and 'almost drown'," but then he reconsiders: "No, I won't fall into this male competitive trap." Realizing that Ivan's idea of a perfect moment is "death," Gray chooses not to follow his friend's self-destructive, self-indulgent masculine lead. For one of the few times in his life, Gray resists the competitive urges that have caused so much personal anxiety and self-doubt.

This perfect moment is his and no one else's. Gray's pursuit of that moment is a pursuit of the indescribable, that thing generally called the sublime. For the moment, he experiences the vastness of creation beyond even the greatest of human imaginations to grasp. The quest is perhaps motivated by a self-indulgent desire, but the experience momentarily places him outside of or beyond not only himself but also all the petty concerns of being "of" or "in" the world at large, beyond concerns of masculinity, power, even the fear of death. Put another way, this brief experience captures the kind of ecstatic moment that American counterculture longed for back in the 1960s, a dream of Woodstock utopia without the fatal memory of Altamont or Charles Manson. Gray's perfect moment, fleetingly found in Thailand, might fleetingly be found and experienced still, but within that experience is also the point that total abandon is the only way to attain such perfection. The danger, as Gray himself realizes, is annihilation. And it reminds us rather poignantly that the ecstatic dream of paradise is not of this world. Gray will eventually find more sustainable, though perhaps less spectacular, perfect moments later in his life. At this stage his sublime experiences are rare. And their increasing rarity in human existence, it seems, has been caused by humanity itself.

Recall that upon meeting Roland Joffe, Gray is given a lesson on Southeast Asian culture. It was a culture of generosity, says Joffe, "that knew how to have a good time," but "because it was such a beautiful, gentle land, they'd lost touch with evil." In a virtually complete state of innocence, they were vulnerable to the horrors of modernity without any ability to do other than suffer under waves of bewildering oppression. When in 1966 the United States decided to destroy North Vietnamese sanctuaries in Cambodia, the action created a political vacuum in Cambodia that was filled by a band of fanatics driven by "a back-to-the-land, racist consciousness beyond anything Hitler had ever dreamed of." The Khmer Rouge, filled with "strict Maoist doctrine [and] a perverse little bit of Rousseau," brought with them the seeds of an ideology bent on creating its own paradise, but the result was a living hell.

Several points are crucial here, but foremost among them is that Gray once again relays these telling observations at second hand. They are summaries of the conversations with Joffe: "Leave it to a Brit to tell you your own history." Gray becomes a curious, absorbed conveyor of the history lesson, marveling at the story but able to remain in a continued state of noncommitment. None of what Gray reports requires him to offer an opinion of the tales' accuracy or to either endorse or reject the rather leftist position from which the tales are told. In fact, through two diversionary tales, Gray reports both a growing suspicion that the liberal agenda was wrong (or incomplete) as well as a confession that he is just not someone willing to take a stand. The first involves his meeting a basically deranged American serviceman on a train back in the U.S. Northeast corridor, after which he wonders, "Maybe I'm the one who's brainwashed. Maybe I've been hanging out with liberals too long. I mean, after all this time I thought I was a conscientious pacifist but maybe I've been deluding myself. Maybe I'm just a passive-aggressive unconscious coward, and like any good liberal, I should question everything." This Hamlet-like self-doubt is coupled with the general question, "When did I last make a stand, any kind of a stand, about anything?" A second story involving that cowardly run-in with his obnoxious neighbors leads Gray to wonder, "How do we begin to approach the so-called Cold War (or Now-Heating-Up War) between Russia and America if I can't even resolve the Hot War down on North Moore and Greenwich in Lower Manhattan?" Doubting his ability ever to really believe in anything and therefore unable to take a stand on any position, Gray is left incapable of activism of any kind, ironically exhibiting some of the very qualities Joffe assigned to the naïvely innocent Thais and Cambodians. Gray finds himself in an oppressor's position but with an oppressing incapacity to do anything about it.

This condition of resignation fairly accurately identifies the general situation that even privileged participants in our Western world are increasingly experiencing. We may be conscious of a cultural pathology of oppression but are immobilized by an overpowering sense of impotence. Gray's own impotence is enhanced by his growing awareness of oppression everywhere he looks. But that overwhelming impotence seems perhaps on the verge of changing as *Swimming to Cambodia* progresses. The title itself touches on the nearly sublime monumentality of coming to terms with truth and responsibility. Gray reports in the introduction: "I titled this work *Swimming to Cambodia* when I realized that to try to imagine what went on in that country during the gruesome period from 1966 to the present would be a task equal to swimming there from New York."

Important as Gray's traveloguelike experiences in Thailand are to his agenda, filming *The Killing Fields* adds yet another layer to this performance piece. The film dramatizes and critiques U.S. complicity in the atrocities set off by America's "secret" bombing of Cambodia in the early 1970s. But even as the film was being created in the 1980s, its production rather unwittingly duplicated the attitudes that led to those abuses. What occurs in the 1980s is far less catastrophic, but the fact that we have failed to change our prejudiced attitudes toward less fortunate fellow human beings does little more than lay the groundwork for future catastrophes. *Swimming to Cambodia* uses the filming of *The Killing Fields* to go beyond demonstrating what *The Killing Fields* itself attempts to present. While *The Killing Fields* documents the devastating results of America's misuse of its military and political power, *Swimming to Cambodia* gets to the roots of the problem by showing that the "innocent" and even well-intended acts of Western camera crews, directors, and actors are little better.

This oppressive manipulation of the other is panoramically illustrated by an innocent observation from Gray. Recalling an ascent in a helicopter, he states, "I saw, my God, how much area the film covered!" The massive project overruns vast territory, often without regard for the damage it will leave behind. But the film controls more than that physical territory. It has panoramic economic control and, from that, psychological and ethical control as well. To make this point, Gray the artist begins from the purely narcissistic and subjective perspective and moves to a level that first reveals the film's well-intended efforts to portray the monumental destruction of war generated by the West. And then he shows how the film industry's design turns in upon itself and becomes an oppressive invasion of that same curiously alien, non-Western culture. The initial, apparently noble effort to document the cruelties of oppression has turned into oppression by using the very tools of disregard, control, and domination it has chosen to critique.

Though Gray's narcissistic performance shell doesn't provide direct commentary, Gray the artist clearly has abandoned narcissism in this monologue. The piece makes the point that oppression, intentional or not, is endemic to Western culture. *Swimming to Cambodia* offers a multilayered critique, challenging the oppression of *The Killing Fields* even as *The Killing Fields* documents the oppression of Pol Pot. Vera Dike put it nicely in her review of *Swimming to Cambodia*: "What in *The Killing Fields* had seemed a complete, integrated rendition of reality is now disrupted. Gray's words serve to break the seamless flow of images, cracking them open like eggshells." The authority of *The Killing Fields* itself is undermined, very much the same way the Wooster Group critiqued the buried roots of oppression in works by artists like Eugene O'Neill.

Gray's critique then returns to America and eventually to Hollywood. His experiences back in America parallel in many ways what he witnessed in Thailand, though it's not as if he hadn't been forewarned. After all, even as he fantasizes about a film career in Hollywood, he returns to the opulent squalor of several of his Bridgehampton friends, which he "recognized . . . from all the Michelob ads I'd seen on TV." The community is familiar to him even before he gets there, thanks to the superficial fantasies generated by film and television. Looking at one of the houses in this pristine community, he sees rot beneath the surface: "It was one of those turn-of-the-century houses that used to have a family in it back in the days of families, and now it was filled with beautiful couples all on the verge of breaking up, and lonely singles who had just broken up and didn't feel ready to re-commit just yet."

Seeing the ugliness under the surfaces, however, doesn't keep Gray from going to Los Angeles to pursue his dream of achieving the same level of material wealth. He hoped to succeed by feeding off his new-found celebrity, literally capitalizing on this hollow phenomenon of fame so valorized by contemporary culture.

Thankfully, Gray seems to be headed into the Hollywood waste-land with eyes wide open, even to the point that he recognizes it as a sort of vast, tantalizing but ultimately hollow Holy Land: "Now, who are the holy people in the West? Actors and actresses. . . . And in our utilitarian, materialistic world, where is Mecca for these holy people of the West? It's Hollywood. And where does their immortality have its being? On film. The image set forever in celluloid. And who is God? The camera. The ever-present, omniscient third eye. And what is the Holy Eucharist? Money!"

Behind or beneath the surface, nothing exists. Much as he came to discover in *The Tooth of Crime* during his Performance Group days, Gray clearly sees that the images that captivate our culture have no real substance. They take meaning, drain it of true value, and repackage it for market consumption. "Image is everything," as the Madison Avenue slogan goes. In the case of *The Killing Fields*, for example, Hollywood can vent its liberal outrage at past American transgressions while further humiliating the very people it pretends to defend—the Southeast Asians—by paying them lower wages, treating the men like coolies, and turning the women into prostitutes.

But even though Gray is aware of this industrial-strength deception and its deadening effects on the American imagination, he goes to Los Angeles anyway, hoping to beat the devil at his own game. He negotiates the superhighways that have paved over former fields of agricultural value, feeling that he is on the way to fulfilling his dream of a life where after a hard day at the studio, he would "rest and be with and sleep with, my little Renée. My little sweetie. And soon the beautiful children would come along and there'd be fun with them on weekends out in the high desert, or downwind, surfing off Venice. And we'd make it." He feels on the verge of living the American Dream, heaven on earth. He's forgotten all the suffering of others that is necessary in order for the few beneficiaries to live lives of carefree abandon, wealthy beyond imagination. He even forgets that the beneficiaries end in broken Bridgehampton homes, more often than not. The allure, however, remains overpowering for Gray and does for most of us as well, even when fully aware of its many snares and traps.

Here is where Gray almost surrealistically turns the table. Early in the monologue several events set us up for the ending. While on the beaches of Thailand with Renée (who comes for a brief visit) and Ivan ("Devil in my Ear"), Gray gets high, and the experience instantly turns into the terror of uncontrollable vomiting: "And so it went; vomit-cover-mask, vomit-cover-mask, until I looked down to see that I had built an entire corpse in the sand and it was my corpse. It was my own decomposing corpse staring back at me, and I could see the teeth pushing through the rotting lips and the ribs coming through the decomposing flesh of my side."

The memory residue of this image continues like the lingering memory of the Bomb in *Sex and Death to the Age 14*. Shortly into Part Two, Gray introduces us to Hang Ngor, a Cambodian survivor of Khmer Rouge atrocities who has been hired to work in the film. Spalding eventually asks him about his past:

> "They put! Plastic! Plastic bag. Over my head!"
> "And then?"
> "And then. They take me. They tie me to a cross. And burn my legs. And burn me right here."
> ". . . . What were you thinking about?"
> "I know. If I tell the truth. I'm one hundred percent dead. Now I'm only ninety-eight percent dead. The truth. Hundred percent dead."

Traces of these horrific remembrances surface in Gray's monologue-closing story of a dream in which he's babysitting a boy: "There was this huge fireplace, and the boy kept playing a game where he would run into the fireplace and get partially consumed by the flames and then run out—just before he was completely consumed—and re-constitute himself." Finally the boy is "completely in flames," and Gray "grabbed the fire-poker to try to pull him out and . . . nothing. It just went right through the flames; there was no substance. And the flames burned down and left this pile of gray ash on the hearth." Then Gray turns to see "a straw boy, an effigy of the real boy," and blows the ash into the effigy's side, bringing it to life. And the effigy's "face had this great, ear-to-ear, joyous, all-knowing, friendly smile as he shook his head. And I realized that he hadn't wanted to come back, that he had chosen to be consumed by flames."

Gray doesn't explain the dream, once again leaving it to activate his audience into making connections. Reflecting the joyous faces of the Thais and Cambodians, the friendly, smiling but hollow boy is much like those hotel servants and prostitutes, devoured over and over by their recurring Western victimization. It's a chilling connection. And then, too, we can see Gray as the straw boy, himself lacking substance throughout the performance and perpetually seeming to be filled with some of the *gray* ashes of substance in which the straw boy seems to have lost faith.

The story continues. Gray recalls that in the dream he tries to report the horrible babysitting event, but no one believes him. One friend tells him he should have found "a witness with authority." When he locates the straw boy's mother, who is with Gray's former lover and Wooster Group colleague, Elizabeth LeCompte, he can't tell the story but instead says, "THE REASON I'M UPSET IS THAT I WAS JUST IN A NEW SAM PECKINPAH MOVIE OF CHEKHOV'S *SEAGULL*." And Gray says he's upset because "I CAN'T REMEMBER DOING IT." The overall suggestion here is that without a memory that can organize our experiences into meaningful sequences, life itself has no meaning. Simply living day to day is not enough. Add to that the point that without a witness to confirm one's life, its meaning is reduced to isolated events of no ultimate significance. Life means nothing if it doesn't involve and affect others. Truth that has no witness, as Hang Ngor attests, will simply consume and self-destruct. And a world that refuses to bear full witness to the atrocities that occur on a daily basis becomes a hollow, lifeless place.

Gray ends the monologue, "And I knew all the time I was telling this story that it was a cover for the real story, the Straw Boy Story, which, for some reason, I found impossible to tell." But Gray the artist *has* told the Straw Boy Story through the many diversionary tales that Gray the performer had generated in the making of *Swimming to Cambodia*. He has told the truth but told it slant (to paraphrase Emily Dickinson) and thereby allows his audience to include our own stories in his.

At the end of the shorter version recorded as the movie (the published text is longer), Gray allows the same point to be made slightly differently and a bit more directly. Drawing on an observation recorded toward the end of Part One of the published version, he announces at the end of the monologue, without comment: "And just as I was dozing off in the Pleasure Prison, I had a flash. An inkling. I suddenly thought I knew what it was that killed Marilyn Monroe." Gray's insider's view as privileged Western male has revealed, it *appears*, exactly how destructively oppressive the indulgences of privileged power can be, even within the ranks of the privileged. The Straw Boy, Hang Ngor, Marilyn Monroe, and Gray himself have all been divested of their three-dimensionality and converted to empty versions of their former real selves. The world of performance has prevailed over the world of real living. To succeed in this world requires certain performances on our part, but that process destroys what makes us who we are.

What was once a glistening but empty *representation* of the real has actually erased the real and become a reasonable and finally acceptable facsimile. It's a trap that Gray can't find a way out of. And presumably neither can we, which means fleeting "perfect moments" are the only thing that seems worth pursuing. It's the American condition, tantalizing but deadly, that Gray has identified.

6

An American Success Story

Coping After Cambodia

With the major success of *Swimming to Cambodia*, Gray became a recognized face in the American cultural mainstream. Now more than ever, he needed to find ways to avoid being swallowed up by his growing celebrity status. Clearly sensing the dangers of being consumed by a world hungry to use him for its own profitable ends, Gray entered a phase where he'd try to maintain his personal integrity and not succumb to the allure of filthy lucre. He needed to be wary of becoming like so many people who start out with noble intentions but get overwhelmed by Hollywood's comforts and flatteries.

Rivkala's Ring

A hint of how Gray would deal with his new status comes shortly after the success of *Swimming to Cambodia*. Gray was among seven playwrights commissioned by John Houseman's The Acting Company to use Anton Chekhov short stories "as a cue for the creation of short theatrical pieces to be produced by the Company as a part of its repertory season." Gray used Chekhov's "The Witch," a story about an unhappy couple isolated in a Russian snowstorm when a lost postman and his assistant arrive for shelter. The husband suspects witchcraft on his wife's part. During every major storm in the past three years of their marriage, men rather mysteriously arrive, breaking the tedium of their lives and, he thinks, satisfying the carnal desires of his wife.

True to the idea that the stories should serve as "cues," Gray almost entirely abandons the original story, choosing instead to focus on the qualities of the husband to generate a monologue. Seeing something of himself in the husband, Gray reports: "I see the character as a kind of manic-y paranoid person who's spinning off these kind of paranoid delusions, trying to make order out of a very frightening and chaotic existence. So I see it fashioned after my character, the character of Spalding Gray that I do in the monologues." The result, *Rivkala's Ring*, is a monologue to be performed by an actor who will try to capture the spirit of Gray's performance persona onstage. Gray even suggests in his preface that the performer go to Lincoln Center for the Performing Arts to see a filmed version of *47 Beds*. The only real connection with Chekhov is an oblique reference to Russia as the ancestral land of Gray's girlfriend Renée, who possesses a ring from her grandmother, Rivkala.

The Gray character, simply identified as "The Person," opens the monologue by telling the audience what happened on the day the Chekhov short story arrived for him to review. He's in Hollywood and remembers seeing two things: his first missing child announcement on a milk container and a drowned rat in his apartment complex pool. The weather is rough. A Santa Ana wind is ripping through the city, paralleling the storm in the Chekhov story, revealing what "The Person" calls "raw indifferent nature." But the indifference that swirls around both "The Person" and Chekhov's husband is an indifference neither is willing to accept. They need explanations for the apparently disconnected randomness that unfolds in their lives.

"The Person" tries to make sense of his world in a manner paralleling the husband's efforts to make sense of the coincidental visitations. For Chekhov's husband, the answer is that his wife is a manipulating witch. "The Person," however, has a different strategy. The dead rat on the day of the story's arrival reminds "The Person" of another rat he encountered earlier in New York, but first he relates the events of the arrival day. In true Gray fashion, "The Person" connects going to a Japanese restaurant that day with recalling V-J Day as a child (recalling the opening of *Sex and Death to the Age 14*), and he still curiously feels "a little guilty about the bomb and all." Then, once home, "The Person" turns on the television to find a documentary on General MacArthur "taking over Japan after World War II." Thinking it "strange," he gets no sympathy from Renée, who sees only coincidence and no meaning in the combination. This late-evening television event is then followed by "The Person" telling us of his insomnia, generated by anxiety, which he tries to assuage by watching the late news. He tells us that "if I can't sleep because of anxiety, I seek a more anxious state outside of myself." The main news story involves the AIDS epidemic, with the disease described as the failure of "our immune system . . . to tell the difference between what was itself and what was not itself. . . . what they call 'organic paranoia'." He then extends this "relationshipal problem" to the fundamental problem existing between the superpowers, Russia and the United States. This leads him to observe that "the more that goes to protecting the outside, the less that goes to protecting the inside."

Other memories line up and interconnect, including the sleep-inducing effects of eating turkey and the recollection that someone once said that democracy left America in 1963. Then "The Person" tells us that he has a tradition of visiting unfamiliar parts of the city when his California friend comes to New York. They must visit areas unfamiliar to both men so they're on equal experiential footing. This leads to a recollection that they both once encountered a hole in the ground (on the corner of Spring Street and West Broadway) filled with cash, twenty dollars of which the California friend picks up. The recollection leads to something of a thematic point for the monologue: "It's become one of those 'spots' that are forever marked in the city. No matter how much I try to be here and now and see the spot for what it is, I can't get that blowing money out of my mind." "The Person" recalls another event when he and Renée came upon a "fresh" suicide; returning to the spot always returns "The Person" to that grisly time and event. From the recollection of the suicide, "The Person" recalls a late-night news story of a near catastrophic airline accident. The pilot saves the day, "The Person" tells us, which prompts him to recall "one of those new-age positive thinkers" who's always saying, "When you meet reality, you do one of three things: you fight it, you flee it, or you flow."

"The Person" then recounts the tale of his encounter with a rat in New York City, as promised at the beginning of the monologue, which ties into the dead rat found the morning of the arrival of the Chekhov story. It was on a Halloween day just after he'd broken a mirror and feared seven years' bad luck. Returning home later that day, he comes face to face with the rat in the apartment building stairwell, cornered by each other in their surprise. They both run "around and around till somehow the rat disappeared." As unlikely as the next connection appears to be, "The Person" next reports admiring Christ because he had "some sort of charcoal filter system in his psyche which enabled him to filter out evil karma or responses to it." Unable to be "Christlike," he has to tell Renée of the rat, which frightens her into a needless panic when she next has to climb the stairs. She manages to overcome her fears quite handily, but "The Person" can't overcome a sense that it all "was a kind of black omen." To settle him down, Renée pulls out her grandmother's (Rivkala's) ring and tells "The Person" to kiss the ring. The result is that "a burden was lifted from my mind. . . . I knew that the seven years' bad luck had been lifted, or counteracted by Rivkala's ring."

As "The Person" returns us to Hollywood, just before going to bed on the evening of the day the story arrives, he feels something of old Russian peasant simplicity unite him and Renée: "And for one brief instant, we were one as the nuclear wind tore at the palms and split the moon through the Venetian blinds." The "moral" to the story appears to be that the simple magic of love can overcome all fear.

But there's more to the monologue than this rather trite happy end. The construction of the monologue itself is something of a magic act, with Gray's imagination at work connecting random thoughts and empty coincidences and generating a sense of order out of apparent disorder. Life is meaningless without imagination and memory working together to make sense out of apparent senselessness.

This conclusion curiously works beyond what Chekhov's "The Witch" presents. In the Chekhov story, as the husband finally settles down to bed with his wife, he feels a sort of bewitching attraction and is irresistibly drawn to her, but as he strokes her neck, she elbows him in the nose, and though "the pain in his nose was soon over . . . the torture in his heart remained." The story ends with love and imagination operating on separate planes, while Gray's monologue combines imagination and love to generate a sort of witchcraft that outdistances anything Chekhov's husband experiences. Connecting the two forces connects "The Person" and Renée, making them both complete and content even as the world swirls indifferently around them. Though perhaps a little too romantically conveyed, this diversion from headier preoccupations seems to capture Gray at his most uncomplicated best. He seems to be telling us that the whirlwind that was Hollywood won't have a damaging effect on him; his household with Renée is all he needs.

The Loneliness of Coping with Monsters

Gray's *Swimming to Cambodia* celebrity also resulted in a book contract. It was to be a novel based on his life. The problem was that Gray had signed on to a project that really wasn't within his comfort zone, given that novels require long hours of isolation in front of a blank piece of paper, and Spalding was, more than most, a very social person uncomfortable with isolation. Without the give-and-take he enjoyed with his audiences, writing a novel was going to be a new and not entirely satisfying experience. He knew it was going to be different, though he might not have been aware of the full extent of the difference until it was too late. In later years, he was able to summarize the differences between creating for performance and creating for publication pretty succinctly: "An audience is more of a resonator than sitting in a room dealing with just a wall and yourself."

The book that he eventually wrote became a massive "monster in a box" of several thousand pages that then needed to be edited down to a manageable (and successful) novel based pretty much on Gray's life. The phrase became the title of the monologue that

Monster in a Box. (Photo copyright Paula Court, courtesy of Paula Court.)

followed *Swimming to Cambodia*. *Monster in a Box* (1991) centers around Gray's newfound writer's life of solitude and the results of coping with that unnerving isolation. Happily back in front of an audience, Gray feeds on the disorientation of his novelist experiment and may even have helped him to complete the task, giving him a sort of public sanctuary from the self-imposed imprisonment that is the writer's lot.

Gray opens *Monster in a Box* by explaining that the monster in the box was the result of a project his agent had convinced him to write and that he in his vanity had agreed to do. The eventual result was Gray's novel *Impossible Vacation* (published in 1992). In his monologue he quickly acknowledges that he "didn't know how I was going to write a novel because I don't know how to make anything up, so I thought I'd write a book instead." The point is repeated throughout the monologue, highlighting the idea that Gray's memory rather than his imagination is the starting point for all of his narratives. So he finally tries to settle down and write a thinly veiled autobiographical "book" he could pass off as a novel.

Despite his problems writing the novel, part of the reason he agreed to do it stems from the fact that his original goal in life—as early as 1959—was to go to New York and "become a writer, inspired then by Thomas Wolfe": "I moved to New York City, but I didn't become a writer. I got involved in theater instead, and theater led to monologues, and the monologues led to publications, and the publications led to my getting a literary agent, and one day my literary agent said to me, '*I think you have a novel in you*.'" Demonstrating a flair for falling victim to distractions of all sorts and deferring to others when it comes to making decisions, Gray confesses that the monologue ultimately "is all about the interruptions that happened to me while I was trying to write the book." Hot on the heels of his popular success with the film of *Swimming to Cambodia*, Gray is exposed to all sorts of interruptions, distractions, and temptations, many of which he indulges in without any real sense of control. He just does what suits him at the moment, without a plan and without any sense of needing to save his energy to write his novel.

What Gray never does throughout the monologue is defend his numerous indulgent distractions. On a positive note, however, it's entirely possible for his audience to see something admirable in Gray's choice *not* to organize his life but to let things fall where they might. Allowing life to come to him rather than the more controlling other way around, Gray experiences things that wouldn't have happened if he had done the logical, sensible thing of getting down to the business of writing. Though never actually stated, living life as it comes seems to be one of the main themes of the monologue and is in fact a theme of Gray's entire career and life. What we see in *Monster in a Box* is a performer virtually given the keys to the empire but really refusing to be converted into some sort of power-hungry egotist. Throughout his post-*Cambodia* odyssey, he is invited to sign a $3 million entertainment deal, take on various film projects, and attend numerous filmings and film festivals. Among the many offers placed in front of him, he accepts small roles in *Clara's Heart* with Whoopi Goldberg and *Beaches* with Bette Midler. And the largest talent agency in Los Angeles (CAA) offers to represent him.

But throughout this bombardment of tantalizing invitations to become part of the power elite, and despite evidence that his famous indecision would make him vulnerable to the many siren calls he hears, Gray remains surprisingly aloof even as he revels in all the possibilities. We begin to sense a sort of chaotic, disorderly control on Gray's part that actually keeps him from being completely sucked into the life-draining opportunities offered by the Hollywood dream factory. The result of this curious balancing act is that Gray absorbs some of the privileges of celebrity while still being able *not* to pay with his soul. And the balancing act places him in the unique position of observer from both sides of the velvet rope that separates the haves from the have-nots. It's a balancing act that can—and does—lead to all sorts of doubts and uncertainties on Gray's part, since he's really not a member of any one group or class of people. In some ways a full-blown celebrity

but also able to walk the streets like a common man, he has the ultimate freedom to do what strikes him at the moment, yet he always
wonders if he's made the right choices. Freedom sounds so attractive,
but for Gray, at least, it has its downside. Relying on his own intuitions
and always suspicious that they're taking him the wrong way, Gray
seems always just on the verge of a nervous breakdown.

Curiously, in fact, in the published monologue's preface, Gray
notes that a representative from the National Foundation for Mental
Health, after seeing *Monster in a Box*, asked that he become their
"national spokesperson," observing, "We feel that we've never heard
anyone so articulate about their mental illness." Torn by his uncertainties and self-doubt, Gray finds a kindred spirit in the character Celia Copplestone from T. S. Eliot's *The Cocktail Party*, drawing
on his experiences with this play when he was creating the Wooster
Group's *Nayatt School*. A particular favorite of his, Celia even surfaces
in *Swimming to Cambodia*. In *Monster in a Box* she seems particularly
appropriate, since Gray is concentrating on his own mental state in a
way only touched on in that earlier monologue. Generally speaking,
Gray's interest in Celia fittingly recurs throughout his career, since
what she shares on the stage resonates with Gray's work and life. His
favorite lines, recited in *Monster in a Box*, are:

> I should really like to think there's something wrong with me—
> Because, if there isn't, then there's something wrong,
> Or at least, very different from what it seemed to be,
> With the world itself—and that's much more frightening!
> That would be terrible! So I'd rather believe
> There is something wrong with me, that could be put right.

The implication is that Gray's behavior appears to be in the wrong
only because he's being judged by the wrong standards. And if our
culture's standards are what's warped, if our culture is wrong, then
that would be much more terrible than merely having poor Spalding
slightly off the beam. It's enough to drive a sensitive soul to madness,

much as it drove Celia to a suicidal end. Gray himself sometimes seems to be walking a fine line. And maybe more of us than currently care to admit it are walking with Gray.

Gray actually tries to deal with this unique brand of madness in his own disarming way, by summarizing his rather comical symptoms, including sweaty feet, dry mouth, and even uncontrollable barking. He goes to a Freudian psychoanalyst that he likes very much, but he's uncertain about the hoped-for results: "I know the cure is supposed to be the transformation of hysterical misery into common unhappiness. And God knows I have a lot of hysterical misery, but I'm not sure I want to let go of it." To be normalized means accepting "common unhappiness," what seems to be a general cultural condition. Surely that's a "wrong" goal to strive for. And Gray isn't willing to live life by half even if "hysterical misery" is the only alternative. Then again, as we see in Gray's monologue, these aren't necessarily the only options.

First, we should recall Gray's preference for performance over the isolating occupation of being a writer. Accepting the job of writing the book, Gray muses, "I thought the monologues were making me too extroverted. I wanted to pull back into my more introverted self and go back in and explore the private self, the shadow self, the part I hadn't been in touch with for twenty years." He adds, "I just wanted to go away to a writer's colony and just write—no living, just writing." But his almost abnormally extroverted lust for living overwhelms him. It is *the* central reason for his inability to master the monster in the box and leads him to "suffer" all the living interruptions that come his way. Lonely and alone, he abandons a comfortable, peaceful writing colony to accept a project in Los Angeles. Gray comes to realize, however, that Los Angeles has its own brand of isolation. Its automobile and interstate highway culture leaves him disconnected and alone, much in the same way he reports in *Rivkala's Ring*. He needs to be connected to other human beings.

At first, he tries to overcome this sense of isolation by accepting a string of invitations to Hollywood business lunches on the heels of his success with *Swimming to Cambodia*. To get back into his comfort zone, he considers doing an HBO special collecting interviews with people abducted by UFOs. He eventually turns to three projects that will connect him far more realistically to the world around him. They involve the lives of have-nots found in Los Angeles, Nicaragua, and the Soviet Union and together turn a significant chunk of *Monster in a Box* into a collage of observations, a portrait of disenfranchisement hidden in the shadows of American plenty.

Gray officially goes to Los Angeles to do the first project, cosponsored by the Mark Taper Forum and the NEA called "L.A.: The Other." He's been commissioned to find "interesting people to be interviewed on stage about living in Los Angeles. The only criteria being that these people could in no way be involved in the film industry." In this fast-paced, quick-hustle freeway world, Gray tells us that his hired assistant, a native of L.A., has what Gray calls "a thirty-five-mile-an-hour consciousness": anything or anyone going more slowly is invisible. Though Gray sees this as a uniquely Los Angeles trait, it could also be a pretty fair summary of most places in the United States. The invisible people who fall under the scan of his assistant's consciousness are the ones he will need to seek out and interview. And once he starts looking, there are plenty of them.

The humor of this segment involves Gray's summary of these people and their lives. They include a 325-pound man who claimed to be a bodily vessel for an extraterrestrial, three valley girls whose religion is automobiles, a Skid Row denizen since 1904, and Charles Manson's lawyer. Unique and quirky in their own ways, Gray later writes in a postscript to *Monster in a Box* (entitled "Other *Others*"): "Not everyone I interviewed on the Mark Taper forum stage in Los Angeles was as weird as I make them out to be in the monologue. To some extent I understand now how I was taking an easy shot at their idiosyncrasies. But, on the other hand, their odd stories make for good drama." Under the spell of privilege as Gray the performer, Gray the artist does concede that his monologue slips into moments of insensitivity and even admits that he drew his audiences into a heartless sort of collusion by having them laugh at what Gray reports. If by some chance, however, Gray's audience recognized their insensitivity and felt uncomfortable in their seats, then he would have succeeded at beginning a process that might lead them to the sorts of awakenings that were fast becoming Gray's hallmark. He wants us to laugh, but he seems also to hope that the laughter becomes a bit uncomfortable as we recognize that we're laughing at other people's misfortunes. That, to my mind, is why Gray adds the written postscript, "Other Others"—as an extra hint just in case we don't "get it."

Along those same lines, in the monologue, Gray is next intrigued by a project that requires a fact-finding mission to Nicaragua, and it becomes yet another interruption to the isolation of writing. It also nicely complements the insensitivity that he locates in Los Angeles with the Mark Taper project. In Nicaragua, he hears stories from "the mothers of the heroes and the martyrs" of the recent revolution so brutally put down by U.S.-supported counterrevolutionaries. These mothers are touching and simple, though once again Gray rather callously judges them as "something like a combination of an A.A. meeting and a very perverse performance art piece, because they have been testifying, innumerable times, about the horrors that have been inflicted on their loved ones." But he's also "feeling guilty for being down there for Columbia Pictures." The contradictory responses are perhaps natural, given that the experience is beyond Gray the performer's comfort zone but not beyond Gray the artist's curiosity to expand that zone of understanding. Humor in performance cloaks a rising empathy on Gray's part, evidenced by his unwillingness simply to dismiss what he witnesses, either in L.A. or in Nicaragua. Exposure to suffering seems to be generating an unexpected degree of fellow-feeling.

In fact, as Christmas approaches, Gray actually makes a momentary turn to empathy, though at this early stage in his awakening, he's too ill-equipped to fully convert to feeling for those around him: "I wanted to help people needier than I. I thought that's what the problem was—why I was so hypochondriacal—I was surrounding myself with myself too much, I was being too narcissistic. Put it aside, help others, help needier people." The epiphany dims quickly, however, when people keep telling him that he's not stable enough to help others but rather needs to help himself. As a result, he abandons his goal of reaching out to other people and seeks psychoanalytic help, which he is fast coming to realize guarantees little in the way of personal redemption. But Gray's instincts are positioning him for a slow turn to a more balanced and more inclusive awareness of a need to reach out to others in order to find himself.

The third project is attending a film festival in Russia that wants to show *Swimming to Cambodia* along with *Hoosiers*, *Rumblefish*, *Cool Hand Luke*, *Children of a Lesser God*, *The Empire Strikes Back*, *An Officer and a Gentleman*, *The Wizard of Oz*, and *Splash!*, all presumably representations of what it is to be "American." Gray goes with a pretty distinguished group that includes Carrie Fisher, Darryl Hannah, Marlee Matlin, Matt Dillon, and Richard Gere.

Amid self-indulgent searches for hard-to-find vodka and the satisfaction he gets from being recognized by a touring group of American adolescents, Gray stumbles into two unscheduled encounters with Russian audiences. Asked to talk impromptu about *The Killing Fields*, he fields a question about how the film is relevant to Russians by responding: "Well . . . I would say that the parallels between you guys and Cambodia is, uh—Afghanistan, of course? What do you think about Afghanistan? Why aren't you in the streets protesting?" His suggestion sparks general enthusiasm within the theater as the audience erupts with claims that they had not been informed of events in Afghanistan, that Americans know more about the situation there, "and it turned into a very open, passionate, fiery question-and-answer session." Gray inadvertently becomes a politicized lightning rod, bringing him into the center of a discussion of repression and oppression. And though the encounter seems on the surface to be a random event in Gray's life, it is connected to his encounters with oppression on the streets of L.A. and in the villages in Nicaragua. Here too the long arm of American influence has found its way into controversy, given that the United States had been supporting Afghani "freedom fighters" against these very same Russians. Without irony but in the most unusual of places, Gray becomes revitalized by this massive personal diversion. Psychotherapy couldn't fix his anxieties about life and living, but getting out with other people at least begins to heal the man. And learning about America from halfway around the world is not a bad bonus.

At another point during his trip to Russia, a screening of *Swimming to Cambodia* is set up without its Russian translation (Gray suspects the taped translation was confiscated in retaliation for his earlier political incitement), and audience members understandably begin leaving in disgust. Gray lures the audience back in by shutting down the film and (through a translator) offering to answer questions instead. One of the questions he receives is, "Why are you so armored?" Correctly presuming that the questioner means "reserved," Gray decides to open up as he has done so many times back in America, by telling "the Russian audience a true story about how just that morning I got thrown out of the Hermitage Museum." His visit to the unusually warm museum caused Gray to sweat since he was wearing long silk underwear to keep from freezing outdoors. While talking to a group of American tourists who identified him because of his recent appearance back home on the David Letterman show, he rolls up his pants legs so he won't overheat, exposing his long underwear. Two matronly Soviet guards grab him and throw him out of the museum because, he later finds out, they think he is "imitating royalty." Gray concludes, "I told this to the Russian audience and they said, 'This could be true'." Experiencing even this very minor infringement on his rights as a human being places Gray in an empathetic relationship with his Russian audience.

This comically confusing encounter with Russian authority gives Gray a sense of the Russian daily experience and leaves him grateful for his privileged existence in America: "We get back to New York City. We get back to that island off the coast of America, Manhattan.

And I am so happy to be back. I am cured from all that Russian common unhappiness. I am so happy to be back in the land of freedom of speech, freedom of the press, that I bow down and kiss the Monster." Gray seems at least temporarily cured of his anxieties through his experiences in Russia and elsewhere. He seems at peace, to the point that he actually has the energy to complete the novel.

But first Gray receives one more interruption, the chance to play the Stage Manager in New York's Lincoln Center production of Thornton Wilder's *Our Town*. The director, Greg Mosher, wants Gray to be "the stage manager of the eighties . . . a farewell to all the sentimental *Our Towns* . . . a farewell to the Hallmark card of *Our Town*." Gray accepts, writing in the mornings and rehearsing in the afternoons. He'd hoped the opening-night reviews would say something like, "He has that special something that translates Grover's Corners into contemporary America," but instead they pan him and most of the production. Devastated, he returns to the theater for the second night's performance to see the entire cast upbeat rather than crushed, because these stage professionals have chosen simply not to read reviews until after the run. One actor actually chides Spalding, saying, "actors never read their reviews. Maybe you read yours because you're a writer." Gray accepts the point, decides he's an actor more than a writer, and basks in positive audience response (they must not have read the reviews either) and his own pleasure in the production rather than feeling tormented by "official" opinions.

Ultimately, the experience of the living theater brings Spalding fully back to life, giving him balance, minimizing his phobias, and allowing him the perspective to get his novel done without going crazy. He's even begun to accept his mother's death. The memory of her suicide had until recently blocked his progress as a novelist because in many ways it blocked his progress as a person. Living overcomes the roadblock even if it doesn't explain why things happen as they do. This getting on with life defeats the apparent meaningless of death, even death by suicide. If Gray's earlier experiences haven't made the point clear, his experience with *Our Town*—particularly the elegiac final scene in the graveyard—seems to have brought it all into perspective.

Central to this return to health and to living is what Gray called a "unifying accident" during one of the performances, "in which something so strange happens in the play, that it suddenly unites the audience in the realization that we are all here together at this one moment in time. It's not television. It's not the movies. And it probably won't be repeated the following night." As Gray enters into the graveyard speech, the audience is of course "waitin' for something they feel is comin'. Something important and great." And something does happen: one of the boys (playing Wally Webb) projectile vomits, utterly disrupting the play's moment of peaceful reflection upon life, death, and the hereafter. The physical here and now literally asserts itself in this somber reflective moment, reminding us with perfectly spontaneous timing that life has its own processes beyond human control, even at the most simple levels. To add to the point, Gray points out that a young boy in the audience broke the embarrassed silence: "He knows what he saw. . . . He is laughing!" Gray completes the play, but the unifying accident and the young boy's response become the final catalyst for his return from the edges of madness to the full presence of living, a step closer to knowing who he is.

Shortly after the run of *Our Town*, Gray gets to the end of his book, where the character Brewster finally makes it to "paradise," to Bali. Here Brewster thinks he should write a short story about his feelings: "But looking up at the stars, he suddenly feels so peaceful, so present, he thinks maybe he should skip the story and try to take a vacation instead." Gray too has returned to an equilibrium that positions him to move beyond accepting a "common unhappiness" that we're told is the best we can expect from this world. Happiness is other people, and reaching out to others may be the best way to discover or recover what's missing within.

That his experiences in *Monster in a Box* led Gray to a greater, less judgmental appreciation of others is confirmed in his "Other Others" postscript to the monologue's published text. He ends the postscript by talking about an *Interviewing an Audience* interview he had with Raymond Harai, one of the denizens of "what, in some more romantic times in America, might have been called Skid Row." Gray humanizes Harai's experience with notable sensitivity and ends the interview by asking Harai if he'd like to add anything, to which "he answered by saying, 'Yeah, I don't know why you hire a guy like me. I'm no good for nothing, only thing I can tell you is your palm says you are making a great success in early future.' And Raymond gently took my left hand and pointed to a confluence of lines that created a star-shaped asterisk I had never noticed before, right in the center of my left palm."

Allusions to Christ's suffering notwithstanding, perhaps the greatest point of contact between the privileged Gray and down-and-out Raymond is the literal point of contact itself, the touch between the two men. Coming back to a normal or "right" life, as Gray seems to be doing in *Monster in a Box*, he is also coming back to an empathetic acceptance of others, taking a step away from egocentric self-absorption. That turn might ultimately heal Gray, but it might also map a path for a larger *cultural* recovery.

What to Do with the Eye/I? *Gray's Anatomy*

The theater is a particularly fruitful place to deal with human consciousness. It's certainly a central theme of Spalding Gray's work. In a 1999 interview, he observes a subtle but important distinction about what goes on in his monologues. They are "a condensation of a lot of memories. It's really like collage art, because I'm cutting and pasting my memory. Everyone that has a memory is creative, because you're recreating the original event through memory. People don't realize that. They have the fantasy that they're in touch with the original event."

Gray continues: "The human consciousness has a structure. What I'm looking for is the random structure that comes through remembering over and over the same event—you know, repeating the story. It takes what I call 'heightened composition'." Packed into his monologues, full of engaging stories drawn from memory, Gray presents his consciousness for his audience to study and evaluate. It's placed on the table for us to dissect. But while this may have been his major focus in the Wooster Group days, he eventually came to realize that consciousness can't operate in a void. We need to recognize that it functions in a world that bombards it moment to moment, forcing it to adjust, alter, and renew its memory as it copes with present events. In other words, memory changes as it copes each moment with new events that the present feeds it. As a result, consciousness and the memories it generates are plastic, forever changing, not because we're getting closer to or farther from "truth," but because we are forever working to incorporate our past selves into the present world. That is what Gray does in his monologues. He builds—or tries to build—a consciousness that will fit into the world.

Swimming to Cambodia focused more on the world at large and worked to squeeze Gray's consciousness into it. *Gray's Anatomy* (1993) works the other way around. It begins with consciousness and tries to absorb the world into it. Either process, in theory, should work, though as we'll see in his later monologues, letting them ebb and flow together as suits the moment seems to work better than artificially highlighting one over the other. In any case, all of Gray's works engages the issue of comprehending the nature of consciousness by disengaging the ego-centered self from its belief that it can best survive by building up walls against the world outside. What needs to occur, and what began to occur in *Monster in a Box*, is for consciousness to reach out to the world and the people who inhabit it. Consciousness needs to connect to the world and feed it while feeding off of it. This give-and-take is the path that will lead to a healthy consciousness. Every other strategy amounts to little more than a fool's errand, especially those egotistical self-help strategies that our culture tries to feed us on a daily basis.

One of the more devious strategies that our culture tries to feed us is that the mind and the body are separate pieces of the self. And

from there we're often indoctrinated to believe that the mind is su-
perior to the body. This mind-body split is famously known as Cartesian dualism, but it erupted in Western thought way before René
Descartes formalized the matter in the 1600s. It's ingrained in our
Judeo-Christian tradition as a matter of soul, spirit, or consciousness
versus our bodies and the world in which that body survives. Soul is
pure and eternal while bodies decay and are temporary. We should
treasure our souls and, at best, tolerate our bodies and the physical world into which we've been thrust. This cultural indoctrination
leads to a general contempt for the world around us in favor of some
perfection beyond this literally putrifying place of uncertainty, insecurity, change, and inevitable death.

Gray suffers from this perception about the separation between
the world of spirit/soul/consciousness and the physical world as
much as anyone. The dilemma leaves him riddled with phobias resulting from guilt about his interest in the pleasures of the body.
Having been brought up to believe that the soul is the essence of the
self, Gray has to believe that something surely is "wrong" with a man
who so thoroughly enjoys the pleasures of the flesh. In fact, Gray
struggles from an even more radically Cartesian antibody perspective
than the typical Westerner. As he notes in an interview, "Growing up
a Christian Scientist, it took so long for me to realize I had a body."
In *Gray's Anatomy* he seems finally to come to terms with his body—
its pleasures and pains—presenting on the stage his transformation
from a confused, "hung up" sensualist to a man assured of himself
and working his way into an integrated sense of selfhood.

According to this dualist suspicion of the world, touch, smell,
and taste engage us too dangerously with that world. We should
invest all our energies in keeping a distance from this world and
turning as much as possible to the world of pure consciousness. So
goes the traditional argument. But for a skeptic like Gray—even
a tentative and guilt-ridden skeptic—perhaps the most important
and most daunting task is to find a way to merge the two worlds

into one. *Monster in a Box* demonstrates the extent to which the world-abandoning, monastic isolation of novel writing can destroy rather than purify the spirit. It seems that the soul actually needs the body and the world to sustain its health! Gray's *Monster in a Box* experience suggests the extent to which full immersion in the world around us can actually save us from our "better" but misdirected otherworldly intentions. *Gray's Anatomy* goes a step further. It's Gray's effort to understand how to position himself to reintegrate and reconnect with the physical. In *Gray's Anatomy*, he studies how consciousness works best when it's connected to the senses that hook us up to the world around us.

Gray's Anatomy concentrates on Gray's almost manic fear that he is losing his vision as a result of a condition known as a macular pucker. It's no small coincidence that a good portion of the events in this monologue overlap with those in *Monster in a Box*, because he comes to realize that his increasing loss of vision begins while he's trying to complete the novel *Impossible Vacation*. The two monologues interweave and prepare Gray to springboard into his subsequent phase, his actual recovery from this "split personality" in *It's a Slippery Slope* and *Morning, Noon and Night*.

Gray's Anatomy involves Gray's many colorful efforts to preserve the failing vision in his left eye (he calls it his "feminine eye"), that thing medically described as "macula pucker." His ocular specialist describes the problem, rather mystifyingly, as "a distortion of the interior limiting membrane secondary to the posterior hyloid face contraction. But the posterior hyloid, which was attached to the optic nerve macula, and major vessels of the retina, have remained attached and intact." The full description is significant because Gray is setting up a basic contrast between the advances of the Western scientific process and a variety of nontraditional alternative procedures he will attempt. Furthermore, his doctor's cold analysis hints at the way Cartesian dualism affects us in our treatment of the body. Reminiscent of the cold analysis of a suffering human patient/specimen in *Rumstick Road*, this doctor's reduction of the eye to a physical,

Publicity photo for *Gray's Anatomy*. (Photo copyright Nigel Dickson, courtesy of Nigel Dickson.)

jellied mass ignores the feelings of the "I" to which this "eye" belongs. Western medicine decides to fix the functional deficiency of the part without making any attempt to understand the complex whole. The recommended eye operation medically reflects the way Western culture psychologically works to restore the "I": by isolating its parts and working to fix its many individual deficiencies without much regard for the whole being.

Gray tells us that possible causes for his ocular degeneration abound. For example, he recalls a case of trauma to this eye experienced way back in 1976. He even thinks the degeneration might be psychologically explained as the psychosomatic result of his Oedipal complex at work: "Not that I'd ever been aware of sleeping with my mother, but Freud says that the denial of some state of affairs is an implicit acknowledgment of it." The reference seems entirely appropriate given the blinding fate that Oedipus suffered. Yet another possibility is metaphysical, namely that Gray's current work project, writing that novel, has left him spiritually vulnerable to infection, especially given that the book is being written in the first person, which Gray concludes "was too much *I, I, I, I, I, I I I I I I I I i i i i i.*" It may also be the case that writing this autobiographical book has emotionally and physically stressed him to the point of blindness: "It was about my mother's suicide, and I felt I really had never properly grieved for her, or mourned her, and what happened was, my eye—my left eye just cried in a big way. It just exploded into one big tear from reading that painful section of the book over and over again. The entire vitreous humor just wept." Of course, this obsession with himself is itself a sort of myopia reflecting Gray's own metaphorical blindness to the rest of the world. The macula pucker is just one major coincidental *physical* reminder of his *spiritual* blindness to the world around him.

The fact is that, whatever the cause may be, going blind literally threatens Gray's very existence, given that without his eyes he can't see to observe and can't observe to report. Without perception he wouldn't have any material, and without material he wouldn't be able to perform. And if he were no longer perceived by an audience, he would essentially cease to exist. Gray doesn't actually say it, but he's drawing on the perspective of the eighteenth-century philosopher George Berkeley, who argued, "To be is to be perceived." His panic is far more than merely "professional." So while he's right that his career is in jeopardy, he's also touching on the larger point that his career is the thing that actually makes and continually salvages his life, especially his life with other people, without whom he wouldn't even exist. Without the theater, he'd become less real as a human being, not to mention less real as an artist. Without the activity of the *eye*—both his own and others'—the *I* would cease to be.

So on to fixing the problem. Not entirely comfortable with the cold analytic certainty of the first doctor, Gray moves quickly to get a second opinion and locates a Chinese American doctor who announces, to Gray's great satisfaction, that the condition is "idiopathic," meaning "no known cause." Gray loves this basically guiltless diagnosis: it's probably not his fault, or at least the blame can't be traced. He's further comforted when he's told that surgery is not immediately necessary. The doctor tells him he can try alternative therapies, but then adds, "And then we'll have to operate." And there's one more possibility: according to the doctor, there's "a one percent chance of the whole condition just clearing up on its own."

Gray's meeting with this doctor marks the beginning of a long, humorous string of attempts to avoid having to go under the knife, though he seems to be the only person who thinks there's any hope of escaping the torments of Western medicine. When Gray reports to his therapist that he'll be searching for alternative remedies, the therapist rather unpleasantly insists: "All things are contingent, and there is also chaos. . . . In other words . . . shit happens. Give up on this magical thinking and this airy-fairy Disneyland kind of let's pretend and your Hollywood la-la fantasy, please. Do the right thing. Get the operation. Hmmn?" But Gray goes off on his own, wondering why he should let someone "cut into the window of my soul." In his airy-fairy way, Gray is absolutely right to at least try to resist.

Gray goes through an odyssey of six different kinds of alternative therapies, the first fairly close to home as he recruits a Christian Science practitioner, drawing on his childhood and family experience. The "therapy" involves a sort of speech-act procedure wherein the patient calls the illness an "error." It's better not to actually name the condition an illness "because to name it gives it power." Then the practitioner prays for a healing that erases the "error." But Gray confesses a distinct lack of faith, noting that he can't entirely give up on the idea of an eventual medical cure, which leads the practitioner to remind Gray that "we can't be duplicitous in our faith. You have to make up your mind whether to go with a Christian Science practitioner or a doctor, but you can't divide your faith that way." It's an either/or world: either have spiritual faith or faith in material science. You can't believe in both. This is an attitude that Gray will eventually abandon. But first he moves on to other alternatives.

The next one is going to an Indian sweat lodge in Minnesota, which involves a set of Native American ritual acts. Gray goes with a sense of unworthiness, given his heritage: "All my ancestors—who were they? Pilgrims. What did they do shortly after they came to America? Kill the Indians. Where was I going? Into an Indian sweat lodge." He sees that the procedure does appear to have curative power, releasing the fears that grip those ahead of him. But when it comes to his turn, stifled by the heat of the sweat lodge, he misses his opportunity by asking for the wrong thing: "I want to give away the fear that I'm about to have a heart attack at this very moment." Despite his Pilgrim roots and to his utter amazement, his fear disappears instantly when another participant takes it on and scrambles from the lodge. His host asks afterward, why "when the time came for you to give away your eye condition, you started babbling about a heart attack!" Gray answers, "I realized that I was still the child who acts on his most immediate needs." It's likely that Gray's request to satisfy an immediate need succeeded because he didn't have time to reflect upon and doubt what he was doing. No skeptical thoughts had time to overwhelm his childlike moment of blind faith in the opportunity at hand. Gray probably realizes as much and doesn't retry the sweat lodge.

He next goes to a Brazilian healer in Oakland, California, who tells him that "someone worked black magic on you three years ago" and proposes a two-month regimen of exorcism. Gray is unimpressed. He next tries an eccentric nutritional ophthalmologist in Poughkeepsie, New York, who determines that Gray "better give up everything. I think you'd better give up all canned goods, give up all tobacco, give up drinking alcohol, any marijuana, any coffee, please, give up caffeine, all that, and just eat raw vegetables." For a while he follows the advice, but after sitting through a particularly unsavory food combining lecture (where he is accused of cooking his vegetables), he gives up on this option as well. Finally, he turns to a faith healer in the Philippines, a man named "Pini Lopa, also known as the 'Elvis Presley of psychic surgeons'." The report Gray hears is that Lopa basically puts on an ecstatic show of reaching into bodies and orifices, pulling out the transgressing organ in a smoothly choreographed, blood-and-guts-spattering daily extravaganza. Before going to him, Gray says to himself, "No judgment! No judgment! I'm just going to hang in here, take it easy." However, he's "completely unprepared for" what he sees, adding, "I couldn't believe my eye." Back at his hotel, trying to muster up the nerve to participate, Gray is told by a local waiter: "Oh, sir, if you go to Pini Lopa and you believe, you will be healed. But if you do not believe you must go home, because you must believe in order to get healed." The point that Gray has been missing all along, of course, is, "I don't believe in anything. Doubt is my bottom line. The only thing I don't doubt is my own doubt."

We see that, rather than just failing eyesight, Gray suffers from an even more pervasive pathology of skepticism. That his skepticism is coincidentally combined with his failing vision—as opposed, say, to a bad back or arthritis—is a brilliant interconnection, given that in a world where seeing is believing, Gray is having problems seeing or believing. And while Gray clearly knows that modern medicine lacks an incorporating spiritual element, he has come to understand that disembodied spiritualism also lacks what he's looking for. He has effectively "skepticked" himself into a corner.

The unspoken result is that by monologue's end Gray is now aware that the spiritual thing is not worth much unless it's also attached to some physical reality, and vice versa. This is a big jump for dealing with not only his eye problem but also the far more important matter of understanding how the world actually operates and where his "I" fits into that world. These two things, spirituality and physicality, somehow need to work together, being interdependent. There's a living element in the physical world and a physical element to the spiritual world. One without the other simply can't be. He discovers this sense of integration even as he's losing the opportunity to experience and enjoy it, since without vision he'll be separated from the world he's beginning to understand is so important to his spiritual well-being. It's a point that Gray has toyed with as early as his Wooster Group days, when he observed that he had met certain mystics who claimed they could escape from themselves, "but I think they're still in their body and they're still coming from themselves." Without their bodies, Gray concludes, they simply don't exist.

Gray seems intuitively to have understood this point his whole life, longing for the physical in ways that can't be labeled anything other than mystical. To find yourself you must first create a context for yourself. Health and physical well-being depend on it. And consciousness is nothing if it's not consciousness of something, meaning that this "something"—the world and people around us—*really* matters. Floating in some never-space of abstraction is a self-deluding course of action if you're trying to find yourself or discover who you really are. In *Gray's Anatomy*, Gray begins to focus on this quest even as he's losing visual focus on the world around him. Or maybe it's *because* he's losing his eagle-eyed ability to interact with others that has finally led him to realize the importance of the world around him. In a long, roundabout way, Gray is revealing to us that he's learning that the world is more than a plaything designed for him and us all to find our sensualist "perfect moments." Rather, true perfect moments are "spiritual" events that include the body too. Now, perhaps, he's one step closer to making that connection. Like the sages of old, Gray sees best only after being blinded. Or nearly blinded.

So Gray comes to realize that consciousness is not some mystical out-of-body manifestation but an extension of the material and concrete world around us, and it's designed to work integratively with whatever appears to be outside of itself. Without grounding in the body, mind is lost, and really, so is the body. But when they work in harmony the result is a rare spiritual/physical gratification, the kind of ecstasy, in fact, that everyone had been looking for back in the 1960s. Finding that perfect moment was one of Gray's childish obsessions in *Swimming to Cambodia*. Amid all the suffering and death he learns about while working on *The Killing Fields*, he still puts most of his energy into selfishly looking for the perfect moment. An unintentional baptism by nearly drowning in the Indian Ocean is the result. But it's at that point that this childish man has actually found himself, fully immersed in the world that gives him identity. In a similar manner, Gray's pursuit of ocular well-being in *Gray's Anatomy* leaps beyond egotistical boundaries from the eye to the I and eventually toward a more completely encompassing sense of spiritual well-being. He is coming to realize that whenever it happens that he has or will experience a perfect moment, it would be characterized by this blend of the physical and the spiritual.

In its discussion of the term "idiopathy," *Gray's Anatomy* takes us to another related point. Idiopathy has stuck in Gray's mind for some time primarily because it goes so solidly against one of the most Western concepts, the belief that everything has a cause and effect. Idiopathy implies a faith of its own sort, that the world sometimes operates in a mysterious fashion not altogether comprehensible by "scientific" human reason. There's more to heaven and earth, it appears, than good science can uncover. In a manner of speaking, then, Gray has hit upon a term that explains that faith is necessary in order to live in the world. It certainly explains why Gray is so comfortable "explaining" the world around him through nearly impossibly coincidental twists and turns of good and bad fortune. Attempting to make sense of the world sometimes works and sometimes doesn't, because of the fabric of the universe itself rather than some personal failing. Some things just can't be explained, so don't worry about it. Realizing this is difficult, if not impossible for most, and Gray is no exception. But by *Gray's Anatomy*, he's getting better at it. His consciousness grapples with the world until the two come together. And increasingly, he's able to accept mystery, the unexplainable, into his vision. A sort of material religion seems to have begun to infect his consciousness.

Upon his return to New York and at another visit to his first doctor's office, Gray sees Richard Nixon leaving the examining room, which triggers a rapid series of events: "It was seeing Richard Nixon come out of my doctor's office that gave me the faith and courage to have the operation." "Faith" seems at first sight an ill-placed word, for this brief encounter hardly includes anything that seems to inspire faith. And the encounter does nothing really to explain why Gray has changed his mind and decided to have the operation. But if nothing else, sighting Nixon returns Gray to thinking about the imperfections that fill our world, from the top down. Is there anything in the world that we can point to and rationally declare we really know? Perhaps there's cause for faith once factual certainty is understood to be ultimately unattainable by reason. Reason can discredit trickery and illusion, but at times faith-based trickery and illusion may have power beyond reason. Maybe. But if we abandon reason, aren't we abandoning the very foundation of Western thought in general and America in particular? How can we live without reason? Gray seems to have begun to ask, how can we live without faith?

So Gray comes upon Nixon, whose public disgrace decades earlier should have given the man "no reason" to live. But this Nixon, an American icon who is anything but valorized as an American ideal, seems to inspire Gray with the faith to carry on against all reason and logic, which no longer seem as all-powerful as he once thought them to be. Idiopathy might explain more than reason ever could. At very least, it "explains" Gray's eye condition, and maybe his "I" condition as well.

So he puts his faith in "American" medicine, though interestingly administered by a "Chinese" doctor. But there's more. Immediately after Gray's statement about Nixon, he adds, "I also couldn't have done it without Renée," his girlfriend, who seems always to be there to ground him in the world from which he so frequently separates himself. The ensuing operation neither improves nor destroys Gray's vision, but he doesn't seem bothered by it as he would've been earlier. He rather serenely accepts the neither-gain-nor-loss results. What we see here is not resignation so much as contentment with what is.

Gray notes while sitting in the doctor's waiting room, "I believe in magic. I believe that there has to be real magic if there are tricks in the world, because what is a trick, if not an imitation of real magic?" Following the operation, perhaps something "magic" does occur, though not in the spectacular or mystical fashion that Gray had been seeking: "I wanted Jesus to walk into that waiting room the way that he used to in the old days with the multitude and *Bing!* The blind shall see." But though this of course doesn't happen, following his operation he is instructed to keep his face pointed downward for two weeks (with a patch over his left eye) to avoid damage to his recuperating eye: "I had to walk with my head down, eat with my chin to my chest. . . . We [Gray and Renée] applied for the Blind Program, so I could go get books on tape at the Library for the Blind, unabridged books. I remember looking at the dog shit and bubble gum on the sidewalk as I walked up to get *The Miracle Worker*, Renée guiding me." No Helen Keller to be sure, Gray nonetheless has been forced not only to compensate for vision loss but also—for two weeks at least—to look downward, literally toward the ground on which he treads, to concentrate on the earth beneath his feet rather than the phobias in his head or any philosophies sent down from mountains on high. With the right attitude, even dog shit and bubble gum, it appears, have a sort of "magic." So this strange contentment of an otherwise manically paranoid individual may have an explanation beyond merely that Gray was too exhausted to think about things anymore. We can almost explain the strange idiopathy of his transformation.

And an additional bit of support runs throughout the monologues, reminiscent of the straw boy in *Swimming to Cambodia*. Gray tells us partway through that he owns a Balinese scroll picture of a man with no head but eyes in his chest, literally an embodiment of vision. Gray says that this talisman has proven magic powers, discovered when

Gray was in the woods of his writer's colony. And because of what happened there, "I knew there was magic in the world." But Gray never fully explains his point. Rather, the monologue ends with two events. One involves Gray accepting Renée's suggestion that they marry when she explains it's the logical thing to do: "When you were in the hospital, every time I tried to get access to you, they wouldn't let me see you, because I was the girlfriend. Now you're going to get older, and you're going to get sicker a lot more and you'll be in the hospital again. I think it's time we got married." A good logical, but hardly romantic, reason. They get married, and Gray tells us that he "brought down the little Balinese man to be a witness," supplying a hoped-for talisman of good luck to complement the good sense of it all. It completes a circle that includes good old American common sense with a rather "magic" leap of faith into the great unknown of matrimony.

The other event occurs before the wedding. Gray nearly drowns while swimming in the ocean and is saved by two men on the beach who Renée forces to go out and save him even though they don't know anything about lifesaving techniques. But they bring a boogie board with them, and Gray says, "When I see that yellow boogie board, it's like a gift from heaven." Maybe it was, but it wouldn't have reached him if it hadn't been for the two men and Renée. Then Gray tells us that the two heroes comically note after the rescue that "they recognized me from the *Swimming to Cambodia* poster, the way my head was bobbing half out of the water!" To that Gray adds a final note: "Art imitates life; life imitates art!"

So the eye operation neither helps nor hurts Gray's vision, but he doesn't grieve over this material stalemate, where Western science neither triumphs nor exactly fails. Miracles will not occur—neither spiritual nor medical—existence continues, and selfhood remains intact. But Gray has calmed down. His paranoid near-paralysis has left him: "I'm happy to have right eye vision . . . I'm on the lookout for pinkies [that is, pinkie fingers] when I dance." And dancing is hardly an act of despair. Rather, it's an expression of the great insight his bout with blindness has given him: "I began to realize that there are tricks in the world, and there's magic in the world. But there's also reality."

What has happened is that the operation restored Gray's failing "I," no longer obsessive and resistant but responsive and accepting of the changes of life. Diving headlong into life, he says that following his wedding he completely disregarded the injunctions of that nutritional ophthalmologist in Poughkeepsie: "I drank vodka and I drank white wine and I ate big fish. I ate steamed vegetables and I ate wedding cake. I drank coffee and I smoked a cigar. I drank brandy. And I ate and I drank and I smoked . . . *everything* that could make me blind." Gray's prospects seem to be looking up. A new religion stripped of mystical trapping and grounded in the physical reality that surrounds us might be precisely what the world needs.

7

Coming to Terms with
the American Dream

As early as 1981, Spalding Gray was proposing a hopeful resolution to his work in the theater. It was a quaint, All-American kind of fantasy:

> Often I have the fantasy that my work will lead me back full circle
> to where I started and I will know the place for the first time. I
> fantasize that if I am true to it it will be the graceful vehicle which
> will return me to life. Oh, what longings; I will move to Oregon.
> I will teach sixth grade. I will fall in love. I will marry. I will have
> three children and I will not reflect. I will die when I die. It will go
> on without me and without my endless commentary.

Though by the turn of the millennium he doesn't wind up teaching sixth grade in Oregon, he does become a family man with three kids, though the path to that destination turns out to be entirely unorthodox and a good deal bumpier than most would like. But it works, in the long run, for Gray, to the point that by 1999, he tells us, he'd finally abandoned the therapy he'd almost religiously relied upon throughout most of his adult life. His life after *Gray's Anatomy*, though by no means easy, finally reached a real level of personal contentment, Gray's own version of the American Dream.

That involvement in therapy up to the mid-1990s is central to his 1996 monologue, *It's a Slippery Slope*, which he describes as "the most deeply felt of the monologues," mainly because so much of what goes on is so emotionally disorienting. And the breakthroughs he describes led in turn in 1999 to *Morning, Noon and Night*, his most poignant and touching monologue about life in the fold of his new life and family. It appears that he at last found his place in the world and would no longer need to continue his manic search for himself. In fact, after the successful Broadway run of *Morning, Noon and Night*, Gray says he was pretty determined to do what he claimed he wanted to do back in 1981, put an end to his endless reflections and commentary and turn to a full-time life of just living. In 2002, he reports, "I think *Morning, Noon and Night* is the end for a while. But I would have said that after *Slippery Slope*. But I really think it more so now because I don't want to use my family as an ongoing soap opera. I don't want to turn my children into characters."

More to the point is that with *Morning, Noon and Night* Gray had come full circle. Or perhaps more accurately, Gray's life had come "full spiral" since it made a return to something like the family life of his childhood, but with the added bonus of being a distinct improvement from where it all began. He had by all accounts finally settled down, but his life had spiraled *up* to a more satisfying and higher level than where it had begun, back in Barrington, Rhode Island. He settled into the fold of a loving family, one that offered him a genuine beacon of hope amid all the quiet desperation he'd dealt with ever since childhood. It seems that until that tragically random and ironically accidental day in 2001 on a byway in Ireland—while, of all things, he was on *vacation*—Gray had at long last found what he was looking for. And he shows us something of what we possibly should be looking for as well, amid all the glittering detritus of that thing called American culture.

Setting the Stage for the Final Acts

Gray's participation in the Wooster Group, an offshoot of Richard Schechner's famous Performance Garage showed signs of where he would later go with his career and his life. First and foremost, he would never fully abandon his cultural roots and offer some rebellious assault on his world by declaring himself an outsider and filling himself with contempt for the world. He seems to have seen early on that an agenda of cultural assault made from some sort of moral high ground might have been an invigorating 1960s/'70s agenda, but that heyday of countercultural activism was really a fundamentally inauthentic movement of very limited value. In fact, Gray began to realize that the best way to face and critique flawed American culture was to confront it from within, and what better object of study than his middle-class self to get at the roots of culture's woes? As a white heterosexual Western European male, Gray was never really in a position to step out of his own skin and be someone other than a man basically to the manor born. He had to accept that his life of comfort and relative security was built on gender, racial, and other injustices that the 1960s and 1970s were targeting. And that leads to the heart of Gray's dilemma as a socially sensitive citizen of America: how to challenge the injustices that built the world of white male privilege he was born into without basically condemning who he was in the process. With the Wooster Group, he critiqued American culture and himself as its beneficiary. But when he moved beyond the Wooster Group, he did so in part to come to terms with the realization that to change the world, he'd first have to find a way to change himself. Otherwise, the likelihood of larger-scale change seems slim.

As noted earlier, *Point Judith* was the Wooster Group's send-off of Spalding Gray into the theater world on his own. And it was a macho-bravado piece that presented a portrait of male misogyny that our culture seems to condone. It is a curious sort of thing to do for a man so needy, hungry for love, and slow to anger. It seems that Gray needed to get over his "effeminate" sensitivity or to embrace it and invent a type of manhood that he could be comfortable living.

Consider the following: it seems that Gray's years in analysis may have led him to conclude that psychoanalysis was based on an assumption that in order to be "normal," you had to be pretty much like everyone else. Psychoanalysis works to generate patterns of behavior in humans that conform to *cultural* prescriptions. Buried under almost all forms of analysis are assumptions that human beings are by nature aggressive and invest most of their energy in individual self-preservation at the expense of everyone and everything around them. For example, according to Freud (and this is a pretty big generalization), any success at achieving selfhood requires escaping the influence of the maternal with the assistance of paternal forces of self-separation. In other words, get away from Mama and join the competitive company of other men. To be is a matter of being able to stand your own two feet, to assert independence, and to conform to our culture's demands that we be autonomous individuals able to defend ourselves against the onslaught of others.

But let's reconsider for a moment Gray's roots. He was lovingly raised by his mother, who is the center of much attention throughout his work. If, as Freudian and Lacanian analysis may argue, he failed sufficiently or effectively to break with this maternal influence, he would never have been able to enter the cultural fold as a fully functioning autonomous male. And that seems to have been the case, given that his mother committed suicide in 1967 while he was "selfishly" vacationing in Mexico. He never achieves any real closure with his mother, and he is therefore never able to move on, haunted by that event as Gray is for his remaining days.

But it is entirely possible to break with conventional cultural wisdom and to see this interdependent relationship as entirely healthy. Maybe the maternalistic dependence that we are told we're supposed to break away from is not so dangerous as culture tells us it is. In fact, perhaps the "need" to declare independence from our mothers and everyone else is a cultural myth that is centrally responsible for our culture's repeated unsuccessful attempts to create a world that values community over individual autonomy. When Gray finally abandons therapy, then, it may be less a case of being "cured" in any accepted sense of the term than that he's finally become strong enough simply to reject what therapy was trying to do to him. To paraphrase Celia

Copplestone (and T. S. Eliot), maybe it *is* the case that culture is wrong. Gray might have somehow decided that his health depended not on asserting his autonomy but on breaking with cultural prescriptions of masculine behavior and doing the unconventional thing of working ("effeminately"?) to bridge the gap between himself and others.

As noted earlier, *Gray's Anatomy* concentrates on Gray's unsuccessful attempt to reclaim a partial loss of vision in his left eye. He fears losing his vision altogether and thereby his powers of observation, his livelihood, and even his *being*. All his efforts to save his left eye merely slow the loss, yet by the monologue's end he comes to accept it, glad that he still has at least some of his sight. At least early on in the monologue, Gray believes that sight is his most important sense, which explains why he has such an overwhelming sense of panic at the prospect of losing it. Sight, of course, is not our only sense, but it is the only sense that doesn't require actual contact with the dirty, sloppy world around us. Through sight we can stand aside and participate in the world without really being part of it. Because sight doesn't require actual contact, of all the senses it's the one that preserves the illusion that we are (or can be) separate from everything we observe. So the accomplishment in *Gray's Anatomy* is that Gray has come to realize the importance of the world around him, though he hasn't yet realized the importance of fully diving in and actually making deep contact with the world around him. At this point he's still a squeamish New Englander. It could be that in *Gray's Anatomy* he's beginning to understand this, and that explains why the prospect of losing his sight might not have been quite as devastating as it might have been earlier. The next step comes in *It's a Slippery Slope*, where Gray finally comes to realize that his body is an integrated system designed to make full and direct contact with the world around him. It takes more than mere perception to make the world go round.

Gray's Slide to "Sanity": *It's a Slippery Slope*

In *It's a Slippery Slope* (1996), Gray shows a darker and far more selfish side to his behavior. In this "most deeply felt of monologues," Gray lays bare some of his greatest personal failings, including infidelity and what amounts to child abandonment. Coping with these serious ethical lapses in behavior, Gray concedes, "I was heavily judged for *It's a Slippery Slope*" by audiences, fans, and reviewers. He continues: "I got my first hate letters—and I thought I had grown up! I thought that the work had finally matured. . . . During *Slippery Slope*, I got ones [i.e., letters] that were so angry that I almost couldn't go onstage—from women, about the betrayal factor, and sneaking around, and infidelities, and all of that. I began to feel that the work was more complex because of that."

What Gray seems to have experienced through the events revealed in the monologue, through developing the monologue itself, and finally from the responses he got was all of a piece. It all comes together to make manifest the point that the "harmlessly" adolescent behavior throughout most of his monologues, charming in its desperate confusion and misdirected bravado, were actions whose impact actually had harmful effects on the people and the world around Gray. Simply showing us that he hadn't *intended* to hurt anyone isn't good enough, which Gray of course had learned during his Wooster Group days. In *It's a Slippery Slope*, Gray comes fully to terms with the fact that he would have to pay the price for his self-obsessed cruelties. Choosing not to gloss over his behavior, *It's a Slippery Slope* put Gray under a critical light to which he hadn't exposed himself in his more benign earlier works, and this brutal self-exposure was a far more certain sign that Gray was growing up than he ever offered before. If he experienced something of a political awakening in *Swimming to Cambodia*, Gray would now be forced into an awakening of even greater, more fully embracing magnitude.

In *Gray's Anatomy*, Gray broke from his reliance on sight and the stifling illusion of separation that that reliance breeds. In its place, Gray moves in *It's a Slippery Slope* to full body contact with his world by learning to ski. It should be added here that virtually all of Gray's work has been engaged with his body and its involvement in the world. But that earlier involvement has been primarily an

It's a Slippery Slope. (Photo copyright Paula Court, courtesy of Paula Court.)

involvement leading to personal conquest, dominion, and the pursuit of a sensualist's perfect moments to be enjoyed by the masculine tyrant wannabe, Spalding Gray. Hints of the delusional value of these goals abound throughout Gray's earlier works, but *It's a Slippery Slope* takes the guilt earned in these earlier works to a level of release that Gray seems not to have been prepared to face earlier. It takes strength to face your failings, and Gray seems ready to face the music.

Part of the dubious legacy of his earlier overreliance on sight is that its distinguishing illusion of difference leads to the delusion of the superiority of one's consciousness over everything else, everything seen. This is the point where Gray begins *It's a Slippery Slope*. But his series of betrayals of numerous women in the piece embroils him in the world in ways he had previously not experienced. Gray's apparent ability to betray Ramona (in earlier monologues she was Renée) and then to deny assistance to the pregnant Kathie likely stems from a cultural inclination to believe that the feminine is inferior to the masculine. We're allowed to betray the female body whenever it's convenient, especially since we've been taught to devalue the importance of the physical over the spiritual. And from there, betraying the entire female is a minor step further. In short, there are only sentimental or romantic reasons to treat the feminine as anything other than objects for masculine manipulation. And Gray buys into this attitude, or tries to, only to suffer devastating results that very likely wouldn't have affected a more "manly" male as much. Gray is catatonically overwhelmed by guilt when his infidelities are discovered, providing at least nominal evidence that he had not been fully socialized to accept his cultural role as master of his domain. His sensitivity betrays him.

But he tries to master himself and those around him. Gray reminds us in the monologue that the matter of masculine control of the feminine surfaced even at the very beginning of his seventeen-year relationship with Ramona. It all begins on an unsettling first date when Ramona "mixed all the wrong drinks, and just as I got in bed with her, she said, 'Excuse me, but I think I'm going to throw up.'" Gray continues, "I ran and grabbed a big cooking pot from the kitchen and held her while she filled it up. I was able to be very nurturing and I came to feel that holding Ramona while she threw up was the first real bond of our love, and I think that because of this, I tried to make her throw up for the rest of the relationship. Only then could I express my love."

Love, in fact, was really little more than control. But Gray—being Gray—wouldn't be fully able to maintain his dominant masculine position because, as he notes, both he and Ramona were cases of "arrested development going on just under the surface of our adult appearance." Gray adds: "Both Ramona's father and my mother had been seductive and invasive parents. They did not mirror well, did not establish healthy boundaries. They were great greedy consumers of their children. . . . I think the night Ramona and I met, the two kids inside us cried out for each other, and we came together initially to try to reparent the needy child inside us both." To a large degree, neither Gray nor Ramona was "properly" masculinized or feminized by their culture's standards, though from Gray's perspective this opportunity to be a man/father and control his female/child girlfriend involved a sense of control that he at least tried to master throughout the confused relationship.

Since this power relationship resulted primarily from the fact that Gray wasn't adequately brought up to be a man's man, the relationship waffled between Gray being dominant and Gray wanting to be a premasculinized man-child nurtured by this woman-mother. This intertwined, entirely confusing, and contradictory relationship reflects the confusing impulses that haunted Spalding Gray throughout his life. How to overcome or reconcile the conflict is his ultimate goal, maybe even the thing that he hopes he'll capture in one of his perfect moments.

But until then, he has this relationship to manage. Apparently, all goes more or less well between Spalding and Ramona for quite some time, but it eventually all comes down in what Gray calls "a very big crash." The closer he gets to his fifty-second birthday (the age Spalding's mother and Ramona's father both died), "the more I began to fragment. . . . I started to disintegrate and go into a number of personalities." One personality, suggested above, was that of a two-year-old: "I had become very good at casting [Ramona] as a mother." Another fragment of his self took on the "uncontrollable, obsessive reenactment" of his mother's madness. And, he adds:

> What complicated things even more was that because I'm an actor who plays himself, there's a hazy line between what my act is and what my authentic behavior is. So I did not know if I was acting crazy or really crazy, or both, which I think must be a form of madness right there. In short, I was deeply confused and alienated from what I felt and thought about anything.

Then there was the fantasy played out in the world beyond Ramona, that of his affair with Kathie. That separate reality created yet another Spalding Gray, "which I ended up calling the sixteen-year-old, because I was having what felt like a sixteen-year-old's affair with Kathie, whom I had met on the road and who had sent me letters and her phone number when she moved to New York for a new job. I did drop in to visit her and we had more than tea." Clearly Gray's life was spiraling out of control, fragmenting and spinning beyond a center of gravity that he was trying so hard to manage.

Even as he was fragmenting in real life, his career was more successful than ever. But even this public success had the sort of hollowness that was so solidly captured in the character Crow in Shepard's *The Tooth of Crime*, that formative play of Gray's younger days. For Gray as for Crow, the price of success was loss of selfhood and personal identity. And success drew him and Ramona into an existence that had no foundation: "For me the roll I was on became the roll 'we' were on, and I got so caught in my image that I didn't know how to get back. There was no substantial self, no private self left to come back to. Both Ramona and I were living in this floating bubble, the public persona of Spalding Gray." Even the theater seemed to be betraying Gray. He had completely lost his center.

Desperate to reclaim some sense of order, Gray decides to act on Ramona's growing interest in making their life official by getting married. He rather mock-benevolently points out that "I felt I should be able to give that to her as a gift." But he betrays his "grownup" side by impregnating Kathie, with whom he'd continued an affair even as he was agreeing to marry Ramona. The crash occurs when Ramona learns the full scope of his infidelity, seemingly accidentally revealed by Gray himself through a careless act of confession. Gray is "caught," and his world collapses: "What followed was two days of highly dramatic hysteria. I was rolling on the floor like an apologizing animal." Then, "over the months I became more and more disintegrated, to the point where I even lost my inner witness; I have no real narrative memory of the chaotic events that transpired." Having lost his storytelling abilities and even his defining "inner witness," Gray suffers the consequences of trying to consume the physical world as a "man" bent on callous self-gratification. But nagging personal guilt ruins his ability to master the world without care or concern for those he masters. He's just not built for that sort of life.

Presumably, if Gray had been more properly masculinized according to cultural standards, this collapse would have been only a minor and temporary setback followed by other callous escapades. This, however, is not the path for Gray, filled with what culture likely would describe as a confusing sense of regret, remorse, and sentimental guilt. But as torturous as all of this appears, these contradictions in behavior are actually signs that he might yet find salvation outside of what his culture tells him to do.

All of this is intriguing autobiography, at least for some of us. But what Gray does in the monologue to expand beyond mere dear-diary material is run this material alongside a story line that takes on a sort of mythic, or at least poetic, quality. It begins with the title. As any audience member could see, Gray's life was, figuratively speaking, slipping down a slippery slope toward catastrophe. But Gray uses the idea of a slippery slope and moves to a different level. His decision to learn to ski puts him literally onto the slippery slopes of the Colorado Rockies even as his personal life is sliding down its own slippery slope. The literal slippery slope, however, puts Gray in touch with his physical self in a crisp, clean, Colorado Rockies manner that runs against his more lurid personal indulgences in physical self-gratification. The experience will ultimately avalanche away his domestic troubles and lead him to another domestic arrangement that will be his salvation.

Skiing requires fully conscious attention and full-bodied coordination. In the best of situations, the skier folds into the mountain, almost becoming a part of its terrain and contours. Gray eventually masters the sport and finds it exhilarating: "Now I was experiencing the mountain as a whole body. My own body was heating up in relation to this mountain. My breath was coming into the rhythm of that giant. I was turned on." Interestingly, this exhilaration occurs on Ajax Mountain, which happens to stand next to a slope called Buttermilk Mountain. Gray describes them in nearly Freudian terms as "Ajax, the big daddy; and beside it Buttermilk, lying like an elegant reclining lady—you can ski over her breasts and thighs—and then go over and get beat up by the 'father' at the end of the day." Gray learns on the forgiving, maternally embracing runs of Buttermilk and then takes on the challenges of the big daddy.

What is also interesting is that Gray is successful against Ajax because he's learned not to think but to feel. Connection with the physical (and even "feminine") world, contact with his environment, brings him to life on these slopes. It's an intentionally mindless triumph of unencumbered matter over confused and self-doubting mind. Freed from all his obsessions while on the slope, Gray escapes the need to describe his accomplishment as a manly triumph over some titanic foe. Instead, he's simply happy to have experienced a pretty perfect moment, though surprisingly he doesn't seem to recognize or label it as one.

From here, however, Gray goes a step further, getting completely away form his "Freudian" adventure in the Colorado Rockies and actually doing what he's always found difficult: going home again. Toward the end of the performance, Gray reports finally having the opportunity to tackle the far less sensational slopes of his "home" country in New England, in Vermont in particular. At first disappointed by the lack of masculine Rocky Mountain-style grandeur, he leaves his hotel—named of all things the Buttermilk Inn—and advances on the slopes, but this time he's with his newfound family, Kathie and her daughter, after having more or less reconciled all the interpersonal fiascos that plagued him earlier in the monologue. And this experience on his home turf surprisingly frees him of all those previous anxieties; he succeeds on the slopes much as he had on Ajax.

But on Ajax he needed to reduce himself to near automatic pilot, clearing his mind of everything in order to master the rugged Western slopes. This time he doesn't need to clear his head first: "And I'm thinking this and skiing at the same time." Vermont offers a less spectacular physical challenge, but it involves and liberates the *whole* Spalding Gray, mind and body together. Surrounded by "family" and getting that feeling of being "at home" in New England for once in his adult life, Gray takes the moment to give rather than to take: he calls out to Kathie's daughter, "Go for it, Marissa," and immediately realizes that he has found a "totally supportive, non-ironic . . . wholesome cheerleader voice" for the first time in his life.

In this monologue, Gray recounts how his life had spiraled out of control on all kinds of levels. He betrays Ramona and their marriage vows. He betrays Kathie by refusing to stand by her as she bears his son. His career seems to be turning into a hollow sham, leaving him lost on the stage as well as in life. But working through it all, he rides down that slippery slope of life, crashing but getting up and trying again, until at long last it all comes together in a perfect ride down a mountain, giving him the feeling of being one with the world around him in nothing less than an unlabeled perfect moment.

Gray ends the monologue by observing, "You know, I've returned to New England and I'm no longer a puritan, if you define a puritan as someone who is constantly haunted by the sneaking suspicion that someone, somewhere else, is having a good time." With friendly strangers on Ajax in Colorado, a physically fine-tuned Gray fully experienced the pleasures of the world swept free of guilt, self-doubt, and concerns about doing the right thing according to standards he's never been comfortable with. And the joy of full-bodied mindlessness is no small thing. But then with family in Vermont, a full-bodied but also fully minded and newly familied Gray finds pleasure in a multilayered oneness he never quite experienced before. *Living* life rather than *reflecting* on it or just *observing* it from a distance, Gray has found at least one moment when he can be and feel himself without worrying about how he *should* be and feel. And that is a truly big thing.

Gray's Joycean Odyssey: *Morning, Noon and Night*

Morning, Noon and Night (1999) takes Gray to his healthiest by continuing the process of full engagement with the world in ways he never would have expected. Following the strategy used by James

Morning, Noon and Night. Family photo used for the published monologue's cover. (Photo copyright Noah Greenberg, courtesy of Noah Greenberg.)

Joyce in his masterpiece novel *Ulysses*, Gray creates a monologue covering a single day but filled with integrated recollections of the past to create what he calls "a complicated present." This single day, in essence, becomes a summary of Gray's complete life. Reflecting on the Sag Harbor Bridge and looking at the panorama before him, Gray says that he's finally able to be in the "present and in the past at the same time. It was because the place was so familiar in a very old sense and yet, at the same time, new." This description of a sort of dance between past and present explains what Gray had been trying to do in his monologues all along, but hadn't achieved in a fully harmonious way. But in *Morning, Noon and Night*, Gray additionally learns the vital trick of embracing the present and allowing it to override the past, rather than allowing the past to oppress and immobilize the present.

The past had been something of a prison for Gray, but he realized early on that it couldn't, or at least shouldn't, be abandoned. Although 1960s activism may have advocated abandoning the past and starting fresh, Gray never really was a child of the '60s, and he almost instinctively knew that ignoring the past was a foolishly naïve option. But facing it full-on would've been enough to make him wish the naïve option were possible. However, in *Morning, Noon and Night*, we see Gray handling the past with healthy respect, not the debilitating fear he often experienced, which frequently prevented him from fully appreciating the present. The present, for Gray, has finally become the thing that incorporates everything. It's no longer just some moment soon to be swallowed up by the past and added to his catalogue of experiences to draw upon for reflection and performance. The present, not the past, is the thing that everything leads to, and so experience—finally—trumps reflection for Gray. At long last life becomes the focus, including and absorbing the experience of his monologues, not the other way around.

This whole concept ties into Gray's perspective that his life is circular, but in that circularity Gray learns that his life needs to be less a matter of *getting* somewhere than of recognizing the value and beauty of *being* somewhere even while continuing in full motion forward. On that bridge, "I felt as if I had returned to the place that I started from and was about to know it for the first time. Circles are, I think, so important to me, or to us. Circles are important because we only live once. Repeating, or coming around full circle, gives us the feeling of rebirth, of living again." Crucial here is that for Gray, finally, his life has begun to imitate his art. He is now beginning to understand that he needs to find the same sort of exhilaration in life that he has previously only found onstage, where "the moment" was everything. Realizing life to be "all transiency, impermanence, and change," he concludes, "the only appropriate thing to do was be in motion, so I got on my bike and I rode."

Tapping into the cyclical nature that he now sees his life to be, it's an easy step to see everything in the span of a single day, and this thought actually increases Gray's sense of personal contentment. Toward day's end, he reflects, "It's not been a bad day, really. The thought of it happening over and over again is just too much for me to let in," and so he proceeds simply to enjoying the moment without fearfully trying to take in the bigger picture or to see it all as fulfilling some grand design or leading to some inevitable end. In previous times, that "end," of course, was death, the source of all Gray's fears—and humanity's too.

In a dream Gray has about a conversation with death, the voice of death tells Gray, "Try enjoying life for a change. See if you can, and remember, tend your gardens. By all means, tend your gardens." Ironically, hearing a disembodied breath encouraging him to indulge an embodied life literally brings Gray to life following the dream— and it is what happens in the monologue in general. Gray bursts "awake like Ebenezer Scrooge" and begins fully to *smell, feel, hear,* and *taste* life anew: "I can smell the dinner. . . . And I feel the word 'delicious' in my head and it feels like a ripe fruit. I hear the warm buzz of the family below. . . . Oh, for a drink or two or three." Rather than looking for the odd perfect moment, Gray has come to learn that there's a sort of perfection in *all* moments. He's become an embodied being fully cognizant and appreciative of all moments before him.

What has happened, fundamentally, is that he's left his abstracting and isolating intellectualizing behind and is determined to embrace the living world around him. What has moved him into this awakening, clearly, has been the birth of his two sons and adoption of an older daughter. He recalls about the birth of his son, Theo: "Before I had children, I was the typical cynic, thinking the earth is overpopulated by a stupid, unconscious, polluting disease called humanity. Or, we have made such a mess of the world, who in their right mind would want to bring a child into it? Now all this was wiped away by this child we were calling Theo—a basic miracle." Gray has taken a leap of faith that defeats the cynicism of a rational, reflective mind. Logic fills him with the thought that "with only one life to live, why bring more life into the world to be responsible for? It's absurd. It's ridiculous, I think. Why complicate your life with more life that you're responsible for?" Logically speaking, it's clearly an absurd proposition to even think that life is for the giving rather than for the taking.

But in *Morning, Noon and Night*, at long last, Gray has gone beyond logic, thinking of others rather than, typically, only of himself: "I love my children, but they could only be accidents born out of blind passion. I could never have had a child if I had to think about it. I know that now. I also think of all the single working mothers and I think, oh, pray, pray, for the single mothers. How do they do it? Bless them." "Blind passion" is, of course, a telling phrase given that Gray's (re)birth into the world began with the macula pucker that had obsessed him in *Gray's Anatomy*. Reaching out to others rather than just trying to observe or manipulate others for his own pleasure, Gray has entered into a way of being part of the world that had previously been only an infrequent occurrence for his formerly paranoid self-indulgent self.

As he reports the birth of Theo, his second son, Gray comes to understand the nearly universal significance of human interdependence and begins to come to terms with his lifelong reluctance or inability to declare his own personal independence from others, regardless of how hard he tried. He sees clearly that his independence, his autonomy, has been a foolish, unnatural, and even inhuman thing to pursue. Theo is a completely dependent being. And Gray responds in fatherly ways to the baby's cries for help. It's natural, necessary, and mutually satisfying. Needing to be needed gives purpose to his life.

This is a point Gray could not have learned from his father, a distant man who left emotional response to his wife. This is not to say that Gray's father was a failure. In fact, by cultural standards, Gray's dad basically fulfilled his duties as a man, husband, and father in this world. But Gray sensed, early on, that this model of manly and fatherly behavior was problematic at best, as he suggests when he brings up a childhood memory of his brother Rocky's first fear-of-death experience: "Then at last Mom and Dad calmed Rocky down and Dad went to bed and Mom turned out the light and sat there in the dark beside Rocky." Earlier in the monologue, Gray tells us with a touch of sadness that Dad had had no real role model for fatherhood since his own dad (Gray's grandfather) had abandoned the family while Dad was still pretty young. Dad seemed to have almost no alternative than to duplicate the ideal of fatherly distance. Acculturated as we generally are to defer direct physical and emotional need to the mother, we learn that the father is supposed to stand outside that relationship and "lay down the law," becoming the boundary-maker who trains children to conform and be able eventually to go it alone. Gray's father, however, abdicates even this dubious paternal responsibility. That dooms Spalding to forty-plus years of confusion, but it also *ultimately* leaves him open to a singular personal transformation given that he was never fully *programmed* to be a "man." After forty-plus years of wandering alone and trying to discover himself, Gray finally locates his own version of what it means to be a man. And expressing love for others is part of it.

Gray relates an event in his adolescence when he has a car accident but rather miraculously survives. Not getting the expected response from his dad, young Spalding is left completely confused: "At that moment, I really didn't know if he wanted me dead because he was so angry or was thankful that I was still alive." Gray's dad fails to lay down the law for the adolescent Spalding at this point: "He did not punish me in a corporal way or in any other way. He left me pretty much on my own to punish myself." And then Gray makes the devastating point by saying that this pattern of self-punishment is something he's "done a pretty good job of over the years." If Gray's father had provided the current culturally expected response of punishment—at that moment and presumably others during Gray's adolescence—perhaps Spalding would have developed into a less neurotic individual. This is not to suggest that Spalding would have been *happy* if Dad had done his job, only that perhaps he would have been more *normal*, a culturally acceptable aggressive, autonomous male.

In an interview around the period that he was doing *Morning, Noon and Night*, Gray acknowledges having read the works of psychologist D. W. Winnicott and seems dedicated to helping his children achieve what Winnicott calls "reality-acceptance," the thing so crucial for a normal existence. Moving away from infant fantasy and into an eventual recognition of how to interact with the world is typically initiated by what Winnicott calls the "good-enough" mother. It's a perspective, of course, that conforms to cultural biases involving the roles of mothers. Gray understands the idea of "reality-acceptance" and even the idea of the "good-enough" mother, especially given his troubled relationship with his own mother. But this new Spalding Gray seems more than willing to share the role with Kathie, choosing not to be the distant father that he's "supposed" to be.

Gray reminds us in the monologue of his familiarity with Winnicott when he tells the story of son Forrest's "omnipotent fantasy" to devour his father by literally biting into Gray's flesh. This act of unacceptable aggression leads Gray to slap his son for the first and only time. But rather than letting things stand as a lesson on boundaries for Forrest, Gray goes unconventional: "As soon as he started to cry, I grabbed him and held him and told him how sorry I was and how much I loved him." Gray becomes simultaneously law-giver and emotional nurturer.

Winnicott very crucially minimizes the role of the father, basically endorsing the distant role of the male as a good provider: "He can provide a space. . . . Properly protected by her man, the mother is saved from having to turn outwards to deal with her surroundings at a time when she is wanting to turn inwards" to serve her children. This point clearly ties into what bothered Gray when he worried about single mothers. But Winnicott's minimal role of the male as good provider is distinctly not the role Gray sees for himself. He takes on duties typically reserved for the male's feminine counterpart, directed by that ever-present but largely ignored sense that he needs to play a more active role in the world around him. His own children give him the exhilarating opportunity. *Morning, Noon and Night* shows Gray, the once reluctant father, diving into tasks that our culture encourages men to leave for the mother to cope with. So the sort of traditional father-son relationship that Gray experienced when he was a child, incomplete in so many ways, may actually have led to Gray's salvation even after it generated nearly forty years of neurotic, needy behavior and symptom-treating analysis.

As we hear throughout Gray's monologues, love is extended to Gray through his mother, but his experience with love as maternal takes turns that are equally confusing. Begin with the fact that his mother almost literally smothered him with attention and affection, add to it the fact that she frequently slipped in and out of insanity as she headed toward her almost inevitable suicide, and the result of a neurotically needy, egocentric son seems inevitable.

But, ironically, thanks to Gray's father's unwillingness or inability to imprint the culturally endorsed masculine ethos upon him, Gray has the opportunity to do something rather singular. As we've seen in *Gray's Anatomy*, Gray moves away from a purely sighted vision of existence, opening himself to the prospect of jumping from an isolating and masculinized mind's-eye view of the world to a position valuing the rather feminized (by culture's accounting) possibility of accepting the full physical embrace of the world around him. He makes the leap in *It's a Slippery Slope*, where the world is no longer an alien other to be conquered but something of a womb to fall into fully immersed, as he does toward the end of that monologue. By the end of *It's a Slippery Slope*, Gray has moved from pursuing the "idea" of Man—with a capital M—to becoming the reality of man—with a lowercase m.

That process of becoming a lowercase man becomes complete in *Morning, Noon and Night*, in which he learns the affective value of love as a gift, not as something to seek as a hollow sensualist. He's now recognized his need for others, as always, but also realizes he has much to offer others as well. In fact, he's discovered that love can only be received after it has been given. From this revelation, Gray adapts one attitude from his father, that disinclination to be a "cop" to his children. But in Gray's hands, this disinclination has a positive effect on his children. As noted with the car accident scene, Gray's dad fails to lay down any sort of "law." Given that he also fails to substitute anything like an expression of love, Gray was left in a sort of ethical void and fills it with guilt. But from one singular action on Dad's part, Gray takes away one key lesson. He recounts an adolescent occasion when his brother Rocky decides to run away to Maine and become a lumberjack, but is thwarted literally by the law in the form of state troopers at the state line and is returned home. Rather than enforce any sort of parental mandate, Dad does something quietly ingenious. He brings in a load of logs and a hand saw and tells Rocky, "You want to be a lumberjack? Well, there you are. Start cutting." Spalding drily reports: "Rocky would soon graduate summa cum laude from Brown University."

Later, when Spalding has his own crises with his own sons, he reports, "I never wanted to have children in the first place because I never wanted to have to act like a cop. I never wanted to be someone else's superego." Then to his obstinate son, he says, "Forrest, I don't want to be your boss. I want to be your guide." Unlike his own dad, Spalding has maintained open lines of communication so that he can *talk* to his son and clearly express his love for Forrest in such a way that Forrest can place some trust in Spalding's offered guidance. Spalding's dad had not established this contact. "As far as my father went," says Spalding, "Mom always seemed to be his emotional go-between. She'd be the one who told me that my father loved me and was proud of me. I never remember it coming from him." Expressed, emoted, affective, physical love was the missing foundational element in this father-son relationship, as it in fact has been in American culture in general.

Finally, the unbounded foundational love Gray develops for his newborn Theo radiates to his older son, Forrest, to his stepdaughter,

Marissa, and to his new life partner, Kathie. The patriarchal law has effectively been replaced by "maternal" affection. It's not a guy thing or a girl thing. And it's not something that recognizes a nature/nurture struggle or that pits maternal nature against paternal law. Rather, it's an advocacy of a full "ecology" of interplay, void of issues of power and dominion. At the end of the piece, Gray still suffers as we all do from a fear of death and from numerous other "lesser" anxieties, but as he notes, "Then it is stopped by the love I feel for my son standing there below me." Concern for the present is more important in the end than obsession with the future, especially if that obsession might drown out the chance for present joy.

We can, of course, go back to the general complaint that all we have seen in this monologue is an egotistical performer bragging about his family life. This is the same kind of charge that has been levied against Gray throughout his career. I'd like to suggest, however, that we need to get beyond seeing Gray as talking only about himself, and see him, rather, as a performer who talks about us all as he talks about himself. Gray has conveyed through his own life's odyssey what a "man" must do to find his place in the world. More is required than confessing personal complicity in how the world has unfolded, though that's a very important step. It's more than getting psychoanalytic or personal self-help, which at best only patches the wounds of one lost soul and does little to deal with our culture's deeper afflictions. Gray learns that our bodies can teach us the value of our embodiedness and therefore our need to deal with the world around us not as a playland to be abused but as a place we need to nurture and that will nurture us in return. From that recognition forward, so much else begins to make sense.

Gray has admitted his self-indulgent tendencies throughout his performance career, not least in *Morning, Noon and Night*: "If I am guilty of anything, it is living in my head more with the world that never was and never will be than I am in the world that is." But although his other monologues hint at a change, this one confirms it.

Having once enjoyed engaging the "chaos" he found on the streets of New York City, he admits that it could only be enjoyed "as long as I could limp back to a nurturing woman and our quiet little nest together." He could do as much because "I was content to cope with the city and be in pursuit of art either as an observer or as a practitioner." But coming into a family way, Gray's life itself took center stage in his consciousness, primarily in the form of what he called the "double chaos" of city life plus screaming kids in his nest. Learning to cope rather than "to get out," as his instincts tell him to do, transformed him from the artist who experienced life for his work into an artist who experienced life for its pleasures.

Even his affection for Kathie turns him more toward an appreciation of and engagement with "other," given her background as an Irish/Italian American Catholic, part of a group of people Gray had always seen as "exotic" creatures "from the other side of the track." The Catholic women especially "overwhelmed" him "by their sensuality and that exotic smell of garlic on their breaths." Early in life Gray was tantalized by these attractive others but felt them to be dangerous and to be avoided. Kathie destroys his WASPish hunger for the isolating security that he seems to have experienced in previous relationships. Even that shattered marriage with Ramona/Renée because of his affair with Kathie works toward Gray's eventual emancipation from encultured ideas of selfhood.

Though once lured to look for perfect moments during vacations far from home, Gray begins to find them in the most unexpected and even traditional of settings. "Oh, the stupefying clutter of it all!" His early sentiments reveal his aversion to "the real world" in favor of the attractions laid before him in a theatrical lifestyle of make-believe: "People were imperfect and rarely dramatic enough for me. . . . Also, I wasn't real interested in replicating the traditional family structure I'd grown up in. I was not interested in creating my own American nuclear family." What he finds, ironically, is that life *was* dramatic enough and that "drama" *could* be found most substantially and thoroughly within the American nuclear family.

Gray no longer needs to look for the perfect moments that so obsessed him earlier in life. He's now replaced the search with a recognition that "awesome" things occur in daily life. Gray first announces in a fatherly show of contempt for adolescent lingo, "I won't let the word 'awesome' into the house, not until something awesome happens." But "awesome" does enter his life in the least expected of ways when he takes little Theo outside: "I look down at his head as though I'm looking down into a viewfinder, as though I am looking out through his eyes. I stand still and feel him give off a little shudder as he enters into what I can only call an 'awesome state'." Later Gray recalls one of his own more self-aware encounters with "awe" in the form of an early childhood confrontation with a wild bear: "When I got to my brother Rocky on the trail, I told him the story not so much in a state of fear but in a state of awe. In fact, I would venture to say the experience was awesome." The recollection could only occur to this newly transformed man, seeing the world through the eyes of a child once again for the first time.

In that new state of being, Gray shares the final passage of the monologue, a domestic duplication of the perfect moment he reported in *Swimming to Cambodia*. That earlier moment involved his drifting in the Indian Ocean unbounded by fear of annihilation even as annihilation seemed immanent. In *Morning, Noon and Night*, it's less spectacular but no less poignant:

> At that moment, when I am just about to let the love I feel for Forrest into my heart, I have a vision of what hell could be for me. Dying by chance (a vein in my brain pops for no apparent reason, just pops), I see my body lying on the floor of that men's room and I feel some leftover part of me trying to make it to some great all-consuming union, like a sperm swimming toward an egg. Then it is stopped by the love I feel for my son standing there below me. It's that earthly love I still feel for Forrest that keeps the part of me that needs to dissolve from dissolving. This spirit of mine can neither come nor go, but just lingers in the limbo of love.

Gray finds a level of sublime ecstasy that recognizes death. But where the Indian Ocean was perfect because Gray was swept into momentary oblivion by its majesty, here perfection overcomes death through love for an "other."

And that love returns him to life rather than to the panic of drowning that Gray felt after his Indian Ocean perfect moment. In the monologue Gray intriguingly refers to T. S. Eliot's "The Love Song of J. Alfred Prufrock," speaking of "a patient etherized upon a table," reminding us once again of that table way back in *The Rhode Island Trilogy*. But it's also a fitting allusion, given that Eliot's poem ends with human voices awakening a dreamer and causing him to drown. But Gray's experience has human voices awakening him to life, the very beings he'd thought would consume him utterly, children themselves. Gray even calls little Theo "My new bliss-eye," recalling both the famous command by renowned anthropologist Joseph Campbell—"Find your Bliss"—and the notion that Gray's fear of losing his sight will be replaced by a confidence that his children will fill in the picture.

One of the final scenes of the monologue recounts Gray's whole family overcoming a dispute at the dinner table not by arguing but by turning it into a blissful act of union by breaking into dance: "The fire in the fireplace is still burning well and the whole family is dancing." Gray had earlier pointed out that "the existential moralists have always been my heroes. They seem to have the courage to try to do the right thing in the face of what appears to be endless relativity." If one considers that "the right thing" first and foremost involves human contact, interaction, and taking responsibility for the well-being of others, then Gray's family dance (in production he actually rises from his desk and dances) is more than a mindless "Chumbawamba": it is a literal materialization of what he has more or less been doing with language his whole career, but never better: engaging and embracing others in a "dance" of give-and-take, leading and then following, as each situation and moment warrants. With more than a little help from his family, Gray has loved and danced his way back to life.

Order or Chance: *Life Interrupted*

On June 22, 2001, Spalding Gray was in a crippling car accident in Ireland while on holiday celebrating his sixtieth birthday. (He arrived in Ireland only the day before.) Until the accident, it appeared that Gray's chaotic life had settled into a loving family arrangement in which he was quite happy. *Morning, Noon and Night* is testament to his having finally found a life filled with the eruption of many perfect moments that he'd always searched for. Family, friends, a home, and a successful career, Gray was finally living the American Dream after so many false starts.

Until the accident, it seemed that Gray's career was about to take a new direction. In his last—incomplete—monologue, *Life Interrupted* (published 2005), he notes that when asked before the accident if he was working on a new monologue, he'd answer, "No, there's nothing on the table, really, nothing new. My life is without crisis and usually they're based on crisis, and I don't have anything planned at all. Things are going smoothly." In a 1999 interview with Richard Schechner, Gray answered the same question by noting, "I think *Morning, Noon and Night* is the end for a while. But I would have said that after *Slippery Slope*. But I really think it more so now because I don't want to use my family as an ongoing soap opera. I don't want to turn my children into characters." *Life Interrupted* even begins, "I didn't think there'd be another monologue, and I'm not still sure if there is. I had settled down into domesticity and a quiet life out in Sag Harbor and didn't want to continue making family soap opera."

Ironically, the accident provided Gray with new material, and he did in fact find the time and inclination to work on the piece after the accident, even when he didn't quite have the energy to polish his efforts. The monologue is clearly a work in progress, evidenced by the fact that its structure is almost exclusively chronologically ordered, with fewer than a half dozen of Gray's trademark diversionary flashback memories tying into the events begun on that fateful June 22. This is not Gray at his best, but that should not come as a surprise.

The date of the accident itself—June 22—is pretty significant in Gray's musings, and perhaps so is the primarily chronological structure. Gray and his family arrive in Ireland on "the longest day of the year, June 21, 2001," the beginning of the first summer in the new millennium (if one considers 2001 the beginning of the millennium). What seems important is that June 22 marks the point just beyond the high point of a life's seasonal journey. The day after the longest day of the year is the beginning of a phase of increasingly shorter days that will eventually lead to the longest night of the year, marking the beginning of winter—and the onset of death. Almost everything Gray's memory presents in the monologue prior to his description of the accident seems to foretell ominous events. The family goes to a monastery "where the Vikings used to come and . . . burn the books and kill the priests." They witness a "kind of Hamletesque" cemetery scene and hear numerous "funeral announcements on the radio": "So there was a lot of death in the air that day." They even talk at dinner that evening about a friend who had been in a car accident in Australia, commenting on the nightmare of receiving medical aid in a foreign country, precisely what was about to afflict Gray and his family.

In a stroke of irony that seems to have infected Gray's life—or perhaps destiny—"on the last long walk I'd ever take in my life," Gray sees a distressed calf in an open field, finds the owner, and suggests that the owner contact a veterinarian to relieve the calf's pain. That vet will be the driver of the vehicle that changes Gray's life forever. Gray's kindly recommendation turns out to seal his fate on that patch of road the locals call the "black spot" because of its dangers to motorists. ("Black Spot" was originally the title of the monologue.) Being at the wrong spot at the wrong time, Gray and his friends are blindsided by the speeding vet's van. Despite the randomness of the event, Gray's mind connects all the pieces and can't escape the "feeling that it's my fault entirely," though his only notable failing was not wearing his seat belt in the back seat of the car. The only way, of course, for him to feel this guilt is to think that somehow he'd been enjoying himself entirely too much and needed to be "punished" for this transgression. A foolish thought to be sure, but it's the kind of sentiment that haunted Gray the New England Puritan his entire life, and now he seems to have proof that he was correct all along.

The point here is that Gray continues to try to make sense of the world around him, even when it all seems senseless. He focuses on the horrors of medical treatment in rural Ireland, noting that the resident doctors failed to notice his serious head injury: "We're dealing with the hip. We didn't check on the head." His time in Irish hands and surrounded by Irish patients becomes a study in contrast between the Irish and American way of seeing the world. The Irish he meets turn out to be fatalists who accept their conditions by drinking and watching television, which contrasts with the American take-control attitude best demonstrated by Kathie, who hustles around and demands better care. While he is horrified by the callous, chaotic, and unsanitary treatment—"it all reminded me of a Brueghel painting"—Irish resignation and acceptance strikes Gray as singularly curious. Whatever their afflictions, and many are pretty serious, they seem to accept their suffering without complaint. So, when "mere" depression sets in following his brain surgery, Gray senses the futility in complaining to his Irish attendants: "I didn't know if they'd acknowledge the condition, or recognize it. I mean, does a fish know it's swimming in water? I had done a monologue over there called *It's a Slippery Slope*, in which I talked about divorce, depression, and skiing, and it wasn't a big hit. None of those three things were a hit in Ireland." And one of Gray's new Irish friends tells him that when it comes to depression, "an Irishman wouldn't give it a second thought. He'd just go about his business. You Americans are too health conscious."

One of the reasons Gray visits Ireland is to get back to his roots, going further back even than to his Puritan-American ancestry. But, seemingly anesthetized to pain and depression, the Irish finally are not the people Gray can actually call "my people." Though he hears the story of how his Scottish ancestors settled in Ireland before coming to the United States, he's come to realize that he's fully *American*, and he cures himself of one thing, at least, his nostalgia for the "old country." (He'd visited Ireland six times before.) And it's not just genetic roots that Gray was trying to recover by visiting the Emerald Isle. He senses that his blarney gift of storytelling had its roots in his Irish connection as well. But this too turns out to be a problematic idea, since even the sentimental vision of the Irish being a race of storytellers seems inaccurate. An Irish patient bedded next to Gray complains "about how TVs have stolen the Irish storytelling. There just isn't the same power of the storytelling because the people aren't in bars carrying on, they're in the bars watching television." Apparently, whatever gift there once had been in ancient Irish culture has succumbed to the tantalizing forces of the modern world. These people have been charmed away from the very communal undertakings that once made their culture so vibrant. The nostalgic ideal is dead even in the place it was most likely to be found.

Finally, Gray is taken out of the hospital and on an "outing" by Kathie, but what he sees is a pretty sad sampling of the great Irish outdoors that he'd been hoping for, little better than "a construction zone." But despite what seems to be an entirely gloomy experience, the optimist in Gray seems to surface, at least momentarily: "It was beautiful. I saw the clouds at last, the horizon, the sky. I had been looking out at an air shaft for three weeks. When a bird flew across, it was a hopeful moment." Gray has by no means despaired at this point. He returns to his room and sees—"pinnacle of pinnacles"—a TV episode of *The Simpsons* that refers to Gray and his monologues.

The head wound that is finally identified is described by Gray in a way reminiscent of *Gray's Anatomy*: "It's an orbital fracture of my eye so it's an open passageway to the brain and they simply can't have that, there's got to be an operation." In lighter days under different circumstances, this physical fact—like the macular pucker of his eye—would likely by itself have been inspiration for a monologue. A description of visual bypass and the outside world's direct access to his brain would very likely have inspired commentary that such a condition was what Gray had longed for his whole life. It could be imagined to be an opportunity to experience unimpeded direct knowledge of the world around him.

But, not quite at full imaginative power, Gray misses a great opportunity to play with this point in his monologue, and that's not a good sign. Instead, he turns to musings more closely related to his physical rather than metaphysical condition. He's returned to the United States, to the same hospital where "Andy Warhol died . . . under dubious circumstances," which leads Gray to "think about death" on the eve of his operation and to recall with admiration the stoicism his son Forrest demonstrates whenever he's under pressure.

But when he awakens from the operation, he turns to big-picture matters: "I think about coincidence and fate. What if I had left my glasses in the restaurant, or my wallet, and had just gone back there. Two minutes. How many accidents had I narrowly missed because of forgetfulness? Is it sheer chance?" Then, in a demonstration of his still solid mental imagination, Gray wonders at the fact that the driver who caused the accident was named Daniel Murphy, and the agent who just sold their Sag Harbor home ("another calamity") was also Daniel Murphy. Plus, the Irish Arts Council head who helped them in Ireland was a Patrick Murphy, and his New York nurse was Patricia Murphy. Out of these coincidences, Gray asks, "Was I in the grip of some overwhelming form of Murphy's Law? I couldn't figure it out. I was getting pretty paranoid."

The whole integrated chronology of *Life Interrupted* leads Gray to his final musings on order and chance: "Is it [all] a coincidence? I don't know. Is it fate?" He turns to probably the only source available to him in the hospital for some help:

> Webster's Unabridged defines fate as "the power supposed to determine the outcome of events before they occur. Inevitable necessity."
>
> Destiny: "Depending on a superior cause. Uncontrollable, according to the Stoics."

Hmm.

"Every event is determined by fate." It gives me the creeps. I don't like it. My therapist believes in such things. I wonder if I should trust her.

For Gray, art has provided a way to control, arrange, and order his life. It helped him to generate order out of chaos. His imagination embraced the physical world he first saw and then, later, he generated a dynamic interplay that brought the mysteries of the world into some sort of comprehensible focus. But here, with his body's pains tormenting his body's mind, Gray finds himself in no condition to pull it all together and decides to bring the monologue to an end. At that moment of utter confusion—though *not*, apparently, of despair—Gray concludes his work with a confession "that it's been difficult to say what exactly one should do and should not do in this world of relativistic, movable-feast morality." But even as he has conceded this point throughout his career, he had until this moment been able to beacon forth ways of looking, listening, feeling. And that was his tantalizing strength, even amid almost paralyzing self-doubt.

Life Interrupted does offer advice to his audience, though it's nothing close to the observations often buried like gems in his previous works: "Always wear your seat belt in the back seat of your car. . . . And whatever you do, get an American Express platinum card . . . so you can be medevacked the *fuck* out of a foreign country if you get in an accident." Until the body can be mended back to health, until the body no longer torments the mind with its pain and suffering, little more can or should be expected.

8

Gray Beyond the Stage

We are all fortunate that Spalding Gray left us some of himself in videos and books. He had the good fortune to work with quality film directors like Jonathan Demme (*Swimming to Cambodia*) and Steven Soderbergh (*Gray's Anatomy*), among others, bringing his presence into movie houses and living rooms even before he left the stage for good. These films seem to be a logical end to a long process of creation. Gray himself regularly noted that his monologues "start as performance art and then when I understand . . . what I'm doing, I begin to act." Having finally settled into a routine, his actual performance run still had a freshness to it, largely because his monologues weren't actually memorized but took slightly different turns each night. That freshness also found its way into his filmed performances, making his performance and acting legacy a lasting one.

But Gray left another legacy, in the form of written words. Although there will never be someone quite so good at performing Spalding Gray as Spalding Gray himself, his monologues do provide a trace of him that others can at least try to capture in performance. Gray encouraged other performers to experiment with his works. He observed in 1999 that theater classes frequently do his monologues, "and someone staged *Swimming to Cambodia* in Germany. I welcome that kind of thing." After his death, Gray's widow, Kathie Russo, successfully compiled monologic vignettes and created *Spalding Gray: Stories Left to Tell* (2007), using a small cast to present Gray's words to an appreciative off-Broadway audience. The production earned one actor, Ain Gordon, an OBIE Award.

Even though they're no longer brought to life by his ironic presence on the stage, Gray's published monologues stand out as entertaining and valuable in their own right. They masterfully capture his persona's ironic stances, paranoias, and rising epiphanies as he mixes his memories of personal events into the larger cultural occurrences of late twentieth-century America. In his writings we have Gray's chronicles of the times, generated by using actual events in his life to come to terms with his own place in the world and suggesting the "place" we all must find in our lives. Like his performances but even without his stage presence, his writings capture a consciousness that recognizes its surroundings and marks Gray as a witness intent on generating a union and communion with others. Strictly speaking, what he wrote is not autobiography because rather than mere accumulations of facts, it is more like reconstructions of remembered engagements with life and living. Through him, we see America as a living and breathing thing of which we *all* are part.

A "Novel": *Impossible Vacation*

In *Monster in a Box,* Gray shares with us the many diversionary experiences he tried out while trying to write his novel, *Impossible Vacation* (1992). About the novel he said, "I didn't know how I was going to write a novel because I didn't know how to make anything up, so I thought I'd write a book instead." The result is a novel generally based on Gray's life where only the names seem to have changed, including even Gray's own character, named Brewster North. But far more importantly, what we see in the novel is a craft that goes well beyond merely retelling Gray's life under the thin disguise of changed names.

Two general points help to explain the novel as a whole. First, it literally begins and ends with the same three sentences: "And I half dreamed and half remembered Mom's never-ending passion for the sea. We were all on our way to Gram's summer house in Sakonnet, Rhode Island, in our wooden-slatted '38 Ford beach wagon. What a car!" Life, for Gray, is a clearly cyclical thing, and memories repeat themselves in a back-and-forth pattern that exists in a creative jumble even as time moves forward. The second point is that within and alongside this framing loop of memory, the narrative goes basically from beginning to end, relying more on chronology than on the loops and warps of time and memory that Gray presents in his monologues. There's a purpose for that decision, given that Gray has Brewster regularly remind the reader that the odyssey he experiences has a built-in destiny to it. Watching melted snow runoff from the window of a bus while visiting the Himalayas and descending literally from the top of the world, Brewster observes:

> I wanted now to flow down with it, follow it down the mountain all the way to New York. I had no idea where it was leading me until I at last found myself at the bottom of the earth, lying naked in a cool stream. I had no idea about the long, dark, confusing route that would lead at last to the bottom of the Grand Canyon. Had I known ahead of time, I doubt I would have gotten on that bus in Ladakh at all. But one day in late June, Meg and I got on that bus and started down. We started home.

No fewer than six times does Brewster refer to this downward journey, from the high, vaulted Edenic ideal of northern India to the floor of the American Grand Canyon. This downstream pattern is one of a near infinity of possible ways of seeing his world, but it's a pattern that works for Gray, helping him to bring his many apparently random life experiences into some semblance of order. And that seems to have been the point both of the novel and of Gray's searching life in general. To find meaning means to be able to make sense of memory. That's Gray's life in art.

For example, prior to moving up in elevation to the Himalayan plateaus, Brewster provides a lengthy observation:

> As I look back at that very turbulent period, I see me, in my quest for a vacation . . . [fall] from a place where I could look out over the surface of the planet to a place where I looked up at the vast layers of the inside of Mother Earth. It was a long and crazy fall that took a little over one year, almost ruined me, and finally ripped Meg and me apart. If you see any thread of meaning in it, so much the better. I'd have to call it some sort of penance. It was as though I felt compelled to create my own punishment, my own personal religion with its own sins and retributions. I was creating my own punishments for the fact that I hadn't saved my mother. I was attempting to put myself through what she had gone through—a fast and total disorientation of the senses.

And, finally, by the novel's end, lying in a stream in the canyon, his journey complete, he says, "I knew my fall was completed. I was at the end of that long, crazy fit of perpetual motion. I had fallen from the top of the world to the bottom, from the Himalayan breast of the Mother to the deep, deep place of her canyon."

His own mother remains deeply embedded in Gray's memory. Unable to alter history, Gray of course is unable to alter his relationship with his mother or to avert her eventual suicide. But what Gray can do is raise his life experiences to meaningful levels that nearly approach mythology itself. From major events like his mom's suicide to minor happenings throughout his life, by giving them order, he gives himself the opportunity to tolerate the memories that he can't escape. That's how Gray's art saved him from a life of overwhelmingly consuming regret. If there's a reason for something, then there's less need for guilt.

Brewster's own life is intertwined in the novel with the life of America in general, as most of Gray's work invariably is. One of the many characters Brewster meets along the way is the self-named Mustang Sally, one of many free spirits who have made Santa Cruz, California their home. When Sally and Brewster eventually say their good-byes as Brewster prepares to travel across America back to New York, Mustang Sally calls America "Mother." This spurs Brewster to muse, "I could hardly think of what was left of America as a mother, but for her sake I put on a smile and tried." We find out that the novel is set in 1976, the American bicentennial. It's a year of American celebration but also a year of American crisis, including recession and post-Vietnam War self-doubt. Through Brewster we see Gray experiencing a parallel series of paradoxical feelings, confident in his roots but full of doubt regarding how he is (or is not) living up to expectations.

Brewster's particular life and America's bicentennial self-promotion frequently collide, especially when Brewster is particularly hungry to make sense of his life. For example, halfway through his narrative, on his way to his dad and new stepmother's house, Brewster observes, "I've lost the linear order of my memory, and so I'm assuming I was very confused in that bicentennial summer." While home, Brewster reacquaints himself with his detached father, giving him numerous subtle barbs regarding Dad's lack of personal warmth and ultimate complicity in the suicide of Brewster's mom. Gray's own guilt remains high, especially since he has to live with the fact that he ran away from home (in his twenties) to escape his mom and was actually on vacation in Mexico when she committed suicide. Brewster's similar highly dysfunctional recollections destroy his ability to seek meaningful employment (he abandoned his mother to go to Houston to become an actor), a meaningful/satisfying vacation (since he was on his first vacation when Mom died), or meaningful relationships (all his girlfriends remind him of Mom). Dealing with this triangulation is central to Brewster's life.

Longing for a sense of belonging and a sense of well-being and comfort, Brewster tries all sorts of "cures." A flash of memory surfaces when he is in an Amsterdam bathhouse about to indulge in sex with another man. He reflects upon the "gruntings and moanings and the strangest of primordial smells," commenting:

> It wasn't bad. It was only new, or maybe not so much new as it was tapping some deep recollection of how everything must have first smelled when I was squeezing out of Mom, that one and only time, and then just for a moment I had a flash of how incredible my birth had been, how I had been right down in it all. Dad had only put his cock in there, and maybe his tongue, but I and my brothers had actually lived inside that place, and we had swum out of it, squeezed out of it. We had the whole experience. And that, I thought, was where I remembered this smell from.

This first memory of the world and of his bond to his mother is what Brewster longs to recapture. Everything was in order then, even the simple perfection of his mother. But as his mother began to disintegrate, so did Brewster's chances of smoothly transferring into a normal life on his own.

D. W. Winnicott, the psychoanalyst whose work Gray read with increasing interest as he grew older, describes a stage of infant disillusionment that is crucial to adult normalcy. It involves the mother needing to wean her child "by adapting less and less completely, gradually, according to the infant's growing ability to deal with her failure." Most of the opening of the novel reveals the extent to which Brewster's (Gray's) mom did not properly psychologically wean him, insisting instead that they remain interdependent even until her suicide, well into Brewster's twenties. This relationship leaves Brewster longing for what he remembered at birth, that perfect sense of being and belonging that apparently "properly" socialized citizens have given up on (or outgrown) long ago. This is Brewster's/Gray's singular torment. But it's also what inspires

Brewster/Gray. Brewster/Gray refuses to give up on finding what was lost.

Brewster does go through occasional phases that approach normalcy, like when he settles into New York with Meg for a "life of moderation and in-betweens." It parallels the life of his grandfather Benton (his mom's dad), who "did nothing in excess. . . . He was excessively unexcessive." But the longing for a return to the totally immersed harmony of an unbounded life of interdependence, like what he experienced with his mother as a newborn child, remains strong.

Brewster believes he's found that when he meets Rex (presumably a fictionalized version of Richard Schechner) and joins his group as it prepares *The Tower*, a performance based on the biblical Tower of Babel. It is set in a mythic or biblical time when all humanity was once united in total harmony by a common language. But when *The Tower* is taken on the road, audiences attack the piece as pornographic, and the experience quickly "turned into the story of the Expulsion" instead: "We had come face-to-face with America and they had found us lacking." This rejection leads Brewster to lose faith in Rex, his group, and American idealism in general in a single blow.

Brewster next tries LSD, sex, and a Zen retreat, and while all provide him with glimpses of what he seeks, none is sustainable or complete. Throughout the novel Brewster refers to a longing for Bali and its much-advertised life of paradise. It is his reprise whenever the current solution fails. Curiously, though, he never literally makes it to Bali.

Brewster instead goes to India in hopes of finding answers at the ashram of Shree Rajneesh. He hears from the Bhagwan that "if you are in agony and anxiety and pain I want you to realize that it is because you have chosen it. . . . You have to realize that only in sorrow can you *be*. When you are in ecstasy you disappear. Suffering gives you a definition. It makes you feel solid." Brewster concedes that he exists through his sorrow, and he also concedes, "To take it away would be to take away me." But then he notes, "I'm sure that's the way Mom must have felt the night she got up, climbed into the car, and started it for the last time." But while he may want to lose himself in the world, to immerse himself in experience, he doesn't want to obliterate himself into nonbeing. That is the option his mom selected. But that occurred only after she'd found no escape from the entrapment of stultifying marriage and a self-condemning religion (Christian Science). Perhaps as a result of being the child of "excessively unexcessive" parents, Brewster's mom was perpetually in need of intimacy, of contact with others. It's this need that had her clinging to her children—and especially to Brewster—and it's what led to disturbing reactions on the part of her children, in particular Brewster. But Brewster observes: "I'm not saying Mom did this consciously, but some dark unconscious shadow was operating through her, a shadow that she never came to recognize because of her constant search for the divine transcendent life. That shadow was a part of her, but she could not see it, because in Christian Science she was taught only to look for the light side, only for the good." Like the Bhagwan, Mom could only see that darkness and suffering was a self-inflicted delusion to be overcome through positive escapism. Her inability to overcome the darkness was her own fault. Or so she thought.

The Bhagwan promotes another equally disturbing idea: the value of fully living in the moment, with utter disregard for the past or the future. Brewster fully rejects the idea of forgetting the past, though he often finds himself pursuing exactly the kind of anesthesia that Rajneesh prescribes: "What does Rajneesh mean by 'Live in the moment, forget the past,' and then he goes and sells you video tapes of your past moments with him! All moments are not equal! There are some that will stand out in memory, and we have a memory for a reason." Blissful forgetfulness may lead to a sort of peace, but it also obliterates the self that is generated by memory. Finally, the entire process of obliterating self-consciousness and self-awareness, tantalizing as it may be, seems to generate as many problems as it promises to cure.

India will never fulfill Brewster's longings, a point made clear the moment he first sets foot on that subcontinent: "This was an overpopulated world, and it immediately brought up those old colonialist attitudes in me: There must be some order imposed here immediately. There are too many people in the world! Humankind is a virus that must be stopped! . . . I never sensed my father in me more—that constant, almost fascistic craving he had for order and control at all cost." His Western mind is simply not equipped to understand, much less to embrace, the Indian solution to the world's woes. Transcendence may be an ideal often placed before us, but it seems ultimately unattainable for the Western mind. Other alternatives surely must be available.

Brewster and Meg try one more option that India has to offer. They leave the overpopulated cities and travel into the wide-open, undeveloped spaces of Kashmir, described at first as something like the American Wild West. But then Brewster sees it as much more, fully blossoming with innocence and charm. As Brewster and Meg move into Ladakh, near the Tibetan border, they enter a "miraculous landscape" that, Brewster reports, "cured me of thoughts of my past and future. Like the sea, it washed all thoughts out of my mind." Taking in the awe-inspiring, simple beauty of the rugged landscape and expansive night sky, Brewster observes, "I was just seeing, and seeing was believing." This is only a momentary revelation, however. It is quickly overshadowed by Brewster's native host introducing them to his "household shrine," which Brewster describes as "an in-house, all-purpose, connected, working religion, complete and without doubt." He continues:

No TV or telephone on snowbound winter days, but infinite connection of mind instead. No one worshiped in that room alone. They worshiped with all of the snowbound Ladakhans scattered in their mud abodes. It was a giant connection through ritual and prayer, and this is when I had my first dose of loneliness, as I looked back on America, and saw that we were only connected by machines now.

The rituals and practices marketed in the Indian lowlands for Western tourists seeking "truth" is here simply and quietly supplanted by a virtually prelapsarian worldview uncorrupted by modern worldly concerns. Brewster reports he began to suffer from "scopophilia": "I was caught in my eyes, looking and looking, looking at all these happy people everywhere, and I was getting very lonely because I knew that I was not one of them." Seeing may be believing, but (as *Gray's Anatomy* demonstrated) it isn't living. The result is: "I had the feeling that in order to be happy anywhere I had to get back to America, to figure out what went wrong and why I couldn't smile in the streets of New York and say 'Good day, good day' to all the people passing by there. Let the people in Ladakh carry on in their own happiness without me. I knew it was impossible to ever be a part of them." Brewster needs to find an American equivalent in order to hope for happiness. Importing it would be impossible.

Brewster does take something from his experiences in India besides a feeling of being an outsider amid an urge to belong. As he tries to find himself by engaging in a same-sex encounter in the baths of Amsterdam, he observes, "I hadn't realized that my time in India had feminized me." Entering that strange new world of India with the eyes of a colonialist oppressor inclining toward bringing order to India's chaos, he grows receptive to the forces that operate and even somehow cohere in India without the domineering imposition of Western systems of rationality. It seems that what singularly impresses Brewster is India's chaotic order, which for many is a contradiction in terms. He sees an order that functions on a sort of sliding scale between radical, rationalist, Western order and irrational Eastern disorder, between actively masculine (Western) power and control and passively feminine (Eastern) response and adaptation. Brewster did, of course, previously intuit such a dichotomy, but he only sensed it as an either/or proposition: either be a man or—impossible for him—be a woman. Subscribing to this Western cultural way of seeing things, he struggled to assume his position in the world as an orderly masculine being, sensing all along that he wasn't fully suited to it. His disinclination, coupled with some feminizing finishing touches from his time in India, results in Brewster's realization that he has to come to terms with his previously buried feminized center. It's a realization that leads him to fall into a passively receptive sexual encounter in the Amsterdam bathhouse, controlled by another man.

But even on his return to New York, he hasn't yet fully comprehended the potential of becoming a male with "feminized" sensibilities, still seeing his choices as being either a "man" or a needy and embarrassing feminized freak of nature: "God, was Meg organized. If I was chaos, she was all order and meaning. She got me through customs and had even made plans ahead of time for our friend Barney to pick us up at the airport." He is clearly wounded by any thought that he might be less than a fully organized, independent man.

Brewster looks for that ideal of composure and masculine self-assurance by trying to capture a freeze-frame life of order that he envisions as he reads Keats's famous poem, "Ode on a Grecian Urn." During his stint as an art model, frozen in a sensual but self-assured pose before the admiring gaze of art students, he says, "I'd turn into a soft, languid statue, like one of the figures on Keats's Grecian urn. I'd sit in the most delicious places, the place of greatest hope, the purest, most delicious place of suspended desire and anticipation, that place just before action destroys perfection and leads to completion of desire and the inevitable corruption and disappointment of consequence." And later, while in Ladakh, he observes, "suddenly that enigmatic end to Keats's 'Ode on a Grecian Urn' made sense, as it crossed my mind like a little ticker tape: '"Beauty is truth, truth beauty,"—that is all/Ye know on earth, and all ye need to know'." It's a tantalizing dream of a stable life without chance or risk of failure, an existence without the dangers of, but also without the opportunities for, change. Finally, it really isn't "life" at all but a mere idealized fiction of life, an existence separated from anything that involves past, present, or future.

Unbeknownst to the Brewster caught up in Keatsian longings for static, orderly, changeless infinity is a vast new alternative. Always interested in storytelling and frequently in an on-again, off-again occupation as an actor, Brewster ultimately succeeds at incorporating time back into his existence, not by way of Rajneesh's proposal—to obliterate the past and only live in the present—and not by Keats's dream of timeless perfection, but by learning to incorporate all time (past, present, and future) into ongoing moments of presence. In fact, when he is struggling with Rajneesh's message, he meets a woman, Melvy, who reminds him: "[Marcel] Proust had demonstrated how the present always turns into the past before you can make any statement about it. . . . She was adamant about Proust and how well he'd written of how there can be no peace of mind when it comes to love because all love is only the beginning of more desire, which is endless." Living life, of which love is the pinnacle, mandates forever moving forward into inevitable pasts even as one exists in the present.

Ultimately Brewster seems to learn this once he returns to New York, recovers from his nervous breakdown, and begins working with a less-than-helpful therapist, when "in some simple pop-psychology way, I had an epiphany." He realizes that "running away to the Alamo Theatre" in Houston to escape his mother's decline and breakdown "had inhibited and prevented me from fighting for the role of Konstantin Gavrilovich in that production of *The Sea Gull* years ago." He adds, "I had flown the nest to become a successful actor and I had failed, and now I had to go back and succeed on my own terms. I had slipped into a postadolescent passive state of unproductive fantasy, which I'd not been able to come out of for years. I had to stage my own version of *The Sea Gull*, and only when I did that would I be cured." He engages in what amounts to a Wooster Group-style performance, using *The Sea Gull* as inspiration and incorporating the play into his own experiences. He essentially brings the past into the present by blending his life into art. Furthermore, he also bridges the chasm between the masculine and feminine.

Before making a full commitment to doing the play, Brewster dreams that "Meg and I were both standing naked and her belly was very full, and I was standing there with my hand on her belly and I was all three of us. I was me and I was Meg and I was the child in her." He concludes: "I knew, too, that this dream meant I was to play all the characters in *The Sea Gull* and that Meg would direct it and we would be pregnant together with this play. I know this may sound like a big leap to you, but believe me . . . I was sure that I had to be directed by Meg in our experimental version of *The Sea Gull* to clear myself of the past." He describes the results: "In the end, our production of *The Sea Gull* was a mad deconstruction, a rambling hodgepodge of mixed emotion, straightforward acting, and a lot of direct autobiographical address. Meg in her own ingenious ordering way had been able to frame it and put it all together." The production becomes a minor success. It also becomes a means of emancipation for Brewster from the haunting memories of his mother. And ultimately, it helps him to break his dependence on his mother surrogate, Meg. He has found a way to order his chaotic life and is able to go on a cross-country journey to California on his own, leaving Meg, his stormy mistress, Sherry, and his dependence anxieties behind. Healthy interdependence, it appears, can only be achieved by first breaking the *need* to rely on one-way flows of dependence and nurture.

In California, Brewster meets and is paternally drawn to a young child, Shanti, at which time "the whole world fell into place" as a result of falling "totally in love with this little kid." It seems that Brewster, finally, has found a way to move beyond his own phobias of self-preservation and for once to project beyond himself in the world at large, as presumably he had done in those heady days performing his version of *The Sea Gull*. Brewster, it seems, is finally evolving into a self able to turn outward rather than remain inwardly focused, and the outward turn results in a healthy affection for an other from which he expects nothing in return and thereby receives far more than ever expected. It is a turn toward two-way input and output that accepts and even cherishes the unexpected without fear of consequences. Brewster actually begins to look forward to the unexpected.

As Brewster is returning to New York City, he has a run-in with the law, is thrown into a Las Vegas jail, and spends eight days there until he finally makes bail. This would have been a cataclysmic event for the former Brewster. But surprisingly, it doesn't destroy the current Brewster. Rather, "for the first time in months I was experiencing a feeling of being centered." He adds, "I sensed that this was a necessary break from my perpetual motion. I now had a new order, a new force upon me." In addition to accepting this new imposition of order upon himself—in the form of a jail cell—he comes to understand how to "manage" time, as he is required to wake up at 5:30 a.m. each day simply to do nothing: "Maybe that's what they meant by 'doing time.' They did time to you. They made you feel time." If his art helped Brewster feel the moment as an onstage performer, here in lockup Brewster feels time by watching it go by and being aware of it for perhaps the first time. Even the uncertainty attached to embracing this decay-generating phenomenon doesn't unsettle him. Among the things he does in jail is write letters he will never mail, including one to Rajneesh, where Brewster tells him that "he was wrong and Proust was right—there is no such thing as being in the present." Brewster realizes that the "present" is an infinite accumulation of presents collectively known as the past. The self performs in the present, but the present is nothing more than memories recollected and re-collecting in each present moment. Brewster observes, "I was beginning to be aware of how my imagination was often more vivid and exciting than the actual experiences I had in the outside world, that the essence of my life was imagining the places I was not in. . . . For the first time in years I felt a strange freedom. I felt incredibly free in the Las Vegas jail." Imagination as repository for memories brings past and present together and brings Brewster finally to life, in of all places a prison cell. His life is now minus the anxiety that comes when time seems to be squandered. And the burden of the past also is lifted as his memories are given their due, permitted to be recalled but not to enchain and entrap him.

Freed from his jail cell, Brewster travels to the Grand Canyon, that physical low point toward which he's been headed ever since leaving the Himalayan top of the world. Having completed his hike down the Grand Canyon, Brewster announces "everything came together in the present" and then concludes: "For the first time in my life, I realized something mattered to me. It was the sharing of this story, the story of all this, the true story of some of the things that happened to me while living on this earth." And as noted earlier, the novel ends literally as it began, but the ending hooks up to the opening with entirely new meaning: the novel that opens without direction, meaning, order, now reopens at its conclusion, filled with direction, meaning, and order. Life lived only for the moment pales in comparison to a life now lived and simultaneously consciously appreciated as it slips into the past. Brewster experiences a "Matisse-like chain dance" of presents turning to pasts that pave the way for still more presents. Having begun in the clouds of idealistic abstractions, Brewster finds himself in the majestic bowels of the American landscape, lying in a stream that for him figuratively began on the slopes of the world's highest mountains. Brewster has literally come back down to earth. And in it, he finds full contentment.

Gray's Novel Perspective: East Meets West

The long descent from the heights of the Himalayas into the bowels of the American Southwest that Gray traces in *Impossible Vacation* can be seen as akin to the spiritual venture Gray pursued throughout his works. He was introduced to Buddhism by Richard Schechner in the late 1960s and continued yoga exercises throughout his life. While fully subscribing to Buddhism seemed never to interest Gray, he was influenced by it and incorporated many of its ideas into his art. Even though he was lured into its embrace on many occasions in his work, Buddhism never seemed to take permanent hold. One possible reason is that Gray was always on the lookout for a "native" explanation to life, a way of looking at the world that aligned with his Western, American upbringing.

His upbringing was of a rather unusual sort, given that his mother converted to Christian Science as a young adult and raised her children to be Christian Scientists. It's a rationalist, fundamentalist form of Christianity that, according to founder Mary Baker Eddy, reveals truth "by demonstration—by healing both disease and sin." The physical and the spiritual have curious attachments; Eddy reports having uncovered the secrets to "the treatment of disease as well as sin," both of which "lose their reality in human consciousness and disappear as naturally and as necessarily as darkness gives place to light and sin to reformation." Key to this entwinement of the physical and spiritual is the belief that "the discords of corporeal sense must yield to the harmony of spiritual sense." In other words, the body interferes with the progress of human spirituality and must be subordinated even to the point that its "illnesses" must be cured by faith rather than by physical treatments prescribed by the medical profession. Escaping physical ills by physical cures simply reinforces attachment to the physical. And that's the thing most to be avoided.

If Gray ever had faith in this view of existence, it deteriorated as he watched his almost fanatically dedicated mother slip deeper and deeper into insanity against all the faith-filled, nonphysical assurances that Christian Science could offer. Gray's practical skepticism, however, seems to have been only part of the problem he had with Christian Science, since it argued so radically against his own emerging beliefs in the centrality of the body. If the spiritual world is good and real while the physical world is its opposite, then the best we can do is merely tolerate our time in the physical world. This radical dualism troubled Gray throughout his life.

Eastern religions, in their popular forms at least, recognize dualistic elements like body and soul, mind and spirit, good and evil, consciousness and unconsciousness, life and death. However, they see these elements not as dualities in the manner that Westerners see them. It's not a matter of something being either one or the other. Rather, Eastern thought sees these elements as *polarities*, parts of a long continuum of greater or lesser being. So body and soul are interdependent elements, and one without the other is virtually impossible. Pursuing the purity of one to the exclusion of the other is nothing more than human folly. The idea of a fully integrated existence that embraces everything in a dynamic dance along a sliding scale of forever becoming—that is what struck Gray as crucial.

Gray's life was full of extremes along these various polarized scales of being. He often sought things like pure mind, soul, or consciousness and then turned with equal dedication to mindlessly pure physicality. Experiencing those extremes certainly offered him a whole universe of riveting stories to tap into. But he eventually came to realize that the tantalizing pursuit of excess merely identified boundaries within which he would need to find his "place." In *Impossible Vacation*, he expresses his amazement at the contentment he *witnessed* at the top of the world. But from there he begins a long descent that lands him in the middle of the geological origins of America. And there, for the first time, he actually *experiences* contentment. It's as if Gray carried that Eastern concept of adjustable polarities with him in his descent into "America" and injected the American landscape—at its bedrock—with a newly integrated vision of existence. No longer seeking a life of extremes, he settles into a life that embraces everything surrounding him, combining the spiritual and the physical into one interconnected experience. This seems to be the picture that Gray offers us in *Impossible Vacation*. He imports an "immigrant" idea of integrated harmony and strives to make it "American."

This is also the picture that Gray created throughout his career on the stage. He first haltingly tries to embrace the Western/American concept of dualism, doing his best to choose one side over the other. But he always slips into almost despairing indecision because he's simply not built to make such a choice. What seems to be a human failing, however, invariably leads to his salvation. He and we come to realize that Gray's struggles actually identifies a misdirected American *culture* rather than a misdirected, truant *citizen* of that culture. The culture works to segregate and then privilege one side over the other, encouraging us either to pursue creature comfort *or* spiritual well-being. But rarely (if ever) do the two unite. Struggling to reconcile this "split personality" that is our culture, Spalding Gray eventually finds contentment in an integration that America seems to have given up on but would do well to reclaim. That, finally, is where Gray wants America to go.

Postscript

An American Original

In 2000, Gray went to Broadway and took on the role of Bill Russell, an idealistic U.S. presidential candidate, in Gore Vidal's 1960 political drama, *The Best Man*. Russell has a skeleton in his closet—having recently sought therapy for a nervous breakdown—and his unscrupulous opponent, Joe Cantrell (played by Chris Noth), intends to use that information to discredit Russell. In a final twist of selflessness, Russell decides to go public with his past, withdraw from the race, and back a third candidate against Cantrell. The play fittingly reminds us of Gray's own idealism, his affection for the "American way," and his desire to do the right thing in life as well as in his art.

On June 22, 2001, Spalding Gray was in a crippling car accident in Ireland while on holiday celebrating his sixtieth birthday. His recuperation never successfully alleviated the excruciating pain, and he is reported to have unsuccessfully attempted suicide on at least three occasions. In September 2002, it's reported that while at his Long Island home, he took his small sailboat out and jumped into the sound, but climbed back aboard when he wasn't overtaken by ocean swells. A week later he contemplates jumping off the Sag Harbor Bridge, but a concerned woman alerts police, and he is talked out of jumping. On October 15, 2003, Spalding does jump from the Sag

Harbor Bridge after talking to a passerby, but a police officer and a civilian pull him from the water.

On Saturday, January 10, 2004, reported to be the coldest day of the winter, Gray is last seen at his SoHo apartment shortly after 6:30 p.m. He had just gone to see the film *Big Fish* with his family and stayed in town to catch a flight to Aspen, Colorado, for a skiing holiday with friends. Later that evening (around 1:00 a.m., now January 11), Gray calls his six-year-old son, Theo, to say how much he loves him. A couple reports having talked to Spalding on the Staten Island ferry on that January 10 evening. A worker recalls having seen him on the ferry several days earlier. Some later thought he was on the ferry planning his jump. On March 8, 2004, Gray's body is pulled from East River.

Although he clearly had been obsessed with death since his mother's 1967 suicide, it didn't seem that Gray was destined to the same end. Until the accident in Ireland, his chaotic life had settled into a loving family arrangement that made Gray quite happy with living and less interested in generating new monologues. Ironically, the accident provided Gray with material to add to his career, and he had in fact found time, energy, and inclination to work on a new piece, *Life Interrupted*, after the accident.

But the pain and subsequent unsuccessful surgeries and treatments were just too much for Spalding to continue to endure. Trying to pinpoint why he took his life is very likely an idle task. Some say he was influenced by *Big Fish*, a film about a man who decides literally to dive into his own imagination and escape the inevitable doom of his declining health. Whether this was *the* reason or *a* reason, whether Gray's death had anything to do with his mother's suicide, or whether it was simply a matter of ending the pain, we'll never know for sure. Maybe it was simply "idiopathic," a term that Gray seemed to like, meaning having no actual or single known cause.

Whatever the case may be, Gray's own work is a testament to his own recognition of the vast complexities involved in understanding the motives behind human behavior. In an interview with David

Savran in the early 1980s, Gray spoke of how human action is often the result of a complicated matrix of reasons:

> I don't think there's any one reason for my mother's suicide. And there's no reason for my collapse after India. It was a collision of events, including diet, that sometimes happens in peoples' lives. And if they're young enough, they're resilient. I think that death is often about that, many things colliding. For my mother, many things collided over a two-year period. And for me it was over a two-year period, too, '76 and '77, the life experience from which the material for the monologue *India and After* was taken.

In *Rumstick Road*, Gray and LeCompte used a tape-recorded conversation between Gray and his mother's psychiatrist, who coldly and clinically defends the failed treatment she's been given and then tries to comfort Spalding by saying, "Don't be frightened by a hereditary disposition. . . . You may not necessarily get it." The fact that he did commit suicide, of course, does not necessarily confirm that he had a hereditary disposition.

Matters of body and spirit may actually reduce themselves to heredity in some instances, perhaps even in this instance, but the matrix of complex interactions that was Gray's life suggests that more than mere heredity was involved. What we do know is that Spalding Gray touched many lives, as a man, a father, a husband, and an artist. He touched everyone he came in contact with.

Life Interrupted reminds us all that the typical American urge to build walls and fortify defenses against life's unexpected turns really is little more than classic self-deception. Life comes at us from too many angles and too quickly to ward off, control, or defend against. The myth of the strong masculine American boldly striding across the landscape in full control of his destiny is just that: a myth. Throughout his career Spalding Gray put that myth to the test, trying it on for size and seeing if it "fit" him like it was supposed to. And when it didn't, he struggled to determine whether the misfit was his fault

Spalding Gray (1941–2004). (Photo by W. Demastes.)

or whether it was because the cut of the cloth that he was trying on was somehow wrong.

In the end, Gray left it up to his audiences to decide whether he was just a quirky eccentric or whether his "eccentricities" were more a matter of a confused cultural perspective. Maybe within a less individualized world picture, Gray was the most normal and sane man in our midst, and maybe what he showed us were the flaws inherent in that thing known as self-confident, monolithic, colossal "America." Have we been trying to be something that we're really not supposed to try to be? Is it possible that the masculine cult of stand-alone autonomy needs to be reassessed and modified? Maybe the "American" way of dealing with the world should be replaced with a more integrated awareness that life is best when living is done with and around others. Maybe that individualized American pursuit of happiness should be replaced with something like the pursuit of group harmony, communal contentment, or even something as retrograde and "old fashioned" as family bliss. Spalding Gray found his happiness in the fold of a fairly traditional family unit, but he adjusted certain roles and challenged certain conventions within that institution. And by doing so he showed us that America is perhaps less in need of some countercultural, 1960s-style revolution than it is in need of major self-evaluation, increased self-awareness, and a willingness to adjust itself without necessarily altering what it is at heart. If freedom is the American dream, along with it should go an abiding sense of American responsibility. Privilege has its pleasures, but it also comes with duties and obligations. *That*, in the final analysis, seems to have been Spalding Gray's "message" in a nutshell. Gray's art took us through all the complexities, pitfalls, and paradoxes of unearthing and then trying to live up to this rather simple idea, reminding us all in his monologues that most things in life are truly easier said than done.

Then there was that other message, Gray's insistence that memory is the essence of life. If true—and it's a hard point to reject—then we all should be comforted to know that the best part of Spalding Gray lives on in the vivid, rich, and varied memories he left for us to visit and revisit for years to come.

Appendix

Gray Chronologized

1941
Spalding Rockwell Gray born June 5, in Barrington, Rhode Island.

1960
In his senior year of high school, earns a role in *The Curious Savage* by John Patrick and is encouraged by director Ruth Hartz.

1961
Graduates from boarding school in Maine, at nearly age twenty.
Matriculates at Boston University. Fails to gain admission into the theater program and transfers to Emerson College.

1965
Graduates from Emerson College.
Secures a repertory position at the Alley Theatre, Houston, Texas. Plays lead angel in *The World of Sholom Aleichem* and improvises offstage sounds for *The Seagull*. Earns Actor's Equity card.

1967
Meets Elizabeth LeCompte in Saratoga, New York, where Gray has a role in Tennessee Williams's *The Battle of Angels* at the

Café Lena Gallery Theatre. Elizabeth graduates from Skidmore College. Travels with her to San Miguel, Mexico, that summer.

Spalding's mother, Bette Gray, commits suicide following a second nervous breakdown, while Spalding is in Mexico.

Spalding and Elizabeth move to 6th Street and Avenue D, New York City.

1968

Earns an off-Broadway role in *Tom Paine* by Tom O'Horgan (March).

Earns an off-Broadway role in Robert Lowell's adaptation of Nathaniel Hawthorne's *Endecott and the Red Cross* (May).

Richard Schechner's The Performance Group buys the Performing Garage at 33 Wooster Street in SoHo and produces *Dionysus in 69*. Spalding and Elizabeth LeCompte admire the work.

1970

Spalding is called by Schechner to audition as a replacement for MacDuff in The Performance Group's *Makbeth* four days prior to opening. He wins the part, joins the Group, and later plays Malcolm. Elizabeth LeCompte joins The Performance Group shortly thereafter.

Gray and LeCompte work with Schechner on *Commune* (opens December 17).

Film credit: "Radical" in *Cowards.*

1972

Film credit: "Radical at Party" in *Love-In '72.*

1973

Performs as "Hoss" in The Performance Group's production of Sam Shepard's *The Tooth of Crime* (premiere March 7).

Film credit: "George" in *The Farmer's Daughter.*

1974

With LeCompte and two other members of The Performance Group, begins development of *Sakonnet Point*, the first piece of what will become *The Rhode Island Trilogy*, a LeCompte/Gray collaboration loosely based on Gray's life.

1975

Performs as "Swiss Cheese" in The Performance Group's production of Brecht's *Mother Courage and Her Children* (premiere February 24).

Sakonnet Point (part of *The Rhode Island Trilogy*) performed, the inaugural production of what will become The Wooster Group.

1976

Goes to India with The Performance Group, staging *Mother Courage* throughout the country. Returns home suffering from a nervous breakdown.

Film credits: "Rick Carson" in *Little Orphan Dusty*; "Airline Passenger" (uncredited) in *The Opening of Misty Beethoven*.

1977

With LeCompte, officially cofounds The Wooster Group.

Rumstick Road (part of *The Rhode Island Trilogy*) performed.

TV credit: "Himself" in *Saturday Night Live* (Episode #2.22).

1978

Performs in The Performance Group's production of Terry Curtis Fox's *Cops*.

Nayatt School (part of *The Rhode Island Trilogy*) performed.

Film credit: "Client" (uncredited) in *Maraschino Cherry*.

1979

Serves as artist-in-residence at Bennington College.

Meets and begins living with Renée Shafransky.

Performs as "Bishop" in The Performance Group's production of Genet's *The Balcony*.

Point Judith (epilogue to *The Rhode Island Trilogy*) performed, his last Wooster Group piece.

Performs *India and After (America)*, his first work unaffiliated with The Wooster Group.

Performs first actual monologue, *Sex and Death to the Age 14*.

1980

Richard Schechner leaves The Performance Group, which disbands
and leaves all properties to The Wooster Group (the actual
corporate name of the company even during the Performance
Group years).
First performs *Interviewing an Audience*.
First performs *A Personal History of the American Theatre*.

1981

First performs *In Search of the Monkey Girl*.

1983

Film credit: "Voice" in *Variety*.

1984

Film credit: "United States Consul" in *The Killing Fields*.

1985

Swimming to Cambodia first performed and published.
Film credits: "Himself" in *The Communists Are Comfortable*; "Terry
Norfolk" in *Hard Choices*; "Dr. Rodney" in *Seven Minutes in
Heaven*; "Travel Agent" in *Almost You*.

1986

Marissa Maier, Spalding's future stepdaughter, is born. They will
first meet in 1990.
Rivkala's Ring, a one-person play commissioned and performed
by The Acting Company, based on a short story by Chekhov, is
published in the collection *Orchards*.
Sex and Death to the Age 14 published.
Film credit: "Earl Culver" in *True Stories*.
TV credits: "Himself" in *Late Night with David Letterman* (30
July); "Talk Show Host (Voice)" in *What You Mean We? (Alive
from Off Center)*.

1987

Spalding Gray's Swimming to Cambodia, directed by Jonathan
    Demme (film), released.
TV credits: "Talk Show Host (Voice)" in *What You Mean We?*;
    "Edward Niles" in *I Confess (Spenser for Hire)*; "Gary" in *Bedtime
    Story (Trying Times)*.

1988

Performs as "Stage Manager" in Tony-award winning revival of
    Thornton Wilder's *Our Town* (Lincoln Center).
Spalding Gray: Terrors of Pleasure, directed by Thomas Schlamme
    (film), released.
Film credits: "Reverend T. J. Cardew" in *Stars and Bars*; "Dr. Peter
    Epstein" in *Clara's Heart*; "Dr. Richard Milstein" in *Beaches*.

1989

Film credit: "Himself" in *Heavy Petting.*
TV credit: "Stage Manager" in *Our Town.*

1990

Film credit: "Himself" in *Caffe Lena.*
TV credit: "Frank Goodrich" in *The Image.*

1991

Marries Renée Shafransky.
Monster in a Box opens on Broadway.
TV credit: "Hobart" in *To Save a Child.*

1992

Spalding's father, Rockwell Gray, dies.
Kathie Russo gives birth to Spalding's child, Forrest, culminating an
    affair begun two years earlier.
Monster in a Box, directed by Nick Broomfield (film), released.
Monster in a Box published.

Impossible Vacation (novel) published.
Film credit: "Dr. Erdman" in *Straight Talk.*

1993
Gray's Anatomy opens on Broadway and is published.
Film credits: "Priest" in *Twenty Bucks*; "Doctor" in *The Pickle*; "Mr.
    Mungo in Room 310" in *King of the Hill.*
TV credit: "Sayre" in *Zelda.*

1994
Film credit: "Paul Bladden" in *The Paper.*

1995
Divorces Renée Shafransky.
Film credits: "Walter Curl" in *Bad Company*; "Jeremy Watt" in
    Beyond Rangoon; "Louis" in *Drunks.*

1996
It's a Slippery Slope opens on Broadway.
Gray's Anatomy, directed by Steven Soderbergh (film), released.
Film credits: "Jimmy Zip" in *Jimmy Zip*; "Simon Veatch" in
    Diabolique; "Jack's Dad" in *Glory Daze.*

1997
Theo, Spalding's second son, is born.
In an interview, provides his own epitaph: "An American Original:
    Troubled, Inner-Directed, and Cannot Type."
It's a Slippery Slope published.
Film credit: "Alfred" in *Bliss.*
TV credits: "Voice" in *The Telephone (The American Experience)*;
    "Dr. Jack Miller" in eight episodes of *The Nanny.*

1998
TV credit: "Dr. Jack Miller" in one episode of *The Nanny.*

1999
Morning, Noon and Night opens on Broadway.

TV credits: "Himself" in *New York: A Documentary Film (The American Experience)*; "Himself" in *The 20th Century: Yesterday's Tomorrows*; "Professor Beaumont" in *Out of Their League (The Mike O'Malley Show)*.

2000
Performs in revival of Gore Vidal's 1960 political drama *The Best Man* on Broadway.
Morning, Noon and Night published.

2001
Is crippled in an automobile accident in Ireland (June 22).
Film credits: "Mr. Miranda" in *Julie Johnson*; "Scooter McCrae" in *Revolution #9*; "Professor Jackson" in *How High*; "Dr. Geisler" in *Kate and Leopold*.

2003
Marries Kathie Russo.
Film credit: "Dr. Calhoun" in *The Paper Mache Chase*.

2004
Goes missing (January 11).
Gray's body is pulled from the East River (March 8).

2005
Life Interrupted published.

2006
Leftover Stories to Tell, codirected by Kathleen Russo and Lucy Sexton, is performed in New York and Los Angeles, featuring varied casts reading from excerpted work left by Spalding Gray.
New York Mayor Michael Bloomberg declares June 5 "Spalding Gray Day," celebrating what would have been Gray's sixty-fifth birthday.

2007
Spalding Gray: Stories Left to Tell, based on excerpts from Gray's monologues, opens off Broadway at the Minetta Lane Theatre.

Concept by Kathie Russo, directed by Lucy Sexton. Ain Gordon wins OBIE Award for his role as "Journals."

2009

Life Interrupted, directed by Steven Soderbergh (film), scheduled to be released.

Notes

Foreword: Spalding

   x   "After the breakup": Richard Schechner, *Environmental Theater* (New York: Hawthorn Books, 1973), 273–274.

  xi   "Oh the entrances from the wings": The complete text of *Commune* plus director's notes can be found in *The Radical Theatre Notebook*, ed. Arthur Sainer (1975; reprint, New York: Applause Books, 2000), 172–221.

xiii   "In *Commune* I played": Quoted in Richard Schechner, "My Art in Life: Interviewing Spalding Gray," *The Drama Review* 46, no. 4 (2002): 160.

xiii   "[In *Tooth*] I do a very long soliloquy": Quoted in Schechner, "My Art in Life," 161.

1. Taking Middle America to SoHo

 16   "experienced a memory film," "no trouble editing," and "Very interesting": Spalding Gray, *Sex and Death to the Age 14* (New York: Vintage, 1986), x. Emphasis added.

 16   "can remember sitting up": Quoted in Judy Lauren Richheimer, "Spaulding [*sic*] Gray: A Personal History," *Other Stages* (16 Dec. 1982): 4.

20   "Traditional/New" chart: Richard Schechner, "Happenings,"
      1968, in Richard Schechner, *Public Domain: Essays on the The-
      atre* (Indianapolis: Bobbs-Merrill, 1969), 146. Reprinted by
      permission of Richard Schechner.

23   "First we sang the play": Richard Schechner, *Environmental
      Theater* (New York: Hawthorn Books, 1973), 234.

2. Incubating "Spalding Gray": The Wooster Group

32   "to be myself first": Spalding Gray, *Sex and Death to the Age 14*
      (New York: Vintage, 1986), xi.

33   "Richard Schechner . . . was a liberator": Spalding Gray,
      "About *Three Places in Rhode Island*," *The Drama Review* 23,
      no. 1 (1979): 32–33.

34   "it is a group autobiography": Gray, "About *Three Places*," 34.

34   "a silent mood piece," and "was about the child learning":
      Gray, *Sex and Death*, xi.

35   "improvisations were set and scored": Gray, *Sex and Death*, xi.

35   "took on no outside character," Gray, *Sex and Death*, xi.

35   "Much of *Nayatt School*": Gray, *Sex and Death*, xi.

37   "as a series of simple actions": Gray, "About *Three Places*," 36.

37   "what the audience saw": Gray, "About *Three Places*," 36.

38   "It became not the art": Gray, "About *Three Places*," 35.

39   "By chance": Gray, "About *Three Places*," 35.

39   "all of *Sakonnet Point*.": Gray, "About *Three Places*," 36.

39   "is more evocative in style": James Bierman, "*Three Places in
      Rhode Island*," *The Drama Review* 23, no. 1 (1979): 14 .

39   "value lay not in any": Arnold Aronson, "*Sakonnet Point*," *The
      Drama Review* 19, no. 4 (1975): 35.

40   "Often, what the audience saw": Gray, "About *Three Places*," 36.

40   "I think *Sakonnet Point* was": Gray, "About *Three Places*,"
      36–37.

40   "was very involving": Gray, "About *Three Places*," 37.

41   "Although the basis": Gray, "About *Three Places*," 38.

41   "confessional. . . . was also an act": Gray, "About *Three Places*,"
      38.

42   "Finally, if it is therapeutic": Gray, "About *Three Places*," 39.

42   "I felt and believed": Gray, "About *Three Places*," 39.

42   "the good-enough mother": Richard Schechner, "My Art in Life: Interviewing Spalding Gray," *The Drama Review* 46, no. 4 (December 2002): 171.

42   "There is no possibility whatever": D. W. Winnicott, *Playing and Reality* (New York: Basic Books, 1971), 10.

43   "I had a pretty normal": Quoted in Schechner, "My Art in Life," 155.

43   "are not just about the loss": Spalding Gray, "Perpetual Saturdays," *Performing Arts Journal* 6, no. 1 (1981): 42.

43   "I fantasize that if" and "the very act of": Gray, "Perpetual Saturdays," 48.

47   "an action that seemed" and "It was just a nice move": David Savran, *Breaking the Rules: The Wooster Group* (New York: Theatre Communications Group, 1986), 65.

47   "We worked on the situation": Spalding Gray, "Playwright's Notes," *Performing Arts Journal* 3, no. 2 (1978): 90.

54   "I'd like to register" and "to make a point of including": Michael Feingold, "Bad Rap," review of *Rumstick Road*, *Village Voice* (21 April 1980): 84.

55   "brutal act perhaps" and "but at the time": Spalding Gray, "Theatre's Brutal Acts," *Village Voice* (28 April 1980): 29.

55   "I don't like being made to participate": Michael Feingold, Response, *Village Voice* (28 April 1980): 29.

57   "Spalding was too sympathetic": Quoted in Savran, *Breaking the Rules*, 150.

57   "Spalding's a very wonderfully": Quoted in Savran, *Breaking the Rules*, 151.

3. Finding His American Voice: Gray's Early Monologues

62   "'Drop your character": Quoted in Richard Schechner, "My Art in Life: Interviewing Spalding Gray," *The Drama Review* 46, no. 4 (Winter 2002): 161.

62   "I really looked forward to it": Quoted in Schechner, "My Art in Life," 161.

62   "unlike his colleagues": Don Shewey, "The Year of Spalding Famously," *Village Voice* (13 November 1984): 99.

63   "It would be": Vincent Canby, "Soloists on the Big Screen," *New York Times* (22 March 1987): sec. 2, 19.

66   "I see the character": Spalding Gray, preface to *Rivkala's Ring*, in *Orchards: Seven Stories by Anton Chekhov and Seven Plays They Inspired* (New York: Knopf, 1986), 159.

68   "a very intense period": Quoted in David Savran, *Breaking the Rules: The Wooster Group* (New York: Theatre Communications Group, 1986), 71.

71   "When, for example": Savran, *Breaking the Rules*, 74.

72   "I hang out with the audience": Quoted in Schechner, "My Art in Life," 169.

73   "brings me back": Quoted in Judy Lauren Richheimer, "Spaulding [*sic*] Gray: A Personal History," *Other Stages* (16 Dec. 1982): 4.

73   "that says, 'What's going on'": Quoted in Schechner, "My Art in Life," 169.

74   "a feeling that the world" and "I told her I thought": Spalding Gray, *Sex and Death to the Age 14* (New York: Vintage, 1986), xii.

74   "transitional object" and "transitional phenomenon": Schechner, "My Art in Life," 171.

74   "inner reality": D. W. Winnicott, *Playing and Reality* (New York: Basic Books, 1971), 2.

4. Rediscovering America: Gray's Early "Autobiographical" Monologues

81   "When I sit down to talk": Quoted in Richard Schechner, "My Art in Life: Interviewing Spalding Gray," *The Drama Review* 46, no. 4 (Winter 2002): 166.

83   "For me there is nothing larger": Spalding Gray, "Perpetual Saturdays," *Performing Arts Journal* 6, no. 1 (1981): 48.

83 "Unfortunately, I simply" and "I have no doubt": David Guy, "From the Heart," *New York Times* (4 May 1986): sec. 7, 32.

85 "I can remember riding beside": Spalding Gray, *Sex and Death to the Age 14* (New York: Vintage, 1986), 3.

86 "the first death": Gray, *Sex and Death*, 3.

86 "knock ourselves out": Gray, *Sex and Death*, 4.

86 "and after the dog died": Gray, *Sex and Death*, 5.

86 "She said they were thinking": Gray, *Sex and Death*, 5.

86 "Their play seemed random": Spalding Gray, "Children of Paradise: Working with Kids," *Performing Arts Journal* 5, no. 1 (1980): 62.

87 "Out of nowhere, I said": Gray, *Sex and Death*, 31.

89 "One was of Prince Charles": Gray, *Sex and Death*, 20.

90 "My mother was a Christian Scientist": Gray, *Sex and Death*, 36.

90 "My father owned": Gray, *Sex and Death*, 53.

90 "I was a virgin": Gray, *Sex and Death*, 67.

91 "I knew my racing.": Gray, *Sex and Death*, 65.

92 "And shortly after": Gray, *Sex and Death*, 78.

93 "In order to calm myself": Gray, *Sex and Death*, 82.

94 "Usually, when I go to visit": Gray, *Sex and Death*, 81–82.

94 "became sexually obsessed": Gray, *Sex and Death*, 81.

94 "the following day" and "ends up in a Zendo": Gray, *Sex and Death*, 86.

94 "that all this time" and "When I realized": Gray, *Sex and Death*, 87.

95 "She . . . said that after we die": Gray, *Sex and Death*, 91.

97 "authentic experience": Gray, *Sex and Death*, 104.

98 "So I started making up": Gray, *Sex and Death*, 104.

99 "Hell City": Gray, *Sex and Death*), 105.

99 "an automatic ice machine": Gray, *Sex and Death*, 105–106.

99 "then I realized": Gray, *Sex and Death*, 107.

99 "a chance to reflect": Gray, *Sex and Death*, 111.

100 "For the first time": Gray, *Sex and Death*, 115.

100 "I wonder if": Gray, *Sex and Death*, 116.

101   "memories, stories, and associations": Spalding Gray, "excerpts from *A Personal History of the American Theatre*," *Performing Arts Journal* 8, no. 1 (1984): 36. A taped performance of *A Personal History of the American Theatre* (dated November 28, 1982) is in the Billy Rose Collection of the New York Public Library.

101   "The names of all these plays": Gray, "excerpts from *A Personal History of the American Theatre*," 36.

101   "I think that certain people": Gray, "excerpts from *A Personal History of the American Theatre*," 37.

102   "how he felt": Gray, *Sex and Death*, 149.

102   "people were throwing": Gray, *Sex and Death*, 122.

103   "Rocky is a specialist": Gray, *Sex and Death*, 123.

103   "This looks like": Gray, *Sex and Death*, 124.

103   "I drank can after can": Gray, *Sex and Death*, 125.

103   "at the last minute": Gray, *Sex and Death*, 126.

103   "a magic protective circle": Gray, *Sex and Death*, 126.

103   "true Western town": Gray, *Sex and Death*, 127.

103   "was nothing like": Gray, *Sex and Death*, 129.

104   "They told stories": Gray, *Sex and Death*, 130.

104   "the perfect lake": Gray, *Sex and Death*, 132.

104   "the city of encounter groups": Gray, *Sex and Death*, 138.

105   "He asked me out": Gray, *Sex and Death*, 139.

105   "Most of the time": Gray, *Sex and Death*, 139.

105   "I'd been feeling more": Gray, *Sex and Death*, 140.

106   "Sam picked me up": Gray, *Sex and Death*, 140.

106   "made this total freak shot": Gray, *Sex and Death*, 140.

106   "Sam took a long pause": Gray, *Sex and Death*, 140–141.

106   "I felt like a good guy": Gray, *Sex and Death*, 141.

106   "didn't want to compare": Gray, *Sex and Death*, 141.

107   "been locked up": Gray, *Sex and Death*, 148.

107   "I figured nobody": Gray, *Sex and Death*, 149.

107   "interviewing the audience": Gray, *Sex and Death*, 154.

108   "At first I saw": Gray, *Sex and Death*, 153.

108   "I'm thinking": Gray, *Sex and Death*, 154.

108   "The rest of the play": Gray, *Sex and Death*, 154.

108   "because my favorite" and "made me feel": Gray, *Sex and Death*, 154.

109   "Land's End": Gray, *Sex and Death*, 159.

109   "Loosen up your tie": Gray, *Sex and Death*, 164.

109   "wearing a tie" and "they couldn't understand": Gray, *Sex and Death*, 164.

109   "I couldn't get in touch" and "as I saw the pond": Gray, *Sex and Death*, 166.

109   "visions of witchcraft": Gray, *Sex and Death*, 167.

109   "stuck my cock deep": Gray, *Sex and Death*, 167.

109   "I wonder": Gray, *Sex and Death*, 167–168.

110   "wife's grandparents": Gray, *Sex and Death*, 180.

110   "They thought I was" and "the next day": Gray, *Sex and Death*, 198.

110   "Moving in was no big": Gray, *Sex and Death*, 210–211.

112   "states that matter": Gray, *Sex and Death*, 210–211.

112   "the spiritual plane": Gray, *Sex and Death*, 221.

112   "it might be possible": Gray, *Sex and Death*, 221.

112   "maybe instead of going": Gray, *Sex and Death*, 222.

113   "Well, I was disappointed": Gray, *Sex and Death*, 237.

113   "Mr. Gray, life": Gray, *Sex and Death*, 237.

113   "And a lightbulb": Gray, *Sex and Death*, 237.

5. Paradise Lost and Found: The Road to Cambodia

116   "It was almost six months": Spalding Gray, *Swimming to Cambodia* (New York: Theatre Communications Group Press, 1985), xvi.

116   "I thought": Quoted in Richard Schechner, "My Art in Life: Interviewing Spalding Gray," *The Drama Review* 46, no. 4 (Winter 2002): 168.

119   "People writing reviews": Quoted in Deborah Mason, "New Wave Confidence," *Vogue* (May 1986): 82.

119   "All of the monologues" and "But such allegorical relation-
       ships": James Leverett, "Introduction," in Gray, *Swimming to
       Cambodia*, xi.

119   "Now, I was really": Gray, *Swimming to Cambodia*, 64.

120   "beginning to feel more": Gray, *Swimming to Cambodia*, 64.

121   "I felt a kind of": Gray, *Swimming to Cambodia*, 212.

121   "the Little King": Gray, *Swimming to Cambodia*, 13.

121   "this act of will": Gray, *Swimming to Cambodia*, 13.

123   "It was the first day off": Gray, *Swimming to Cambodia*, 3.

123   "a class thing": Gray, *Swimming to Cambodia*, 86.

123   "the British electricians": Gray, *Swimming to Cambodia*, 4.

123   "the actors didn't buy": Gray, *Swimming to Cambodia*, 86.

124   "you could very easily": Gray, *Swimming to Cambodia*, 87.

124   "Joy was my": Gray, *Swimming to Cambodia*, 103.

124   "a slightly drained": Gray, *Swimming to Cambodia*, 104.

124   "yes, I've heard": Gray, *Swimming to Cambodia*, 187.

124   "cool, business-as-usual": Gray, *Swimming to Cambodia*, 87.

124   "I treated Renée": Gray, *Swimming to Cambodia*, 107.

125   "a Cambodian who": Gray, *Swimming to Cambodia*, 69.

125   "And God knows": Gray, *Swimming to Cambodia*, 79.

125   "was making the same": Gray, *Swimming to Cambodia*, 91.

126   "find the most responsible": Gray, *Swimming to Cambodia*,
       76.

126   "Real People": Gray, *Swimming to Cambodia*, 77.

126   "And then there was": Gray, *Swimming to Cambodia*, 79.

126   "I wanted to say goodbye": Gray, *Swimming to Cambodia*,
       101.

126   "And when I got" and "Go back, Spalding": Gray, *Swimming
       to Cambodia*, 102.

126   "The film was": Gray, *Swimming to Cambodia*, 97–98.

127   "I wanted to be": Gray, *Swimming to Cambodia*, 98.

127   "a good storyteller": Gray, *Swimming to Cambodia*, 97.

127   "Yeah! Suffer": Gray, *Swimming to Cambodia*), 98.

127   "I suddenly and clearly": Gray, *Swimming to Cambodia*, 121.

127   "I would be a changed man": Gray, *Swimming to Cambodia*, 106.

128   "I fled from the table" and "I'm supposed to be in": Gray, *Swimming to Cambodia*, 106.

128   "It was like": Gray, *Swimming to Cambodia*, 72.

128   "water buffalo posing": Gray, *Swimming to Cambodia*, 73.

128   "It was all like": Gray, *Swimming to Cambodia*, 90.

129   "better bus": Gray, *Swimming to Cambodia*, 71.

129   "I was with these real": Gray, *Swimming to Cambodia*, 77.

129   "can just get on": Gray, *Swimming to Cambodia*, 77.

129   "the kind of guy": Gray, *Swimming to Cambodia*, 93.

129   "Cosmic Consciousness": Gray, *Swimming to Cambodia*, 92.

129   "Boat People": Gray, *Swimming to Cambodia*, 92.

130   "But was it": Gray, *Swimming to Cambodia*, 92.

130   "I don't know": Gray, *Swimming to Cambodia*, 32.

130   "Oh my God": Gray, *Swimming to Cambodia*, 74.

130   "the big stuff": Gray, *Swimming to Cambodia*, 80.

130   "Suddenly, there was no time": Gray, *Swimming to Cambodia*, 80.

131   "was all very out of time": Gray, *Swimming to Cambodia*, 80.

131   "I fell back into time": Gray, *Swimming to Cambodia*, 81.

131   "Now I'm going to have to go": Gray, *Swimming to Cambodia*, 81.

132   "that knew how to": Gray, *Swimming to Cambodia*, 15.

132   "a back-to-the-land": Gray, *Swimming to Cambodia*, 17.

132   "strict Maoist": Gray, *Swimming to Cambodia*, 17.

132   "Leave it to a Brit": Gray, *Swimming to Cambodia*, 17.

132   "Maybe I'm the one": Gray, *Swimming to Cambodia*, 27.

133   "When did I last make": Gray, *Swimming to Cambodia*, 27.

133   "How do we begin": Gray, *Swimming to Cambodia*, 33.

133   "I titled this work": Gray, *Swimming to Cambodia*, xvi.

134   "I saw, my God": Gray, *Swimming to Cambodia*, 55.

134   "What in *The Killing Fields*": Vera Dike, "Cinema: Critical/ Mass," *Art in America* (January 1988): 39.

135   "recognized . . . from all the Michelob ads": Gray, *Swimming to Cambodia*, 107.

135   "It was one of those turn-of-the-century": Gray, *Swimming to Cambodia*, 107.

135   "Now, who are the holy people": Gray, *Swimming to Cambodia*, 115.

136   "rest and be with": Gray, *Swimming to Cambodia*, 124.

136   "And so it went": Gray, *Swimming to Cambodia*, 124.

137   "'They put! Plastic!'": Gray, *Swimming to Cambodia*, 85.

137   "There was this huge": Gray, *Swimming to Cambodia*), 125–126.

137   "completely in flames," and "grabbed the fire-poker": Gray, *Swimming to Cambodia*, 125.

137   "a straw boy" and "face had this great": Gray, *Swimming to Cambodia*, 126.

138   "a witness": Gray, *Swimming to Cambodia*, 126.

138   "THE REASON I'M UPSET": Gray, *Swimming to Cambodia*, 127.

138   "I CAN'T REMEMBER": Gray, *Swimming to Cambodia*, 127.

138   "And I knew": Gray, *Swimming to Cambodia*, 127.

139   "And just as I was dozing off": Gray, *Swimming to Cambodia*, 127.

6. An American "Success" Story: Coping After Cambodia

141   "as a cue": John Houseman, foreword, in *Orchards: Seven Stories by Anton Chekhov and Seven Plays They Inspired* (New York: Knopf, 1986), n.p.

142   "I see the character": Spalding Gray, *Rivkala's Ring*, in *Orchards: Seven Stories by Anton Chekhov and Seven Plays They Inspired* (New York: Knopf, 1986), 159.

142   "raw indifferent nature": Gray, *Rivkala's Ring*, 160–161.

143   "a little guilty about": Gray, *Rivkala's Ring*, 162.

143   "taking over Japan": Gray, *Rivkala's Ring*, 163.

143   "if I can't sleep": Gray, *Rivkala's Ring*, 163.

143   "our immune system": Gray, *Rivkala's Ring*, 164.

143   "the more that goes": Gray, *Rivkala's Ring*, 164.

143   "It's become one of those": Gray, *Rivkala's Ring*, 169.

144   "one of those new-age positive thinkers" and "When you meet reality": Gray, *Rivkala's Ring*, 171.

144   "around and around": Gray, *Rivkala's Ring*, 173.

144   "some sort of charcoal filter": Gray, *Rivkala's Ring*, 173.

144   "was a kind of black omen": Gray, *Rivkala's Ring*, 174.

144   "a burden was lifted": Gray, *Rivkala's Ring*, 174.

144   "And for one brief instant": Gray, *Rivkala's Ring*, 175.

145   "the pain in his nose": Gray, *Rivkala's Ring*, 175.

145   "An audience is more": Quoted in Richard Schechner, "My Art in Life: Interviewing Spalding Gray," *The Drama Review* 46, no. 4 (Winter 2002): 165.

147   "didn't know how I was": Spalding Gray, *Monster in a Box* (New York: Vintage, 1992), 4.

147   "become a writer": Gray, *Monster in a Box*, 3.

147   "I moved to New York City": Gray, *Monster in a Box*, 3–4.

147   "is all about the interruptions": Gray, *Monster in a Box*, 5.

149   "I should really like to think": Gray, *Monster in a Box*, 24.

150   "I know the cure": Gray, *Monster in a Box*, 46.

150   "I thought the monologues": Gray, *Monster in a Box*, 6.

151   "interesting people": Gray, *Monster in a Box*, 7.

151   "a thirty-five-mile-an-hour consciousness": Gray, *Monster in a Box*, 10.

151   "Not everyone I interviewed": Gray, *Monster in a Box*, 72.

152   "the mothers of the heroes": Gray, *Monster in a Box*, 25.

152   "something like a combination": Gray, *Monster in a Box*, 26.

152   "feeling guilty": Gray, *Monster in a Box*, 26.

152   "I wanted to help": Gray, *Monster in a Box*, 37.

153   "Well . . . I would say": Gray, *Monster in a Box*, 52–53.

153   "and it turned into": Gray, *Monster in a Box*, 53.

154   "Why are you": Gray, *Monster in a Box*, 56–57.

154   "I told this to": Gray, *Monster in a Box*, 59.

154   "We get back to New York City": Gray, *Monster in a Box*, 62.

155   "the stage manager": Gray, *Monster in a Box*, 64.

155   "He has that special": Gray, *Monster in a Box*, 65.

155   "actors never read": Gray, *Monster in a Box*, 66.

156   "unifying accident": Gray, *Monster in a Box*, 69–70.

156   "waitin' for something": Gray, *Monster in a Box*, 70.

156   "He knows what he saw": Gray, *Monster in a Box*, 70.

156   "But looking up at the stars": Gray, *Monster in a Box*, 71.

157   "what, in some more romantic times": Gray, *Monster in a Box*, 76.

157   "he answered by saying": Gray, *Monster in a Box*, 81.

157   "a condensation of a lot": Spalding Gray, "Spalding Gray, New York, February 9, 1999," in Steve Capra, *Theater Voices: Conversations on the Stage* (Lanham, MD: Scarecrow Press, 2004), 113–114.

157   "The human consciousness": Gray, "Spalding Gray, New York, February 9, 1999," 117.

159   "Growing up a Christian Scientist": Quoted in Eleanor Wachtel, "Spalding Gray," interview, *Writers and Company* (Toronto: Knopf Canada, 1993), 39.

160   "feminine eye": Spalding Gray, *Gray's Anatomy* (New York: Vintage, 1993), 11.

160   "macula pucker": Gray, *Gray's Anatomy*, 9.

160   "a distortion of the interior": Gray, *Gray's Anatomy*, 8.

162   "Not that I'd ever": Gray, *Gray's Anatomy*, 11.

162   "was too much": Gray, *Gray's Anatomy*, 11.

162   "It was about my mother's suicide"; Gray, *Gray's Anatomy*, 10–11.

163   "idiopathic": Gray, *Gray's Anatomy*, 12.

163   "And then": Gray, *Gray's Anatomy*, 13.

163   "a one percent chance": Gray, *Gray's Anatomy*, 12.

163   "All things are contingent": Gray, *Gray's Anatomy*, 19.

163   "cut into the window": Gray, *Gray's Anatomy*, 19.

163 "because to name it": Gray, *Gray's Anatomy*, 17.

164 "we can't be duplicitous": Gray, *Gray's Anatomy*, 18.

164 "All my ancestors": Gray, *Gray's Anatomy*, 27.

164 "I want to give away": Gray, *Gray's Anatomy*, 30.

164 "when the time came": Gray, *Gray's Anatomy*, 32.

164 "I realized that I was": Gray, *Gray's Anatomy*, 32.

164 "someone worked black magic": Gray, *Gray's Anatomy*, 37.

164 "better give up everything": Gray, *Gray's Anatomy*, 48.

165 "Pini Lopa": Gray, *Gray's Anatomy*, 60.

165 "No judgment": Gray, *Gray's Anatomy*, 61.

165 "completely unprepared for": Gray, *Gray's Anatomy*, 63.

165 "Oh, sir, if you go": Gray, *Gray's Anatomy*, 65.

165 "I don't believe": Gray, *Gray's Anatomy*, 66.

166 "but I think they're still": Quoted in David Savran, *Breaking the Rules: The Wooster Group* (New York: Theatre Communications Group, 1986), 63.

168 "It was seeing Richard Nixon": Gray, *Gray's Anatomy*, 71.

168 "I also couldn't have done it": Gray, *Gray's Anatomy*, 71.

169 "I believe in magic": Gray, *Gray's Anatomy*, 54–55.

169 "I wanted Jesus": Gray, *Gray's Anatomy*, 54.

169 "I had to walk": Gray, *Gray's Anatomy*, 72–73.

170 "I knew there was magic": Gray, *Gray's Anatomy*, 58.

170 "When you were in the hospital": Gray, *Gray's Anatomy*, 74.

170 "brought down the little": Gray, *Gray's Anatomy*, 79.

170 "When I see that": Gray, *Gray's Anatomy*, 77.

170 "they recognized me": Gray, *Gray's Anatomy*, 77.

170 "Art imitates life": Gray, *Gray's Anatomy*, 77.

170 "I'm happy to have": Gray, *Gray's Anatomy*, 74.

171 "I began to realize": Gray, *Gray's Anatomy*, 74.

171 "I drank vodka": Gray, *Gray's Anatomy*, 79–80.

7. Coming to Terms with the American Dream

173 "Often I have the fantasy": Spalding Gray, "Perpetual Saturdays," *Performing Arts Journal* 6, no. 1 (1981): 48.

174 "the most deeply felt": Quoted in Richard Schechner, "My Art in Life: Interviewing Spalding Gray," *The Drama Review* 46, no. 4 (Winter 2002): 172.

174 "I think *Morning, Noon and Night*": Quoted in Schechner, "My Art in Life," 173.

178 "I was heavily judged": Spalding Gray, "Spalding Gray, New York, February 9, 1999," in Steve Capra, *Theater Voices: Conversations on the Stage* (Lanham, MD: Scarecrow Press, 2004), 115.

178 "I got my first hate letters": Gray, "Spalding Gray, New York, February 9, 1999,", 115–116.

180 "mixed all the wrong drinks": Spalding Gray, *It's a Slippery Slope* (New York: Noonday Press, 1997), 47–48.

180 "I ran and grabbed a big": Gray, *It's a Slippery Slope*, 48.

180 "arrested development": Gray, *It's a Slippery Slope*, 48.

180 "Both Ramona's father": Gray, *It's a Slippery Slope*, 48.

181 "a very big crash": Gray, *It's a Slippery Slope*, 52.

181 "the more I began to fragment": Gray, *It's a Slippery Slope*, 52.

181 "I had become": Gray, *It's a Slippery Slope*, 52.

181 "uncontrollable, obsessive reenactment": Gray, *It's a Slippery Slope*, 53.

181 "What complicated things": Gray, *It's a Slippery Slope*, 53.

181 "which I ended up calling": Gray, *It's a Slippery Slope*, 56.

182 "For me the roll": Gray, *It's a Slippery Slope*, 58.

182 "I felt I should": Gray, *It's a Slippery Slope*, 60.

182 "What followed": Gray, *It's a Slippery Slope*, 74.

182 "over the months": Gray, *It's a Slippery Slope*, 76.

183 "Now I was experiencing": Gray, *It's a Slippery Slope*, 45.

183 "Ajax, the big daddy": Gray, *It's a Slippery Slope*, 35.

184 "And I'm thinking": Gray, *It's a Slippery Slope*, 96.

"Go for it": Gray, *It's a Slippery Slope*, 102.

185 "You know": Gray, *It's a Slippery Slope*, 105.

186 "a complicated present": Spalding Gray, *Morning, Noon and Night* (New York: Farrar, Straus & Giroux, 1999), 75.

186   "present and in the past": Gray, *Morning, Noon and Night*, 75.

187   "I felt as if": Gray, *Morning, Noon and Night*, 75–76.

187   "all transiency, impermanence, and change": Gray, *Morning, Noon and Night*, 76.

188   "It's not been a bad day": Gray, *Morning, Noon and Night*, 76.

188   "Try enjoying life": Gray, *Morning, Noon and Night*, 130.

188   "awake like Ebenezer Scrooge": Gray, *Morning, Noon and Night*, 131.

188   "Before I had children": Gray, *Morning, Noon and Night*, 26.

188   "with only one life": Gray, *Morning, Noon and Night*, 145.

189   "I love my children": Gray, *Morning, Noon and Night*, 145.

190   "Then at last Mom and Dad": Gray, *Morning, Noon and Night*, 124–125.

190   "At that moment": Gray, *Morning, Noon and Night*, 47.

190   "done a pretty good job": Gray, *Morning, Noon and Night*, 47.

191   "reality-acceptance": See Schechner, "My Art in Life," 173.

191   "omnipotent fantasy": Gray, *Morning, Noon and Night*, 50.

191   "As soon as he started": Gray, *Morning, Noon and Night*, 51.

191   "He can provide": D. W. Winnicott, *The Child, the Family and the Outside World* (London: Penguin, 1964), 25.

193   "You want to be a lumberjack": Gray, *Morning, Noon and Night*, 45.

193   "Rocky would soon": Gray, *Morning, Noon and Night*, 45.

193   "I never wanted": Gray, *Morning, Noon and Night*, 136.

193   "Forrest, I don't want": Gray, *Morning, Noon and Night*, 137.

193   "As far as my father went": Gray, *Morning, Noon and Night*, 128.

194   "Then it is stopped": Gray, *Morning, Noon and Night*, 151.

194   "If I am guilty": Gray, *Morning, Noon and Night*, 26.

195   "as long as I": Gray, *Morning, Noon and Night*, 28.

195   "I was content": Gray, *Morning, Noon and Night*, 28.

195   "exotic . . . from the other": Gray, *Morning, Noon and Night*, 39.

195   "overwhelmed . . . by their sensuality": Gray, *Morning, Noon and Night*, 39.

195   "Oh, the stupefying": Gray, *Morning, Noon and Night*, 72.

195   "the real world": Gray, *Morning, Noon and Night*, 79.

195   "People were imperfect": Gray, *Morning, Noon and Night*, 79.

196   "I won't let the word": Gray, *Morning, Noon and Night*, 56.

196   "I look down at his head": Gray, *Morning, Noon and Night*, 65–66.

196   "When I got to my brother": Gray, *Morning, Noon and Night*, 105.

196   "At that moment": Gray, *Morning, Noon and Night*, 151.

197   "a patient etherized": Gray, *Morning, Noon and Night*, 131.

197   "My new bliss-eye": Gray, *Morning, Noon and Night*, 66.

197   "The fire in the fireplace": Gray, *Morning, Noon and Night*, 142.

197   "the existential moralists": Gray, *Morning, Noon and Night*, 120.

198   "No, there's nothing": Spalding Gray, *Life Interrupted: The Unfinished Monologue* (New York: Crown, 2005), 57.

198   "I think *Morning, Noon and Night* is the end": Quoted in Schechner, "My Art in Life," 173.

198   "I didn't think": Gray, *Life Interrupted*, 53.

199   "the longest day": Gray, *Life Interrupted*, 57.

199   "where the Vikings": Gray, *Life Interrupted*, 58.

199   "kind of Hamletesque. . . . funeral announcements": Gray, *Life Interrupted*, 58.

199   "So there was": Gray, *Life Interrupted*, 59.

199   "on the last long walk": Gray, *Life Interrupted*, 59.

199   "black spot": Gray, *Life Interrupted*, 62.

199   "feeling that it's my fault": Gray, *Life Interrupted*, 64.

200   "We're dealing": Gray, *Life Interrupted*, 83.

200   "it all reminded me": Gray, *Life Interrupted*, 67.

200   "I didn't know": Gray, *Life Interrupted*, 75.

200   "an Irishman": Gray, *Life Interrupted*, 75.

201   "about how TVs": Gray, *Life Interrupted*, 77.

201   "a construction zone": Gray, *Life Interrupted*, 79.

201   "It was beautiful": Gray, *Life Interrupted*, 79.

201   "pinnacle of pinnacles": Gray, *Life Interrupted*, 79.

201   "It's an orbital fracture": Gray, *Life Interrupted*, 86.

202   "Andy Warhol died": Gray, *Life Interrupted*, 89.

202   "I think about": Gray, *Life Interrupted*, 88.

202   "another calamity": Gray, *Life Interrupted*, 89.

202   "Was I in the grip": Gray, *Life Interrupted*, 89.

202   "Is it [all] a coincidence": Gray, *Life Interrupted*, 91.

202   "Webster's Unabridged": Gray, *Life Interrupted*, 91.

203   "that it's been difficult": Gray, *Life Interrupted*, 92.

203   "Always wear your seat belt": Gray, *Life Interrupted*, 92.

8. Gray Beyond the Stage

205   "start as performance art": Quoted in Richard Schechner, "My Art in Life: Interviewing Spalding Gray," *The Drama Review* 46, no. 4 (December 2002): 168.

205   "and someone staged": Quoted in Schechner, "My Art in Life," 171.

205   "I didn't know": Spalding Gray, *Monster in a Box* (New York: Vintage, 1992), 4.

207   "And I half dreamed": Spalding Gray, *Impossible Vacation* (New York: Vintage, 1993), 3, 228.

207   "I wanted now": Gray, *Impossible Vacation*, 122.

208   "As I look back": Gray, *Impossible Vacation*, 112–113.

208   "I knew my fall": Gray, *Impossible Vacation*, 227.

209   "I could hardly think": Gray, *Impossible Vacation*, 210.

209   "I've lost the linear order": Gray, *Impossible Vacation*, 159.

210   "gruntings and moanings. . . . It wasn't bad": Gray, *Impossible Vacation*, 135.

210   "by adapting less": D. W. Winnicott, *Collected Papers: Through Paediatrics to Psycho-Analysis*, 2nd ed. (London: Tavistock Publications, 1975), 238.

211   "life of moderation": Gray, *Impossible Vacation*, 63.

211   "did nothing in excess": Gray, *Impossible Vacation*, 73.

211   "turned into the story": Gray, *Impossible Vacation*, 72.

211   "We had come face-to-face": Gray, *Impossible Vacation*, 72.

211   "if you are in agony": Gray, *Impossible Vacation*,, 102.

211   "To take it away": Gray, *Impossible Vacation*, 103.

211   "I'm sure that's the way": Gray, *Impossible Vacation*, 103.

212   "I'm not saying Mom": Gray, *Impossible Vacation*, 65–66.

212   "What does Rajneesh": Gray, *Impossible Vacation*, 106.

213   "This was an overpopulated world": Gray, *Impossible Vacation*, 94.

213   "miraculous landscape . . . cured me": Gray, *Impossible Vacation*, 113.

213   "I was just seeing": Gray, *Impossible Vacation*, 117.

213   "household shrine . . . an in-house": Gray, *Impossible Vacation*, 119.

213   "No TV or telephone": Gray, *Impossible Vacation*, 119.

214   "scopophilia. . . . I was caught": Gray, *Impossible Vacation*, 120.

214   "I had the feeling": Gray, *Impossible Vacation*, 121–122.

214   "I hadn't realized": Gray, *Impossible Vacation*, 133.

215   "God, was Meg organized": Gray, *Impossible Vacation*, 142.

215   "I'd turn into a soft": Gray, *Impossible Vacation*, 45.

215   "suddenly that enigmatic": Gray, *Impossible Vacation*, 117–118.

216   "[Marcel] Proust had demonstrated": Gray, *Impossible Vacation*, 104–105.

216   "in some simple": Gray, *Impossible Vacation*, 181.

216   "running away . . . had inhibited and prevented. . . . I had flown": Gray, *Impossible Vacation*, 181.

217   "Meg and I. . . . I knew, too": Gray, *Impossible Vacation*, 181.

217   "In the end": Spalding Gray, *Impossible Vacation*, 183.

217   "the whole world. . . . totally in love": Gray, *Impossible Vacation*, 203.

218   "for the first time . . . I sensed": Gray, *Impossible Vacation*, 219.

218   "Maybe that's": Gray, *Impossible Vacation*, 219.

218   "he was wrong": Gray, *Impossible Vacation*, 220.

218   "I was beginning": Gray, *Impossible Vacation*, 223.

219   "everything came together. . . . For the first time": Gray, *Impossible Vacation*, 228.

219   "Matisse-like chain dance": Gray, *Impossible Vacation*, 227.

220   "by demonstration": Mary Baker Eddy, *Science and Health with Keys to the Scriptures* (1875) (Boston: Trustees under the Will of Mary Baker G. Eddy, 1934), viii.

220   "the treatment": Eddy, *Science and Health with Keys to the Scriptures,* viii.

220   "lose their reality": Eddy, *Science and Health with Keys to the Scriptures,* xi.

220   "the discords": Eddy, *Science and Health with Keys to the Scriptures,* viii.

Postscript: An American Original

225   "I don't think there's": Quoted in David Savran, *Breaking the Rules: The Wooster Group* (New York: Theatre Communications Group, 1986), 71.

225   "don't be frightened": Spalding Gray and Elizabeth LeCompte, "Rumstick Road," *Performing Arts Journal* 3, no. 2 (1978): 111.

Bibliography

Gray's Monologues

Gray, Spalding. "excerpts from A Personal History of the American Theatre." *Performing Arts Journal* 8, no. 1 (1984): 36–50.

———. *Swimming to Cambodia*. New York: Theatre Communications Group, 1985.

———. *Rivkala's Ring*. In *Orchards: Seven Stories by Anton Chekhov and Seven Plays They Inspired*. New York: Knopf, 1986, 157–175.

———. *Sex and Death to the Age 14*. New York: Vintage, 1986.

———. "'Gray's Anatomy': A Preview." *The New York Times*, 17 May 1992, sec. 6:1, 42–48.

———. *Monster in a Box*. New York: Vintage, 1992.

———. *Gray's Anatomy*. New York: Vintage, 1993.

———. *It's a Slippery Slope*. New York: Noonday Press, 1997.

———. *Morning, Noon and Night*. New York: Farrar, Straus & Giroux, 1999.

———. *Life Interrupted: The Unfinished Monologue*. New York: Crown, 2005.

Gray's Novel

Gray, Spalding. *Impossible Vacation*. New York: Vintage, 1993.

Other Pieces by Gray

Gray, Spalding. "About *Three Places in Rhode Island*." *The Drama Review* 23, no. 1 (1979): 35.

———. "Children of Paradise. Working with Kids." *Performing Arts Journal* 5, no. 1 (1980): 61–74.

———. "Theater's Brutal Acts." *The Village Voice,* 28 April 1980, 29.

———. "Perpetual Saturdays." *Performing Arts Journal* 6, no. 1 (1981): 46–49.

———. "A Child's Christmas on Rumstick Road." *The New York Times,* 25 December 1991, 31.

———. "Inside Out: The Dalai Lama Interviewed by Spalding Gray." *Tricycle: The Buddhist Review* 1, no. 1 (Premier Issue) (Fall 1991): 34–42.

———. "Let's Get Undepressed." *The New York Times*, 17 January 1993, sec. 7:15, 16.

———. "53." In *250 Ways to Make America Better: Great Ideas on How We Can Improve Our Country*. Ed. *George* Magazine. Comp. Carolyn Mackler. New York: Villard, 1999, 64.

———. "Spalding Gray, New York, February 9, 1999." In Steve Capra, *Theater Voices: Conversations on the Stage*. Lanham, MD: Scarecrow Press, 2004, 113–119.

Gray, Spalding, and Elizabeth LeCompte. "Rumstick Road." *Performing Arts Journal* 3, no. 2 (Fall 1978): 92–115.

———. "Special Section: The Making of a Trilogy." *Performing Arts Journal* 3, no. 2 (Fall 1978): 80–91.

Gray, Spalding, and Randal Levenson. *In Search of the Monkey Girl*. New York: Aperture, 1982.

Works About Gray

A good deal of the material in this section consists of performance reviews and newspaper publicity relating to Gray. Less numerous are articles and book sections analyzing and evaluating Gray's work. Among those, the most informative are by Aronson, Auslander, Brewer, Demastes, Savran, Schechner, Shank, Vanden Heuvel, and Vorlicky.

Aronson, Arnold. *American Avant-Garde Theatre: A History*. London: Routledge, 2000.

Auslander, Philip. *Presence and Resistance: Postmodernism and Cultural Politics in Contemporary American Performance*. Ann Arbor: University of Michigan Press, 1992.

Banes, Sally. "A Couple of Grays Sitting Around Talking." Revs. of *In Search of the Monkey Girl* and *Interviewing an Audience*. *The Village Voice*, 18 January 1983, 95.

Barron, James. "Another Anatomy Lesson." *The New York Times*, 6 July 2001, B-2.

———. "Police Tracing Clues in Spalding Gray Case." *The New York Times*, 14 January 2004, B-3.

———. "Tip on Spalding Gray Sighting Investigated." *The New York Times*, 15 January 2005, B-3.

Brewer, Gay. "Talking His Way Back to Life: Spalding Gray and the Embodied Voice." *Contemporary Literature* 37, no. 2 (1996): 237–238.

Callens, Johan, ed. *The Wooster Group and Its Traditions*. Bruxelles: P.I.E.-Peter Lang, 2004.

Canby, Vincent. "Soloists on the Big Screen." *The New York Times*, 22 March 1987, 2:19.

Coe, Robert. "Telling Tales." *Vanity Fair* (August 1985):94–96.

Dace, Tish. "Setting the Record Straight: Wooster Group Funding Slashed." *Other Stages*, 14 January 1982, 5.

Demastes, William W. "Spalding Gray's *Swimming to Cambodia* and the Evolution of an Ironic Presence." *Theatre Journal* 41, no. 1 (March 1989): 75–94.

DeVries, Hilary. "His New Favorite Subject—Him." *Los Angeles Times*, 11 November 1990, Calendar:3, 93.

Dewan, Shaila K., and Jesse McKinley. "Body of Spalding Gray Found; Monologuist and Actor was 62." *The New York Times*, 9 March 2005, A-1, B-7.

Feingold, Michael. "Bad Rap." Rev. of *Rumstick Road*. *The Village Voice*, 21 April 1980, 84.

Freedman, Samuel G. "3 U.S. Theater Artists Plan a Visit to Vietnam." *The New York Times*, 18 April 1986, C-19.

Garcia, Guy. "Spoken Word Finds a New Partner in Music: James Taylor and Spalding Gray Team up in Recording Studio." *The New York Times,* 24 May 1998, sec. 2:33, 34.

Gener, Randy. "Comp d'Oeil." *The Village Voice,* 14 December 1993, 106, 108.

Gussow, Mel. "Theater: Spalding Gray's '*47 Beds*'." *The New York Times*, 12 December 1981, 21.

———. "The Theater: 'Sex and Death'." *The New York Times*, 30 October 1982, sec. 1:15.

———. "Stage: Spalding Gray as Storyteller." Rev. of *Swimming to Cambodia. The New York Times*, 16 November 1984, C-3.

———. "Critic's Notebook." *The New York Times,* 29 May 1986, C-1.

———. "Theater: Spalding Gray." Rev. of *Terrors of Pleasure. The New York Times*, 15 May 1986, C-19.

Guy, David. "From the Heart." Rev. of *Sex and Death to the Age 14. The New York Times*, 4 May 1986, sec. 7:32.

Isherwood, Charles. "Exit Talking: Spalding Gray Left Something Typically Dark and Funny to Remember Him By." Rev. of *Life Interrupted. The New York Times*, 23 October 2005, sec 7:13.

Kakutani, Michiko. "That Spalding Gray Novel Isn't a Monster, After All." Rev. of *Impossible Vacation. The New York Times,* 22 May 1992, C-25.

Klein, Alvin. "Spalding Gray and His Children." *The New York Times*, 20 February 2000, sec. 14:12.

Klosterman, Chuck. "To Tell the Truth: He Did Reality Before She Did Reality TV." *The New York Times,* 26 Dec. 2004, sec. 6:55.

Korzon, Dave. "Spalding Gray, Leftover Stories Told: Kathie Russo Talks About Her Husband's Legacy." *The Rambler* (November/December 2006): 8–11.

Marks, Peter. "Negotiating the Twists in Skiing and Life." Rev. of *It's a Slippery Slope. The New York Times,* 11 November 1996, C-11, C-12.

McGuigan, Cathleen. "Gray's Eminence: An Endless Supply of Stories." *Newsweek,* 28 July 1986, 69.

Morris, Bob. "The Unnoticed Mr. Gray." *The New York Times*, 25 July 1993, sec 9:7.

Nightingale, Benedict. "He Is a Few of His Favorite Things." Revs. of *Impossible Vacation* and *Monster in a Box. The New York Times*, 12 July 1992, sec. 7:9.

O'Connor, John J. "Spalding Gray on HBO." Rev. of *On Location: Terrors of Pleasure. The New York Times*, 14 December 1987, C-21.

Patterson, John S. "Solo Performance as Autobiography." *The Villager,* 26 November 1981.

———. "Spalding Gray: Chronicles." *Other Stages,* 14 January 1982, 6.

Pogrebin, Robin. "A Mellower Monologist, Trying Home Life." *The New York Times,* 27 December 1999, E-1, E-5.

Reviews of "God is Dead My Radio" and "What Happened on the Way Here?" *The Christian Science Monitor*, 12 February 1981, 19.

Richheimer, Judy Lauren. "Spaulding [*sic*] Gray: A Personal History." *Other Stages*, 16 December 1982, 4.

Rothstein, Mervyn. "A New Face in Grover's Corners." *The New York Times,* 4 December 1988, sec. 2:1, 10.

Salamon, Julie. "Spalding Gray: A Storyteller on the Big Screen." *The Wall Street Journal,* 12 March 1987, 30.

Savran, David. *Breaking the Rules: The Wooster Group*. New York: Theatre Communications Group, 1986.

Schechner, Richard. "The Politics of Ecstasy" (1968). In *Public Domain: Essays on the Theatre*. Indianapolis: Bobb-Merrill, 1969, 209–228.

———. *Environmental Theater*. New York: Hawthorn Books, 1973.

———. *The End of Humanism: Writings on Performance*. New York: Performing Arts Journal Publications, 1982.

———. "Magnitudes of Performance" (1986). In *Performance Theory,* rev. and expanded ed. New York: Routledge, 1988, 251–288.

————. "My Art in Life: Interviewing Spalding Gray." *The Drama Review* 46, no. 4 (December 2002): 154–174.

Shank, Theodore. *Beyond the Boundaries: American Alternative Theatre.* 1982; reprint, Ann Arbor: University of Michigan Press, 2002.

Shewey, Don. "A Spinner of Tales Moves Into the Mainstream." *The New York Times,* 11 May 1986, sec. 2:7, 8.

————. "Chekhov's Stories Through the Eyes of Seven Playwrights." *The New York Times,* 25 August 1985, sec. 2:4, 26.

————. "The Year of Spalding Famously." *The Village Voice,* 13 November 1984, 99, 107.

Simpson, Mona. "Somebody to Talk About: The Performance Artist Spalding Gray May Hit It Big with His Epic-Monologue Feature Film." *The New York Times,* 8 March 1987, sec. 6:40, 92.

Smith, Sid. "'Talking Man': Spalding Gray Sails Along with a Flow of Words in His New Show." *Chicago Tribune,* 4 September 1990, sec. 5:3.

Solway, Diane. "Creative Couples: Is Love Blind?" *The New York Times,* 19 July 1987, sec. 2:1, 14, 15.

Sterritt, David. "Adventures Way off Broadway." *The Christian Science Monitor,* 23 September 1980, 18.

————. "New Directions in American Theater." *The Christian Science Monitor,* 3 May 1979, 12–13.

"Swimming to Washington and Moscow With Gray." *The New York Times,* 24 April 1987, C-8.

"270 are Named Guggenheim Fellows." *The New York Times,* 7 April 1985, 33.

Vanden Heuvel, Michael. *Performing Drama/Dramatizing Performance: Alternative Theater and the Dramatic Text.* Ann Arbor: University of Michigan Press, 1991.

Vorlicky, Robert H. "Marking Change, Marking America: Contemporary Performance and Men's Autobiographical Selves." In *Performing America: Cultural Nationalism in American Theater,* ed. Jeffrey D. Mason and J. Ellen Gainor. Ann Arbor: University of Michigan Press, 1999, 193–209.

Wachtel, Eleanor. "Spalding Gray." In *Writers and Company.* Toronto: Knopf Canada, 1993.

Weber, Bruce. "At Lunch with Spalding Gray: A Life Based on a True Story." *The New York Times,* 8 December 1991, C-1, C-10.

———. "Spalding Gray Remembered in Tribute at Lincoln Center." *The New York Times*, 14 April 2004, C-15.

Witchel, Alex. "Yes, Spalding Gray, This Is Your Life…" *The New York Times,* 11 November 1990, sec. 2:8, 34.

General Studies About Culture, Philosophy, and Psychology

Theories about postmodernism and the human condition often tie directly into what Spalding Gray was doing on the stage. Baudrillard's concept of the simulacra, for instance, explains much of Gray's sense of hollowness as an actor, and the kinds of cultural impediments he faced as he struggled to develop a sense of personal authenticity. Jameson and Lyotard highlight the cultural conditions in general, and Butler's work nicely highlights the gender issues that troubled Gray for most of his career.

Brennan and Oliver each propose ways to escape the "postmodern condition," and their works also focus on matters that concerned Gray, from the need to *feel* life to the need to experience it with and around others. Gray may have fallen prey to that condition on numerous occasions, but he eventually came to many of the same conclusions as they did.

Winnicott's works are cited below because so many of his ideas on the psychology of the family seemed to appeal to Gray, at least later in life when he finally discovered Winnicott's works. Mary Baker Eddy's Christian Science book is included because it was so influential in Gray's mother's life, and therefore on Gray's life as well. Gray's interest in Eastern religions, particularly in Buddhism and the Tibetan Book of the Dead, was extensive. Lauf's analysis is a solid, if rather academic summary.

Roach's article "It" discusses the qualities necessary in order for someone to be said to have "it," that quality of humble charisma that draws us all into some mysterious spell of attraction the way Gray did.

Baudrillard, Jean. *Symbolic Exchange and Death.* 1976; reprint, London: Sage, 1993.
———. *Simulacra and Simulation.* Tr. Sheila Faria Glaser. 1981; reprint, Ann Arbor: University of Michigan Press, 1994.
Brennan, Teresa. *The Transmission of Affect.* Ithaca, NY: Cornell University Press, 2004.
Butler, Judith. *Bodies That Matter: On the Discursive Limits of "Sex."* New York: Routledge, 1993.
Eddy, Mary Baker. *Science and Health with Keys to the Scriptures* (1875). Boston: Trustees Under the Will of Mary Baker G. Eddy, 1934.
Jacobs, Michael. *D. W. Winnicott.* London: Sage, 1995.
Jameson, Fredric. "Postmodernism, or The Cultural Logic of Late Capitalism." *New Left Review* 146 (1984): 53–92.
Lauf, Detlef Ingo. *Secret Doctrines of the Tibetan Book of the Dead.* Tr. Graham Parkes. Boulder, CO: Shambhala Press, 1977.
Lyotard, Jean-François. "Notes on the Critical Function of the Work of Art." In *Driftworks,* trans. Susan Hanson. New York: Semiotext[e], 1984, 78.
———. *The Postmodern Condition: A Report on Knowledge* (1979). Tr. Geoff Bennington and Brian Massumi. Minneapolis: University of Minnesota Press, 1984.
Oliver, Kelly. *Family Values: Subjects Between Culture and Nature.* New York: Routledge, 1997.
———. *Witnessing: Beyond Recognition.* Minneapolis: University of Minnesota Press, 2001.
Roach, Joseph. "It." *Theatre Journal* 56, no. 4 (December 2004): 555–568.
Winnicott, D. W. *The Child, the Family and the Outside World.* London: Penguin, 1964.
———. *Playing and Reality.* New York: Basic Books, 1971.
———. *Collected Papers: Through Paediatrics to Psycho-Analysis.* 2nd ed. London: Tavistock, 1975, 240.

Index

Grateful acknowledgment is made to the following for permission to reprint previously published material:

PAJ Publications: Excerpts from "Perpetual Saturdays" by Spalding Gray from *Performing Arts Journal* (volume 6: number 1, 1981). Used by permission.

Random House, Inc.: Excerpts from *Life Interrupted: The Unfinished Monologue* by Spalding Gray. Copyright © 2005 by the Estate of Spalding Gray. Used by permission of Crown Publishers, a division of Random House, Inc. (U.S., Canada, P.I., Open Market, and E.U. rights). Excerpts from *Gray's Anatomy* by Spalding Gray. Copyright © 1993 by Spalding Gray. Used by permission of Vintage Books, a division of Random House, Inc. (U.S., Canada, P.I., Open Market, and E.U. rights). Excerpts from *Impossible Vacation: A Novel* by Spalding Gray. Copyright © 1992 by Spalding Gray. Used by permission of Alfred A. Knopf, a division of Random House, Inc. (U.S., Canada, P.I., Open Market, and E.U. rights). Excerpts from *Monster in a Box* by Spalding Gray. Copyright © 1991 by Spalding Gray. Used by permission of Alfred A. Knopf, a division of Random House, Inc. (U.S., Canada, P.I., Open Market, and E.U. rights). Excerpts from "Rivkala's Ring" by Spalding Gray. Copyright © 1986 by Spalding Gray. From *Orchards: Seven Stories by Anton Chekhov and Seven Plays They Have Inspired* by Anton Chekhov et al. Used by permission of Alfred A. Knopf, a division of Random House, Inc. Excerpts from *Sex and Death to the Age 14* by Spalding Gray. Copyright © 1986 by Spalding Gray. Used by permission of Vintage Books, a division of Random House, Inc. (U.S., Canada, P.I., Open Market, and E.U. rights).

Kathie Russo: Quotes from the published works of Spalding Gray. Used by permission.

TDR: The Drama Review: Excerpts from "About *Three Places in Rhode Island*" by Spalding Gray from *TDR* (volume 23: issue 1, T81, March 1979). Used by permission. Excerpts from "My Life in Art: Interviewing Spalding Gray" by Richard Schechner from *TDR* (volume 46: issue 4, T176, Winter 2002). Used by permission.

Theatre Communications Group: Excerpts from *Swimming to Cambodia* by Spalding Gray, published by Theatre Communications Group in 1985. Used by permission of Theatre Communications Group. Excerpts from *Breaking the Rules: The Wooster Group* by David Savran, published by Theatre Communications Group in 1986. Used by permission of Theatre Communications Group.

The author also expresses gratitude to the following for quoted materials:

Farrar, Strauss and Giroux, LLC: Excerpts from *It's a Slippery Slope* by Spalding Gray, published by Farrar, Strauss and Giroux/Noonday Press in 1997. Excerpts from *Morning, Noon and Night* by Spalding Gray, published by Farrar, Straus and Giroux in 1999.

International Creative Management: Excerpts from *Gray's Anatomy* by Spalding Gray. Copyright © 1993 by Spalding Gray (U.K. rights). Excerpts from *Impossible Vacation: A Novel* by Spalding Gray. Copyright © 1992 by Spalding Gray (U.K. rights). Excerpts from *Monster in a Box* by Spalding Gray. Copyright © 1991 by Spalding Gray (U.K. rights). Excerpts from *Sex and Death to the Age 14* by Spalding Gray. Copyright © 1986 by Spalding Gray (U.K. rights).

William Morris Agency: Excerpts from *Life Interrupted: The Unfinished Monologue* by Spalding Gray. Copyright © 2005 by the Estate of Spalding Gray (U.K. rights).

Every reasonable effort has been made to contact copyright holders and secure permissions. Omissions can be remedied in future editions.

ONE GOD FOR ALL

DIL R BANU

authorHOUSE®

AuthorHouse™
1663 Liberty Drive
Bloomington, IN 47403
www.authorhouse.com
Phone: 1 (800) 839-8640

Published by AuthorHouse 05/01/2015

ISBN: 978-1-4969-1157-5 (sc)
ISBN: 978-1-5049-0835-1 (hc)
ISBN: 978-1-4969-1156-8 (e)

Library of Congress Control Number: 2014908684

Print information available on the last page.

DEDICATION

*This book is exclusively meant for and dedicated to all
God-loving and truth-seeking people of all religions
who truly believe in God and also hope to return to
Him safely following His revealed guidance.*

BOOK REVIEW:
ONE GOD FOR ALL
BY DIL R. BANU

Reading Ms Banu's manuscript, I was reminded of a conversation I had about 30 year ago when a dear friend of mine asked if I believed in God. At that time I was still an Evangelical Christian (at least on paper) living in Switzerland. I have since converted to Islam and live in the US.

My answer was and I can remember time, setting and circumstances as if it just happened yesterday: "Yes I believe in God but I have a hard time believing in Jesus as God's son and the entire Trinity approach."

Looking back obviously makes one see much clearer and it proves that God's guidance set me off in the right direction many years before becoming a Muslim. It is indeed the concept of "tawhid", believing in the One and only God, which like no other fundament of our joint belief system as the three monotheistic religions, is at the heart of our salvation. The mere fact that we do talk about monotheism as the binding link between all of us suggests, God is One and only One.

I believe this book to focus on the most essential issue that guides us as believers in God. I am not very familiar with the Bible so this book allows Muslims valuable insights in its teachings and therefore a broader horizon to discuss issues of "tawhid" in an informed dialogue with Christian colleagues and friends. On the other hand it invites Christians to get a good overview of the Quran's teachings touching the most important common issue of our joint faith without reading the entire Book which of course is very much recommended nonetheless.

The book by Dil Banu as she herself suggests, is not one more scholarly attempt to clarify the commonalities and differences most notably between the Christian and Islamic practice of "tawhid" but chooses a very unique and refreshing approach by ways of a dozen letters addressed to the well-known Reverend Franklin Graham in response to his assertions that we do not worship the same God. Furthermore, it lives of its dialogues between the Author and various missionaries which visit her to make their case for Trinity and Jesus as the only way for salvation.

Many books, as the author admits herself, have been written on the topic. However, the unique approach to writing this book and the strong focus on the essential arguments for a truly monotheistic "tawhid" as prescribed by God in the Quran and the Bible, make *"One God for All"* a book that I can recommend very highly to Christians and Muslims alike to read.

Allow me to just quote one sign (ayah) of the Quran here in conclusion: Ibrahim (14:52): "Here is a message for mankind. Let them take warning therefrom. And let them know that HE Is (no other than) One God: Let men of understanding take heed."

Blessed are those who treasure this truth in their souls.

Eduard Tschan, PhD., Senior Adviser Community
Health Workers, at American Red Cross previously Country
Director in Haiti for the International Red Cross.

In our times of strife and alienation, the author presents a fresh argument for harmony and togetherness. She has a deep understanding of the human mind through ages in which God eternally leaves His unifying marks. God's Omnipresence binds our ageless humanity on one hand, and on the other, it directs us to His singular message of Unity. The author essentially focuses on the Unity of God, and articulates its dimensions from the vantage point of her Islamic conviction. In so doing, she places other religions vis-à-vis Islam and vice versa. In keeping with the spirit of Islam, she never indulges in the denigration of the other. She does encounter anti-Islamism that we see in vogue. Her style is unapologetic and straight to the point. She takes the antagonists to the task. But her tone, all throughout, is one of reconciliation. She seeks to make her audience understand her belief-system, i. e. Islam, and in turn, understand the misunderstanding of Islam by her audience.

Her audience, obviously, is Western (if not exclusively), and as such, her arguments flourish in the Western context. She does leave room for the watchful non-Western Muslim and non-Muslim readers to get hold of that context. The book addressing timeless issues is quintessentially timely.

Muhammad Mashreque has been a professor of English at Allen University, Columbia, SC. Besides, he works with such organizations as uniting adherents of the Faith (i. e. CAIR), and promoting ethnic-racial harmony (i.e. SPLC).

One God for All is an interesting and contemplative work, delving deep into the ancient texts of both the Bible and the Quran, to uncover the ties which bind Christianity and Islam to each other, and the origins from which differing practices and beliefs have stemmed. People of all religious backgrounds can benefit from this thorough and informative text. One God for All surprises us with its hidden gems of knowledge, sure to intrigue and enlighten even the most learned of readers.

Christina Keating Sami
Maryland

Writing a book on comparative religion is a very challenging task, as one must be well-versed in different religions. Mrs. Banu has spent much of her life reading and researching different books on Islam, Christianity, Judaism, and other religions. Finally, she has presented us with this version. The very name "One God for All" says that we all worship the same God. However, there are many deviations and misconceptions among different groups in some beliefs.

Mrs. Banu has tried to eliminate those misconceptions by taking verses from the Bible including both the Old and the New Testament and the Qur'an. This has presented a unique opportunity for the readers of all faiths to judge for themselves what the truth could be.

In this world of conflict and confusion, we all are looking for reconciliation and peace. I hope Mrs. Banu's efforts will lead many of us in that direction. I congratulate the author and the publisher for taking up the challenge of publishing this book, and I hope they are successful in their endeavors.

Dr. Mohammad Q. Islam
Maryland

Though D. R. Banu's letters are addressed specially to Reverend Sir Franklin Graham, it will surely capture a wide audience to engage in the same conversation with her. Her dire need to clarify the rather widely debated topic; do the Muslims, Jews and the Christians worship the same God? will unravel the misconceptions laid out in the Religious world of today. This question was probably the catalyst that started her conversations with Reverend Sir Franklin Graham.

With current technologies and overload of information, Dil Banu's letters are simple and yet meticulously detailed to give the reader the understanding of the fundamental beliefs of the Muslims who share the same Abrahamic faith with both the Jews and the Christians.

Her collection of letters are well organized and easy to read. She also provides good resources from both the Quranic and Biblical texts which confirms her beliefs and statements. These texts will guide the reader to pay attention to factual details.

"Remember this everlasting covenant of God which He meant to be obeyed and observed by Abraham and by all his progeny" (Letter-3), is the cornerstone of her letter which becomes the connecting factor that will unite those who share the same Abrahamic faith.

Though religious toleration is highly encouraged in her letters, the author is certainly unapologetic in stating her firm belief in worshipping the same One God of the Judeo-Christian Faith.

Merriam-Webster Encyclopedia of World Religions (page 747) defines: Islamic monotheism is more literal and uncompromising than that of any other religion. Allah is confessed being one, eternal, unbegotten, unequaled and beyond partnership of any kind.

A well-researched and comparative reading, written passionately.

Diyana Abdullah
Richmond, Virginia

We are parents of two school kids and teachers by profession. From our long experience as both parents and teachers, we strongly feel that this book "One God For All," is a must read book for the young generations of all religions especially the Christians and the Muslims when they are in so much confusion, contempt and distrust. We believe this book will help them to identify the root or heritage of their own faith and also make them to look at each other with love, respect and trust.

We also thank the author and the Publisher both to present us with such an enlightening and thought-provoking book as this. We also look forward to see her next book in reply to the evangelist's comment against Islam.

Md. Ziaul Haque Chowdhury &
Towhida Yesmin Chowdhury
Maryland

CONTENTS

PREFACE

IN THE NAME OF GOD, THE COMPASSIONATE, THE MERCIFUL

I think, a book like this requires a preface so that my prospective readers know in advance what motivated an old, ordinary, and unknown woman like me to write about such a highly sensitive, speculative and metaphysical subject as God.

But before I come to that, I would like to mention first the contents of this book, *One God for All*, is actually meant for the common Christians who worship God, along with Jesus. But people of other religions, who believe in God and in the eternal life through following His revealed guidance, may also find this book refreshing and worth reading.

This book is a kind of religious journal. I have reported here truthfully what I have observed, studied, learned or felt about the religious faith of the devoted Christians-both ordinary and elite, while living with them as my neighbors, coworkers, and friends for more than a decade (Twelve years have passed since then). I think, I need to add here a few things about me and some of my experiences to help my readers to know what is my true intention behind this writing.

I am a non-Arab Muslim by birth and practice. My homeland is Bangladesh-a beautiful country in South-East Asia. I was fifty when I came to America-the land of my childhood dream through OP-1 Visa. I came here not only from a different race and religion than most Americans, but also with a bagful of different customs, culture, language, and lifestyle. But I was lucky enough to have with me the maturity of my age and also a way of life of a practicing Muslim which helped me greatly to adjust myself with those changes of the Western culture while keeping my old ways of life unchanged. Besides that, I had a long experience of teaching in one of the prestigious schools of our country, and I think it helped me to get a job of a substitute teacher in the local elementary schools, soon after I came here.

But after a year or so, I gave up teaching and opened a licensed family day care in my rented apartment, where all my neighbors were Christians. I still am grateful to God for helping me choose the job of a child-care provider over the job of a teacher, because this change of job made a turning point in my life. I had a keen fascination for religion and the people of other religions since my teen age. So naturally, I became very happy and excited when I came in close contact with bunches of cute and lovely kids of some Christian families along with their kind, caring and helpful parents, after I started running my daycare. But there was other reason that made me feel more close to them.

People of the Book

I had known about Jesus and his followers in details from my mid-twenties, when I first started reading the meaning of the Holy Quran- the text of which God revealed to His last Prophet Muhammad in Arabic, about fourteen hundred years ago. In many places of the Quran, I found both the Jews and the Christians were addressed by God as the "People of the Book," because they also received their Holy books, the Torah, the Psalms, and the Gospel, through Moses, David, and Jesus, respectively.

The Quran has also addressed Abraham as the father and the leader of many nations and called him frequently as the upholder of pure and pristine monotheism, where God is claimed to be the One and Only and none has the right to be worshipped except Him. The Quran also tells us that the Jews, the Christians, and the Muslims have inherited the basic essence of their faith through Abraham. May be, it is for that long and deep-rooted link or heritage of our faith, I felt myself very much connected with my Christian neighbors and friends, even though I knew there was a heaven-to-earth differences in what we both believe and practice in the name of the same God.

The Christians are nearest in affection to the Muslims

But I tried to ignore those differences after I came to know them closely while living my day to day life with them as my neighbors and friends. I found them so kind, loving, friendly, and helpful that they often reminded me of that particular verse of the Quran where God has mentioned about them saying, *"You will find nearest in affection to the believers [Muslims] are those who say: "We are Christians." (5:82)*

But as the days went on, I began to feel a strong urge inside me to tell them what the Quran has really said about Jesus, and what he truly preached and practiced himself by the command of God and what he never taught. But somehow I could not. I found religion was a very delicate and sensitive subject and the topic of my discussion was even more critical. How could I tell them that they were following something in the name of Jesus that he never taught? Then, one day, to my utter surprise, the chance of talking about Jesus came to me quite unexpectedly.

No Jesus, no Heaven

It was a year or so after I began my day care, Christian missionaries started visiting me unannounced. They used to come in a group consisting of two to three men, women, young and old both. The sole purpose of their visit was, I soon learned, to make me alert of my salvation and how could I attain it through having faith in Jesus. They also flooded me with books, booklets, magazines, leaflets, and flyers whenever they came to visit me. As religion was my favorite subject, I used to read them all most willingly from cover to cover, and I felt amazed to know the bottom line of all those printed materials was one and the same. It was "No Jesus, No Heaven."

Most of them remained unaware of the mainstream Islam

But I felt more astonished to know that most of my missionary friends remained unaware of the mainstream Islam and therefore, the name of Muhammad, as the last Prophet of God, and the name of the Quran, as the last and final guidebook of God, also remained unknown to most of them. Or, if they knew anything at all, it was either wrong or misleading. As for example, many of them mistook Muhammad, the prophet of Islam in the seventh century Arabian desert, for Elijah Muhammad, a black American and the founder of Nation of Islam in Chicago only a few decades before.

I tried to correct those mistakes as humbly as possible and I also tried to inform them of some basic things about Islam to which one-fourth population of the world now adheres. Still, I preferred to talk to them more about Jesus than anything else. I found them quite pleased, when I described to them what the Quran says in adoration of Mary and her son, Jesus, including his miraculous birth, the miracles he performed, and the special status or rank that he and his mother received from God as a favor to them. But they began to visit me less after I started telling them that Jesus was not a deity or an inseparable part of God as they believed. Rather, he was a noble and a righteous human being who God chose as His messenger for the guidance of his own people-the misguided Jews.

But, soon I understood my mistake. I was telling them about Jesus as I learnt from the Quran-the Book we believe as the last and the final guidebook of God, but they believe it is only the Bible which contains true guidance of God. Some of my missionary friends also told me that they would not believe anything to be true, if they did not find it in their Holy Bible or find it inconsistent or contradictory to its teaching. So I thought, they might have listened to me carefully, if I could tell them about Jesus or his teaching from their own Gospel, the book they believed undoubtedly as the true account of Jesus' own words and deeds. As soon as I understood it, I took the study of the Bible very seriously.

One of my missionary friends gave me a copy of Bible in the King James Version which I used to read in a sporadic manner. In this way, I completed most of the chapters of the first four Gospels. But to establish Jesus as a messenger of God, and like all his predecessors and his successor Muhammad, he was also sent to proclaim the worship of One True God among his people and to help them live their lives through keeping His commands, I needed to read both parts of the Bible minutely. With this intention in mind, I started reading the Bible from Genesis, the first book of the Old Testament.

Both Parts of the Bible proclaim: God is One and Only

Frankly speaking, my faith in the Holy Quran became stronger and more intensified when I found both parts of the Holy Bible proclaim God being One and Only and no one was equal or worthy of worship besides Him. It was then, I felt for the first time to share this common heritage of our faith with the followers of Jesus Christ through my writing.

My old hobby of taking notes or synopsis from what I read or heard on religious and spiritual matters, seemed to be very helpful to carry out the project of my writing. I also had a huge stock of booklets, papers, leaflets, magazines and flyers that I collected so far in the last few years since my missionary friends began visiting me. Besides that, I had dozens of notepads where I jotted down the sum and substance of our conversations after they left. I just needed to arrange them according to the contents of my writing.

But all my spirit or inspiration fused off instantly when I told some of my close Muslim friends about the subject of writing, and she told me point-blank, it would be a sheer waste of my valuable time, labor and money. She also gave me a convincing explanation to justify her point. Finally she said that hundreds of well-researched and most valuable books were written on the same subject since Jesus left, so it would matter the least to his followers, if another book of the same kind was added to the list or not.

Though, I disliked her advice, I did not mind to ponder over the matter once again seriously.

Prayer followed by an anti-Islamic propaganda

After Mr. Bush won the election, I was watching the live telecast program of his presidential inauguration on January 20, 2001. In that ceremony, Reverend Franklin Graham, the well-reputed evangelist and a missionary of America, offered a prayer that I found very interesting. I felt elated, as he offered his prayer just like a Muslim. He said, "Now, O Lord, we dedicate this presidential inaugural ceremony to You. May this be the beginning of a new dawn for America as we humble ourselves before You and acknowledge You alone as our Lord, our Savior, and our Redeemer." And then, of course, he finished his prayer like a devoted Christian, saying, "We pray this in the name of the Father, and of the Son, the Lord Jesus Christ, and of the Holy Spirit. Amen."

While listening to the last part of his prayer, I asked myself wondering, how could a great evangelist like Rev. Graham, make his prayer in the name of three Gods, right after he acknowledged God alone as being their Lord, Savior, and Redeemer?

But I did not know then, more surprises were waiting for me. In the same occasion, Rev. Graham chose to volunteer some unsolicited comment about the God of the Muslims and their religion, Islam. He said bluntly and boldly: "The god of Islam is not the same God of the Christians or the Judeo-Christian faith. It is a different god, and I believe Islam is a very evil and a very wicked religion."

He made this comment prior to 9/11, and so I had no clue what he really intended to mean by this "different god" of the Muslims or what made him blurt out with this kind of slanderous comment against their religion Islam which is now adhered by one-fourth population of the world? But whatever his intention was, it worked as a jump-start for me. I instantly felt that I could begin now with my long-pending project of writing. I felt so, because by his comment, the evangelist made it quite clear that the Muslims worshipped some kind of pagan god or goddess of the uncivilized world and also practiced a kind of monstrous religion called Islam. I found his comment not only wrong, but it was completely misleading and malicious.

I thanked God most gratefully for making me wait so long, until the time and situation became absolutely ready and right for me. I also thanked the evangelist in silence to make my work easy for me, because it is through him I could now prove to his people with the help of both Bible and Quran that the Muslims never worshipped any 'different god' from the God of the Judeo-Christian Faith, it is in fact the Christians who did. With this intention in mind, I started writing to the evangelist some open letters on my website nonebutonegod.com, opposing the first part of his comment where he said, "The god of Islam is not the same God of the Christians or the Judeo-Christian Faith. It is a different god."

This book, "One God For All" contains more or less the same material, as I originally posted on my website about thirteen years before.

If God permits, I intend to take care of the last part of his comment in my next book to prove Islam is not a very evil and a very wicked religion, as the evangelist believes, it should on the other hand, be preached and practiced by all, as the terminator of all evils.

ACKNOWLEDGEMENTS

I took this project of writing absolutely in the name of God and for the sake of His pleasure. So, I first thank God most humbly and gratefully to help me fulfill my mission with His constant care, mercy and guidance.

I also offer my heartfelt thanks to all my learned reviewers who, in spite of their busy schedule, have spent their valuable time in reading my manuscript and also for writing their kind notes of appreciation to enhance the value and worth of my book. May God always help them make the best use of their knowledge and wisdom freely and for His Cause.

I feel very happy to convey my special thanks to the editorial, production and sales staff of the Author House Publication, for their courage, cooperation and generous support to publish this book and to make it available for both my Christian and non-Christian friends, throughout the world. May God help them all to achieve the best.

Last, but not the least, I like to remember my Lord in endless gratitude for blessing me with a loving, caring and a responsible daughter and a son, along with their supportive families. My daughter-in-law showed me first how to type in the lap and other things related to it, thus saving me forever from the tedious and time-killing job of writing by hand. My daughter, who is my honest critic and guide, tolerated me patiently through all the changes and corrections that I often made on my website for the last seven years. May God put them all under His constant care, mercy and guidance and also keep them happy and safe, both here and hereafter. I also wish the same for all my relatives, friends and neighbors who stood by me when I first came here as an immigrant and needed their help most.

Reference and Information

The primary sources of my knowledge, information, and reference are our Holy Scriptures-the Quran and the Bible. For the Bible, I consulted the King James Version (KJV), the Revised Standard Version (RSV), and the New International Version (NIV), but I quoted the verses of the Bible mostly from KJV.

For the Quran, I consulted the meaning and interpretation of Ibn Kathir, Mufty Muhammad Shafi, Dr. Muhammad Taqi-ud-Din al-Hilali and Muhammad Muhsin Khan, A. Yusuf Ali, Muhammad M. Pickthal, and Muhammad Farooq-i-Azam Malik. But I quoted the meaning of the verses mostly from the last three books. In this connection, I also like to admit honestly that sometimes I copied their translations as it is, but sometimes I copied them combining all, but always keeping their meaning intact. I did so only to make it sound plain, simple and easily understood by the common and ordinary people of the Western world.

Other Sources

In addition to that, *Merriam-Webster's Encyclopedia of World Religions*, *The Concise Encyclopedia of Islam* by Cyril Glasse, the complete works of Ahmed Deedat, and many other valuable books written by the most learned, open-minded and well-reputed scholars of both Eastern and the Western World also helped me greatly to explore, inquire, and understand the basic truth about God and of His eternal message that He revealed through all His messengers for the guidance of mankind. I have also added a list of books in a bibliography that I used for study, information or reference, at the end of my writing.

<u>Last of all, I hope my Muslim friends would not forget to invoke God for His peace and blessing upon Muhammad and all His messengers whenever they come across with their blessed names.</u>

SUMMARY OF THE CONTENTS

Letter 1. The God of Judeo-Christian Faith vs. The God of Islam

- Is "the God of Islam" different from "the God of the Judeo-Christian faith," as the Rev. Franklin Graham intended to mean?
- Why do the Muslims call God Allah? Is Allah different from God?
- Why Allah is the most appropriate name of all that man has ever invoked to remember or to worship his Supreme Lord, the Creator, and the Sustainer of the entire heavens and earth?

Letter 2. The Holy Quran Says: "God is One and Only"

- What has God said about Himself and His guidance in the Holy Quran, through His last Prophet Muhammad?
- Why could no one in the entire heavens and earth be equal to God or worthy of worship besides Him?

Letter 3. Both Parts of the Holy Bible Proclaim: "God is One and Only"

- What has God declared about Himself in the Old Testament through all His prophets before the arrival of Jesus?
- Did Jesus say anything about God or His guidance that was new or different from the teaching of all his predecessors or his successor Muhammad?

Letter 4. Muhammad Was Sent after Jesus Reviving Abraham's Faith, in Islam

- Did Muhammad ever ask his people to worship a different god from the God of Jesus, Moses, Abraham, or from any of his predecessors who were sent before him?
- What is Islamic monotheism? Why is it believed to be an eternal truth in the guidance of God being preached and practiced by all His messengers, including both Jesus and Muhammad?
- Who among the Jews, the Christians, and the Muslims can truly claim Abraham as their patriarch?

Letter 5. Jesus' Comforter was Muhammad, the Prophet of Islam

- Who did Jesus really mean to be his Comforter? Was he Muhammad, the Prophet of Islam, or the Holy Ghost?
- Why can Jesus' Comforter be no one else other than his successor, Muhammad?

Letter 6. True Meaning and Implication of the Name "Christ" and "Word"

- Why are there so many myths and misconceptions about the name "Christ?" What has the Holy Bible said about it?
- What has the Holy Quran said about the name Christ through his testifier Muhammad?
- Why Jesus was called the "Word of God" in the Bible and the Quran both? Did God really appear in the form of Jesus?
- What does *Grolier's Encyclopedia* say on Jesus' incarnation?

Letter 7. Jesus Declared Himself "A Prophet of God" in the Gospel and also in the Quran

- Who was Jesus and why he was sent for?
- What did our Holy Scriptures- the Gospel and the Quran, really say about Jesus?
- What did the Anglican bishops in England say about Jesus in their survey in 1984?

Letter 8. "Son of God" vs. "Son of man"

- Why did Jesus call God his Father and himself His Son?
- By calling himself the Son of God, did Jesus really mean he was truly begotten by God, as his followers claim?
- What did the people of Jesus' time really mean by the phrases "Son of God" and "Son of man"?
- What has the Quran said about Jesus' followers' claiming him as the Son of God?

Letter 9. Trinity Was Invented after Jesus left, He Never Taught It

- Did Jesus ever teach his people the doctrine of the Trinity or ask them to worship one God in the union of three (God, Jesus, and the Holy Ghost) or three Gods as one and the same?
- How did Jesus' true followers react when the Trinity was first inserted into their faith by the Council of Nicaea in 325 CE (about 325 years after Jesus' ascent to heaven)?
- What has the Quran said about the doctrine of the Trinity through Jesus' testifier Muhammad?

Letter 10. Some misunderstood and misinterpreted statements of Jesus

- What are those statements of Jesus that might confuse his followers and make them worship him as God or along with God by ignoring the crystal clear message of the first commandment?
- Did not Jesus tell his people repeatedly that he was but a servant of God, and he said or did nothing but by the will or the command of God?
- What has the Quran said in general about the deviation of the people from the easy and straight path of God to the invented path of men?

Letter 11. Jesus Never Said or Did Anything but by the Command of God

- Can any evangelist explain how God and Jesus be regarded as one and the same in those verses of Math (5:48; 11:25; 19:17; 27:46); Mark (3:35; 10:27; 11:22; 12:29-30); Luke (4:8) and John (8:42; 17:3, 20:17)?
- Why Jesus' miraculous birth and the miracles he performed could not make him God or His equal?
- How does the episode of the fig tree make Jesus' human status distinctly clear from the unattainable status of God?

Letter 12. Our "Only Way to Heaven" as Described in the Bible and the Quran

- Did God say anywhere in the Bible or in the Quran that Adam was responsible for the sin of mankind?
- Did not the Bible and the Quran tell us repeatedly that man was responsible for his own deeds and no one would bear the burden of others?

- What does a man truly require for the remission of his sin? What does the Bible and the Quran say about it?
- What has God said about our only way to heaven in both our Holy Scriptures-the Bible and the Quran?
- Does the Gospel bear any acceptable evidence in support of Jesus' atonement or his resurrection, which his followers are required to believe for the remission of their sin and for their eternal life in heaven?

THE GOD OF THE JUDEO-CHRISTIAN FAITH VS. THE GOD OF ISLAM

*And argue not with the people of the Books (Jews and the Christians),
except in a better way unless it is with those of them who inflict
wrong, and say (to them): We believe in that which has been revealed
to us and in that which has been revealed to you; our God and your
God is the Same One God, and to Him we submit as Muslims.*
—Holy Quran 29:46

Much Respected Reverend Franklin Graham:

It is needless to say I strongly dispute your comment that Muslims worship a "different god" from the God of the Judeo-Christian faith. But before I enter into that, I would like to draw your attention to one basic thing needed to determine the truth of a disputed, doubtful, or a controversial issue.

As a man of great learning, wisdom, and insight, you must know that truth itself is self-evident. It does not require any evidence to prove *truth* to be true. If we never learned about the rotation of the earth on its axis, it still would remain true until the end of the creation. But the scientists needed to provide sufficient proof, evidence, and reasonable explanation to establish it as true or to make it acceptable to others.

But for some reason, however, you have overlooked this fact and did not give any evidence or explanation of why you think the God of the Muslims is different from the God of the Jews or the Christians. In your speech at President Bush's inauguration, of which I have a printed transcript, you wrote "the god of Islam"—using a lowercase "g"—but "the God of the Judeo-Christian faith" with a capital G. By this tricky change in the letter G, you made your intention quite clear. Along with it, you also commented that Islam was a "very evil and a very wicked religion," and that made your mission complete. The common Christians who believe everything that their evangelists utter to them and who know very little if anything about Islam, the Quran, or Muhammad, might assume the Muslims worship some god or goddess like the pagans of the ancient world and practice some religion which is barbaric in nature.

Reverend, with this preconceived idea or impression about the God of Islam, I don't expect your people to go through my arguments to see what kind of God the Muslims really worship or where exactly the God of Islam differs from the God of the Judeo-Christian faith. In spite of that, I would like to hope that some of them might reflect upon the contents of this letter and next three where I have tried to prove with the help of both Bible and Quran that the God of Islam and the God of the Judeo-Christian faith is one and the same. With this hope in mind, I like to begin first what we truly mean by the God of the Judeo-Christian faith and the God of Islam.

The very name indicates that the God of the Judeo-Christian faith refers absolutely to the same one God worshipped by Moses and Jesus and their true followers, the Jews and the Christians, respectively. Similarly, the God of Islam refers exclusively to the God worshipped by Muhammad, the prophet of Islam, and his followers, the Muslims.

Muhammad worshipped the same One God of all his predecessors

According to the recorded history of the Semitic religion, language, and culture, the God of the Judeo-Christian faith and the God of

Islam is one and the same. The eternal truth in the guidance of God, which He sent through all His messengers beginning with Adam, the father of mankind, until His last messenger, Muhammad, was *Tawhid* (in Arabic), the meaning of which is pure and pristine monotheism, where God is claimed to be One and Only, and none has the right to be worshipped except Him.

Muhammad, the last prophet of God, left the same message in Islam about fourteen hundred years ago, and his followers, the Muslims, still worship the same one God of all His messengers including Abraham, Moses, Jesus and Muhammad. I'll try to justify the truth of my claim with clear and concrete evidence from our Holy Scriptures-the Bible and the Quran both. I think, this is the only way a sensible person could determine whether Muslims worship the same one God of the Judeo-Christian Faith or a "different god" as you intended to mean.

> **A note to readers:**
>
> On the basis of the evangelists comment, I would keep this discussion exclusively in between the Christians and the Muslims. Except for reference, I would not involve the Jews or the people of other religions, with this disputed issue.

The contents of my letters

Reverend, I intend to present the entire topic of my discussion in twelve letters. In the first four letters, I will try to establish that the Muslims have always worshipped and still worship the same One God as He described Himself in His Holy Scriptures -the Torah, the Gospel, and the Quran through all His messengers beginning from Adam to Muhammad and all who were sent in between for the guidance of His people. And, in the rest of my letters, I intend to prove with the help of the Bible and the Quran both that it is in fact, the Christians who worship 'different god' from the God of the Judeo-Christian faith by forsaking the eternal truth of the first commandment and by making Jesus an object of worship along with One True God.

The topic of my first letter is Allah

As God is the cornerstone of this topic, I would like to explain here a bit why the Muslims all over the world call or invoke God as Allah. I think to discuss the God of Islam without mentioning the name Allah, would be like teaching a language without teaching its alphabet or smelling a rose without having its fragrance. To all Muslims, the name Allah itself is the touchstone of their faith, without which its true essence, spirit, or ecstasy could never be felt or understood.

While talking to my missionary friends over the past few years, I had a chance to know the common Christians here in America have lots of misconceptions about the name Allah. But I felt astonished to know that many elite and well reputed people here in America also belonged to them, at least in this particular field of knowledge.

After that fateful day of September 11, 2001, Lieutenant General William G. Boykin said once clearly and confidently that his God meaning the God of the Christians were real and bigger than the God of the Muslims, called Allah. But like you, he also did not bother to explain how he found Allah or the God of the Muslims, being fake or smaller than the God of the Christians.

Even a responsible US senator once said, when referring to the fatal incidents of 9/11, that the God of the Christians sacrificed His own Son to show His love for them and to take them to heaven, but the God of the Muslims who they call Allah, wanted them to sacrifice their lives to show their love for Him and to go to heaven.

So, I think it is for the information of all I need to explain first, why the Muslims call the object of their worship Allah instead of God or by any other name.

Allah and God Are Synonymous

Allah is the proper name of the same one God in Arabic. So, it is not confined to Islam alone. All Arabic-speaking people, including the Jews and the Christians of the Arab countries, also call Him Allah instead of God or by any other name. The non-Arab Muslims, like me and others all over the world, also call Him Allah, because this name has frequently been used in the text of the Holy Quran, which God revealed to Muhammad in his native language Arabic. In other word, "Allah" and "God" are synonymous.

Muslims believe absolutely that the name "Allah" refers to none but the one true God, Who created mankind with a definite purpose, made them dwell on earth for a while to fulfill that purpose, and finally wanted them back to heaven, their eternal abode from this transitory station of their life.

The name Allah was known in the Pre-Islamic Arab

The pagans of pre-Islamic Arabia, who gradually indulged themselves in idol worship by forgetting the pure monotheistic faith of Abraham, Ishmael and Isaac, also invoked their supreme deity by the name Allah. Not only that, in case of any emergency, importance, or religious obligation, they used to take their oath or to make their sacrifices in the name of Allah. In other words, the name Allah was known to the Arabs and was used by them long before the Quran was revealed to Muhammad. As for example, the name of Muhammad's own father was Abd Allah, meaning the slave or the servant of God. But when the people got completely derailed from the practice of pure monotheism to the pagan practice of polytheism, they made Allah remote or passive and began to ask His favor only through their associates or other deities, whom they worshipped by different names.

The name Allah existed in the Vedic scriptures

The name Allah existed even in the Veda, the oldest known scriptures of ancient India, during the period of 1500–1200 BCE.

In the 9:67:30 and 3:30:10 mantras, or the verses, of Rigveda, the name Allah was described as being one, omnipresent and omniscient. Let me quote a few of them:

"That Allah is One, Who enters the hearts of men and knows their secrets." (Atharvaveda 10:9:29)

"The Lord of the Universe is One; He is the Soul of every living being, He is immanent in every form of life; He directs all actions, He is above all; He is everyone's Refuge, He sees all, He knows all; no epithet is applicable to Him." (Shetash-water Upanishad, 6:11)

"The Supreme Being manifests the manifest. He fulfills the desire of the good-natured. He is the Lord. He is Omnipresent. He is Worthy of all praises. He is the Object of all respect. He is Rich. He is the Greatest. He is the Creator of everything and has the knowledge of everything." (Rigveda 2:1:3)

YAWH and Elohim were also synonymous to Allah

In the Hebrew Scriptures of Torah (The Old Testament of the Bible), God never introduced Himself as God, quite naturally, because all the messengers of God were known to receive His message in their own native languages. Since none of them was English-speaking, it is more than obvious that the name of God as "God" were unknown to them.

The Hebrew Bible used two names for the same one God. One was known as YAWH and the other was Elohim. And both of these names have always been translated in English as Lord God. But in a broader and a deeper sense, both the names carry one universal truth about God's being one, eternal and absolute.

It is also interesting to note here that the Jews considered the name of God to be too holy to utter, so they refrained totally from articulating it. Even their chief rabbis (the spiritual leaders of the Jewish congregation) did not allow this ineffable name to be heard any way or anywhere. As a result of that, they eventually forgot how the name of YAWH or Elohim was pronounced.

YAWH became Jehovah in course of time

It is now known that both the Hebrew and Arabic languages, which the Jews and the Arabs inherited from a common linguistic source, tradition, and culture, go long back to their religious and spiritual leader Abraham. Both the languages shared some common characteristics.

Originally, both Hebrew and Arabic were written without any vowel sign, which made no problem for the native people. They could read at ease, even without vowels. But later, they started using vowels for the benefit of the outsiders who had different native languages. Accordingly, YAWH, when it was spelled in writing with the use of vowels, became YeHoWaH.

So YAWH, Yehova, or Yahuwa all referred to God in both Hebrew and Arabic. "Ya" is a vocative and an exclamatory particle in both Hebrew and Arabic meaning "Oh!"

Similarly, Huwa, or Hu, means *He* in both Hebrew and Arabic. So by YAWH or Yahuwa, we find 'Oh, He!' which the Jews used for God without uttering His name. But when a popular trend developed with the European translators to replace the Y for J, the name YeHoWaH changed into Jehovah.

As for example, Yael, Yehuda, Yusuf, Yunus, and Yesus became Joel, Judah, Joseph, Jonah, and Jesus, respectively, after being translated into English

It was between the sixth and tenth centuries that YAWH, the unpronounced name of God of the Hebrew Bible, became Jehovah, a Judeo-Christian name for God.

Centuries later, in 1931, Joseph Franklin Rutherford, popularly known as Judge Rutherford, founded a new cult upon this very name and called it Jehovah's Witnesses, to reaffirm Jehovah as the true God and to identify those who witnessed in this name as God's especially accredited followers.

Elohim, the plural form of Eloah used to mean One God

Though Elohim is the plural form of Eloah, it also was used to mean the same one God in Hebrew. It is also important to note that there are two types of plural in the Hebrew and Arabic languages. One indicates number, and the other shows honor or respect, as in the case of any royal proclamation. Elohim is a plural form of a noun but is singular in meaning, when it is used for One True God. Both Hebrew and Arabic have this particular characteristic and therefore none of my readers should be confused with those Quranic verses where God used "We" instead of "I" while delivering His message to Muhammad through Gabriel. I needed to mention it here because while reading the verses of the Quran, many a scholar of the Western world often get confused about this characteristic of the Arabic language and mistake "We" for the Trinity (Father, Son, and Holy Spirit). But nowhere in the Quran, the name of God has been mentioned in the plural form.

For example, in the verse 105 of chapter 4, God declares through Muhammad, saying,

"We have revealed to you the Book with the Truth so that you may judge between people in accordance with the Right Way which Allah has shown to you, so be not advocate for those who betray trust."

Reverend, I would like to draw your attention to the following chart, which will explain how the name of One God has been used in both Hebrew and Arabic language.

HEBREW	ARABIC	ENGLISH
Elah	Ilah	God
Ikhud	Ahud	One
YaHuwa	YaHuwa	Oh He
Huwa El Elah	Huwallah	He is God

In fact, all the prophets of God, including Jesus, were familiar with the name Allah. They used the name of God in their own languages, which was synonymous to Allah. Or, the name sounded closer to Allah than God or any other known name of God.

In the Hebrew Bible, the name of Allah as Elah or Alah appears in almost all the verses of the first chapter of Genesis.

Jesus invoked God as E-li or E-lo-i

In the Gospel, which Jesus received from God in his native language Aramaic, we heard him to invoke desperately the name of his eternal Lord as E-li or E-lo-i in Matthew 27:46 and Mark 15:34. Reverend, don't you think they sound closer to Elah, Alah, or Allah than to God or any other name of God? I think any expert linguist in Hebrew, Aramaic, or Arabic would find the name of E-li, E-lo-i, Elohim, Al, El, Al-le-lu-ia, Alloah, Elah, Alah, or Allah originated from the same root and also meant the same one, eternal, absolute, and self-existing Divine Being. In other words, they all represent the one single Arabic word, Allah-the original, unchanged, and immortal name of the Almighty God. Not only that, the name has also remained intact under all circumstances and against all transgression made by men in the scriptures of God, except His last Guidebook the Quran, the text of which has remained unchanged word for word for the last fourteen hundred years. And, we believe it will remain so until the end of the world, according to the promise of God that He made in the Quran (15:9) through His last Prophet Muhammad.

On Alleluia—Points to Ponder

Reverend, we find this word "alleluia" in the book of Revelation 19:1-the last book of the New Testament. This verse describes a vision of John, a disciple of Jesus, when he heard the angels in heaven say "alleluia" in praise of God. Christians, in general, also exclaim "alleluia" when they go into some sorts of ecstasy or excitement. I think they do so, however, without knowing the true meaning or the implication of that word. Based on your comment about the God of Islam, I think you are also unaware of its meaning as well. By the exclamation "alleluia," they actually express their feeling of joy or gratitude to God, simply calling Him "Oh Allah!" the way a devoted Muslim does.

As previously mentioned, in both the Hebrew and Arabic languages, "Ya" is used as a vocative or an exclamatory particle, meaning "Oh!" Accordingly, any Arab or Jew would pronounce *alleluia* as "Ya-Alle-Lu," meaning "Oh Eli, Alle, Elah, Alah or Allah."

Sir, don't you think this explanation matches with Allah much better than with God or any other name of God invoked or worshipped by men until now?

In this connection, I also like to mention here, the Scofield Reference Bible, in English, edited by Rev. C. I. Scofield, DD (doctor of divinity), along with a team of eight consulting editors, all DDs, found "Alah" to be more appropriate while translating the Hebrew word "Elah" from the book of Genesis. But later, "Alah" was wiped out mysteriously from recent publication of the New Scofield Reference Bible, as well as from the authorized King James Version. But no one can suppress the truth for long, especially when it concerns God and the eternal truth of His guidance, because God has His own unique way to save the truth for them who really seek for it.

The name Allah is unique and immutable

Allah is undoubtedly a unique and an immutable name for a number of good reasons.

First, the name Allah is as eternal as Allah Himself. This name has remained unchanged and immutable since God first revealed this name for Him, to be invoked and worshipped by men.

Second, Allah has no corresponding word in English or in any other known language of the world.

Third, no new or corresponding word can be made from Allah, as it is done with the name God. For example, the words god, goddess, godfather, godson, and godly have been made from the word God.

Fourth, the name Allah has neither any plural nor any masculine or feminine form, as we have with God.

The name is considered as the key to salvation

Reverend, the name is most amazing of all for one particular reason. (I have borrowed this explanation mostly from *The Concise Encyclopedia of Islam* by Cyril Glasse, page 37.) Muhammad Busharah, a representative of a Moroccan Darqawi Shaykh in the beginning of this century, observed an overwhelming presence of One True God, along with the basic truth of His guidance in this unique Arabic name Allah, which is spelled as alif, laam, laam, and haa. Let us see how.

In Arabic, the name of Allah begins with its first letter *Alif,* which also looks like the Arabic first numeral one (1), representing, undoubtedly, His being one and the first.

Now, if we remove the first letter alif from the name Allah, the remaining letters will be read in Arabic like "Lillah," meaning toward Allah or for the sake of Allah.

Then, if we remove the second letter, which is the first *laam*, it will be read in Arabic like "Lahu," meaning to Him.

And, if we remove the third letter, which is the second *laam*, the only letter that remains is Ha, which, vocalized, becomes the name

"Huwa," meaning He-the name of the essence referring again to none but God Himself.

You may also be amazed to know that when we invoke the name of Allah, its form gradually melts into breath itself. The same happens to the dying man whose soul is resolved into breathing alone and leaves the body with the last breath. In this way, the name itself remains with us until our last breath, reminding us constantly of One and Only God and of His one designated path, so that we could return to Him safely and without being confused or misled.

I think, this information is enough for a sensible and open-minded person to know and understand why the Muslims find the name 'Allah' more appropriate to worship or invoke while asking for His help, mercy or guidance. But it is also a fact that besides the name Allah, the Quran has also described many other beautiful names of God denoting His unique essence and attributes through His last Prophet Muhammad.

> Allah! There is no God but He. To Him belong the most beautiful names (20:8).

LETTER 2

THE HOLY QURAN SAYS GOD IS ONE AND ONLY

∞

Your God is One God; there is no one worthy of worship except Him,
the Compassionate, the Merciful.
—Quran 2:163

∞

Reverend Franklin Graham:

In this letter, I intend to tell you about Allah, or the God of Islam, as He has described Himself in the Quran through His last prophet, Muhammad. There are countless verses in the Quran in which God makes Himself known to us through His unique essence and attributes. I hope this will help you to know clearly and correctly what kind of God the Muslims really worship, obey and adore.

But before that, I need to mention here two things related to the meaning or the translation of the Quran. First, except for the Quran in Arabic text, which Muhammad received directly from God through Gabriel, the Muslims do not regard its meaning or the translation in other languages as the Quran or the revealed Book of God. They mention them as the meaning of the Quran in English and French, etc.

Second, the Quran has 114 *Suras*, or chapters, consisting of verses of unequal length. While quoting from the Quran, the number of the chapter is placed first, followed by a colon and the number of the verse or verses. For example, the numbers in the parenthesis (14:31-34) indicate verses 31 to 34 have been quoted from the chapter 14, the title of which is Ibrahim.

With this little note of information, now I would like to draw your attention to the meaning and translation of the following verses of the Quran where you will find how the God of Islam has made Himself and the basic truth of His guidance, known to the people through His last Prophet Muhammad.

God is One and without any partner

"Allah Himself has testified to the fact that there is no God but Him and so do the angels and those who are well grounded in knowledge standing firm on justice. There is no God except Him, the Mighty, the Wise." (3:18)

"[To Muhammad] Say: He is Allah, The One and Only. Allah, The Eternal, The Absolute; He begets not, nor is He begotten; And there is none comparable to Him." (112:1–4)

"All that exists on the earth will perish, but the Face of your Lord will remain full of Majesty and Glory." (55:26–27)

"This is a Message for the mankind: let them take warning from there, and let them know that He is the One and Only God: and let the men of understanding take heed." (14:52)

"[To Muhammad] Say: O mankind! I am the Messenger of Allah towards all of you from Him to whom belongs the kingdom of the heavens and the earth. There is no god but Him." (7:158)

"Allah is He, beside Him there is no other god, The Knower of all things both secret and open. He is Most Gracious, Most Merciful. Allah is He, besides Him there is no other god. The Sovereign, the Holy One, The Source

of Peace, the Guardian of Faith, The Preserver of Security, the Exalted in Might, The Irresistible, the Supreme: Glory be to Allah! High is He above the partners they ascribe to Him. He is Allah, the Creator, the Evolver, the Modeler. To whom belong the Most Beautiful Names: All that is in the heavens and the earth declare His glory: And He is the All-Mighty, the All-Wise." (59:22–24)

"Allah! There is no god but Him; The Living, The Eternal. He has revealed to you this Book [the Quran] with the Truth, confirming the scripture which preceded it, as He revealed the Torah and the Gospel before this." (3:2–3)

Reverend, there are many oft-repeated verses in the Quran like the last one I quoted above, where we are told clearly and categorically that the Bible including both its Old and the New Part, carry the same eternal truth about God's being One and worshipping none but Him. We shall check the truth in the next letter.

God is Omnipotent, Omnipresent and Omniscient

"Allah! There is no god but Him: the Living, the Eternal. Neither slumbers nor sleep overtakes Him. To Him belongs all that is in the heavens and in the earth. Who is he that can intercede with Him without His permission? He knows what is before them and what is behind them. And they encompass nothing of His knowledge except what He pleases. His throne extends over the heavens and the earth, and He feels no fatigue in preserving them. And He is the Most High, the Supreme." (2:255)

"He Alone has the keys of the unforeseen treasures, of which no one knows except Him. He knows whatever is in the land and in the sea; there is not a single leaf that falls without His knowledge, there is neither a grain in the darkness of the earth nor anything fresh or dry but is written in a Clear Record." (6:59)

By this clear record, the Quran refers to al-Lawh al-Mahfuz, meaning the guarded tablet, or the Glorious Book, which has recorded everything that exists in the entire heavens and earth and every event that has taken place from the beginning to the day of resurrection manifesting Gods overall knowledge and authority over them. It is also called the Mother Book.

"No vision can grasp Him while He grasps all visions. He is the Subtle, the Aware." (6:102–103)

"He has the knowledge of all that goes into the earth and that which comes out of it; and all of that which comes down from heaven and that ascends to it." (34:2)

"God is He Who has created seven Firmaments and of the earth a similar number. His Command descends through them: that you may know that Allah has power over all things, and that Allah comprehends all things in His knowledge." (65:12)

God is the Creator of all

Reverend, in the following verses of the Quran, God describes Himself as being the sole Creator of the heavens and earth and everything that comes in between.

"All praises be to Allah, the One Who has created the heavens and the earth and made the darkness and the light; yet the unbelievers set up equal partners with their Lord. He is the One Who has created you from clay,

then decreed a fixed term of life and set a deadline for you Himself; yet you go on doubting!" (6:1–2)

"Allah is the One Who raised the heavens without any pillars that you can see, then firmly established Him on the throne of authority and subjected the sun and the moon to His Law, each one pursuing its course for an appointed time. He regulates all affairs. He has spelled out His revelations so that you may believe in meeting your Lord." (13:2)

"He is the One Who spread out the earth and placed thereon mountains and rivers, created fruits of every kind in pairs, two and two, and makes the night cover the day. Certainly, in these things there are signs for those who use their common sense." (13:3)

"He brings out the living from the dead and the dead from the Living, and gives life to the earth after its death. Likewise you shall be brought forth to life after your death." (30:19)

"Verily, whenever He intends doing a thing, He says to it Be and it is!" (36:82)

God Is the Planner and the Controller of Everything

"The sun runs its course which is predetermined by the Almighty, the All-Knowing. As for the moon, We have designed phases for it till it again becomes like an old dry palm branch. Neither it is possible for the sun to overtake the moon, nor for the night to outstrip the day: each floats along in its own orbit (According to the Law of God). When Allah commands, there is none to reverse His Command and He is swift in taking accountability. Allah is the Master of all planning. He knows the actions of every soul." (13:41)

"Allah is the creator of all things and He is the Guardian and Disposer of all affairs." (39:62)

"He is the One Who has given you life, will cause you to die and then will bring you back to life again." (22:66)

God Is the Provider and the Sustainer of All

Reverend, in the following verses of the Quran, we shall see that God of Islam is not only the Creator of all or the master of all planning, but He is also the provider and the sustainer of every living thing that exists on, above, or under the earth.

"We send the fertilizing winds and send down water from the sky for you to drink; and it is not you who own the storage of this wealth." (15:22)

"We have spread out the earth and set mountains upon it; and caused to grow therein every suitable thing in due proportion. And we have provided therein means of subsistence for you and for those whom you do not provide." (15:19–20)

"Let man reflect on the food he eats, how we pour down rainwater in abundance and cleave the soil asunder. How we bring forth grain, grapes and nutritious vegetations, olives and dates, lush gardens, fruit and fodder, as a mean of sustenance for you and for your cattle." (80:24–32)

"How many creatures are there that do not carry their provisions with them. Allah provides them as He provides for you." (29:60)

On God's Endless Favors, Mercy, and Forgiveness

"Allah brought you forth from the wombs of your mothers when you knew nothing, and He gave you hearing, sight and intelligence so that you might give thanks to Allah." (16:78)

"It is Allah, Who has created the heavens and the earth. He sends down rain from the sky with which He brings forth fruits for your sustenance. He

has made the ships subservient to you, which may sail through the sea by His Command; and likewise the rivers are made for your benefit. The sun and the moon are also assigned for your benefit, which diligently pursue their courses to cause the night and day for your service. He has given you all that you could ask for and if you want to count the favors of Allah, you will never be able to count them." (14:32-34)

"He has also subjected to you whatever is in between the heavens and the earth: it is all as a favor and kindness from Him. Verily, there are signs in it for those who reflect." (45:13)

"Allah says: O my servants who have transgressed against their souls, do not despair of the mercy of Allah, for Allah forgives all sins: Truly, He is Oft-Forgiving, Most Merciful." (39:53)

No One Is Worthy of Worship Besides God

Reverend, the verses I quoted above are sufficient to know and realize that God alone has the right to be worshipped since no one in the entire heavens and earth could be His equal or worthy of worship besides Him. I have quoted below a few more verses from the Quran with the same eternal message that God wanted all of mankind to remember and follow, so that all could return to Him-their Ultimate Refuge safely.

"O Muhammad, tell them: I am but a human being like you; the revelation is sent to me to declare that your God is One God; therefore, whoever hopes to meet his Lord, let him do good deeds and join no partner in the worship of his Lord." (18:110)

"Invoke no other god besides Allah. There is no god besides Him. Everything is perishable except Him. To Him belongs the judgment and to Him you will be returned." (28:88)

"[To Muhammad] Say: O ignorant! Do you bid me to worship someone other than Allah? But it has already been revealed to you as it was revealed to those before you that if you ascribe a partner to Allah, all your deeds will go in vain and you will surely be among the losers. Therefore, worship Allah and be among His thankful servants." (39:65–66)

"O Prophet, tell them: 'I have been forbidden to invoke them who you invoke besides Allah. How could I do so after clear revelations came to me from my Lord and I have commanded to submit myself to the Lord of the worlds?" (40:66)

"O mankind! Worship your Lord Who created you and created those who came before you. Who has made the earth your couch, and the sky your canopy, and sent down rain from the heavens; and brought forth therewith fruits for your sustenance; Then do not set up rivals unto Allah [in worship] when you know the truth [that He alone has the right to be worshipped]." (2:21–22)

Reverend, on the basis of the above verses, the Muslims, or the followers of Muhammad, believe absolutely that there is none but Allah, whose glory and greatness, wisdom and authority, compassion and kindness, and favors and forgiveness are beyond any measure, and therefore, no one has the right to be worshipped except Him. This is Allah, whom the Muslims worship, obey and constantly seek for His mercy and guidance in every walk of their life.

> He is the Lord of the heavens and the earth, and of all that lies in between, so worship Him, be steadfast in His worship. Do you know anyone who is similar to Him? (Holy Quran 19:65).

BOTH PARTS OF THE HOLY BIBLE PROCLAIM "GOD IS ONE AND ONLY"

Hear, O Israel: The Lord our God is one Lord.
And thou shalt love the Lord thy God
with all thine heart, and with all thy soul, and with all thy might.
—Deuteronomy 6:4–5

Reverend Franklin Graham:

In my last letter, I have described what the Quran says about God and the basic truth of His guidance. The Quran also confirms that both the Old and the New Testament of the Holy Bible contain the same eternal truth of God's being one and worshipping none but Him. But the Muslims do not have to read the Bible to verify the truth, because upon the testimony of Muhammad alone, they already believe it to be absolutely true. In support of my claim, I have quoted below a series of evidence from both parts of the Bible.

The Old Testament of the Bible proclaims: God is One and Only

I will start first with Genesis, the first book of the Holy Bible

"In the beginning, God created the heaven and the earth." (Genesis 1:1)

"And the LORD God formed man of the dust of the ground, and breathed into his nostrils the breath of life; and man became a living soul." (Genesis 2:7)

"But Noah found grace in the eyes of the LORD. These are the generations of Noah: Noah was a just man and perfect in his generations, and Noah walked with God." (Genesis 6:8–9)

The first two verses confirm that no one existed in the beginning, except God Who created heaven and earth and also formed Adam-the father of mankind with dust and made him a complete human being after He breathed His spirit through his nostrils.

The last verse tells us that the path of God was defined from the start and spread of human habitation, but it was followed only by just and righteous persons, like Noah.

God's everlasting covenant with Abraham and his seeds

In the following verses of the Genesis, we shall see that Abraham and his descendants also worshipped the same one God of Adam and Noah and lived their lives by His command.

"And when Abram [Abraham] was ninety years old and nine, the LORD appeared to Abram, and said unto him, I am the Almighty God; walk before me, and be thou perfect." (Genesis 17:1)

Jacob saw a dream and heard God say to him … "And, behold, the LORD stood above it, and said, I am the LORD God of Abraham thy father, and the God of Isaac: the land whereon thou liest, to thee will I give it, and to thy seed." (Genesis 28:13)

"And I will establish my covenant between me and thee and thy seed after thee in their generations for an everlasting covenant, to be a God unto thee, and to thy seed after thee." (Genesis 17:7)

Reverend, kindly remember this everlasting covenant of God, which He meant to be obeyed and observed by Abraham and by all his progeny. The Muslims believe it is "Tawhid" (in Arabic), the meaning of which is Islamic monotheism where God is claimed to be One and Only, and none has the right to be worshipped except Him. We also believe that it is the fundamental truth in the guidance of God which He revealed to all His messengers including both Jesus and Muhammad. In other word, all of them were sent to teach their people to worship none but One God and to live their worldly life through keeping His commands. I'll try to justify my point with some statements of the Old Testament. Let us begin first with Moses- a mighty messenger of God from the tribes of Abraham as well as one of the founding pillars of the Judeo-Christian Faith.

Moses was sent to proclaim God is One and to worship none but Him

"And God spoke unto Moses, and said unto him, I am the LORD: And I appeared unto Abraham, unto Isaac, and unto Jacob, by the name of God Almighty, but by my name Je-ho-vah was I not known to them." (Exodus 6:2–3)

"Who is like unto thee, O LORD among the gods? Who is like thee, glorious in holiness, fearful in praises, doing wonders?" (Exodus 15:11)

"The LORD shall reign forever and ever." (Exodus 15:18)

"And God spake all these words saying, I am the LORD thy God, which have brought thee out of the land of Egypt, out of the house of bondage. Thou shalt have no other gods before me. Thou shalt not make unto thee any graven

image, or any likeness of anything that is in heaven above, or that is in the earth beneath, or that is in the water under the earth." (Exodus 20:1–4)

"And the LORD spake unto Moses, saying, Speak unto the children of Israel, and say unto them, I am the LORD your God." (Leviticus 18:1–2)

"Ye shall do my judgments, and keep mine ordinances, to walk therein: I am the LORD your God." (Leviticus 18:4)

"Unto thee it was shewed, that thou mightiest know that the LORD he is God; there is none else beside him." (Deuteronomy 4:35)

"Know therefore this day, and consider it in thine heart, that the LORD he is God in heaven above, and upon the earth beneath: there is none else." (Deuteronomy 4:39)

"Hear, O Israel: The LORD our God is one LORD.. And thou shalt love the LORD thy God with all thine heart, and with all thy soul, and with all thy might." (Deuteronomy 6:4–5)

Reverend, I think the message of the above-quoted verses is crystal clear. It is in fact 'Tawhid' or pure and pristine monotheism, which I already mentioned before. In the following verses of the Old Testament, Moses is seen pleading his people earnestly to obey God and to live their lives by His command and also to warn them about the consequence of their being disobedient to Him.

"Ye shall diligently keep the commandments of the LORD your God, and His testimonies, and His statutes, which He hath commanded thee." (Deuteronomy 6:17)

"And it shall be, if thou do at all forget the LORD thy God, and walk after other gods, and serve them, and worship them, I testify against you this day that ye shall surely perish." (Deuteronomy 8:19)

"Behold, I set before you this day a blessing and a curse; A blessing, if ye obey the commandments of the LORD your God, which I command you this day: And a curse, if you will not obey the commandments of the LORD your God, but turn aside out of the way which I command you this day, to go after other gods, which ye have not known." (Deuteronomy 11:26–28)

The message of the above verses is plain and simple. Like all his predecessors, Moses was also sent to teach his people worship none but One God, to remind them of His reward and blessing, if they obeyed His commands; and of His curse and punishment, if they chose to disobey Him or deviate from His path.

The following statements of the Old Testament tell us what happened after the departure of Moses and Aaron.

"And the children of Israel did evil in the sight of the LORD, and served Ba-a-lim: And they forsook the LORD God of their fathers, which brought them out of the land of Egypt, and followed other gods, of the gods of the people that were round about them, and bowed themselves unto them, and provoked the LORD to anger." (Judges 2:11–12)

But every time it happened so, God has only punished them who He found rebellious, arrogant, and unrepentant for their wrong doing, in spite of His repeated reminder and warning through their respective messengers. But God has always forgiven them and also guided them to His path who He found repent truly and to rectify their wrong doings. Not only that, as a mark of His endless love, mercy and kindness to the ignorant, oblivious, careless and misled people, God has sent His messengers one after another along with His guidance so that they could remember of His path and follow it to return to Him safely.

David surrendered himself completely to the will and command of God

Reverend, in the following verses of the Old Testament, we shall see how David-one of the noble messengers of God, surrendered himself completely to the will and command of God and also expressed his love and gratitude in appreciation of His endless glory and greatness.

"Wherefore thou art great, O LORD God: for there is none like thee, neither is there any god beside thee, according to all that we have heard with our ears." (2 Samuel:7:22)

"And he said, the LORD is my rock, and my fortress, and my deliverer; The God of my rock; in Him will I trust: He is my shield, and the horn of my salvation, my high tower, and my refuge, my saviour ...". (11 Samuel 22:2-3)

"As for God, His way is perfect; the word of the LORD is tried: he is a buckler to all them that trust in Him." (11 Samuel 22:31)

"All the ends of the world shall remember and turn unto the LORD: and all the kindreds of the nations shall worship before thee." (Psalm 22:27)

"Shew me thy ways, O LORD, teach me thy paths. Lead me in thy truth, and teach me: for thou art the God of my salvation; on thee do I wait all the day." (Psalm 25:4–5)

"Thine, O LORD, is the greatness, and the power, and the glory, and the victory, and the majesty: for all that is in the heaven and in the earth is thine; thine is the kingdom, O LORD, and thou art exalted as head above all. Both riches and honor come of thee, and thou reignest over all; and in thine hand is power and might, and in thine hand it is to make great, and to give strength unto all." (1 Chronicles:29:11–12)

In 1Kings 2:3, we find David to advise his son Solomon from his deathbed, saying more or less the same thing as Moses did to his people:

"And keep the charge of the LORD thy God, to walk in his ways, to keep his statutes, and His commandments, and his judgment and His testimonies, as it is written in the law of Moses, that thou mayest prosper in all that thou doest, and whithersoever thou turnest thyself."

Like his father, Solomon was also a self-surrendered servant of God

Like his father David, Solomon was also a self-surrendered servant of God and like him he also tried to do everything only to please God. The following verses of the Old Testament bear clear evidence in support of that.

"And the house which I build is great: for great is our God above all gods. But who is able to build Him an house, seeing the heaven and heaven of heavens cannot contain Him? Who am I then, that I should build Him an house, save only to burn sacrifice before him?"
(11 Chronicles 2:5-6)

Then when a small scaffold was made, Solomon stood upon it and knelt down upon his knees before all the congregation of Israel and spread forth his hands towards heaven saying to God most humbly,

"O LORD God of Israel, there is no God like thee in the heaven, nor in the earth; which keepest covenant, and shewest mercy unto thy servants, that walk before thee with all their hearts." (11 Chronicles 6:14)

Reverend, Muslims also kneel down and spread their hands toward heaven while making their supplication to God, more or less the same way as did Solomon.

What God revealed to His other messengers

We shall now proceed to check what God has revealed to His other messengers before He sent Jesus.

"I, even I, am the LORD; and besides me there is no savior". (Isaiah 43:11)

"Tell ye, and bring them near, yea, let them take counsel together: who hath declared this from ancient time? who hath told it from that time? have not I the LORD? and there is no God else beside me; a just God and a Saviour: there is none beside me." (Isaiah 45:21)

"Remember the former things of old: for I am God, and there is none else; I am God, and there is none like me." (Isaiah 46:9)

"But the LORD is the true God, he is the living God, and an everlasting king: at his wrath the earth shall tremble, and the nations shall not be able to abide his indignation." (Jeremiah 10:10)

"He hath made the earth by his power, he hath established the world by his wisdom, and hath stretched out the heavens by his discretion." (Jeremiah 10:12)

"Can any hide himself in secret places that I shall not see him? saith the LORD. Do not I fill heaven and earth? saith the LORD." (Jeremiah 23:24)

"And, go not after other gods to serve them, and to worship them, and provoke me not to anger with the works of your hands; and I will do you no hurt." (Jeremiah 25:6)

"To the LORD our God belong mercies and forgiveness, though we have rebelled against him." (Daniel 9:9)

"Now therefore, O our God, hear the prayer of thy servant, and his supplications, and cause thy face to shine upon thy sanctuary that is desolate, for the Lord's sake." (Daniel 9:17)

Reverend, the following verses of the Old Testament, also tell us about the same One God from time immemorial who, out of His own mercy, love and compassion, asked His people to think of His glory and greatness, to use their own intelligence and common sense in choosing His path, to repent for their sin, to rectify their wrongdoings, and to return to Him, their only Savior.

"Yet I am the LORD thy God from the land of Egypt, and thou shalt know no god but me: for there is no saviour beside me." (Hosea 13:4)

"Who is wise, and he shall understand these things? prudent, and he shall know them? for the ways of the LORD are right, and the just shall walk in them: but the transgressors shall fall therein." (Hosea 14:9)

"Therefore also now, saith the LORD, turn ye even to me with all your heart, and with fasting, and with weeping, and with mourning: And rend your heart, and not your garments, and turn unto the LORD your God: for he is gracious and merciful, slow to anger, and of great kindness, and repenteth him of the evil." (Joel 2:12–13)

I think, the contents of the verses that I quoted above from different books of the Old Testament are self-evident and conclusive. In that case, no more explanation is required to convince you or anyone that all the recognized messengers of God who were sent before Jesus, worshipped none but One True God, obeyed His commands, and also asked their people do the same. Reverend, it is still the same One God whom the Muslims-the followers of Muhammad, call, invoke, and worship by the name Allah.

The Gospel of Jesus also tells us God is One and Only

Now, I would like to draw your attention to some of the statements of the Gospel, where Jesus, whom we love and respect dearly as a mighty messenger of God, made it absolutely clear that he also worshipped the same One God of all his predecessors, and so did his true followers.

"And Jesus answered him [the scribe], The first of all the commandments is, HEAR O ISRAEL; THE LORD OUR GOD IS ONE LORD: AND THOU SHALT LOVE THE LORD THY GOD WITH ALL THY HEART, AND WITH ALL THY SOUL, AND WITH ALL THY MIND, AND WITH ALL THY STRENGTH: this is the first commandment." (Mark 12:29–30)

"And the scribe said unto him, Well, Master, thou hast said the truth: for there is one God; and there is none other but he:" (Mark 12:32)

Then, in reply to all the lucrative offers of the Satan (Matthew 4:8-9), Jesus said to him in disgust, *"Get thee hence, Satan: for it is written, THOU SHALT WORSHIP THE LORD THY GOD, AND HIM ONLY SHALT THOU SERVE. (Matthew 4:10)*

Jesus says, God Alone is All Perfect

"And behold, one came and said unto him [to Jesus], Good Master, what good thing shall I do, that I may have eternal life?

And he said unto him, Why callest thou me good? There is none good but one, that is, God: but if thou wilt enter into life, keep the commandments." (Matthew 19:16–17)

By this advice to the young man, Jesus made it absolutely clear that it was none but God Who alone is all perfect. And, to have an eternal life, people must live their lives by His commands that He revealed through their respective messengers, from time to time.

Jesus' Clear View on keeping the Commands of God

"Think not that I am come to destroy the law, or the prophets: I am not come to destroy, but to fulfill. For verily I say unto you, Till heaven and earth pass, one jot or one tittle shall in no wise pass from the law, till all be

fulfilled. Whosoever therefore shall break one of these least commandments, and shall teach men so, he shall be called the least in the kingdom of heaven: but whosoever shall do and teach them, the same shall be called great in the kingdom of heaven." (Matthew 5:17–19)

By those commands, Jesus obviously meant the Laws of the Old Testament, which God revealed to Moses for the guidance of his people. In other word, Jesus also worshipped the same one God of David, Moses, Abraham and all his predecessors who were sent before him for the guidance of their people.

And, so did Muhammad, whom God sent after Jesus reviving, rectifying and also restoring forever Abraham's faith of pristine monotheism, in Islam.

To every messenger whom We sent before you (Muhammad), We revealed the same message: There is no god but Me, so worship Me Alone. (Quran 21:25)

LETTER 4

MUHAMMAD WAS SENT AFTER JESUS, REVIVING AND RESTORING ABRAHAM'S FAITH, IN ISLAM

Say (O Muhammad): we believe in God and in what has been revealed to us, and what was sent down to Abraham, Ishmael, Isaac, Jacob and their descendants; and what was given to Moses, Jesus and other prophets from their Lord; We make no distinction between one another among them, and to God we do submit [in Islam].
—Holy Quran 3:84

Reverend Franklin Graham:

You obviously have noticed from my last two letters that God's guidance for mankind, which He revealed through all His messengers, including Jesus and Muhammad, had one thing in common. And, I hope you won't mind if I repeat once again that it is called *Tawhid* in Arabic, the meaning of which is pure and pristine monotheism, where God is claimed to be One and Only, and none has the right to be worshipped except God. It is also called 'Islamic monotheism' since Muhammad- the last Prophet of God was sent with Islam reviving and restoring in it Abraham's primordial faith in the absolute oneness and authority of God and surrendering to none but Him.

According to *Merriam-Webster's Encyclopedia of World Religions* (page 747), Islamic monotheism is more literal and uncompromising than that of any other religion. Allah is confessed as being one, eternal, unbegotten, unequaled, and beyond partnership of any kind.

God chose the name "Islam" and "Muslim"

The Quran tells us God has chosen the name "Islam" for His religion and "Muslim" for its adherents.(2:130–132; 5:3; 22:78). Both names originate from *salaam* in Arabic, which ordinarily means peace or submission for Islam, and calm or submissive for Muslim. But in a broader sense, Islam means a complete surrender or resignation to the will and the command of God. And Muslim refers to a person who submits himself completely to God, while striving for His cause or seeking His pleasure. (3:19- 20, 83–85).

In that sense, all the messengers of God and their true followers were Muslims, and the faith they preached and practiced was Islam, maybe in different name. In my last two letters, I have provided plenty of clear evidence from both our Holy Scriptures-the Quran and the Bible in support of that. We will know about it more through our last prophet Muhammad, as we proceed.

God's guidance to Adam before he was sent to earth

From the description of the Bible and the Quran, we came to know that God made this earth a dwelling place as well as a testing ground for men. He gave them a short and uncertain life along with a reflective mind and freedom of will to choose His path that He showed to them through their respective messengers, or to reject it by the instigation of the Satan. In my last letter, I've described from both parts of the Holy Bible what God revealed to all His prophets for the guidance of their people before the arrival of Muhammad. In this letter, I'd like to mention what the Quran, the last revealed Book of God has said through His last Prophet Muhammad reminding the teaching of his predecessors.

Let us begin first with Adam, who God made in heaven and then sent to earth as His first vicegerent, along with his wife Eve, and Satan, who made them eat the forbidden fruit by disobeying His command. The story of Adam and Eve has been told and retold in many places of the Quran, where we learnt God forgave them both when they repented for their sin and begged Him sincerely for His mercy and forgiveness, and then He sent them to earth, along with Satan as their open enemy, saying clearly:

"Get down from here all of you. Henceforth, there shall come to you guidance from Me, those who accept and follow it, shall have nothing to fear or to regret. But those who reject and defy Our revelation will be inmates of hellfire, wherein they shall live forever." (Quran 2:38–39)

The Quran also tells us the bottom line of His guidance that God revealed to Adam-the father of the mankind has remained the same in the teaching of all His prophets including both Jesus and Muhammad. We shall begin now with Noah and other prophets of God who were sent before Muhammad for the guidance of their people.

Noah and other prophets of God

"We sent Noah to his people. He said:'O my people, worship Allah! You have no other god but Him. I fear for you the punishment of a dreadful day!'" (7:59)

"Elias was surely one of our Messengers. 'Behold, he said to his people: Have you no fear of Allah? Would you invoke Bal (the name of their invented god) and forsake the best of the Creators-Allah Who is your Lord and the Lord of your forefathers?" (37:123–126)

"To the people of Ad We sent their brother Hud. He said: O my people! Worship Allah, You have no other god but Him. You are not but inventors (of falsehood)." (11:50)

"To the tribe of Thamud, We sent their brother Salih, He said, O my people! Worship Allah: You have no other god but Him. It is He Who

created you from the earth and made it a dwelling place for you. So, seek forgiveness from Him and turn to Him in repentance. Surely, my Lord is very close and ready to answer." (11:61)

"To the people of Median We sent their brother Shu'aib who said, O my people! Worship Allah, and look forward to the Last Day, and do not transgress in the land wickedly." (29:36)

Abraham's faith has been reinstated in Islam through Muhammad

In the Quran, Abraham is frequently addressed as *Hanif,* meaning the upright and the upholder of true monotheism. Though he was born in a pagan society, where everyone around him was an idol worshipper, he did not fail to recognize the existence of one true eternal God and His unparalleled glory, greatness, wisdom and authority over everything in the heavens and earth. After this realization, nothing not even the hostility of the pagan leaders including his own arrogant father could prevent him from confessing the truth about God openly to them. We can still feel the strength and the spirit of Abraham's primordial faith in the absolute oneness and authority of God, as he stood all alone against his hostile opponents, confessing loud and clear:

"Verily, I have turned my face, being upright to Him Who has created the heavens and the earth and I am not of the Mushriks." (6:79)

> *Mushrik* is an Arabic term that refers to a person who believes God has a partner or partners and also worships them equally as God or along with God. The Muslims all over the world still make this confession of Abraham in silence, when they stand before God facing Kabah five times a day to say their prayer.

35

"When his people started arguing with him, he [Abraham] said to them: Will you argue with me about Allah when He has guided me Himself? I do not fear those whom you worship in association with Allah. Nothing can happen to me unless it is so willed by my Lord. The knowledge of my Lord encompasses all things. Will you not then admonish yourself?" (6:80)

"Who would forsake the faith of Abraham except him who befools himself? Verily, We chose him in this world, and he will be among the righteous in the Hereafter." (2:130)

"Abraham was neither a Jew nor a Christian but was a Muslim [submitted himself to the will and the command of God], true in faith. He was not one of them who set up partners with God. Surely, those of mankind who have the best claim to Abraham are those who follow him, (in submission to God) and this Prophet [Muhammad] and those who believe with him..." (3:67-68)

"Say [O Muhammad]: As for me, surely my Lord has guided me to a Straight Path, a Right Religion, the faith of Abraham, the upright and he was not of them who were the idolaters.

Say: Surely my prayer, my sacrifice, my life and my death are all for Allah, the Lord of the Worlds." (6:161–162)

Reverend, I think, the message of the verses I've quoted above is clear and conclusive. And I also hope, no more explanation is required to understand who among the Jews, the Christians and the Muslims have the best claim on Abraham as their Patriarch or as the inheritors of his faith. We shall know about it more as we proceed.

Abraham's descendants also followed his legacy

"This was the legacy that Abraham left to his sons. And so did Jacob, when he said: O my sons! God has chosen for you this Deen, therefore, die not unless you are Muslims." (2:132)

> *Deen* is an Arabic word with a complex meaning, but in general, it means religion, a way of life, a set rule or instruction that God prescribed for the guidance of the people through their respective messengers.

"[To Muhammad] Were you present when death approached Jacob? He asked his sons: Who will you worship after me? They replied: We will worship the same One God Who is your Lord and the Lord of your forefathers Abraham, Ishmael and Isaac, and to Him we have surrendered [as Muslims]." (2:133)

"We gave him [Abraham] Isaac and Jacob and guided them all as we guided Noah before them, and among his descendants were David, Solomon, Job, Joseph, Moses and Aaron; thus We reward those who do good to others.

Other descendants include Zechariah, John, Jesus, and Elias; all of them were righteous; and Ishmael, Elisha, Jonah and Lot. We exalted each of them over the mankind.

And we exalted some of their forefathers, their children and their brothers. We chose them for Our service and guided them to the Right Path. (6:85–87)

Joseph- great-grandson of Abraham also spoke of One God

"[Joseph says to the fellow-prisoners,] I follow the ways of my fathers Abraham, Isaac and Jacob; and never could we attribute any partners to Allah: that (comes) of the grace of Allah to us and to mankind: yet most men are not grateful.

O my two companions of the prison! Are many lords differing among themselves better or Allah the One and Irresistible?

If it were not Him, you worship nothing but names which you have named or your fathers for which Allah has sent you no authority: the Command is for none but Allah: He has commanded that you worship none but Him: that is the right religion but most men understand not. (12:38–40)

Moses was sent to proclaim the worship of none but One God

In the following verses of the Quran, we shall see the faith and practices of other messengers of God, whom He sent later from the tribes of Abraham. Let's start with Moses, a mighty messenger and one of the pillars of the Judeo-Christian faith.

"[To Moses] I have chosen thee: listen then to the inspiration (sent to thee).

Verily, I am Allah: there is no god but I. So serve only Me and establish regular prayer for my rememberance.

The final Hour is sure to come. But I will keep it hidden, so that every soul may be rewarded according to its efforts. (20:13–14)

"We gave Moses the Book [Torah] and made it a guide to the children of Israel commanding: Take not other than Me as Disposer of your affairs." *(17:2)*

"Then he [Moses] addressed his people saying, O my people! Your only God is Allah, there is no other god besides Him. His knowledge encompasses everything." (20:97)

"Certainly, We granted to Moses and Aaron the Criterion of right and wrong, a light and a reminder for those people who are righteous." (21:48)

David was a self-surrendered servant of One True God

In the following verses of the Quran, Muhammad is reminded of David's unconditional love, longing and of his adoration in praise of God.

"Bear, O Prophet! with what they (who rejected Muhammad's call to Islam) say and remember Our servant David, the man of strength. Verily, he was ever turning in repentance towards Allah.
We made the mountains to join him in Our praises at evening and the sunrise.
And the birds, too, join him in flocks to sing with him.
We strengthened his kingdom and gave him wisdom and sound judgment." (38:17-20)

Solomon followed in the footsteps of his father

"We gave [in the past] knowledge to David and Solomon: and they both said: Praise be to Allah Who has favored us above many of His servants who believe." (27:15)
"He [Solomon] said: O my Lord! Forgive me and grant me a kingdom similar of which does not belong to any one after me. Surely, you are the Giver. [without any measure]
So, We subjected to him the wind which blew gently to whichever direction he wanted." (38:35–36)

The contents of the above-quoted verses, tell us clearly that David and his son Solomon also worshipped the same One God of Adam, Noah, Abraham, Jacob, Joseph, Moses and other prophets of God who were sent before them for the guidance of their people.

And so did Jesus, the son of Mary.

Jesus also proclaimed God being One and Only, and worshipped none but Him

Reverend, for a number of good reasons, the Quran gives an extra coverage on Mary and especially her son, Jesus, including his miraculous birth, miracles he showed, his death on the cross, his ascent to heaven, his Second Coming, and above all, what he taught his people in the name of God and what they followed in his name after he left. But I intend to quote here only a few of them that tells us Jesus, son of Mary, another indispensable name related to the Judeo-Christian faith, also proclaimed God being One and Only, and worshipped none but Him.

Then, in the footsteps of those prophets, We sent Jesus, the son of Mary, confirming the Law [Torah] that had come before him: And We sent him the Gospel where there was guidance and light and confirmation of the Torah which was sent before him; a guidance and admonition to those who fear Allah." (5:46)

"Surely, they have disbelieved who say: God is the Messiah [Jesus] son of Mary. While Christ said himself, O children of Israel! Worship God, My Lord and your Lord." (5:72)

> But go to my brethren, and say unto them, I ascend unto my Father, and your Father; and to my God, and your God. (John 20:17)

"I (Jesus) am appointed to confirm the Law which was before me and to make lawful some of that which was forbidden to you. I have come to you with a sign from your Lord, So fear Allah, and obey me."(3:50)

"It is not possible for any human being to whom God has given Book, the wisdom and the prophet hood that he would say to the people: worship me instead of God. On the contrary [he would say], be you devoted worshippers of your Almighty God in accordance with your Book that you have been teaching and reading." (3:79)

Muhammad succeeded Jesus confirming the eternal truth of the First Commandment

Reverend, there are many oft-repeated verses in the Quran where we have been told clearly that Muhammad- the last messenger of God succeeded Jesus confirming the eternal truth of the First Commandment. I have quoted below a few of them from different parts of the Quran to justify my claim.

"O Muhammad! We have sent revelations to you just as We sent to Noah, and the Prophets who came after him; We also sent revelations to Abraham, Ishmael, Isaac, Jacob, his descendants, Jesus, Job, Jonah, Aaron and Solomon, and to David We gave the Psalms.

Revelations were also sent to those Messengers whom We have mentioned to you and to those whose names We have not mentioned; To Moses Allah spoke directly." (4:163–164)

"[To Muhammad] Say: O mankind! Verily, I am sent to you all as the messenger of God to whom belongs the kingdom of heavens and the earth. There is no deity but Him. It is He Who gives life and causes death. So, believe in God and His messenger, the unlettered prophet [Muhammad] who believes in God and in His words [what He revealed in the Quran, the Torah and the Gospel]. And follow him so that you may be rightly guided." (7:158)

"… … Say: He is my Lord! There is no god but Him. In Him I put my trust and to Him shall I return." (13:30)

"Your God is One God; there is no one worthy of worship except Him, The Compassionate, The Merciful." (2:163)

"Allah Himself has testified to the fact that there is no god but Him and so do the angels and those who are well grounded in knowledge standing firm on justice. There is no god except Him, the Mighty, the Wise." (3:18)

"The fact is, to every Messenger who We sent before you (Muhammad), We revealed the same message: 'There is no god but Me, so worship Me Alone.'" (21:25)

The Messengers Were Many but the Message Was One

Reverend, the verses I have quoted so far from our Holy Scriptures, the Bible and the Quran, tell us the Messengers of God were many but the Message He revealed through them for the guidance of their people, was one and the same regardless to their time and place, as the whiteness of milk remains the same everywhere in the world, irrespective of the color or the type of cows. It is, as I mentioned before, called *Tawhid*, the meaning of which refers to "Islamic monotheism," since the pure and pristine monotheism of Abraham's faith has been reinstated in Islam through Muhammad-the last Prophet of God.

Man's deviation from the path of God

At this point, any sensible and open-minded person might ask in wonder, how could men deviate from that plain, simple, and straight path of God after it was taught by all His messengers, so clearly, categorically, and consistently, right from the beginning? Should not they have followed the same trodden path of all His Messengers instead of following so many paths which are not only different from one another but sometimes are completely reverse from others?

The Quran has an answer for that. The following verses of the Quran show how the people deviated gradually from one designated path of God to so many different or invented paths of men.

"Mankind were one community and Allah sent Prophets with glad tidings and warnings, and with them He sent the Scripture with the truth to settle the matters in between them where they differed. And the very people to whom it [the Book] was given, started disputes because of rivalry in between one another after the clear proofs had come unto them." (2:213)

"Surely, the true religion in the sight of Allah is Islam [meaning submission to His will and command]. Those who received the Scripture before differed through envy of each other, only after true knowledge had come to them ... ..." (3:19)

"Verily this brotherhood of yours is a single brotherhood and I am your only God, therefore worship Me Alone. But the people have divided their religion into sects in between them-to Us they shall all return." (21:92–93)

There are also numerous verses in the Quran in which people's ego, arrogance, ignorance, ingratitude, obliviousness, pride, prejudice and above all, their love for the material world and heedlessness have been blamed for their deviating from the plain, simple, and straight path of God. Out of many, I have quoted below a few of them.

"[To Muhammad]Ask them: Who provides your sustenance from the heaven and from the earth? Who has control over hearing and sight? Who brings forth the living from the dead and the dead from the living? They will soon reply Allah/God. Say: Why do you not then fear Him for your going against the truth?"(10:31)

43

"If you ask them Who has created the heavens and the earth? They will certainly say: Allah/God. Say: Praise be to Allah! But the fact is most of them do not use their common sense to understand." (31:25)

"It is He Who gives life and causes you die, and in His control is the alternation of the night and day: then why don't you understand?" (23:80)

"The fact is that most of them follow nothing but mere conjecture and conjecture is no way a substitute for the truth. Surely Allah is well aware of what they do." (10:36)

"... ... Those are the ones who have hearts with which they do not understand, they have eyes with which they do not see, they have ears with which they do not hear. They are like animals even worse than them, because they are those who are heedless." (7:179)

Muhammad was sent as the last Reminder and the Warner to mankind

Reverend, there are many verses in the Quran which tell us that God has sent Muhammad to remind His people of the glad tidings that He promised to them in return to their having faith in Him and for keeping His commands as well as to warn them of the fatal consequences that they might face for their disbelief in Him and for defying His commands. I have quoted below a few of them in support of that.

"We have revealed the Quran in Truth, and with the Truth it has come down: and We have sent you [O Muhammad] as a bearer of glad tidings [to the believers] and as a warner [to the unbelievers]. (17:105)

"We have sent you [O Muhammad] only as a bearer of good news and a warner. Say: I ask of you no recompense for this work except that he who wants, may choose the Right Way to His Lord." (25:56–57)

"Tell them [O Muhammad!] I am but a plain warner; And there is no divinity except Allah, the One, the Irresistible, the Lord of the heavens and the earth and all that lies in between them, the Almighty, the Forgiver. Say: This is a supreme message: yet you pay no heed to it." (38:65–68).

"[To Muhammad] Say to them [who ascribes partnership to God]: O ignorant! Do you bid me worship someone other than Allah? And verily, it has been revealed to you which had already been revealed to them before you that if you ascribe a partner to Allah, all your deeds will go in vain and you will surely be among the losers." (39:64–65)

"O Muhammad, tell them: I am but a human being like you; the revelation is sent to me to declare that your God is One God; therefore, whoever hopes to meet his Lord, let him do good deeds and join no partner in the worship of his Lord." (Quran 18:110)

"O Prophet, ask them: Have you ever considered if this Quran is really from Allah and you deny it, who can be more astray than you who have gone too far defying Him." (41:52)

The eternal truth in the guidance of God never changed

Reverend, by this time I have provided countless evidence from both Bible and the Quran to prove Muhammad was neither an imposter nor an inventor of a new faith or cult, as most of your people think of him, unknowingly. Rather, he was also sent with the same eternal truth in the guidance of God about which the Bible has said:

"The grass withereth, the flower fadeth: but the word of our God shall stand forever."
(Isaiah 40:8)

And, the Quran says: *"This has always been our Ways with the apostles who we sent before you: You will find no change in our Ways. (17:77)*

Reverend, with the help of those unchanged and eternal words in both Bible and Quran, I have undoubtedly proved that Muslims never worshipped any 'different god' from the God of the Judeo-Christian Faith, as you claimed. Rather, they always have worshipped and still worship the same One God of all His messengers including both Jesus and Muhammad. In that sense, I have completed my arguments, and I should have stopped here thanking you gratefully for giving me a chance to let your people know about the God of Islam.

But I could not, because while reading our Holy Scriptures-the Bible and the Quran both, I found it is not the Muslims, it is in fact, the Christians who worship 'a different god' from the God of the Judeo-Christian Faith. They do so by making Jesus an object of worship along with One True God or as one the Gods in the Trinity. I think, it is a colossal deviation from the eternal truth of the First Commandment that Jesus preached and practiced all through his life following the footsteps of all his predecessors.

It is absolutely for the sake of truth, I feel myself obliged to share this information with you and my other prospective readers- especially the Christians. I hope, you will give me a chance to correct my mistake, if you find me misquote or misinterpret anything from the Bible, the Quran or any other book that I used for information or reference to establish the truth of my claim.

> O Muhammad, declare: O mankind, the truth has come to you from your Lord! He that follows guidance, does it for his own good, and he that goes astray does so at his own risk; for I am not a custodian over you. (10:108)

LETTER 5

JESUS' COMFORTER IS MUHAMMAD, THE PROPHET OF ISLAM

But when the Comforter is come, whom I will send unto you from the Father, even the Spirit of truth, which proceedeth from the Father, he shall testify of me.
—John 15:26–27

Reverend Franklin Graham:

You may feel surprised to know that the topic I chose for this letter is not Jesus but his Comforter, whom he mentioned in some of his predictions. While talking to his disciples, Jesus told them that his Comforter would come from God to testify of him. I chose to talk about his Comforter first, because I need his testimony to prove that Jesus was not a Deity but a mighty messenger of God, and he did not teach any of those doctrines which his followers now believe in his name as the integral parts of their faith. But before I go into that, we need to check first who Jesus really meant to be his Comforter so that you could accept his testimony to be true and valid.

Jesus' Comforter is not the Holy Ghost, but Muhammad

Following the signs or the indications in Jesus' predictions, the Muslims believe undoubtedly that his Comforter is Muhammad, the last Prophet of God, though you may nullify their claim with his another prediction in John 14:26, where he mentioned clearly his Comforter was the Holy Ghost. [*"But the Comforter which is the Holy Ghost, whom the Father will send in my name, He shall teach you all things, and bring all things to your remembrance, whatsoever I have said unto you"*] In that case, what makes me claim so confidently that Jesus' Comforter is not the Holy Ghost, but Muhammad?

In reply to that, I would ask you to have patience with me until I prove with clear and concrete evidence from the Bible and the Quran both that Jesus meant none but Muhammad to be his Comforter. My first observation or objection is, the Holy Ghost does not match with any of his predictions, while Muhammad does with each of them equally and without any question. I'll now try to justify my claim one by one. Since Jesus mentioned the name of the Holy Ghost as his Comforter, we have to check first who was this Holy Ghost that Jesus meant for his Comforter?

Holy Ghost vs. Holy Spirit

To find this answer, we need to know the true meaning and implication of two translated names in the Bible: the Holy Ghost and the Holy Spirit.

Jesus used to teach his people in his native language, Aramaic, which had been translated first into Hebrew, from Hebrew to Greek and from Greek to English. But as we are concerned only with the English version of the Bible, I'll discuss how the Holy Ghost came into English from the Greek version of the Bible.

The learned scholars of the Western world have detected some confusion while translating the phrase "Holy Ghost" or "Holy Spirit" from Greek to English. They found *pneuma* in Greek is the root word for spirit, and it has no separate word for ghost. So, in many places of the King James and Roman Catholic version of the Bible, the terms Holy Ghost and Holy Spirit both are used to mean the same thing or to serve the same purpose.

In the Revised Standard Version of the Bible, which was reviewed and edited by some thirty-two scholars of the highest eminence and backed by fifty cooperating denominations, the word Ghost was replaced by Spirit. At this point, it is important to note here that both the Bible and the Quran have used the term Spirit for a messenger of God, whom He usually appoints from the angels and also from human beings to carry out His mission on earth or to serve His purpose. Let me justify my point with some instances from both the Bible and the Quran.

"And the Holy Ghost [Spirit] descended in a bodily shape like a dove upon him. [Jesus]" (Luke 3:22)

"And there appeared an angel unto him [Jesus] from the heaven, strengthening him." (Luke 22:43)

"Then Allah will ask: O Jesus son of Mary! Recall my favor upon you and to your mother, how I strengthened you with the Holy Spirit." (Quran 5:110)

"[To Muhammad] Say: The Holy Spirit has brought the revelation from your Lord in truth, in order to strengthen those who believe, and as a guide and glad tidings to the Muslims [who surrender to God]." (Quran 16:102)

Reverend, in many places of the Gospel, the term "Spirit" has been used for the true prophets of God as well as for the false prophets. Jesus was found to caution his disciples about them, saying:

"Beloved, believe not every Spirit, but try the Spirits whether they are of God; because many false Prophets are gone out into the world. Hereby know ye the Spirit of God: Every Spirit that confesseth that Jesus Christ is come in the flesh is of God." (1John 4:1–2)

In this statement of Jesus, we have noticed that he used "Spirit" and the "Prophet" to mean a messenger from humankind regardless to his status. Besides that, in this precautionary notes to his disciples, Jesus also made it absolutely clear that he did not mean any angel or the invisible Holy Ghost to be his Comforter. He meant his Comforter would be a human being and a chosen prophet of God. But since Jesus was aware of the false prophets and also about their false claims to mislead the people from his teaching, he also left for them a clear indication of how to identify a true prophet, or his Comforter, from the false claimants.

Jesus told them the true Prophet of God would remind them who Jesus really was and why he was sent to them. In other word, a true Prophet would never tell them that God appeared to them in the form of Jesus and they should worship him as God. Rather, he would tell them Jesus was a human being-a man of flesh blood and God sent him to earth only to guide them by His commands. In my last letter, you will find ample evidence of what God said about Jesus through his testifier Muhammad.

Now, I like to draw your attention to the other parts of Jesus' prediction that he made about his Comforter in John 14:26.

"He shall teach you all things and bring all things to your remembrance" (John 14:26).

Reverend, this part of Jesus' prediction fits Muhammad perfectly well. Let's see how. Jesus being an inspired messenger of God knew in advance that a day would come after him, when his people would forget what he taught them following the laws of the Torah, and obey the invented doctrines of men which they would teach them in his name. (I would discuss those invented parts of their faith in my next letters). But, as a true and an inspired messenger of God, Jesus also knew that Muhammad-the last Prophet of God would be sent along with His last guidebook- the Quran testifying of his true status and mission and also reminding them of what he really taught them and what he did not teach. So it happened, as he said. To verify the truth, you may read again the last few pages of my last two letters.

By this prediction, Jesus also confirmed indirectly but undoubtedly that he did not mean the Holy Ghost to be his Comforter. How could he mean the invisible Holy Ghost to appear before his people and to bring everything back to their memory?

We shall now check what Jesus said about his Comforter in his other predictions.

In John 16:13-14, Jesus said to his disciples:

"Howbeit when he, the Spirit of Truth, is come, he will guide you into all truth. For he shall not speak of himself; but whatsoever he shall hear, that he shall speak: and he will shew you things to come. He shall glorify me: for he shall receive of mine, and shall show it unto you."

"The Spirit of Truth" describes Muhammad accurately.

Reverend, the 'Spirit of Truth' describes Muhammad accurately. According to all his biographers, both ancient and modern, Arab and non-Arab, Muslims and non-Muslims Muhammad was called *Al Amin* (in Arabic), meaning the truthful or trustworthy, by all his pagan kith and kin, beginning from his very boyhood. They called him so for his being scrupulously honest, truthful, and trustworthy. In other words, his love and commitment for truth and trustworthiness was known to all, long before he claimed himself a prophet of God.

"He will guide you into all truth." (John 16:13)

According to the description of the Holy Scriptures-the Bible and the Quran both, the eternal truth in the guidance of God, is pure and pristine monotheism where God is claimed to be one and only and none has any right to be worshipped except Him.We also came to know that all the messengers of God including both Jesus and Muhammad were sent to establish the worship of one true God among the people.

Jesus' followers worshipped none but One God as long as he lived with them, but after his ascent to heaven, they somehow deviated from the eternal truth of the First Commandment and began to worship

God following the invented doctrines of men. Jesus being an inspired Messenger of God knew it to be inevitable. But, he also knew that God would send His last Messenger Muhammad reviving and restoring the eternal truth of His guidance, in Islam and in His everlasting guidebook the Quran. So, he said to his people through his disciples that when his Comforter would come, he would help them all to recognize the truth in the revealed guidance of God and bring them back to it. I wrote about it in my last two letters supported by countless evidence from the Bible and the Quran both.

We'll now examine another part of Jesus' prediction in John 16:13 where he said:

"For he shall not speak of himself; but whatsoever he shall hear, that shall he speak …"

Based on well-established tradition and Muhammad's biographies-both old and modern, we came to know when or how he received words from God. We have been told that the Angel Gabriel delivered the words of God to him at the age of forty when he was meditating in the solitary cave of the Mount Hira about three miles away from Mecca-his place of birth. Muhammad was illiterate and he did not know how to read or write. So he had to repeat each and every word with Gabriel until he committed them by heart. Then he conveyed the same to the people as he heard from him. In other words, while delivering the words of God, Muhammad did not add anything to them from his own, nor he omitted or held back anything from what he learnt. The Holy Quran has still been carrying the same words as Muhammad received from God through Gabriel about fourteen hundred years ago. At this point, I also like to mention here that through fulfilling this prediction of Jesus, Muhammad has also fulfilled God's promise that He made to Moses about sending a prophet like him, in Deuteronomy 18:18.

> I will raise them up a Prophet from among their brethren, like unto thee, and will put my words in his mouth; and he shall speak unto them all that I shall command him. (Deuteronomy 18:18)

"And he will shew you things to come" (John 16:13).

Reverend, the Holy Ghost does not match this prediction, because the Holy Ghost is known to carry orders of God or His words to His designated persons, but he is not known to make any prediction. But the prophets of God are well known in making prophecies or predictions. In fact, it has been made a criterion to identify a true prophet of God from a false claimant. Predictions made by a true Prophet of God would come true but the predictions of a false prophet would not come to pass. (Duet 18:22)

According to the description of many authentic Hadith (traditions related to Muhammad's own words and deeds, as recounted by his close companions), Muhammad made a series of prophecies, including the signs of the Last Hour and of Jesus' Second Coming. Many of them occurred soon after he left, and many of them have still been occurring in and around us. I have stated below only a few of them that have already occurred and are occurring till today, proving the sanctity of his message and mission both.

- Before his death, Muhammad called his daughter Fatima to his bedside and told her she would be the first among his family to join him after his death. And so it happened. Fatima, who was then only twenty eight, joined her father six months after he left.
- Muhammad predicted the caliphate (the reign of his rightly guided companions) would last for thirty years and then there

would be biting kingship. The history of Islam tells us the prediction of the noble prophet came true, as he said.

- Muhammad predicted Uthman (third caliph of Islam) would be killed while reading the Quran, and so it happened

Reverend, I will quote below a few more predictions that Muhammad made to his people about fourteen hundred years ago, the truth of which is now more than evident.

- Muhammad said the Muslims would conquer Damascus, Jerusalem, Iraq, Persia, Constantinople, and Cyprus, and their religion, Islam, would reach as far as the remotest corners of the world in the East and the West.
- The barefooted Bedouins would compete in building tall buildings.
- The mosques would be built like palaces.
- Killing would increase in such a way that the one who killed would not know why he killed, and the one killed would not know why he was killed.
- Sexual promiscuity would increase and a new disease, which people had not heard of before, would spread among them as a consequence of that.
- Women would appear naked while still being dressed.
- People would hop between cloud and earth. (referring to journey by air).

He [the Spirit of Truth] shall glorify me." (John 16:14)

Reverend, this prediction of Jesus about his Comforter has also been fulfilled through Muhammad. I already have mentioned before that the "Spirit of Truth" refers to Muhammad and we shall now check how Muhammad, who arrived nearly six hundred years after Jesus, glorified him. We will find the answer in the Quran where the name and status of Jesus and also of his mother Mary was raised high through his testifier

Muhammad. Not only that, it is also through Muhammad's testimony in the Quran, Jesus was made free from the accountability of those invented doctrines of men that his followers believed in his name as the integral parts of their faith after he left. (Quran 3:42–55; 4:156-157, 172; 5:46, 72–73, 116–117; 19: 27-36, 88–92; 43:59, 63–64)

Jesus' Comforter will come after he leaves

In John 16:7, Jesus said to his disciples: *"Nevertheless, I tell you the truth; It is expedient for you that I go away; for if I go not away, the Comforter will not come unto you; but if I depart, I will send him unto you."*

In this prediction, Jesus made it absolutely clear that his Comforter would come after his departure, and not before that. So it happened, because no other prophet except Muhammad came after Jesus with a revealed Book like the Quran or a great religion like Islam. The Quran also contains a prophecy of Jesus bearing the good news of Ahmad's arrival, after he leaves. Ahmad is another popular name of Muhammad.

(To Muhammad) "And, remember when Jesus-the son of Mary said, O children of Israel! I am the Messenger of Allah towards you, confirming the Torah which came before me, and to give you glad tidings of a Messenger who will come after me, whose name shall be Ahmad."(61:6)

By this prediction, Jesus also proved undoubtedly that he did not mean the Holy Ghost to be his Comforter, because there are many instances in the Gospel and also in the Quran that tell us the Holy Ghost appeared to Jesus before his departure from earth. (Luke 3:21-22; Quran 5:110)

Jesus' "another Comforter" refers to none but Muhammad

Reverend, we shall now check what Jesus said about his Comforter in other parts of his predictions and try to see how Muhammad could fit with each of them equally well.

While talking to his disciples about the Comforter, Jesus said to them, *"And I will pray the Father, and he shall give you another Comforter that he may abide with you forever." (John 14:16)*

We shall first try to examine what Jesus really meant by 'another Comforter?' The scholars of the Bible used the Greek word *"allon"* for another. It also means "another of the same kind." On the basis of that, we can rightly assume that Jesus wanted his disciples to know and believe that his 'another Comforter' would be someone like him, having the same status or position and the same mission to fulfill. The Quran also tells us to believe and respect all the prophets of God equally and without making any distinction among them. (3:84) Accordingly, we believe Jesus and his successor Muhammad had the same status and both of them were sent to fulfill the same mission which is to establish the worship of One True God among the people and to guide them all to His path.

"He [The Comforter] may abide with you forever"

This last part of Jesus' prediction in John 14:16, also describes Muhammad perfectly well. Some of my missionary friends, however, wanted to know how Muhammad, who came long after Jesus with a different religion, could live forever with his followers. I surprised them saying that Jesus meant the Muslims to be his true followers, because it is only the Muslims, who love and respect Jesus as a mighty messenger of God and also worship God according to the eternal truth of the first commandment that Jesus and his successor Muhammad preached and practiced themselves following the footsteps of all their predecessors. In that case, it is very much expected that Jesus would consider only the Muslims to be his true followers and it is with them his Comforter or Muhammad would live forever.

I have tried to explain to them how Muhammad who has left the world about fourteen hundred years ago, have still been abiding with his followers, and will continue to live until the end of the world. We shall check the truth with some clear and concrete evidence from both Islamic and non-Islamic sources.

Islamic sources

Reverend, the Quran tells the believers that if they really love God and hope to meet Him in their life hereafter, they should obey Muhammad and follow his *Sunnah* meaning the acted examples of his words and deeds that he set for them through keeping the commands of God. (3:31; 33:21; 4:65, 80; 42:52) On the basis of that, the Muslims try to live their lives following the Sunnah of the Prophet or the set examples from his life. Thus the Muslims have kept his name alive in every walk of their life through following him as their role model.

Muhammad's name is also remembered aloud ten times a day in all Muslim countries of the world, when a muezzin (who calls the Muslims five times a day from a local mosque to attend to their prayers) announces some of the prescribed phrases twice. One of them is, "I bear witness that Muhammad is the messenger of God."

The Muslims also make this witness for Muhammad, 9 times a day and also ask God for His peace and blessing upon him 20 times a day while saying their five times obligatory prayers in their homes, mosques, or by the side of a road. Along with those obligatory prayers, they also make many optional and special prayers and all their prayers whether obligatory, optional or special, remain incomplete if they don't make that witness about Muhammad or ask God to bestow His peace and blessing upon him. Besides that, we have no count of how many millions of cell phones, i-pads and computers among 1.25 billion (now 1.6) of his followers today, are now loaded with five times call of prayers along with his sayings or teachings to keep his name alive forever.

You will also not find any name in the entire world which is more popular than the name of Muhammad. You might feel amazed to know that one out of ten from 1.6 billion Muslims in the world, is named after the name of their beloved Prophet Muhammad or Ahmad.

There is also no count of how many tons of books have been written so far on various aspects of Muhammad's life only by the Muslim writers-both Arab and non-Arab to keep his name alive forever in the history of mankind.

Most important of all, the Muslims need to invoke God for His peace and blessing upon Muhammad every time they utter, hear, read or write his name. This remembrance of Muhammad's name aloud or in silence, becomes more intensified and incessant in both Mecca and Medina, the places of his birth and death and especially during the time of Hajj (Pilgrimage attended now by a million once a year in commemoration of Abraham's sacrifice of his son).

According to the projected data of Pew report, if Islam-the latest and the fastest growing religion of the world maintains its current rate of growth, the number of its adherents which is now 1.6 billion, will reach to 1.76 by 2050 and by the end of the century it will be the largest on this planet, claiming one of its three people as Muslim. On the basis of that calculation, we have no doubt in mind that the possibility of Muhammad's living forever with his followers is bound to rocket up, as the days roll by, proving Jesus' prediction about his Comforter in John 14:16, to be absolutely true.

Non-Islamic sources

Reverend, you may believe it or not, but it is also a fact that if the Muslims stop writing about Muhammad or never wrote a word about him, he would still live forever in the writings of non-Muslim scholars especially of the Western World. To save my time and space, I'll quote in brief only a few of them.

Let us begin first with the observation of Thomas Carlyle, a renowned Scottish philosopher, historian and a writer. In his book, *Heroes and Hero-Worship and the Heroic in History* (1840), he paid a rich tribute to Muhammad-the Messenger of God, saying:

"A man of truth and fidelity; true in what he did, in what he spake and thought...."

"A silent great soul, one of that who cannot but be earnest. He was to kindle the world, the world's Maker has ordered so."

"A false man found a religion? Why, a false man cannot build a brick house! ....It will not stand for twelve centuries, (it is fourteen centuries now) to lodge a hundred and eighty millions; (1.6 billion today-the second largest on earth) it will fall straight away......"

"The lies (western slanders) which well-meaning zeal has heaped round this man (Muhammad) are disgraceful to ourselves only."

The History of the Decline and the Fall of Roman Empire (1776) a great book written by Edward Gibbon, the famous European historian and the scholar tells us:

"The Creed of Muhammad is free from the suspicious of ambiguity and the Koran is a glorious Testimony to the unity of God."

"The Apostle of God submitted to the menial offices of the family, he kindled the fire, swept the floor, milked the ewes, and mended with his own hands his shoes and garments."

Reverend Bosworth Smith, an American Protestant Episcopal Bishop and the author of *Mohammad and Mohammadanism* (London 1874) describes:

He (Muhammad) was a Caesar and Pope in one; but he was Pope without the Pope's pretensions, and Caesar without the legions of Caesar: without a standing army, without a bodyguard, without a palace, without a fixed revenue; if ever any man had the right to say that he ruled by the right Divine, it was Mohammad, for he had all the powers without its instruments and without its supports.

John William Draper, MD, LL.D, was a professor of chemistry and physiology and also a distinguished writer of many valuable books on the inconsistencies and the conflict in history and religion. In his book, *A History of the Intellectual Development of Europe* (London 1875), he has said:

"Four years after the death of Justinian, A.D. 569, was born in Mecca, in Arabia, the man who, of all men has exercised the greatest influence upon the human race ...To be the religious head of many empires, to guide the daily life of one-third of the human race, may perhaps justify the title of a Messenger of God."

In his valuable book, *Histoire de la Turquie* (Paris, 1854), Alphonse de Lamartine, a famous French scholar wrote in appreciation of Muhammad:

..... If greatness of purpose, smallness of means and astonishing results are the three criteria of human genius, who could dare compare any great man in history with Muhammad? The most famous men created arms, laws and empires only. They founded, if anything at all, no more than material powers which often crumbled away before their eyes. This man moved not only armies, legislations, empires, peoples, dynasties, but millions of men in one-third of the then inhabited world; and more than that, he moved the altars, the gods, the religions, the ideas, the beliefs and the souls.... Philosopher, Orator, Apostle, Legislator, Conqueror of Ideas, Restorer of Rational Beliefs...the founder of twenty terrestrial empires and of one spiritual empire, that is Muhammad. As regards all standards by which human greatness may be measured, we may all ask, is there any man greater than he?

We may now check what George Bernard Shaw, a renowned Irish author, a playwright and also a noble prize winner, thought of Muhammad and of his religion. In his book, *The Genuine Islam" Vol. 1, No 8 (1936), he said:*

"If any religion had the chance of ruling over England, nay Europe within the next hundred years, it could be Islam. I have always held the religion of Muhammad in high estimation because of its wonderful vitality. It is the only religion which appears to me to possess that assimilating capacity to the changing phases of existence which can make it appeal to every age." .....

"I have studied him-the wonderful man-and in my opinion far from being anti-Christ, he must be called the savior of humanity. I believe that if a man like him were to assume the dictatorship of the modern world, he would succeed in solving its problems in a way that would bring it the much needed peace and happiness."

Jules Masserman, an American Jew and a renowned psychoanalyst and a Professor of Chicago University, also found Muhammad the greatest of all leaders, on the basis of three criteria. In his essay published in Time in July 15, 1974, he said:

Leaders must fulfill three functions. They must provide for the well-being of the lead, provide a social organization in which people feel relatively secure and provide them with one set of beliefs.

People like Louis Pasteur and Jonas Salk are leaders in the first sense. People like Gandhi and Confucius, on one hand, and Alexander, Caesar and Hitler on the other, are leaders in the second and perhaps in the third sense. Jesus and Buddha belong in the third category alone .

Perhaps the greatest leader of all times was Muhammad who combined all three functions. To a lesser degree Moses did the same.

Reverend, I'll end this part with the observation of Michael Hart, an American author and astrophysicist. In his book *The 100, A Ranking of the Most Influential Persons in History* (Carol Publishing Group: New York, 1989), he has reported honestly:

"My choice of Muhammad to lead the list of the world's most influential persons may surprise some readers and may be questioned by others, but he was the only man in history who was supremely successful on both the religious and secular levels. ... Muhammad founded and promulgated one of the world's great religions and became an immensely effective political leader. Today, 13 centuries after his death, his influence is still powerful and pervasive. ... It is the unparalleled combination of secular and religious influence which I feel entitles Muhammad to be considered the most influential single figure in human history.

Reverend, the Muslims believe undoubtedly that it is that single figure in the entire human history that God sent to earth fulfilling Jesus' prayer and prediction both in John 14:16. But, in spite of those crystal clear instances, if you are still in doubt and like to think, *Why Muhammad, Jesus could mean someone else who has not arrived yet?"*

The answer can be sought in the meaning of two Greek words *'periclytos' and paracletos.'*

Periclytos or Paracletos?

But before I go into the meaning or implication of these two Greek words, I should first explain to you the meaning and significance of two Arabic names Muhammad and Ahmad. I already mentioned before that Ahmad is another popular name of Muhammad. Both Muhammad and Ahmad originated from the same root word *himdath or hmd* in the language of Hebrew, Arabic or Aramaic, the meaning of which is "the praised one, the most laudable, desire, desirable or glorified."

In that sense, if Jesus meant Muhammad or Ahmad to be his Comforter, he needed to mention his name in Aramaic as *hmd, himdath,* or *himda*, to mean someone praiseworthy, desirable, or glorified which could correspond directly to the meaning of Muhammad or Ahmad-two well-known names of the Prophet of Islam. The Greek word "Periclytos" also corresponds to the meaning of himdath or hmd in Hebrew, Aramaic or in Arabic. But, it is interesting to note here that the translators of the Bible from Greek to English, chose the word 'paracletos' the meaning of which is comforter, counselor, advocate, kind, friendly, or 'one being sought for help'.

Paracletos is a corrupt reading for Periclytos

According to the observation of the modern and open-minded scholars of the Bible, the Greek word *paracletos* is a corrupt reading for *periclytos*. They think the translators of the Bible from Greek to English chose paracletos over periclytos, either intentionally or unintentionally. But instead of going into that controversy, we can also accept 'paracletos' for Muhammad, because it also describes him perfectly well. Muhammad was also known to his people as a very kind, comforting and a friendly person who they constantly sought for help, advice or guidance long before God lauded him in the Quran, saying, *"We have sent you not, but as a mercy to the mankind" (21:107)*.

Reverend, if you still find this explanation inadequate to accept Muhammad as Jesus' Comforter, and like to wait for someone else who has not arrived yet, in that case, I would request you to look for your answer in another prediction that God made in Haggai, 37th book of the Old Testament.

In the verse 7 and 9 in the book of Haggai, God has declared:

"And, I will shake all nations, and the desire of all nations shall come: and I will fill this house with glory, saith the Lord of the hosts.....
The glory of this latter house shall be greater than of the former, saith the Lord of the hosts: and in this place will I give peace."

Let us identify first who is the man that God has referred here as *the desire of all nations* and then we shall see how other things in the description fit with him like pieces of puzzles. The *desire* in the above quoted verses, has been translated from *himdath or himda* in original Hebrew, the meaning of which I already mentioned before, corresponds directly to the Greek word *periclytos* or the Arabic word *hmd*-the root word of both Muhammad and Ahmad.

this latter house in the verse refers to Ka'bah-the house of God at Mecca where Muhammad was born from the progeny of Ishmael-Abraham's firstborn and *the former house* refers to the house of God at Jerusalem. I think in this modern IT World, it is only a matter of moments to visit both the houses of God and to look for yourself how His house at Mecca was glorified not only from His house at Jerusalem, but also from all the sanctuaries on earth?

Last of all, remains *peace* and it has been translated into English from the Hebrew word *shalom*, the meaning of which is identical with Arabic root word *silm* from where *salaam or the name of Islam*-the latest, purest and the world-shaking religion of God was originated and given to Muhammad at Mecca, nearly six hundred years after Jesus' ascent to heaven.

Reverend, I have no more to say except one thing that on the basis of those crystal clear instances from our Holy Scriptures-the Bible and the Quran both, we believe undoubtedly that Jesus' Comforter is no one else but his Successor Muhammad –the Prophet of Islam. We have been claiming so unopposed, for the last fourteen hundred years, since Muhammad arrived with the Quran testifying of Jesus' true status and mission and also clearing his name from all the myths, misconceptions and invented doctrines of men that his people began cherishing in his name as indispensable parts of their faith, after he left.

I intend to address those issues one by one in the rest of my letters where I will try to justify my claim by the testimony of the Quran that God sent through Jesus' testifier Muhammad and also by the statements of the Gospel-the book you believe absolutely as the true account of Jesus' own words and deeds.

> O Jesus! I will take you and raise you to Myself and clear you [of the falsehood] of those who blasphemy. I will make those who follow you superior to those who reject faith until the Day of Resurrection. Then you all return to Me and I will judge between you in the matters wherein you differ. (Quran 3:55)

TRUE MEANING AND IMPLICATION OF THE NAME "CHRIST" AND "WORD"

Then said Jesus to those Jews which believed on him, If ye continue in my word, then are ye my disciples indeed; And ye shall know the truth, and the truth shall make you free.
—John 8:31–32

Reverend Franklin Graham:

In my last letter, I mentioned that Muhammad was sent after Jesus as his testifier fulfilling his prediction and prayer and making him free from all the myths and misconceptions that his followers began cherishing about him as the integral parts of their faith. In this letter, I intend to discuss some of Jesus' popular names or titles which his followers took to be completely mystic, mysterious, or "divine" in nature, and finally it led them to worship Jesus as God or as His equal. Let us begin with his name "Christ."

While studying our Holy Scriptures, the Bible and the Quran, I find the name Christ is neither mystical nor mysterious. It is rather, a misunderstood or a misinterpreted name. Some of my missionary friends tried to convince me that Jesus was an inseparable part of God. They believed the name Christ was meant exclusively for their Lord, who appeared to them later as God incarnate. According to their explanation, the name Christ was kept hidden by God Himself, from the beginning of His creation, for His only begotten. So when Jesus was born without a father and was referred to in the Bible as the "Christ," some of the overly enthusiastic men took him for the "Son of God or God's only begotten in human flesh."

After I read about it in the Bible, the Quran, and other religious books written by many learned and renowned scholars, both Christians and non-Christians, I found the true meaning and the implication of the name Christ was completely different from what they believed to be absolutely true.

Both "Christ" and "Messiah" are synonymous

The word Christ comes from the Greek word "Christos," meaning anointed or appointed. And Christos was translated into Greek from the Hebrew word "mashiyach," or "messiah," which also means to anoint, to rub, or to appoint. In Arabic, it is called "masih," meaning simply a chosen or appointed messenger of God.

There is a long-rooted tradition among the Jews regarding their religious faith and practices. They used to anoint their prophets, priests, or kings ceremonially before they held their position, rank, or authority. Accordingly, the person who was anointed or appointed in this way was also called messiah or Christ by their people.

There are many instances in the Holy Bible that tell us how the procedure of getting someone anointed took place among the Jews.

"And Moses took the anointing oil, and anointed the tabernacle and all that was therein, and sanctioned them." (Leviticus 8:10)

"Then Samuel took the horn of oil, and anointed him [David] in the midst of his brethren" ... ... (1 Samuel 16:13)

"He is the tower of salvation for his king: and sheweth mercy to his anointed, unto David, and to his seed for evermore." (2 Samuel 22:51)

"Thus saith the Lord to his anointed, to Cyrus, whose right hand I have holden, …" (Isaiah 45:1)

There are many verses in both the Bible and the Quran where we have been told the desperate, deprived, and God-fearing people used to wait eagerly for the arrival of some designated messengers who they called messiahs. The people usually came to know about their arrival through the prediction of other messengers who were sent before them. The example of Moses, Jesus, and Muhammad could be cited, for instance. Common people used to wait eagerly for their promised messiahs to come and to save them from the injustice and suffering in the hands of their oppressors. Accordingly, both "Christ" and "Messiah" are synonymous and refer to a chosen Messenger of God. Let me justify my point in the light of our Holy Scriptures, the Bible and the Quran.

"The woman saith unto him (Jesus), I know that Messias cometh, which is called Christ: when he is come, he will tell us all things. Jesus saith unto her, I that speak unto thee am he." (John 4:25–26)

"And Jesus walked in the temple in Solomon's porch. Then came the Jews round about him, and said unto him, How long dost thou make us to doubt? If thou be the Christ, tell us plainly." (John10:23–24)

"[Remember] When the angels said, O Mary! Verily, Allah gives you the glad tidings of a Word [be] from Him: his name will be Christ Jesus … …" (Quran 3:45)

Other prophets also had God-given names and titles

Reverend, it was not Jesus alone, many other chosen messengers of God also received their names and titles from God Himself. Let me quote here a few instances from the Bible and the Quran.

"And the angel of the Lord said unto her [Hagar], Behold, thou art with child, and shalt bear a son, and shall call his name Ishmael; because the Lord hath heard thy affliction." (Genesis 16:11)

"And God said, Sarah thy wife [by this time God had changed Abram's name to Abraham and his wife, Sarai's, name to Sarah] shall bear thee a son indeed; and thou shalt call his name Isaac" ... ... (Genesis 17:19)

"And God said unto him, Thy name is Jacob: thy name shall not be called any more Jacob, but Israel shall be thy name: and he called his name Israel." (Genesis 35:10)

There are many verses in the Quran, where Abraham was called "Hanif," meaning upright by nature and worshipper of none but the One True God. And in other places, he was also called "Khalilullah," meaning friend of Allah.

"Who can be better in religion than one who submits his whole self to Allah, does good and follows the way of Abraham-the Hanif. For Allah did take Abraham as His Khalil [friend]." (Quran 4:125)

Moses was also called "Kalimullah," meaning "to whom God spoke directly."

"And Messengers We have mentioned to you before, and Messengers We have not mentioned to you, and to Moses Allah spoke directly." (Quran 4:164)

The Quran also tells us that Jesus was named "Masih," meaning the Christ or a designated messenger of God. He was also called "Kalima" meaning "Be" the commanding word of God.

"[Remember] When the angels said, O Mary! Verily, Allah gives you the glad tidings of a Word [Be] from Him: his name will be Christ Jesus." (Quran 3:45)

In many places of the Quran, Muhammad, the last prophet of God, was called "Nabial Ummi," meaning "Unlettered Prophet." He was also addressed as "Khataman nabiun," meaning the "Seal of the Prophets," and also "Rahmatal-lil-aalamiin," meaning a blessing for the whole world.

"Those who follow the Apostle—the unlettered prophet [Muhammad] whom they find mentioned in the Torah and the Gospel; for he commands them what is just and forbids them what is evil." (Quran 7:157)

And the book is delivered to him that is not learned, saying, Read this, I pray thee: and he saith, I am not learned (Isaiah 29:12).

"Muhammad is not the father of any of your men but (he is) the Apostle of Allah and the Seal of the Prophets." (Quran 33:40)

Reverend, it is interesting to note here that Jesus was not given any special name or title, like his predecessors Abraham and Moses or his successor, Muhammad. I think that God, being the omnipresent and omniscient, knew perfectly well that a day would come soon after Jesus, when his followers would worship him as God, by forgetting his true status or position or by ignoring the crystal clear instruction of His first commandment. So by the name "Christ," God simply wanted them to remember that Jesus was only one of His messengers and he was sent to earth for the guidance of his own people, the misguided Jews. (Matthew15:24)

The status of God is unattainable

Muslims believe the status of God is unattainable, because He is the Creator, the Controller and the Sustainer of the entire heavens and earth and everything that comes in between. So the status of God is the highest of all and it could in no way be attained by any of His created things. The Muslims, therefore have no clue at all why Jesus, whom God created in his mother's womb by His command and later chose him for the guidance of his own people, should be worshipped like God for having his name Christ, the meaning of which is Messiah or a chosen messenger of God?

An unexpected visitor

Something quite unexpected happened, when I was in the middle of my writing. I was visited by a young missionary lady with a copy of Bible in her hand. I felt myself quite excited to know that I could share with her certain things about Jesus, especially at that moment, when I was writing about his true status and mission in the light of the Bible and the Quran both.

This woman was probably in her mid-forties, tall, slim, and light-skinned. She also looked very smart and dignified in her white blouse and long black skirt that matched well with her black cap and black shoes. I took a moment to appreciate a perfect blend of beauty and brightness standing right before me, after I opened the door at the first knock.

While walking to the living room, she, let's call her Mrs. Martha Miller, told me she was a teacher of science in the local high school and a volunteer worker for the local Church of the Trinity. I also told her a few things about me. She looked happy when I said to her that I was also a teacher like her before I came to America. But she seemed to me a little reserved when I told her that I was a Muslim and apprehensive when I mentioned to her my special love and respect for Jesus as a mighty messenger of God.

We sat in our living room couches face to face besides a coffee table the top of which was loaded with my lap, a copy of the Bible, two books on the meaning of the Quran in English, several books on Islam and Christianity along with notepads, pencil holders, a bottle of water and a box of soft tissue. Mrs. Miller was kind enough to ignore the mess and exclaimed happily, "Oh, my God, do you read the Bible?"

"Yes Madam. It is a copy of the King James Version."

"Same is mine. But as far as I know your Holy Book is Quran, Right?" She asked me while putting her own copy of the Bible at the corner of the table.

"Right. But a Muslim is required to believe in all the messengers of God equally and what God revealed to them for the guidance of their people."

"Really? But I know many Muslims who practically avoid us when they find us with a Bible in our hand."

"Maybe, they are too busy to waste their time on something which they already know.

"You mean they also read the Bible as they read the Quran?"

"No, I mean they already know from the Quran what God revealed to Jesus, Moses, Abraham and other prophets of God who were sent before Muhammad." Then I added in a hurry, "But my case is different. I've been reading the Bible very seriously for the last one year."

"Very interesting" She remarked. "May I please know why?"

"Sure. I have a website where I've been writing about Jesus as I found him in the Quran and also in the Gospel. So, when I saw you first, I felt you were God-sent, because you arrived at that moment when I was trying to understand a verse in the Gospel that I found very confusing."

"May I please know which verse?"

"It is the first verse in John 1. Do you want me to read?" I picked up the Bible from the table and opened it.

"Just give me a second," she said, while turning over the pages of her Bible. Then she stopped, saying, "Yes, here it is. You may now read."

It was a short verse, but I tried to read it slowly and as correctly as possible with my unavoidable foreign accent. *"In the beginning was the Word, and the Word was with God, and the Word was God."(John 1:1)*

After I finished reading, I said to her politely, "I feel confused, because some of my missionary friends told me the 'Word' in the verse refers to Jesus and God both. Do you think that, too?"

"Yes, absolutely," Mrs. Miller confirmed, making me both shocked and surprised.

"But the verse did not mention anything about Jesus. So I don't understand what makes you think the 'word' here refers to Jesus? And if it does, how could Jesus and God be one and the same?"

"I understand your confusion. But, you need to remember that the verses of the Bible are complementary to one another. So to understand the meaning of verse 1, you also have to read the verse 14 below it." So saying, Mrs. Miller put her index finger on verse 14, which I read no less than twenty times, since I intended to write about Jesus in reply to your comment about the God of Islam being different from the God of the Judeo-Christian Faith.

Then she said, "Okay, let me read the verse and explain to you." And, I heard her read in her soft, sweet, and well-modulated voice. *"And the Word was made flesh, and dwelt among us, (and we beheld his glory, the glory of as of the only begotten of the Father,) full of grace and truth."* (John 1:14)

After she finished reading, she looked up at me and then said with assurance, "I think now you can see the connection, because this verse has mentioned clearly the 'Word,' referring to God in verse 1, was made flesh. It means God appeared Himself in the physical form of Jesus and then dwelled among the people, with full of grace and truth. In that case, what choice do we have but to believe the Word refers to God and Jesus both, meaning both are one or the same?" She sounded absolutely cool and confident.

I kept quiet for a while and then said with a bit hesitation, "Please excuse me of my shortcomings. But there are some elements in verses 1 and 14 that I still find confusing. For example, you said the 'Word' in both the verses refers to God and Jesus equally. But I really don't see how, because the 'Word' did not come into existence by itself. It needed to be made flesh in the physical form of Jesus and be sent to earth to dwell among the people, Right?"

"Yes, it is what the verse said."

"But I really don't understand how the Maker and being made or the Sender and being sent can be accepted as one and the same?"

"I think you have missed here one thing," said Mrs. Miller. "It was God Himself who made Him appear in the form of Jesus. So the question of the Maker and being made does not arise here."

Do you want me believe that it was God Himself who begot Him in the womb of Virgin Mary and then manifested Himself on earth through Jesus? But I kept my question to myself and said to her, "But I still have some confusion. The verse 14 has mentioned *'beholding of his glory, the glory as of the only begotten of the Father'* in parenthesis. Do you have any idea why did God mention His appearance through Jesus in parenthsis?"

"Frankly speaking, this type of question does not bother a true follower of Jesus, because whatever the Bible says, within the parenthesis or without it, we believe and accept them as the words of God, without having any doubt in it."

After this straightforward answer, I thought I should better stop mentioning anything to her from the Gospel, and start telling her what the Quran has said about Jesus' being "the word of God". May be, she would find my explanation more reasonable than what she just explained to me. So, I said to her supporting, "Sure. A true believer should take the words of God very seriously. I think you will be happy to know that we also believe Jesus as the "Word of God"."

"Really?"

"Yes. The Quran has addressed Jesus as the 'word of God' and we also don't mind to believe that he remained with God as His Word from the beginning."

"Then why can't you accept him being equal to God?"

"We can't, because we believe it is not only Jesus, everything in the creation of God has remained with Him in His ultimate plan and then comes into existence according to His will or command. There are many verses in the Quran where we have been told that whenever God wants to do anything, He just says to it, 'Be,' and it is.

> The Originator of the heavens and the earth! When He decrees a matter, He only says to it: Be! And it is. (Quran 2:117)

"Same thing happened when God wanted Mary to conceive her son without a father. He just commanded, "Be," and she conceived. Let me read a few verses of the Quran from my lap in support of that." So saying, I went to a particular file on my lap and read to her three verses that I quoted below.

"She [Mary] said: 'O my Lord! How shall I have a son when no man has ever touched me?' He said: 'Even so. God creates what He wills; when He decides to do anything, He only says to it, 'Be' and it is!" (3:47)

".....Allah gives you [Zachariah] glad tidings of Yahya [John the Baptist] confirming the Word from Allah [meaning the creation of Jesus by His word 'Be']. (3:39)

"Verily, the likeness of Jesus before Allah is as the likeness of Adam. He created him (Adam) from dust, then He said to him: "Be" and he was." (3:59)

After I finished reading, I looked at Mrs. Miller and said, "I hope now you know why the Muslims have no problem accepting Jesus as the 'Word' of God but have a problem accepting him as God?"

Mrs. Miller did not answer.

The Bible says, "Let there be" and the Quran says, "Be"

Luckily, by this time I had completed most of the books of the Bible, beginning with Genesis, and I remembered very well how the creation of God first came into existence. So I said to her politely, "Mrs. Miller, you certainly have read the book of Genesis and also remember how God created light and other things of His creations, Right?"

Mrs. Miller looked apprehensive and said, "Yes I do."

"Then you certainly remember what happened when God wanted to create light. He said, "Let there be light," and there was light. So He said with His other creations. Doesn't it tell us that both in the Bible and the Quran, God used more or less the same commanding word to bring things into existence? So, I don't understand how could we consider the Commander and His commanding word "Be" as one and the same?"

"May I please know, if everything in the world came to existence by His Commanding Word "Be," why then Jesus alone was called the "Word of God?""

"Good question. I also pondered over the matter for quite some time. Then I thought Jesus was called so only to remind his people how his virgin mother conceived him by the will and the command of God so that they could always remember why Jesus was called 'Word' or why he could not be God Incarnate because of his birth."

Mrs. Miller looked at her wristwatch after I stopped and then she said to me apologetically, "I wish I could stay with you longer and talk about Jesus more, but I have to leave now to attend a seminar in my church."

"Sure. But I thank you very much for giving me a chance to talk about Jesus so freely."

"Don't mention it, please. Talking to you about Jesus had also been a great pleasure to me. I think, the more we talk about him, the better we know about him." She picked up her bag and the Bible from the table.

While walking to the door, she surprised me saying, "I'll come again soon. I promise."

"Thanks. I'll be waiting for you."

We shook our hands warmly and she left gracefully after I opened the door and held it for her.

Interpretation of the "Word" as found in the Modern Versions of the Bible.

Reverend, a few weeks after Mrs. Miller left, I had a chance to read the interpretation of the "Word" in John 1.1 and few other verses of the Gospel in some Modern Versions of the Bible, which I like to share with you and with my other readers-both Christians and non-Christians.

Modern scholars of the Bible tell us that in the original Greek manuscript, the Word was used to mean divine or god, and it was never used to mean Divine or God. Accordingly, the New World Translation of the Bible has translated John 1:1 as follows:

"In the beginning was the Word and the Word was with God, and the Word was divine."

The Dictionary of the Bible by John McKenzie translates John 1:1 as follows:

"The word was with God [the Father] and the word was a divine being."

They actually confirm those verses of the Quran where Jesus was addressed as the "word" of God and was described as being noble, chaste, righteous, and close to God.(3:39, 3:45, 3:47)

On Jesus' Incarnation: Points to ponder

Reverend, I think, it will not be irrelevant, if I mention here another essential element of your faith related to Jesus' incarnation, meaning God manifested Himself in flesh through Jesus. I would like to draw your attention to the following statement, which I have quoted below from the *Grolier's Encyclopedia,* for your kind perusal.

Incarnation denotes the embodiment of a deity in human form. The idea occurs frequently in mythology.

In ancient times, certain people, especially kings and priests, were often believed to be divinities. In Hinduism, Vishnu is believed to have nine incarnations, or Avatars. For Christians, the incarnation is a central dogma referring to the belief that the eternal son of God, the second person of the Trinity, became man in the person of Jesus Christ. The incarnation was defined as a doctrine only after long struggles by early Church Council. The Council of Nicaea (325 CE) defined the deity of Christ against Aryanism; the Council of Constantinople (381 CE) defined the full humanity of the incarnate Christ against Apollinarianism; the Council of Ephesus (431 CE) defined the unity of Christ's person against Nestorianism; and the council of Chalcedon (451 CE) defined the two natures of Christ, divine and human, against Eutyches.

The above statement makes it absolutely clear how Jesus, the son of Mary, was gradually turned into a human God or became an object of worship by his followers, after he left.

The only verse quoted so far to validate the doctrine of incarnation was also proved to be a forgery about six centuries after Jesus' ascent to heaven. It is also interesting to note here that after its official injunction to the Christian faith, the Council of Churches needed biblical evidence to fulfill their purpose. They made a subtle change in 1 Timothy 3:16. Please have a look how this verse was read before and after the incarnation was made an essential doctrine of the Christian faith.

1 Timothy 3:16, as read before the sixth-century amendment: *"And without ceremony great is the mystery of **_godliness_**: which was manifest in the flesh, justified in the Spirit, seen of angels, preached unto the gentiles, believed on in the world, received up into glory."*

1 Timothy 3:16, as read after the sixth-century amendment: *"And without controversy great is the mystery of godliness: __God__ was manifest in the flesh, justified in the Spirit, seen of angels, preached unto the Gentiles, believed on in the world, received up into glory."*

Reverend, I hope you will now agree with me that how a subtle change in a word or words may create a heaven to earth difference in the meaning or understanding the message of a particular issue. But for the truth-seeking people, it is a matter of great relief that the modern versions of the Bible, like the Revised Standard Version, have been able to detect those changes and bring them to the knowledge of the public.

> He [Jesus] was no more than a servant: We granted Our favor to him and made him an example to the Children of Israel (Quran 43:59).

JESUS DECLARED HIMSELF A PROPHET OF GOD BOTH IN THE GOSPEL AND IN THE QURAN

———————————— ❧ ————————————

And the multitude said, This is Jesus the prophet of Nazareth of Galilee.
—Matthew 21:11

———————————— ❧ ————————————

Rev. Franklin Graham:

In my third and fourth letter, I have described in details and also with clear proof and evidence from both Bible and the Quran that Jesus was a mighty messenger of God and like all his predecessors and his successor Muhammad, he was also sent to establish the worship of One True God among his people and to help them live their lives through keeping His commands. But in spite of that, his followers ignored what he preached and practiced himself by the command of God and also began to worship him as God or along with God, after he left.

In this letter, I intend to prove with the help of the Gospel and the Quran both that Jesus was but a messenger of God, and he was sent exclusively for the guidance of his own people, the misguided Jews. Please consider the verses that I quoted below from different parts of the Gospel.

Jesus was a prophet of God: Instances from the Gospel

"But he [Jesus] answered and said, I am not sent but unto the lost sheep of the house of Israel." (Matthew 15:24)

"And the multitude said, This is Jesus the prophet of Nazareth of Galilee." (Matthew 21:11)

"But Jesus said unto them, a prophet [referring to himself when his own people offended him by their disrespectful attitude towards him] *is not without honour, but in his own country, and among his own kin, and in his own house." (Mark 6:4)*

"And he [Jesus] said unto them, I must preach the kingdom of God to other cities also: for therefore am I sent." (Luke 4:43)

"And he [Jesus] said unto them, What things? And they said unto him, Concerning Jesus of Nazareth, which was a prophet mighty in deed and word before God and all the people:" (Luke 24:19)

"The woman saith unto him [Jesus], Sir, I perceive that thou art a prophet. (John 4:19)

"The woman saith unto him, I know that Messias cometh, which is called Christ: when he is come, he will tell us all things. Jesus saith unto her, I that speak unto thee am he." (John 4:25–26)

"Then those men, when they had seen the miracle that Jesus did, said, This is of a truth that prophet that should come into the world." (John 6:14)

"Many of the people therefore, when they heard this saying, said, Of a truth this is the Prophet." (John 7:40)

"Ye men of Israel, hear these words; Jesus of Nazareth, a man approved of God among you by miracles and wonders and signs, which God did by him in the midst of you, as ye yourselves also know." (Acts 2:22)

I think, the contents of those quoted verses made it clear to us that Jesus knew himself he was a Prophet of God and why he was sent for. The people of his time knew that, too. If Jesus knew he was God or was equal to God, as you believe, why did he introduce himself falsely as the prophet of God or allow his people to remain in the dark about his true identity or status? The fact is, Jesus had nothing to hide about him, so he told them honestly who he really was and why he was sent for?

Jesus was a prophet of God: Instances from the Quran

In the following verses of the Quran, we shall see what God revealed through Muhammad, testifying of Jesus' true status or mission, was in complete harmony with the statements of the Gospel, I quoted above.

"While he [Zakariya] was standing in a prayer in the chamber, the angel called upon him [saying]: Allah gives you good news of Yahya [John, the Baptist], witnessing the truth of a word [meaning Jesus] from Allah who will be noble, chaste and a Prophet from among the righteous." (3:39)

"Behold! the angels said: "O Mary! Allah has chosen you and purified you, chosen you above the women of all nations. ... God will teach your son the Book, the Wisdom, the Torah, and the Gospel. And will make him a Messenger to the children of Israel ... ." (3:42, 48-49)

While testifying himself as a prophet of God, Jesus spoke to the people from his cradle in response to their slander against Mary, his virgin mother.

"Then she [Mary] pointed to him [her son in the cradle]. They said: How can we talk to one who is a child in the cradle? He [Jesus] said, I

am indeed a servant of God; He has given me revelation and made me a Prophet." (19:29–30)

While reminding people about Jesus' true status and mission, the Quran has said through Muhammad:

"We gave Moses the Book and followed him with a succession of Apostles; We gave Jesus the son of Mary clear Signs and strengthened him with the holy spirit." (2:87)

"Then in the footsteps of those Prophets, We sent Jesus the son of Mary confirming whatever remained intact from the Torah in his time, and gave him the Gospel wherein was guidance and light, corroborating what was revealed in the Torah; a guidance and an abomination to those who fear Allah." (5:46)

"Christ the son of Mary was no more than a Messenger of God; There were many apostles who passed away before him. His mother was a truthful woman." (5:75)

Reverend, on the basis of those statements from the Quran, which God revealed to Muhammad about fourteen hundred years ago, all his followers have accepted, loved, and respected Mary as a chaste, truthful and an illustrious woman of the world and her son, Jesus, as a noble, righteous and a chosen messenger of God, without knowing anything of what the Gospel has really said about him or about his mother.

Jesus was a self-surrendered servant of God

There are many verses in both Bible and the Quran where the messengers of God are addressed as His slaves or servants. Quite naturally. God chose His messengers to accomplish His mission through them, which is to guide His people to His path and to help them return to Him in heaven, the original and eternal home of their parents. So to help the people to achieve their goal, they left nothing unsaid or undone of what God revealed to them for the guidance of their people. It is for their total submission or surrender to the will and command of God, they were often addressed in the Quran as *Ibaa-di-naal Mur-saleen* (in Arabic), meaning *our slaves, the messengers.* I have quoted below some verses from both parts of the Bible and the Quran in support of that.

"Remember Abraham, Isaac, and Israel, thy servants, to whom thou swearest, by thine own self, and saidst unto them, I will multiply your seed as the stars of heaven..." (Exodus 32:13)

"Now after the death of Moses, the servant of the Lord it came to pass, that the Lord spake unto Joshua the son of Nun." (Joshua 1:1)

"And what can David say more unto thee? For thou, Lord God, knowest thy servant." (2 Samuel 7:20)

"And the Lord said unto Satan, Hast thou considered my servant Job, that there is none like him in the earth, a perfect and upright man, one that." (Job 2:3)

"Yet now hear, O Jacob my servant; and Israel, whom I have chosen." (Isaiah 44:1)

"Now therefore, O our God, hear the prayer of thy servant [Daniel], and his supplications, and cause thy face to shine upon thy sanctuary that is desolate, for the Lord's sake." (Daniel 9:17)

"Verily, verily, I say unto you, The servant [Jesus compares himself to a servant] is not greater than his lord; neither he that is sent greater than he that sent him." (John 13:16)

"The God of Abraham, Isaac and Jacob, the God of our fathers, has glorified his Son [servant] Jesus." (Acts 3:13)

"Unto you first God, having raised his Son [servant] Jesus, sent him to bless you, in turning away everyone of you from his inequities." (Acts 3:26)

Of interest is the use or application of two Greek words, *pias* and *paida*, both of which mean son, child, or servant. But while translating the Holy Bible from Greek to English, the translators used these words mostly to suit their own purpose. Out of their excessive love for Jesus, they used "Son" in reference to Jesus and "servant" in reference to all others. Besides that, they also chose to write "Son of God," capitalizing "Son" for Jesus but using a lowercase "s" for others, even though in the original Greek, no such difference exists. I think they did so without realizing that the level of one's closeness to God depends entirely upon the degree or depth of one's submission to His will and command and as well as upon striving for His cause.

The following passages of the Holy Quran, tell us about some of the messengers whom God favored many ways for their total submission to Him.

"We gave [in the past] knowledge to David and Solomon: and they both said: Praise be to Allah Who has favored us above many of His servants who believe!" (27:15)

"We have already promised Our Servants whom We sent as our Messengers that they would certainly be helped." (37:171–172)

"He [Jesus] was no more than a servant. We granted Our favor to him, and We made him an example to the children of Israel. (Through His miraculous birth and the miracles he performed to them in the name of God)" (43:59)

"The Messiah [Jesus] will never be proud to reject to be a slave to God, nor the angels who are nearest [to God]." (4:172)

"Glory to Allah Who did take His Servant [Muhammad] for journey by night from the Sacred Mosque of Mecca to the Farthest Mosque [in Jerusalem*]." (17:1)*

Jesus did everything by the command of God and for the sake of His pleasure

While reading the Gospel, I also came across many verses in which Jesus admitted that he did not speak or do anything on his own but by the command of God. Let me quote below a few of them:

"I can of mine own self do nothing: as I hear, I judge: and my judgment is just; because I seek not mine own will, but the will of the Father which hath sent me." (John 5:30)

"For I have not spoken of myself; but the Father which sent me, he gave me a commandment, what I should say, and what I should speak." (John 12:49)

"And he [God] that sent me is with me: the Father hath not left me alone; for I do always those things that please him." (John 8:29)

Reverend, I think the message of the above quoted verses is loud and clear. Who but the most devoted and dedicated servant of God would try to complete his assigned job in this manner, as did Jesus?

The Gospel also contains a number of verses where we saw Jesus wanted his people to know who he really was and why he was sent for. He wanted them to believe and keep it in mind that he was sent by God along with His guidance and to fulfill His purpose on earth. I have quoted below a few of them.

"And he said unto them, I must preach the kingdom of God to other cities also: for therefore am I sent." (Luke 4:43)

"I must the work the works of him that sent me, ...(John 9:4)

"Jesus cried and said, He that believeth on me, believeth not on me, but on him that sent me." (John 12:44)

"And this is life eternal, that they might know thee the only true God, and Jesus Christ, whom thou has sent.(John 17:3)

Jesus showed his complete adherence to the Laws of Moses

Both the Gospel and the Quran describe Jesus' complete adherence to the Law, which God revealed to Moses for the guidance of his people. I think the following verses that I quoted from the Gospel and the Quran will be enough to justify my point.

"Think not that I am come to destroy the law, or the prophets: I am not come to destroy, but to fulfill.

For verily I say unto you, Till heaven and earth pass, one jot or one tittle shall in no wise pass from the law, till all be fulfilled.

Whosoever therefore shall break one of these least commandments, and shall teach men so, he shall be called the least in the kingdom of heaven: but whosoever shall do and teach them, the same shall be called great in the kingdom of heaven." (Matthew 5:17–19)

"And behold, one came and said unto him, Good Master, what good thing shall I do, that I may have eternal life? And he said unto him, Why callest thou me good? there is none good but one, that is, God: but if thou wilt enter into life, keep the commandments." (Matthew 19:16–17)

"I [Jesus] have come to you to attest the Law [Law of Moses] which was before me and to make lawful to you part of which was forbidden to you before: I have come to you with a Sign from your Lord. So fear Allah and obey me. It is Allah Who is my Lord and your Lord; then worship Him. This is a straight way." (3:50–51)

"Then in the footsteps of those Prophets, We sent Jesus the son of Mary confirming whatever remained intact from the Torah in his time, and gave him the Gospel wherein was guidance and light, corroborating what was revealed in the Torah; a guidance and an abomination to those who fear Allah." (5:46)

Reverend, many of my missionary friends believe Jesus was God incarnate because of his miraculous birth and the miracles he performed before his people. But I think the arrival or existence of a legendary figure described in Hebrews 7:1–4 is more astonishing than Jesus' birth without a father. And, the miracles performed by a prophet in Ezekiel 37 is more stunning than Jesus' bringing a four-days-dead body back to life from his grave. (John 11:39–44)

There are also many clear instances in the Gospel to prove that Jesus was a man of flesh and blood. From the episode of the fig tree, we came to know that like any other ordinary human being, Jesus was also a subject to hunger, anger, ignorance, and obliviousness, including the suffering of pain and feeling of frustration. (Mark 11)

Opinion of the Anglican Bishops about Jesus' true status

On June 25, 1984, the *London Daily News* ran an article titled "Shock Survey of Anglican Bishops," which described a survey report regarding Jesus' true status. A poll, conducted by the religious television show *Credo*, showed that more than half of the Anglican Bishops in England said Christians were not obliged to believe that Jesus Christ was God. The article further stated that nineteen of the thirty-one Bishops agreed that "it is sufficient to regard Jesus as God's supreme agent."

God's "supreme agents" refer to none but the chosen or designated messengers of God who were sent to earth from time to time for the guidance of their people. The Anglican Bishops' comment about Jesus in the survey report in 1984 is similar to that which God said about him in the Quran through his testifier Muhammad about fourteen hundred years ago.

Christ, the son of Mary, was no more than a messenger; Many messengers had already passed away before him. His mother was a truthful woman; they both ate earthly food like other human beings. See how the revelations are made clear to them to know the reality; yet see how they ignore the truth.

Holy Quran (5:75)

LETTER 8

SON OF GOD VS. SON OF MAN

(To Muhammad) Say: He is God,
The One and Only; God, the Self-Sufficient.
He begets not, Nor He is begotten; And there is
none equal or comparable to Him.
—Holy Quran 112:1–4

Reverend Franklin Graham:

In this letter, I intend to discuss whether Jesus was truly the "Son of God" or His "only begotten," as his devoted followers claim about him. Or, he was the "son of man," meaning simply a human being, as we claim. I'll obviously discuss the matter upon the evidence of our Holy Scriptures-the Bible and the Quran both.

As a Muslim, I'd never believe that Jesus called God his Father and him as the son of God to mean he was really begotten by God as a human father begets his children and because of that Jesus and his Father in the heaven are one and the same or they are inseparable part of each other.

We look at this Father-Son relationship in between God and Jesus completely from a different perspective. We believe Jesus called God his Father to show his intense love, longing, or intimate feeling that he always had for Him. It is a kind of feeling that a very concerned, loyal, and grateful son always nourishes in his heart for his most loving, caring, competent, and adorable father. Jesus also knew that his mother conceived him by fulfilling the will and the command of God, and because of that, he might feel himself more close and connected with God when he addressed Him as his Father and him as His son.

The status of God is the highest of all

But I don't need any assumed excuses or explanations to make you accept what we think or believe about this very essential element of your faith. We have Jesus' own statement in the Gospel to find out whether by calling God his Father and him as His son, he ever meant he was equal to his Father or, he had the same status, wisdom, authority and power as his Father in heaven had? Let us examine the contents of the following verses and find out the actual message that Jesus has left in them for our reflection.

"Then answered Jesus and said unto them, Verily, Verily, I say unto you the Son can do nothing of himself, but what he seeth the Father do: for what things soever he doeth, these also doeth the Son likewise.

For the Father loveth the Son, and sheweth him all things that himself doeth: and he will shew him greater works than these, that ye may marvel." (John 5:19–20)

"When Jesus heard that, he said, This sickness is not unto death, but for the glory of God, that the Son of God might be glorified thereby." (John 11:4)

In the above quoted verses, Jesus admitted to his people openly that the Son could do nothing by himself. Whatever astonishing acts he performed to them so far, he did them by the inspiration of Almighty God-his heavenly Father. Jesus also told them that God would show to them more astonishing works through him because of His love for the Son and to make him great or glorified to them. Jesus said so in reference to his bringing Lazarus (one of his devoted followers) back to life from his grave, where he had remained buried for four days. By those instances, Jesus wanted his people to realize the overall power, authority, wisdom and glory of God so that they might love and obey him who He sent to them for their guidance.

This should tell us that the 'Son' who admitted clearly that he could do nothing by himself or needed to be glorified by the 'Father' to draw his peoples' attention, admiration or obedience, could no way be equal to God. By those statements Jesus also made it clear to us that by calling God his Father and him as His Son, he only wanted to feel the intimacy or oneness with God in fulfilling His purpose, but he never meant him being the same or equal to God.

"Son of God" refers to a righteous person

It is interesting to note that the two Greek words 'pias' or 'paida' mean servant, son or child. But while translating them into English the overly enthusiastic translators of the Bible used a capital S for "Son" when referring to Jesus and "servant" or "son" with a small s to mean others. They did so probably without knowing what the people of Jesus' time truly meant when they called someone "Son of God." In the Jewish language and culture, a righteous, a loyal and a God-fearing person was often called the 'Son of God'. I quoted below a few statements from both parts of the Holy Bible to justify my point.

"I [David] will declare the decree: the LORD hath said unto me, Thou art my son; this day have I begotten thee." (Psalm 2:7)

(To Moses) "And thou shalt say unto Pharaoh, Thus saith the LORD, Israel is my son, even my firstborn." (Exodus 4:22)

"He [Solomon] shall build an house for my name; and he shall be my son, and I will be his father." (1 Chronicles 22:10)

"When the morning stars sang together, and all the sons of God shouted for joy." (Job 38:7)

"For as many as they are led by the Spirit of God, they are the sons of God." (Romans 8:14)

And lo a voice from heaven, saying, This is my beloved Son, in whom I am well pleased." (Matthew 3:17)

The verses I quoted above do not show any difference in the status, place or position among the sons of God. Rather, they all have been used for the most noble, righteous, obedient, and beloved persons of God.

Below are two verses from the Gospels of Mark and Luke, concerning a remark by a centurion about Jesus, after he saw him die on the cross.

"And when the centurion, which stood over against him, saw that he [Jesus] so cried out, and gave up the ghost, he said, truly this man was the Son of God." (Mark 15:39)

"Now when the centurion saw what was done, he glorified God, saying, certainly this was a righteous man." (Luke 23:47)

In the Gospel of Luke, the phrase "Son of God" was replaced by a "righteous man," because, people of Jesus' time as I mentioned before, used to address a noble and righteous man as the Son of God.

"Son of man" refers to a human being

Reverend, now, I would like to draw your attention to the phrase "son of man" which Jesus used more frequently than the "Son of God."

The scholars in the Jewish language and culture tell us, that people of Jesus' time, used to call a human being as "son of man." According to the practice of that time, Jesus who was born and brought up in a Jewish family, called himself "son of man," when in reality, he had no human father. By "son of man" Jesus simply meant himself a human being or a man of flesh and blood.

At this point, I also like to mention here that Jesus referred himself as the "son of man" eighty times in the Gospel, whereas he mentioned himself as the "Son of God" only ten times in the Chapters 5 and 11 in the Gospel of John.

In this connection, I also like to point out that as the days unfold and scroll toward more advancement and acknowledgement of truth, the open-minded and the truth-seeking scholars of the Holy Bible are likely to make more progress in identifying Jesus' true status and mission out of those misleading addresses or titles. They already took care many of them either through amendments, elimination, or adding footnotes. Accordingly, some amendments or elimination was made in the most prominent and popular dogma regarding Jesus' status as the 'Son of God'.

In the narration of the New World Translation of the Holy Scriptures, the title Son of God has been eliminated from the Gospel of Mark 1.1.

Another important elimination regarding "Son of God" was made in the Acts of Apostles. The King James Version of the Bible reads: *"And Philip said [to the eunuch], if thou believest with all thine heart, thou mayest. And he answered and said, I believe that Christ is the Son of God." (Acts 8:37)*

But the entire verse has now been eliminated from the New International Version of the Bible, with a footnote at the bottom of the page that tells us this verse was not found in any other ancient manuscripts. So they thought it was added later, as a confession to Jesus' being the Son of God, by some of his overly enthusiastic followers.

The situation got more complex, as the word "begotten" was added to the phrase "Son of God" to raise Jesus' status to being equal to God or to make him being the "Savior of mankind."

"For God so loved the world, that He gave His only Begotten Son, that whosoever believeth in him should not perish, but have everlasting life." (John 3:16)

My missionary friends often quoted this verse in support of their eternal life through believing in Jesus' sacrifice for the sin of the world. But now, the keyword "Begotten" has been removed from the verse from all the modern versions of Bible. They found the word "begotten" came from the Greek word *monogenes*, which actually means "unique" or special. This describes Jesus accurately, because his miraculous birth, the miracles he performed, his crucifixion, his ascent to heaven alive- all these extraordinary episodes of his life, has truly made him a very unique and a special human being in the history of mankind.

In fact, what the most enlightened and open-minded scholars of the Bible have now discovered on Jesus' being the 'only begotten of God' through years of their time, toil, patience and perseverance, the Quran, the last and the final Book of God, denounced it to be a monstrous lie about fourteen hundred years ago, through Jesus' testifier, Muhammad. I've quoted below a few verses from different chapters of the Quran in support of that.

"[To Muhammad] And say: Praise be to Allah Who has not taken unto Himself a son, and Who has no partner in the Sovereignty, nor He needs any protecting friend to support Him. And magnify Him with all magnificence." (17:111)

"And they [the Christians] say: The Most Gracious [Allah] has begotten a son! Indeed they have said a most monstrous lie! For which the skies are ready to burst, the earth is to split asunder and the mountains are to fall in utter ruin, that they ascribe a son to the most Gracious [Allah]. For it is not befitting to the Compassionate God that He should beget a son." (19:88–92)

"They say: 'Allah has begotten a son!' Glory be to Him! He is self-Sufficient! His is all that is in the heavens and earth! Have you any proof for what you say? Would you ascribe to Allah something about which you have no knowledge?" (10:68)

The Quran has addressed Jesus as the son of Mary

Jesus' name has been used in the Quran frequently, and it has mostly been followed by the "son of Mary." We may consider it most easy and appropriate to understand his true identity or status by the scholars and illiterates alike. Let us check how Jesus has been addressed in the Quran through his testifier Muhammad:

"O people of the Book [meaning the Christians]! Do not exceed the limits in your religion, nor say of Allah anything but the truth. The Messiah Jesus, the son of Mary was no more than a Messenger of God." (4:171)

"When the angels said, "O Mary! Indeed Allah gives you the good news of a word from Him, whose name will be the Messiah, Jesus (Jesus Christ), the son of Mary, illustrious in this world and the Hereafter, and among those who are close to Allah.(3:45)

Reverend, according to the statements of the Bible and the Quran both, we came to know that Jesus was a unique and a special son of Mary through his miraculous birth, a son of man, meaning a human being or a son of God meaning a noble, chaste, and a righteous person who God sent to earth as His Messenger for the guidance of his own people-the misguided Jews.

In this connection, I also like to mention here that to save the people from all those fictions or fantasies about God and His Messengers, nowhere in the Quran God was addressed as Father or His Messengers as His sons. They were simply addressed as His prophets, messengers, servants or slaves of God.

It is not befitting to the majesty of Allah that He should beget a son. Glory be to Him! When He determines a matter He only says to it Be and it is. (19:35)

TRINITY WAS INVENTED AFTER JESUS LEFT, HE NEVER TAUGHT IT

For there are three that bear record in heaven, the Father, the Word and the Holy Ghost: And these three are one.
—1 John 5:7

Reverend Franklin Graham:

Christians believe the doctrine of the Trinity to be an integral part of their faith related to the attainment of their most desired salvation. But Muslims believe it is an invented doctrine of men and also a clear blaspheme against One True God and it became a part of Christian Faith after Jesus left. I found it to be absolutely true when I did not come across any single statement in the Gospel where Jesus asked his people to worship him as God in any form or manner. After I learnt that, I felt curious to know how the Christians worship three Gods as one or how the Trinity became a part of the Christian faith, if Jesus never taught it and the Gospel had also no record for it? So naturally, I saved my questions for my missionary friends who used to visit me then off and on.

Several weeks later, a middle-aged white missionary lady, I would call her Mrs. Robinson, agreed to talk when I asked her straight what the Gospel has really said about the Trinity. In reply to my question, she opened her Bible in the King James Version, and said, "You will find it in 1 John 5:7." And then she read it to me after I opened my own copy:

"For there are three that bear record in heaven, the Father, the Word, and the Holy Ghost: And these three are one."

After she finished reading, I said, "Please excuse me for my shortcomings, but I really don't see where in this verse, you are asked to believe in the Father, the Word and the Holy Ghost as three Gods but to worship them as one?"

"It is understood."

"Will you please explain a bit?"

From her slow and laconic explanation, I came to know that Father is God as the Godhead; the Word is God as His only begotten Son, Jesus; and then there is the Holy Ghost or the Holy Spirit. These three are merged into one. Thus, Christians worship one God in the union of three. But I remained in the dark as before.

So I said to her apologetically, "Please don't mind, it still sounds to me very confusing, because I think to be like God, Jesus, and the Holy Ghost should also be like God. I mean, both of them should have the same essence and attributes to become like God or His equal, Right?"

"Right and so they are. We believe the Father, the Son, and the Holy Ghost are made of the same substance, and because of that, they have the same equal majesty and the glory of a fully independent God."

"But, how do you worship three independent Gods as the one or the same God?"

"There lies the mystery. In spite of their being independent, we neither worship them separately, nor worship them together. We worship them as one God in the union of three."

"But how is it possible? I mean, how could they maintain their independence after being merged into one?" I asked her again, trying to hide my frustration.

"It is possible, because, they are merged into one without losing their own independence and glory."

The way she described, it seemed to me the God of the Trinity matched more with a very mysterious, magical, or a supernatural being found in some digital movie, but it could no way match with the God of the Judeo-Christian faith or the God of Islam, as described in our holy scriptures-the Bible and the Quran both.

Besides that, a series of unwanted but unavoidable questions flashed in my mind. I wanted to know how the Father, the Son, and the Holy Ghost function as a fully independent God, while being merged into one?

Or, what is the use of their being independent or having the same substance, glory, and majesty, if they can't do anything separately? And, if they do, then what will happen to their unity?

Or, how could their unity remain intact, when Jesus, one of the inseparable parts of the Trinity died on the Cross and remained buried for three days?

What happened then to the Godhead and the Holy Ghost after Jesus died? Did they die too, with Jesus, and then resurrect after three days along with him? In that case, what happened to the heavens and earth if they remained dead for three days?

Then to distract myself from the flow of those unwanted but unavoidable questions, I said to her, again politely, "But I still have no clue how these three Gods get merged into one without losing their own independence or majesty?"

Trinity to be understood in three different states of water

"I know it is very difficult to understand," Mrs. Robinson said, "especially for the people of other faiths. But I will try to explain it with an example. Just think of water in its three different states: liquid, solid, and steam. Water is liquid, ice is solid, and air is steam. Now, what is the substance we find common in three of them?"

"Water, obviously."

"Similarly, the substance of three Gods is one and the same, just like the water is found common in its three different states. I hope, now you know what it means."

"Sorry," I said, "I feel myself more confused. Let me tell you why? We believe God is Eternal, Almighty and All knowing. So, whatever His substance is, it must remain the same or unchanged under all circumstances. Don't you think so, too?"

"Yes, that is what I meant when I gave the example of water. It also remains unchanged in all its three states."

"But I don't think any essence or attributes of God, if we name it His substance, can be compared with water, because water does not remain the same in its three different states. I mean, when water is changed into ice or steam, it loses its liquidity. Besides that, water does not freeze into ice or change into steam on its own. It must go through certain states or conditions to become ice or steam, Right?"

Mrs. Robinson did not answer. In her silence, I continued, "But it does not happen so with any of the essence, attributes, or the substance of God. I mean, nothing could affect, change, or destroy it any way. In other words, the substance of God remains the same or as it is, when He adds anything new to His creation, eliminates anything from it, or changes anything to something else, Right?"

I felt tensed while waiting for her response, but she remained silent as before. Then, I asked her again casually, "By the by Madam, do you know any other statement of the Gospel where Jesus mentions anything of the Trinity? I mean, to worship God, him, and the Holy Ghost together as One God?"

Mrs. Robinson seemed to relax. She leafed through her Bible and then said, "It is here, last three verses in the last chapter of Matthew."

I opened my Bible and when I looked at those verses, I thanked God in silence. Just a few days ago, while re-reading the last scene of Jesus' Crucifixion in the Gospel of Matthew, Mark, Luke and John, I read them too. So, I remembered very well that Jesus gave those instructions to his disciples after he rose up from his grave and I did not find there any such element that she could use in support of the Trinity. At that moment, I heard her reading the last three verses from the last chapter of Matthew very slowly, softly and uttering each word distinctly clear.

And Jesus came and spake unto them, saying, All power is given unto me in heaven and in earth.

Go ye therefore, and teach all nations, baptizing them in the name of the Father, and of the Son, and of the Holy Ghost.

Teaching them to observe all things whatsoever I have commanded you: And, lo, I am with you, alway, even unto the end of the world. Amen. (Matthew 28:18-20)

After she finished reading, she said politely, "I think, if you look into the meaning of those verses, you will see Jesus wanted us worship the Father, the Son and the Holy Ghost as one God. It means Jesus knew he was an inseparable part of God otherwise -"

"Sorry! I don't see any such indication." I interrupted. "Will you please tell me what makes you think so?"

"Sure. We need to remember here that Jesus gave those commands to his disciples after three days of his resurrection. It tells us like his Father in heaven, Jesus was also eternal or immortal, because he overcame death through his resurrection."

"But I don't see how. You just told me that Jesus resurrected from his grave after three days. In that case, how could you claim he was immortal or eternal like God? Because, we believe God is eternal and All-Knowing and therefore nothing could stop or interrupt Him grasping anything from His knowledge or seeing anything from His vision, even for a moment. So how could Jesus, who died and remained buried for three days, as you claim, be eternal like God or equal to Him?"

From her look, I understood she did not expect this question from me. But a few moments later, she asked me seriously, "Then what do you think of the promise that Jesus made to his disciples about his staying with them 'til the end of the world?"

I also did not expect this question from her. But keeping my surprises to myself, I said to her, "I think, you took the apparent meaning of what Jesus said and overlooked its inherent message. Jesus meant to stay with them till the end of the world through his teaching, morals or spirit. Just think for a moment, how Jesus has been living with you for the last two thousand years? The same way he will always live with his followers until the end of the world, fulfilling his promise. In fact, it is not only Jesus but the Prophets like Abraham, Moses, Muhammad, and other legendary figures of the world are still alive in the hearts of men and will remain so forever in the history of mankind. So what do you think of them? Are they eternal too, as God is?"

Jesus had power over heavens and earth

"But they are not like Jesus," Mrs. Robinson argued. "They did not have power like God, but Jesus had power over heavens and earth."

Mrs. Robinson reminded me of Jesus' claim on having his power, in the verse 18 of Matthew 28. In reply to that, I said to her politely, "I think, you have overlooked one vital clue that Jesus has left in his claim. He said the power over entire heavens and earth was given to him. In other words, Jesus had that power after he received it from God. In that case, how could we claim that the status of the Giver and the given as one or the same?"

"Sorry. I think we are too small to explain the status or the relation of the Father and the Son."

What do you need to explain when the answer is more than obvious? I thought, but I kept my question to myself and said to her instead, "Okay, if for the sake of argument, I believe Jesus was as powerful as God is, but still it does not make him God, because it does not tell us whether Jesus was also as wise as God is, or he could comprehend everything in his knowledge or in his vision as God does."

"How do you know he could not?" Mrs. Robinson sounded a bit frustrated.

"I know it from Jesus' own words in the Gospel. Once, talking to his disciples, Jesus admitted to them honestly that he was unaware of the Last Hour and no one had any knowledge of that except God.(Math 24:36) Besides that, if you read the story of the fig tree in Mark 11, you will also notice that Jesus did not know even the season of the fig and he walked to the tree to appease his hunger, without knowing it had no fruit in it but the leaves. Don't you think, if Jesus were God or His equal, nothing could remain hidden from his knowledge or vision?"

Jesus asked his disciples to baptize all nations in the name of the "Three"

In reply to my question, Mrs. Robinson asked, "Why, then, Jesus asked his disciples to baptize all nations in the name of the "Three"-the Father, the Son, and the Holy Ghost?"

"Do you think, by this command, Jesus meant all nations to worship the Father, the Son, and the Holy Ghost as one God?"

"Isn't it most obvious?" she asked me back. "Otherwise, why we have been worshipping them as one God for the last two thousand years?"

"Do you think that a wrong thing turns to be right if it is believed to be right for hundreds of years?" I was about to ask her. But keeping my question to myself, I said to her, "Yes, you have a point there. But if Jesus really meant so as you said, he must have taught about the Trinity before the Jews made him arrested by the soldiers of Governor Pilate, right?"

"May I please know what difference does it make?" Mrs. Robinson asked me in apprehension.

"A lot, because there is no such statement in the Gospel where Jesus is found teaching anything about the Trinity, before he was detained by them. You can, of course, correct me, if I am wrong."

Mrs. Robinson did not try to correct me.

So, I asked her, "In that case, how could Jesus command his disciples to teach something among the nations that he never taught?

Mrs. Robinson maintained her silence as before. So I continued, "We also have no reason to guess that Jesus might have taught it to his disciples in secret or when no one was around them, because while talking to the high priest about certain charges against him, Jesus made it absolutely clear that he did not teach them anything in secret or in private; he always spoke to them openly. In that case, I think it would be a wild guess if we believe Jesus taught his disciples about the Trinity before his arrest, but the writers of all four Gospels somehow forgot to mention it."

> The high priest then asked Jesus of his disciples, and of his doctrine. Jesus answered him, I spake openly to the world; I ever taught in the synagogue, and in the temple, whither the Jews always resort; and in secret have I said nothing. Why askest thou me? Ask them which heard me, what I have said unto them: behold, they know what I said. (John 18:19-21)

"Then why Jesus asked his disciples to baptize all nations in the name of the Father, the Son, and the Holy Ghost, if he did not mean them as one or the same?" Mrs. Robinson asked me to clarify.

"If you don't mind to listen, I could try to explain it as I understood myself."

"Sure. I'll be happy to know."

"Thanks. As far as I know, baptism is a kind of celebration that you generally observe marking your child's admission in the Church or giving him a name, Right?"

"Right."

"The Baptist of the Churches conducts the ceremony by dipping the child in water or by sprinkling him with water, Right?'

"Yes, a child needs to go through this kind of stuff."

"But you also know very well that baptism is not a mere ceremony, it also has some inner or deeper meaning than admitting the child in the Church or giving his name. It also means to bring some changes in the heart or soul of the child with the light or the spirit of his faith so that he could love and obey his God unconditionally as did Jesus and his true followers. For this reason, it is believed that baptism works better upon the older children when they understand the true meaning of the ceremony. Do you agree with me?"

"Yes." Mrs. Robinson admitted frankly.

"Thanks. Now on the basis of that explanation, we can rightly guess that Jesus did not want his disciples to baptize all nations in the name of the Father, the Son and the Holy Ghost, to give them names or admit them in the church through some ceremony, Right?"

Mrs. Robinson remained silent.

So, I answered for her, "Certainly not. Jesus wanted his disciples to teach all nations about the status of the Father, the Son and the Holy Ghost clearly so that they never got confused or misled, when the false prophets would come after him with their false doctrines to deviate them from the eternal truth of the first commandment that he preached and practiced himself when he was with them . So, to save the nations from this deviation, Jesus left for his disciples two brief instructions before he was raised to heaven."

"By the first instruction, Jesus wanted his disciples to baptize all nations in the name of the Father, the Son and the Holy Ghost. By this he meant to tinge their souls with renewal of their faith in One True God. Jesus' disciples knew perfectly well that the status of God was the highest of all in the entire heavens and earth and no one could be His equal or worthy of worship besides Him. They also knew that Jesus was but a messenger of God and he was sent to his people to guide them by the command of God. They were also aware of the fact that Jesus called God his Father and him as His son out of his excessive love and longing for Him and by this call he never meant him the same or equal to God."

"Similarly, Jesus' disciples also knew that the Holy Ghost or the Holy Spirit was the angel Gabriel —the chief of all angels who used to convey the words of God to His messengers on earth and also to help them to fulfill their mission. According to the description of the Gospel, Jesus' disciples were more familiar with the role of the Holy Ghost than others. They found the Holy Ghost to interfere in Jesus' birth, his baptism, miracles he performed and also with his ascent to heaven. Do you think, with this clear knowledge and understanding about the supreme status and overall authority of God and the distinct and definite role played by both Jesus and the Holy Ghost, his disciples would ever teach the nations to worship the 'Three' as one God?"

In her silence I added, "I think, no explanation is required for Jesus' second instruction. He simply wanted his disciples to teach all nations to obey and observe everything that he preached and practiced himself following the footsteps of all his predecessors. In that case, a sensible person would like to know how could Jesus want his disciples to teach about the Trinity that he never taught them?"

But before she could respond, her cell phone rang. Then, after a brief exchange of words in a very low voice, she said to me apologetically, Sorry, I have to leave now to take my father to his dentist."

"Sure. Family should come first."

Upon the validity of the statement in 1 John 5:7

Reverend, when Mrs. Robinson read the verse in 1 John 5:7 in support of the Trinity, I did not know then that it was discarded long before from the Revised Standard Version of the Bible, edited by a group of thirty-two eminent Christian scholars, as an unauthorized addition to the Greek text of the New Testament. When I first came to know about it, I verified the truth in the Holman Christian Standard Bible and also in the Zondervan New International Version Bible. I found the verse 5:7 from 1 John has been expunged from both the texts and put below as a footnote.

In this connection, sir, I also like to mention here that besides that abrogated verse, the writers of all the four Gospels, even Paul, the self-announced disciple of Jesus and the writer of the last seventeen books of the New Testament, did not mention anything about the Trinity in any of their books. In that case, the most obvious question is how the Trinity became an integral part of the Christian faith, if it was not taught by Jesus or by any of his true disciples or even by Paul? You will find the answer below.

The Trinity was the product of the council of Nicaea

While looking for the answer myself, I came across with some authentic and well-researched books where I found the doctrine of the Trinity was a manmade product of the council of Nicaea and it became an indispensable part of Christian faith about 325 years after Jesus left. It was first presented by Athanasius, an Egyptian deacon from Alexandria, and was accepted by the Council of Nicaea in 325 CE. It was called the Creed of Nicaea. Let me quote here a few lines from the report accepted or approved by the council.

> Whoever wishes to be saved must, above all, keep the Catholic faith. This is what the Catholic faith teaches: We worship one God in the Trinity and the Trinity in unity. We distinguish among the persons, but we do not divide the substance. For the Father is a distinct person; the Son is a distinct person; and the Holy Spirit is a distinct person. Still the Father and the Son and the Holy Spirit have One divinity, equal glory, and coeternal majesty. What the Father is, the Son is, and the Holy Spirit is. ... The Father is eternal, the Son is eternal, and the Holy Spirit is eternal. Nevertheless, there are not three eternal beings, but one eternal being. ... Likewise, the Father is omnipotent, the Son is omnipotent, and the Holy Spirit is omnipotent. Yet there are not three omnipotent beings, but one omnipotent being. Thus the Father is God, the Son is God and the Holy Spirit is God. But there are not three gods but one God. ... For according to the Christian truth, we must profess that each of the persons individually is God; and according to Christian religion we are forbidden to say that there are three gods or lords. But the entire three persons are co-eternal and co-equal with one another.

Reverend, it is interesting to note here that according to the manifesto of the Council of Nicaea, the Christian truth is different from the Christian religion. The Christian truth wants its adherents to profess each of the three persons—the Father, the Son, and the Holy Spirit as being a separate and independent God. But the Christian religion forbids its adherents to call them three gods and to regard the 'three' being one, coeternal and coequal to one another. This was how the eternal truth in the first commandment of God, which was pure and pristine monotheism, got contaminated with the pagan practice of polytheism long after Jesus left.

The Trinity was rejected by the Unitarian Christians

But, we have no reason to believe that Jesus' true followers, the Unitarian Christians or the worshippers of one God, accepted the doctrine of the Trinity, as they were asked to do. According to the authentic report of the historians and religious scholars, we came to know they rejected it at once to be wrong, inappropriate, and above all, as a grave sin of blasphemy. But when the authority of the Council failed to justify their doctrine on the basis of logic, evidence, or acceptable explanation, they tried to force the people to accept it blindly. Not only that, they also began to arrest, torture, burn and kill them who dared to oppose or criticize their doctrine in public.

But, it is also a fact that by the end of the fourth century, the doctrine of the Trinity became assimilated as an indispensable part of the Christian faith, and since then, devoted followers of Jesus Christ have worshipped God in the union of three by ignoring the crystal-clear message of His first commandment which they still find in their Holy Gospel in the teaching of Jesus. (Mark 12:29–30)

What the Quran says about the Trinity?

The Quran, which God revealed to Jesus' Comforter Muhammad about six hundred years after his ascent to heaven, has renounced the doctrine of the Trinity as a clear blaspheme against One True God. There are a number of verses in the Quran that confirm Jesus never asked his people worship him as God or as one of the Gods in the Trinity. Rather, he worshipped the same One God of all his predecessors and also asked his people do the same.

"O people of the Book! [meaning here the Christians] Do not transgress on the limits of your religion. Speak nothing but the truth about Allah. The Messiah Jesus, the son of Mary was no more than a Messenger of Allah and His Word 'Be' which He bestowed upon Mary and a Spirit from Him. So, believe in Allah and His Messenger and do not say Trinity. Stop saying that. Allah is only One Deity." (4:171)

"Certainly they have disbelieved who say: 'Allah is Christ-the son of Mary,' while Christ himself said: 'O children of Israel! Worship Allah; my Lord and your Lord.' whoever commits shirk [to worship God in association with others], Allah will deny him the paradise, and the hellfire will be his home" (5:72).

"They disbelieve who say: God is one of the 'three' in a Trinity. For there is no god except One God. If they desist not from what they say, verily a grievous chastisement will befall the disbelievers among them." (5:73)

"They [Jews and Christians] have taken their rabbis and their priests to be their Lords beside Allah and so they did with Messiah, the son of Mary, though they were commanded [in the Torah and the Gospel] to worship none but One God, besides Whom there is none worthy of worship. Exalted is He from having partners they associate with Him." (9:31)

"O people of the Book! Why do you confound the truth with falsehood and conceal the truth while you know?" (3:71)

"It is not possible for a man whom Allah has given the Book, the Wisdom and the Prophet Hood, that he would say to the people: Worship

me instead of Allah. On the contrary he would say: Be worshippers of your Lord in accordance with the Holy Book you have been teaching and reading. Nor would he command you to take the angels and the prophets as your Lords. Would He order you to disbelieve after you have surrendered to God?" (3:79–80)

Reverend, I think if the members of the Council of Nicaea had any idea that God would reveal the truth about three hundred years later by sending His last prophet Muhammad, and testifying through him about Jesus' true status and mission, clearing his name from all falsehood that they imposed upon him and also protecting his honor in the Quran, His everlasting guidebook, they would have thought twice, before they dared venturing into the laws of God or demeaning the sanctity of any of His chosen messengers.

> (To Muhammad) And declare: The Truth has come and falsehood has vanished, for falsehood by its nature is bound to perish.
>
> (Quran 17:81)

LETTER 10

SOME MISUNDERSTOOD OR MISINTERPRETED STATEMENTS OF JESUS

---

*Therefore speak I to them in parables: because they seeing see not; and
hearing they hear not, neither do they understand. And in them is
fulfilled the Prophecy of Esa-ias, which saith, by hearing ye shall hear, and
shall not understand; and seeing ye shall see, and shall not perceive:*
—Matthew 13:13–14

Rev. Franklin Graham:

In this letter, I like to draw your attention to some of the statements
in the Gospel where many of my missionary friends found clear
indication to believe Jesus and God were one and the same and to
worship them both as one God. But when I studied them myself, I felt
the true meaning of those statements of Jesus got somehow distorted,
after he left.

But before I go into that, I should mention first two important
criteria of Jesus' way or style of teaching. His teaching about God
and His guidance was both transparent and ambiguous. The message
in some of his statements was absolutely plain, simple and easily
understood by the scholars or illiterate alike. But some of them were
truly complicated and confusing for the common and ordinary people

to grasp their inherent meaning. Let me explain the difference with Jesus' own statements in the Gospel.

Clear and Conclusive Verses

"And Jesus answered him [a Jewish scribe] The first of all commandments is, hear, O Israel, the Lord our God is one Lord: and thou shalt love the Lord thy God with all thy heart, and with all thy soul, and with all thy mind and with all thy strength: this is the first commandment." (Mark 12:29–30)

"But Jesus beheld them, and said unto them, With men this is impossible; but with God all things are possible." (Matthew 19:26)

"And Jesus answering saith unto them, Have faith in God." (Mark 11:22)

I think, the message of the above verses is clear and conclusive and understood by the scholars and the illiterates alike.

Complicated and Confusing Verses

The Gospel also contains many statements of Jesus that are allegorical or metaphorical in nature, and therefore, the meaning or the implication of those verses seemed to be complicated and confusing to most of his followers. So, they got easily misled when the shrewd and ill- motivated people misinterpreted those verses in their own way to suit their own purpose. The verses below fall in this category.

"I and my Father are one." (John 10:30)

"I am the way, the truth, and the life: no man cometh unto the Father, but by me." (John 14:6)

"Whoever has seen me has seen the Father." (John 14:9)

Reverend, I will now try to explain those misunderstood or misinterpreted verses and try to look for the inherent or underlying message that Jesus left in them for our reflection. Let me begin first with the verse 30 in John 10, which my missionary friends often quoted to prove Jesus and God were one and the same.

"I and my Father are one." (John 10:30)

I will try to explain this verse in reference to the context. Jesus said it when he faced an unpleasant encounter with the Jews on Solomon's porch in the temple of Jerusalem. They gathered around him and began to ask him persistently to tell them whether he was the Christ or not. (John 10:22–38) But Jesus, being an inspired messenger of God, knew very well of their true motive and intention and why they were insisting him on telling something which they already knew to be true. He also understood that the Jews did not want to accept him as the promised Messiah of God, due to their low faith and also for their drifting away from the path of God. Therefore, to test their faith and to expose their true motive, Jesus said to them certain things that made the intention of their hearts quite clear.

In reply to the Jews' suspicion of him and his mission, Jesus said to them, a little sarcastically, that they surely would have known him by this time if they were his sheep, meaning his true followers. By this statement, he told them indirectly but undoubtedly who he really was and why he was sent for.

> I am not sent but unto the lost sheep of the house of Israel (Matthew 15:24).

In John 10:27–29, Jesus mentioned to the Jews about his true followers' unconditional faith and submission to God and to His commands, which he taught them to guide to His Path. In this

113

connection, he also said to them that in return to his followers' absolute faith and submission to God, he ensured eternal life for them. At this point, some of my missionary friends asked me how Jesus could ensure eternal life for his followers if he were not God?

In reply to their question, I used to tell them that Jesus was a true messenger of God and because of that, he knew perfectly well what the people needed to do to have an eternal life in heaven. On the basis of that, Jesus had no doubt in his mind that God would bless all his true followers with eternal life, as they sincerely tried to live their life through keeping His commands which he taught them. As Jesus helped them to reach their goal through his guidance, he said to the Jews that it was him (as if), who gave them eternal life.

My Father, which gave them me, is greater than all

We shall now check what Jesus said to those aggressive Jews before he made that comment in John 10:30. He said to them: *"My Father, which gave them me, is greater than all; and no man is able to pluck them out of my Father's hand" (John 10:29).*

In this verse, Jesus declared to them openly that his Father was greater than all. After this clear confession, how could he claim himself being equal to God in the very next verse for his saying: "I and my Father are one?" But the Jews, who were mostly ignorant, arrogant, selfish, and apprehensive of Jesus' true mission, obviously failed to understand the inherent meaning of his claim and began to throw stones at him on the charge of blasphemy.

It is, indeed an irony of fate that the same statement which made the Jews throw stones at Jesus with the charge of blasphemy, made his own followers worship him as God or along with God, forsaking the eternal truth of His First Commandment being preached and practiced by all His messengers, including Moses, Jesus and Muhammad.

But in spite of that, Jesus tried to bring the hostile Jews back to their senses by reminding them of a verse in the Old Testament, where God addressed His messengers as gods.

I have said, Ye are gods; and all of you are children of the most High. (Psalm 82:6)

It is interesting to note here that in Psalm 82:6, "gods" was written with a lowercase "g," but for whatever reason, it began with an uppercase G when it was put in Jesus' mouth in the verse 34 in John 10.

Jesus quoted this verse as a reminder to the Jews, so that they could not charge him with blasphemy for claiming himself Son of God. Jesus also wanted them to think why would he compare him with his predecessors if he really meant that he and God were one and the same?

"The Father is in me, and I in him" (John 10:38).

The Jews might have accepted his explanation but could not, because while talking to them about his works which he always tried to do by the inspiration of God, Jesus said to them *again, "that ye may know, and believe, that the Father is in me, and I in him."*

The Jews who were too impatient or too shallow to look for its inherent meaning, misunderstood him once again, became more aggressive, and tried to get hold of him but could not, because this time, Jesus managed to escape to a safer place, as a sensible human being would have done against the assault of a hostile mob.

Now, we shall check what did Jesus really mean when he said, "I and my Father are one" or "the Father is in me and I in him"?

In fact, verses 30 and 38 are metaphorical in nature. Jesus tried to convey to them something different or deeper than its apparent meaning. He wanted them to understand his intimate and unique relation with God that he always had felt inside him since he knew his virgin mother conceived him by the will and the command of God. Besides that, he was also a self-surrendered messenger of God and he submitted himself completely to fulfill His purpose on earth, as he mentioned in John 17:3.

> And this is life eternal, that they might know thee the only true God, and Jesus Christ, whom thou hast sent (John 17:3).

In that case, it is understood that when Jesus said to them, *"I and my Father are one,"* or *"My Father is in me and I in him,"* he meant himself being one or the same with God in fulfilling His purpose. In other word, for his total submission and obedience to God, Jesus always felt himself being united with God to accomplish His will or command on earth. If Jesus meant himself God or His equal, as the suspicious Jews allegedly thought of him, why would he say to them a moment before, "My Father is greater than all"?

Reverend, in spite of that clear confession, if you and your people claim that Jesus made those statements to mean himself God or His equal, in that case, I would like to request you all to ponder over a little with Jesus' prayer to God in John 17:21. In this heart rendering supplication to God Jesus begged Him most humbly to make his beloved disciples be united with them, meaning him and his Father, as one.

"That they all may be one; as thou, Father, art in me, and I in thee, that they also may be one in us..." (John17:21)

Exact number of God: one, two, three or fifteen?

Reverend, can you please tell me honestly what could happen, if twelve of Jesus' disciples be united with God and Jesus as one, fulfilling his prayer? I mean, if Jesus could be your God for his saying, *"I and my Father are one,"* or *'that the Father is in me, and I in him,'* the same way his twelve disciples could also be your Gods after their being united with Jesus and his Father as one. There is of course the Holy Ghost or the Holy Spirit to add with them, too. You certainly don't want me to guess that instead of worshipping Three Gods as one, you actually worship fifteen Gods as one, right?

But to admit frankly, I am still in confusion with the exact number of Gods that you worship as one. I'm confused, because according to the statement of the first commandment (Mark 12:29-30), you were asked to worship none but One God. Then, according to John 1:1, 14 and John 10:30, you claimed Jesus and God were one and the same, which tells us you worship two Gods as One. After that, the Holy Ghost somehow joined with the Two and thus making you worship the Three as one God. In that case, any sensible and open minded person would like to know what is the exact number of Gods that you worship as One? Is it one, two, three or fifteen?

I think, this type of undesirable questions arise when people worship God according to the invented doctrines of men by ignoring the crystal clear commands of God that they still read and teach in their own Holy Book. (Duet 6:4-5), (2 Samuel 7:22),(Isaiah 45:21), (Matthew 4:10) and (Mark 12:29-30).

We will now examine other verses of the Gospel, where Jesus' followers find clear proofs to worship him as God or along with God.

I am the way, the truth, and the life.

Reverend, in verse 6 of John 14, Jesus has claimed: *"I am the way, the truth, and the life: no man cometh unto the Father but by me."*

My missionary friends used to quote this verse in support of Jesus' being equal to God. But, I used to tell them that it were not Jesus alone, all the chosen messengers of God were in fact the way, the truth, and the life to their people. Then I said to them explaining that God made Himself and His Path known to the people only through His Messengers who He sent to them one after another along with His guidance. It was only through them, their people came to know about the life after death, the existence of heaven and hell and the Day of Judgment. It was only the messengers of God who told their people repeatedly what they should do to have eternal life in heaven and what not to do to save them from the fire of hell. In that sense, Jesus who God sent to his people along with His guidance and who told them clearly and categorically what they needed to do to meet God in heaven, was absolutely right when he claimed that no one could go to his Father but through him.

I think, it is like meeting with the president in the White House through his personal attaché. But, if that man claims no one could go to the president but through him, it certainly does not mean that he wanted us to believe him and the president as one and the same.

"he that hath seen me hath seen the Father" (John 14:9).

My missionary friends used to quote this verse to prove Jesus meant him God when he said who had seen him had seen his Father. But I used to tell them that it also belonged to the same kind of metaphorical statement as "the Father is in me, and I in him" or like the one I just explained above. Let us examine what Jesus really meant by his claim in John 14:9.

I believe, that by seeing God through him, Jesus actually meant that his people who truly believed in one and eternal God and also tried to live through keeping His Commands that he preached and practiced himself, would go to heaven where they could see God with their own eyes. As Jesus knew for certain that it was through following his guidance, they would meet God in heaven, he claimed whoever saw him, would see God in heaven. By this comment, Jesus also wanted his people to reflect and realize what could happen to them who saw him but did not obey him or follow his path.

If Jesus really meant himself God for his saying, "Whoever has seen me has seen the Father," he definitely would not make that statement in John 5:37 where he said clearly that no one could ever hear the voice of God, nor could see His shape. I mean, if Jesus and God were one and the same, then how could this description match with Jesus who were heard and seen by multitudes during his life time?

On Jesus' Forgiving People's Sin

Reverend, we shall now check the verse in Mathew 9:2 where my missionary friends found clear evidence in support of Jesus' deity.

"Son, be of good cheer; thy sins be forgiven thee."(Matthew 9:2).

According to the version of my missionary friends, there was none but God who could forgive our sin. Since Jesus forgave the sin of the man sick with palsy, they took him for God. But when I read this verse, I understood its meaning much differently.

The man in question was sick with an incurable disease and he was a sinner, too. But after he suffered for a long time, God, out of His own mercy, wanted to make him free from both his sin and sickness. He empowered Jesus to do it to glorify him in the eyes of his people, so that they could believe and obey him as His messenger. If Jesus really knew he was God and he could forgive sin like God, why did not he tell the man straight "I forgive thy sin," instead of telling him "thy sins be forgiven thee?"

There are other statements in the Gospel (Mark 6:5) which also tell us that except for healing a few sick people by the touch of his hand, Jesus was unable to perform any powerful work in his hometown. Not only that, he also failed to restore eyesight to a blind man at the first attempt. He needed a second try to cure him. (Mark 8:23-25)

If Jesus were God, as you claim, his power would never fail and he would not need a second try to cure the blind.

"Before Abraham was, I am" (John 8:58).

It is another misunderstood or misinterpreted statement of Jesus where he said, "*Verily, verily, I say unto you, before Abraham was, I am.*"

Jesus said it to the Jews who were still suspicious of his true motive and mission and were not yet ready to accept him as the promised Messiah of God.

One of my missionary friends explained that Jesus said "I am" to mean he was God, because in Exodus 3:14, God has declared His name as "I AM." So, my friend expected me to believe that it was a clear indication in favor of Jesus' being equal or co-eternal with God.

> And God said unto Moses, I AM that I AM: and he said, Thus shalt thou say unto the children of Israel, I AM hath sent me unto you (Exodus 3:14).

But I found, it was another metaphorical statement of Jesus which had nothing to do with the "I AM" in Exodus. If Jesus really used it to mean himself God, the translators of the Bible would gladly copy each letter of it in upper case, as we find it written in the book of Exodus. I thought it might be a slip of tongue, Jesus said "I am" when he meant to say "I was."

But when I told it to my missionary friend, he asked me back very politely, how could I explain that when we know Jesus was sent long after Abraham?

"I wish I knew how the chronology of God's chosen messengers is being maintained in the celestial world where the question of time and date does not exist. The Muslims however, believe that God has created first the light or the spirit of Muhammad long before He created Adam, though he was sent last of all messengers. May be, the light or the spirit of Jesus and of all his predecessors were made right after Muhammad in the similar pattern meaning from back to top which finally ended with Adam who was sent first as the father of the mankind. In that sense, Jesus was right, when he said, he was before Abraham was. So, what do you think of that?"

"I appreciate your imagination. But as a true Christian, I take my faith seriously. We only believe what Jesus has said in the Gospel."

"Do you really? Then, how could you believe that by saying "I am" Jesus claimed himself God by denouncing the eternal truth of the first commandment that he preached and practiced himself all through his life?

But keeping my question to myself, I said to him, "You are right. We should take the words of our Holy Books seriously. And as far as I know both our Holy Books-the Bible and the Quran tell us clearly that except God there is none who could be His equal or co-eternal with Him." Then I added, "But if Jesus meant that he was with God as His unexpressed word or command "Be" until he was born, in that case, he might claim himself senior to Abraham.

Reverend, Now, a long time after my conversation with my missionary friend, I feel myself quite happy to share with you an important piece of discovery related to this claim of Jesus in John 8:58. From further study, I luckily came to know that in the Syriac Peshitta version of the Bible, which is considered as one of the oldest known versions, John 8:58 reads, "Before Abraham was, I was."

But I wish I also could tell you how or since when this "I was" got replaced by "I AM,"-the name of the God in Exodus and got tagged with the name of Jesus to make him co-eternal with God?

Test of Faith

Reverend, many a time I've asked myself wondering why Jesus made those statements when he knew that might confuse his own followers or deviate them from the eternal truth of the first commandment of God? I can of course, explain it now with a verse of the Quran, which God revealed through His last Prophet Muhammad, about fourteen hundred years ago.

In verse 3:7, the Quran says:

> He is the One Who has revealed to you [Muhammad] the Book, some of its verses are decisive-they are the foundation of the Book while others are allegorical. Those whose hearts are infected with disbelief follow the allegorical part to mislead others and give their own interpretation, seeking for its hidden meanings, but no one knows its hidden meanings except Allah. … Those who are well grounded in knowledge say: We believe in it; it is all from our Lord. But none will take heed except the people of understanding.

Reverend, if we reflect on the contents of the above passage, we shall see that God wants to test the people's faith in Him, according to the degree, depth, and the integrity of their commitment to His will and command. He wants to do it through the combination of clear and confusing statements in His Scriptures. God says, people whose faith in Him is low, shallow, or shaky usually prefer to go by the self-made interpretation of those allegorical or metaphorical verses, which eventually deviate them from the plain, simple, and straight path of God. But people whose faith in God is pure and perfect, believe everything in the revealed scriptures comes from God, but they only follow those instructions which are plain, simple, easy and straight and also free from all confusion.

For I have not spoken of myself; but the Father which sent me, he gave me a commandment, what I should say, and what I should speak. And I know that his commandment is life everlasting: whatsoever I speak therefore, even as the Father said unto me, so I speak. (John 12:49-50)

LETTER 11

JESUS NEVER SAID OR DID ANYTHING BUT BY THE COMMAND OF GOD

"Touch me not; for I am not yet ascended to my father: but go to my brethren and say unto them, I ascend unto my father, and your father, and to my God, and to your God."
—John 20:17

Reverend Franklin Graham:

In my last letter, I have tried to explain those statements of Jesus that were metaphoric in nature. But his followers misunderstood or misinterpreted them to such an extent that they made him an object of worship and began to worship him along with God by ignoring the crystal clear instruction of the first commandment (Mark 12: 29-30). In this letter, I intend to draw your attention to some of his most plain and simple statements where Jesus made his own status absolutely clear from the eternal and unattainable status of God.

God is greater than all and Jesus, too.

"My Father, which gave them me, is greater than all." (John 10:29)

"... ... ... *If ye loved me, ye would rejoice, because I said, I go unto the Father: For my Father is greater than I.*" *(John 14:28)*

"*Verily, verily, I say unto you, The servant is not greater than his Lord; neither he that is sent greater than he that sent him.*" *(John 13:16)*

Jesus was sent by God for the guidance of his own people.

"*But he [Jesus] answered and said, I am not sent but unto the lost sheep of the house of Israel.*" *(Matthew 15:24)*

"*And he [Jesus] said unto them, I must preach the kingdom of God to other cities also: for therefore am I sent.*" *(Luke 4:43)*

"*I must work the works of him [God] that sent me.*" *(John 9:4)*

"*Jesus cried and said, he that believeth in me, believeth not on me, but on him that sent me.*" *(John 12:44)*

Jesus never said or did anything but by the command of God.

"*Then Jesus said unto them, When ye have lifted up the son of man, then shall ye know that I am he, and that I do nothing of myself; but as my father hath taught me, I speak of these things. And he that sent me is with me: the Father hath not left me alone; for I do always those things that please him.*" *(John 8:28–29)*

"*For I have not spoken of myself, but the Father which sent me, He gave me a commandment, what I should say, and what I should speak. And I know that His commandment is life everlasting: whatsoever I speak therefore, even as the Father said unto me, so I speak.*" *(John 12:49–50)*

Jesus does not judge, but God does.

"He that rejecteth me, and receiveth not my words, hath one that judgeth him: the word that I have spoken, the same shall judge him in the last day." (John 12:48)

Reverend, is it possible that Jesus used the "one" and the "same" in the above verse to mean both him and God as One or the same?

Jesus does not forgive; his Father does.

"Then said Jesus, Father, Father, forgive them; for they know not what they do." (Luke 23:34)

Jesus prayed to God more when he was in agony

"And they came to a place ... and he [Jesus] saith to his disciples, Sit ye here, while I shall pray." (Mark 14:32)

"And it came to pass in those days, that he went out into a mountain to pray, and continued all night in prayer to God." (Luke 6:12)

"And being in an agony he prayed more earnestly: and his sweat was as it were great drops of blood falling down to the ground." (Luke 22:44)

Reverend, in the verses I quoted above, Jesus made it absolutely clear that he often prayed to God and he prayed to Him more when he was in distress. Now the question is, if Jesus and God were one and the same, who prayed to whom?

Jesus taught his disciples how to pray to God.

"And he said unto them, When ye pray, say, Our Father which art in heaven, Hallowed be thy name. Thy kingdom come. Thy will be done, as

in heaven, so in earth. Give us day by day our daily bread. And forgive our sins; for we also forgive everyone that is indebted to us. And lead us not unto temptation; but deliver us from evil." (Luke 11:2–4)

Here we see that Jesus not only prayed to God himself, but he also taught his disciples how to pray to God and to ask Him to forgive their sin, deliver them from evil, protect them from temptation, and to provide them with their daily bread. Do you think Jesus would teach them so if he did not believe himself God was their only Lord, the provider, the protector, the redeemer of their sin, and the disposer of all affairs?

Jesus had nothing on which to lay his head.

"... ... Foxes have holes, and birds of the air have nests, but the Son of man Hath not where to lay his head." (Luke 9:58)

There are plenty of clear verses in the Bible and the Quran both, where God has reminded us repeatedly that He was the Creator of the heavens and the earth and He had overall authority on everything that exists in them or what comes in between. But here we see Jesus, whom you worship as God or as His equal, admitting himself openly that he had no place to lay his head, when foxes and birds have.

Jesus needed strength from heaven.

"And there appeared an angel unto him from heaven, strengthening him." (Luke 22:43)

In the verse 110 of the Chapter 5 in the Quran, God says to Jesus, *"O Jesus, son of Mary! Recall my favor upon you and to your mother, how I strengthened you with the Holy Spirit."*

Reverend, could you please tell us why Jesus needed strength from an angel, if he were God or like God? You have no acceptable answer for that. But according to the description of both the Gospel and the Quran, we came to know, Jesus needed that strength to carry out his assignment as a messenger of God.

Jesus became vulnerable at his last hour

"And he went a little farther, and fell on his face, and prayed, saying, O my father, if it be possible, let this cup pass from me: nevertheless not as I will, but as thou wilt."

"O my father, if this cup may not pass away from me: except I drink it, thy will be done." (Matthew 26:39, 42)

In the above verses, Jesus left a clear message for all of mankind that like a common and an ordinary human being, he could also become helpless and vulnerable in a crucial situation as facing death on the Cross. But then as a true messenger of God, we also find him to surrender himself completely to the will and the command of God and to accept gracefully what He desired for him.

Jesus felt himself deserted of God's mercy.

"And about the ninth hour Jesus cried with a loud voice, saying, E-li, E-li, la`-ma sa-bach` tha-ni? That is to say, my God, my God, why hast thou forsaken me?" (Matthew 27:46)

I think, this one statement in the Gospel is enough to prove that though Jesus was a mighty messenger of God, he was also a mortal human being. So, he could not help himself feeling deserted of God's mercy and crying to Him like a helpless and vulnerable person when he found his death on the Cross was imminent.

Jesus was ignorant of the last hour.

"But of that day and that hour knoweth no man, no, not the angels which are in heaven, neither the Son, but the Father." (Mark 13:32)

In the above quoted statement, we find Jesus has included himself with the rest of mankind who are ignorant of the last hour. Do you think that Jesus, whom you claim as God or His equal, was ignorant of such an important or major event like the end of this existing world? But the fact is that by admitting his own ignorance about the last hour, Jesus proved undoubtedly that he was not God but he was a true messenger of God. And like all His messengers, Jesus also admitted honestly that no one was aware of the last hour except God.

Who is that God Jesus refers to in each of the following verses?

"Hear, O' Israel; the Lord our God is one Lord: and thou shalt love the Lord thy God with all thy heart, and with all thy soul, and with all thy mind, and with all thy strength: this the first commandment." (Mark 12:29–30)

"Get thee behind me, Satan: for it is written, thou shalt worship the Lord thy God, and Him only shall thou serve." (Luke 4:8)

"Jesus said unto them, If God were your Father, ye would love me: for I proceeded forth and came from God; neither came I of myself, but he sent me." (John 8:42)

"'Touch me not; for I am not yet ascended to my father: but go to my brethren and say unto them, I ascend unto my father, and your father, and to my God, and to your God.'" (John 20:17)

"Be ye therefore perfect, even as your Father which is in heaven is perfect." (Matthew 5:48)

"At that time, Jesus answered and said, I thank thee, O Father, Lord of heaven and earth." (Matthew 11:25)

"And he said upon him, Why callest thou me good? There is none good but one, that is, God." (Matthew 19:17)

"For whosoever shall do the will of God, the same is my brother, and my sister, and mother." (Mark 3:35)

"And Jesus looking upon them saith, With men it is impossible, but not with God: for with God all things are possible." (Mark 10:27)

"But of that day and that hour knoweth no man, no, not the angels which are in heaven, neither the Son, but the Father." (Mark 13:32)

"And Jesus answering saith unto them, Have faith in God." (Mark 11:22)

"But now you seek to kill me, a man that hath told you the truth, which I heard of God..."(John 8:40)

"And about the ninth hour Jesus cried with a loud voice, saying, E-li, E-li, la`-ma sa-bach` tha-ni? That is to say, my God, my God, why hast thou forsaken me?" (Matthew 27:46)

Reverend, can you please explain how does the God, Who Jesus mentioned in each and every verse I quoted above, become Jesus and God both equally and at the same time?

Jesus' Miraculous Birth and Miraculous Acts In Support of His Being Equal to God

In spite of those clear evidences or explanation, many of my missionary friends used to claim Jesus was more than a prophet.

"May I please know how much more is it that you could worship him like God?"

In reply to that, one of my young missionary friends, a college student, mentioned to me of Jesus' miraculous birth and I opposed him saying, that Adam's birth was more miraculous than his, because Adam had neither father nor mother. He also did not go through the normal procedure of child-birth like the rest of the mankind. But except for being born to a virgin mother, Jesus' birth was similar to any of us.

> In fact, the example of the birth of Jesus in the sight of God is like the example of Adam who had no father and no mother. He created him out of dust and then said to him: Be and he was. (Quran 3:59)

Looking at his impassive face, I told him again, "Okay, if the instance of the Quran does not impress you that much, then let me read to you first four verses of chapter 7 in the book of Hebrew. I'm sure, you will find it more stunning than Adam's birth without a father or a mother."

On Mel-Chis-E-Dec's arrival

> For this Mel-Chis`-E-Dec, king of Sa`-lem priest of the most high God, who met Abraham returning from the slaughter of the kings, and blessed him;

To whom also Abraham gave a tenth part of all; first being by interpretation King of righteousness, and after that also King of Salem, which is, King of peace;

Without father, without mother, without descent, having neither beginning of days, nor end of life; but made like unto the Son of God; abideth a priest continually.

Now consider how great this man was, unto whom even the patriarch Abraham gave the tenth of the spoils. (Hebrews 7:1–4)

After I finished reading, I asked him, "Don't you think this great man's arrival or existence was more miraculous than Jesus, who people of his time knew very well how he was born and what happened to him in the short span of his life?"

In reply to my question, his missionary friend who came with him reminded me politely of Jesus' miraculous acts particularly of his bringing four-days old dead body of his friend Lazarus out of his grave. After reading that incident in John 11:39-44, he asked, "Who but God controls life and death? If Jesus were not God, how could he bring his four days old dead friend back to life?"

Miracles in the Book of Ezekiel 37, is more stunning than the miracles done by Jesus

I answered his question with another instance from the Bible which was more astonishing than Jesus' bringing four day old dead body back to life. I read to him the first ten verses of Ezekiel 37, where we came across a thrilling description of how a Prophet of God turned a whole valley of dried-up bones of a large army of Israel to stand on their feet, alive. Then I asked them both, "Don't you think if the status of God could be achieved through one's acts of miracles, the other prophet's chance of being God was invariably better than Jesus'?"

When none of them answered, I said, "In fact, it is not only Jesus or the other Prophet, we know of many other messengers of God who also stunned their people by the acts of their miracles. For example, Abraham remained unburned inside the gulf of fire for three days. Moses turned his dry stick into a live python and also made a path in the middle of the sea with the touch of his stick. Similarly, David made the trees and mountains sing with him in praise of God and his son Solomon could change the course of air by his command. Muhammad also made the moon split in half with the sign of his forefinger. But none of their followers worshipped them as God or along with God, because they knew and believed that God empowered His messengers to perform those miracles to make their people realize His power and glory and to follow His path that He showed through them." Then I added, "Jesus' true followers also believed the same about his miracles. Let me justify my point with a verse from the Gospel of John."

"The same [Nicodemus, a ruler of the Jews] came to Jesus by night, and said unto him, Rabbi, we know that thou art a teacher come from God: for no man can do these miracles that thou doest, except God be with him" (John 3:2).

"The Quran also said more or less the same thing through Muhammad who God sent after Jesus as His last Messenger."

"O Jesus, son of Mary! Recount My favor upon you and to your mother, how I strengthened you with the Holy Spirit, so you could speak to the people in cradle ... how you made the figure of a bird out of clay by My permission, and how you breathed into it and changed it into a real bird by My permission. And how you could heal the born blind, and the lepers, by My permission. And how you could bring forth the dead back to life by My permission.... (Quran 5:110).

The episode of the fig tree tells us Jesus was not a deity but a man of flesh and blood

Reverend, I would like to end this letter with the episode of the fig tree, as described in the Gospel of Mark 11, because I think, this one incident could be an eye-opener to them who believe in Jesus' deity and also worship him along with God as one and the same or His equal. On the basis of quoted verses below, I'll try to establish Jesus as a man of flesh and blood who God chose as His messenger and also sent him for the guidance of his own people-the misguided Jews.

> *And on the morrow, when they were come from Bethany, he [Jesus] was hungry:*
> *And seeing a fig tree afar off having leaves, he came, if haply he might find anything thereon: and when he came to it, he found nothing but leaves; for the time of figs was not yet.*
> *And Jesus answered and said unto it, No man eat fruit of thee hereafter forever. And his disciples heard it.*
> *And they came to Jerusalem: And Jesus went into temple, and began to cast out them that sold and bought in the temple, and overthrew the tables of the money exchangers, and the seats of them that sold doves; ...*
> *And in the morning, as they passed by, they saw the fig tree dried up from the roots. (Mark 11:12–15, 20)*

Reverend, while reading of this little episode for the first time, I had a weird feeling about Jesus whom the Muslims love and respect dearly as a mighty messenger of God. I felt weird, because this kind of intolerance, anger, or ill manner was not expected of him, who was often addressed in the Quran as being noble, chaste, righteous, and close to God. How could a rational, righteous, and a beloved person of God curse a tree for its' failing to provide him with untimely fruits to appease his hunger? Did not his predecessors suffer a lot more torture and torment, hatred and hostility, pains and persecution while striving for the cause of God?

God has His own unique way to save the truth or to expose it

Then, it suddenly occurred to me that God always had His own unique way to save the truth of His message and messengers or to expose and establish it against all falsehood. In this small incident of the fig tree, Jesus, who used to say or do everything by the command of God, left many clear indications for his followers to help them to know and remember that he was but a man of flesh and blood who God sent to them as His messenger only to guide them to His Path. So, the question of worshipping Jesus as God in any form or manner does not arise at all. We will now examine those indications that Jesus has left for his people to read, reflect and to know who he really was, why he was sent for and why they should not worship him as God.

I've already mentioned before that Jesus was ignorant of the last hour, but now we came to know that he did not know even the season of the fig. If Jesus were God, God incarnate, or one of the Gods in the Trinity, nothing could escape his knowledge or vision. But as Jesus was a man of flesh and blood, this kind of ignorance, obliviousness, or forgetfulness was quite expected.

If Jesus were God, he would be completely free from all kinds of human needs and weakness, like hunger, thirst, fatigue, or frustration, as God really is. But Jesus was a human being like any of us, so he felt hungry and also became very angry when he saw no fruit in the tree to appease his hunger.

If Jesus was the perfect embodiment of both God and man, as you claim, he should be absolutely patient, polite, calm and considerate when he saw that the fig tree had no fruit besides the leaves. Instead, it made him so angry, upset, and offended that he cursed the fig tree and made it barren forever for no fault of its' own. In addition to that, his outburst with the common and ordinary sales persons in the temple of Jerusalem also seemed to me quite rude for a godly person like him.

I think there are many simple and ordinary persons among us, who would score more points than Jesus in the test of patience, manners, and self-control.

Jesus behaved like that on purpose

In spite of that, I like to believe that Jesus acted like that on purpose and by the inspiration of God. I have quoted before a number of verses from the Gospel where Jesus claimed that he said or did nothing on his own accord but by the will and the command of God. (John 12: 49-50) On the basis of that, I'll try to justify my point with an instance from the Gospel.

In Matthew 15:32–36, we have noticed how Jesus felt the pain of hunger of the multitudes and also fed them in full with a few pieces of bread. In the same way, he could have made the tree full of figs instead of making it barren forever with his curse. But he did not, because he wanted to leave this incident as an eye-opener for all his followers so that they could never mistake him for God but believe he was a man of flesh and blood who God chose to send for the guidance of his own people, the misguided Jews.

"Have faith in God" (Mark 11:22).

While passing by the fig tree next morning, some of Jesus' disciples drew his attention to the dried-up fig tree, which he ignored, saying,

"Have faith in God. For verily I say unto you, That whosoever shall say unto this mountain, Be thou removed, and be thou cast into the sea; and shall not doubt in his heart, but shall believe that those things which he saith shall come to pass; he shall have whatsoever he saith." (Mark 11:22–23)

With this sermon, Jesus appeared again in his true form, the role of a messenger. He sounded cool and confident when he started teaching his disciples how to keep their faith in God without any question or condition and what they could achieve through the strength of their sincere faith. By this statement, Jesus also wanted them to know that turning a green tree to a dry log was nothing in comparison to moving a mountain from its place and throwing it into the sea, if only they could always remain true to their faith in God and keep it intact or uncontaminated under all circumstances.

Along with this instance and advice, Jesus also left for his followers some precautionary notes so that they could never deviate from the eternal truth of the First Commandment especially when the false prophets would come with their invented doctrines to deceive them in his name. I have quoted below only a few of them.

"Beware of the false prophets, which come to you in sheep's clothing, but inwardly they are ravening wolves." (Matthew 7:15)

"Take heed that no man deceive you. For many shall come in my name, saying, I am Christ; and shall deceive many." (Matthew 24:4–5)

"But in vain they do worship me, teaching for doctrines the commandments of men." (Matthew 15:9)

"Not everyone that saith unto me, Lord, Lord, shall enter the kingdom of heaven; but he that doeth the will of my Father which is in heaven." (Matthew 7:21)

"......Every plant, which my heavenly Father hath not planted, shall be rooted up.

Let them alone: they be blind leaders of the blind. And, if the blind lead the blind, both shall fall into the ditch." (Matthew 15:13-14)

"If you love me, keep my commandments." (John 14:15)

"Whosoever therefore shall break one of these least commandments, and shall teach men so, he shall be called the least in the kingdom of heaven." (Matthew 5:9)

"Ask, and it shall be given you; seek, and ye shall find; knock, and it shall be opened unto you". (Mathew 7:7)

"And ye shall know the truth, and the truth shall make you free." (John 8:32)

Reverend, with those guidelines in the Gospel, Jesus also wanted his followers to pay heed to the last Prophet Muhammad who God would send after him fulfilling his prayer and prediction both in John 14:16 and also testifying of his true status and mission in His final and everlasting Guidebook, the Quran.

> Therefore whosoever heareth these sayings of mine, and doeth them, I will liken him unto a wise man, which built his house upon a rock: ...And every one that heareth these sayings of mine, and doeth them not, shall be likened unto a foolish man, which built his house upon the sand: (Matthew 7:24, 26)

LETTER 12

OUR ONLY WAY TO HEAVEN AS DESCRIBED IN THE BIBLE AND THE QURAN BOTH

The soul that sinneth, it shall die. The son shall not bear the iniquity of the father, neither shall the father bear the iniquity of the son: the righteousness of the righteous shall be upon him, and the wickedness of the wicked shall be upon him.
—Ezekiel 18:20

Respected Reverend Franklin Graham:

Early one afternoon on a Labor Day weekend, when I was examining the contents on a file of my lap which I named "Our only way to heaven,"-the last topic of my last letter to you, I was revisited by Mrs. Martha Miller. From my past experience with my other missionary friends, I really did not expect her to visit me again, although she had promised to come before she left. So, you may easily guess how I felt when I opened the door and saw her standing with a sweet smile on her beautiful face right before me? Not only that, with my next and last topic of writing in my head, I again took her to be God sent. So naturally, I thanked her cordially for her second visit and welcomed her in cheerfully.

Discussion on Jesus without his atonement, means nothing to his followers

After we sat down face-to-face in the same living room beside the same coffee table overloaded with my books and other stuffs, she said to me with a polite hesitation, "I think, I chose a wrong time to come. But I was in the neighborhood and I also had some free time, so I thought...."

"Mrs. Miller, I already told you how glad I was to see you. So, feel free and fresh with a glass of cold orange juice and some homemade cookies. Just give me a few moments."

But before I left for the kitchen, she stopped me saying, "Excuse me please. I already overate in my lunch and I have to attend a housewarming party in the evening. So, what do you think, if we now try to nourish our soul with something good than perishing it with excessive drink and food?"

"You said it very well. But I think, most of us don't know even why or when our souls starve and what kind of food it needs for its nourishment?

"Right, I think you should write about it."

"Are you kidding?"

"No, I'm serious. Didn't you tell me last time that you had been writing about Jesus on your website?"

"Yes, you heard me right."

"Doesn't mean you are a writer?"

"I don't think so. You may call me a compiler, because I'm writing about Jesus as I found him in our Holy Scriptures-the Quran and the Gospel both."

"Yes, you told me so. By the by, may I please know what the Quran says about Jesus' sacrifice?"

"To tell you the truth," I said to her being cautious and careful, "the Quran has mentioned about Jesus' crucifixion, but it has not mentioned anything about his sacrifice."

"In that case, how could you write on Jesus' sacrifice if the Quran did not mention anything about it?" Then, without waiting for my answer, she added again softly, "I mean, you may write about Jesus all you want, but I think your writing on Jesus without his atonement will mean nothing to his followers. It will be like a description of the Sun without mentioning its light. I hope, you did not mind to tell you the truth so openly, right?"

"No, not at all. But, may I please know what makes you think so?"

Jesus' true status cannot be measured without his atonement

"I think so, because we believe Jesus' true status cannot be measured without his atonement. It is the only thing that separates him from all other messengers of God, because all of them besides Jesus were sent exclusively for the guidance of their own people. But none of them sacrificed their lives for the sin of their people or for their eternal life in heaven. Only Jesus, the only begotten and beloved son of God, did. I hope, now you know what Jesus' atonement could really mean to his followers and why other things of his life do not matter to them at all?"

In reply to her question, I said to her, "Yes, Mrs. Miller, I got my answer. But I don't understand why Jesus needed to give his life for the sin of others? Aren't men responsible for their own sin?" I asked her to make sure whether she tells me anything new or different from what I already heard from many of my missionary friends. While talking to her, I put a pencil and a notepad before me to jot down the points of our discussion so that I could use them later for my writing.

At first, I did not find anything to scribble as she repeated the same old story that I already knew. She told me how Adam, the father of mankind, disobeyed God by eating a forbidden fruit in the Garden of Eden. Since breaking the law of God was a sin, Adam became the first sinner and because of him all his children were born with the stain of his sin. At this point, I asked her, "You mean every child comes into the world as a sinner, without committing any sin?"

"Yes. Saint Augustine has said, 'No one is clean, not even if his life be only for a day.'"

I wondered how Saint Augustine who came a few centuries after Jesus, knew about it, when Jesus did not! I mean, how could Jesus declare openly that heaven was meant for the children, if he knew they were born with Adam's sin? (Mark 2:5) But I did not ask her, because I needed to listen to her first before I tell her finally what I learnt in the Gospel about Jesus' giving life for the sin of men or for their eternal life in heaven? So keeping my questions to myself, I said to her, "If it is so as you say, it must be a very frightening situation for all of us, Right?"

Both righteous and unrighteous were equal before God

"It was indeed, because it was a sin over which we had no control and from which we had no escape. And, because of that inborn sin, people both righteous and unrighteous fell short equally before the glory of God and were destined for hell."

I understood she was telling me about the Original Sin which Paul, a self-declared disciple of Jesus invented in the name of Jesus (Roman 1:1; 2:16; 3:23-24, 28; 5:12, 17, 19, 21) contradicting his own teaching after he left.(Matthew 5:17-20; 19:16-19)

But as I wanted to know all about it in details, I asked her casually, "You mean because of Adam's sin, a righteous person will also be considered a sinner and be sent to hell along with the unrighteous?"

"Yes, undoubtedly. It is like putting a drop of vinegar in a cup of fresh milk. The same way, the stain of Adam's sin prevented a man from being absolutely holy, in spite of all of his good deeds, thus making him unfit to deserve a place in heaven."

"But, Mrs. Miller continued, "thanks to God for His endless love, kindness, and mercy for mankind. He loved them so much that He did not want any of them be punished in hell."

"Not only that, God also wanted them all to have eternal life in heaven as a free gift from Him. So, He took a unique measure to wash their sin with the holy blood of the sinless. Now, the question is whose blood could be more holy than the blood of His only begotten and beloved Son, Jesus? I hope, now you understand why Jesus was sent to earth or why his giving life on the Cross could really mean to us."

While listening to her, I remembered that the word "begotten" from the phrase "His only begotten Son" in the verse 16 of John 3, has now been removed as an unauthorized interpretation from all the modern versions of the Bible. But without mentioning it, I said to her, "As Muslims, we also believe Jesus was holy and sinless. And, I think I told you before that the Quran did not mention anything about Jesus' atonement or giving his holy blood for the sin of mankind. So to believe in his atonement, as you do, I need to know certain things to make sure why the Quran has not mentioned anything about it." I told her so only to continue our discussion.

"Sure. What do you want to know?"

"As sin is the vital point of our discussion, I like to know first what does the Holy Bible really say about sin?"

"The Bible says sin is breaking the law of God or to do something disobeying His command." she explained.

> Whosoever committeth sin transgresseth also the law; for sin is the transgression of the law (1 John 3:4).

"As far as I remember, the Quran also says the same."

["*If anyone disobeys God and His Messengers, he has indeed strayed clearly in a wrong path.*" (Quran 33:36)]

"Now, my next question is, if sin is a transgression of law or disobedience to God, as it is said in both the Bible and the Quran, doesn't it tell us clearly that whoever disobeys God, commits a sin and becomes a sinner?"

"Sure. There is no question about that."

A newborn child becomes a sinner without committing a sin

"In that case, how could a newborn child become a sinner without being disobedient to God or breaking any of His laws?"

"I think, I already mentioned it to you."

"Yes, you did. But what you said did not match at all with the definition of sin. It matches more with an incurable and transmittable disease, the virus of which might pass through the genes of a sick father to his children. Do you think Adam's sin was a kind of transmittable virus that passed through his progeny, making them all sick, or sinners, until Jesus was sent to atone for it?"

"Yes, it is what we believe. Sin is also a kind of sickness. Man commits sin from the sickness of his heart." Mrs. Miller sounded cool and confident.

"I see your point, but if we believe so, we should also believe that God made Adam, the father of mankind, with a sick heart that was prone to sin. In that case, how could we even blame Adam for his own sin?"

"No, God did not make Adam with a sick heart. He gave him intelligence, insight and freedom of will to choose in between right and wrong. But Adam misused all of it when the devil instigated him to eat the fruit that God forbade him eating. His greed made him sick at heart, which ultimately led him to eat the fruit by disobeying the command of God."

"But like Adam, all his children were also given intelligence and freedom of choice to obey the commands of God or to disobey Him. So isn't it most expected that, like Adam, all his children could also be punished separately for their being disobedient to God? But why would God, Whom we trust absolutely for being most kind, just and fair, make all of mankind accountable for the sin of one man?"

"It is what we find in the book of Roman. It tells us *as for one man's disobedience, all men were made sinners, so by the obedience of one man, they were made righteous.*" (5:19)

I was about to interrupt her saying that it was not the statement of Jesus or any of his true disciples. It was the statement of Paul, who claimed to learn everything from Jesus through his alleged vision. I needed to know what Jesus or his true followers had said about it?" But keeping my thoughts to myself, I tried to listen to her carefully when she said to me explaining, "As by the sin of Adam, all his children became sinners, similarly, by the holy blood of His only son Jesus, God wanted to clean them all from their sin."

God made His only son die to show His endless love for the mankind

Mrs. Miller stopped for a moment and then said again with a tone of absolute confidence. "And, God did it for no other reason but to show His endless love for the world."

"You mean God took Adam's sin as an excuse so that He could use it later to prove His endless love for all by giving His only Son's life for their sin?" I asked her softly and making each word distinctly clear.

"Yes, but it is not an excuse," Mrs. Miller sounded a bit offended. "It is an instance. I think God's love for the mankind has been expressed in full strength through giving His only son's life for them."

While listening to her, I could not help myself feeling sorry for Jesus and his Father both. *Couldn't God show His endless love and mercy to all by simply forgiving their sin and putting them straight to heaven without being so unkind and unjust to His Own innocent son?* But soon I came back to my senses. I remembered clearly of those verses in the Bible and the Quran both to prove the God of Adam, Abraham, Moses, Jesus and Muhammad never took this kind of cruel and ghastly measure to show His endless love for the sin of mankind. But before I come to that, I needed to know more from her about this unique part of Jesus' life so that I could explain my point better. With this intention in mind, I said to her, "In that case, we hope the entire human race are now free from their sin and can go straight to heaven, right?"

"Right, but they need to fulfill certain conditions. They must believe Jesus as their only Savior, and he gave his life for their sin."

"May I please know why? Didn't you just say that God wanted to prove His love for the world by letting His only Son die for their sin? In that case, shouldn't Jesus' holy blood purify them all equally and at the same time, the moment it was shed for them?"

"Yes," she agreed, "but God also wanted them to show their sincere love, gratitude, and obedience to Jesus for what he did for them. I mean, how could you expect them be holy or go to heaven, if they don't even admit that or simply deny it?"

A few pertinent questions with no acceptable answers

"In that case, what do you think of those infants in the Christian family who die without knowing anything about their inborn sin or about Jesus' sacrifice for their sin?"

"Since they were born and died as Christians, we believe they will be saved through the faith of their parents."

"If so, what do you think of them who lived and died with their inborn sin before the arrival of Jesus? Or who died believing in something else as their only way to heaven?"

"I think we should leave the matter entirely to God," she answered. "He would certainly take care of them."

I remained silent for a few moments and then asked her again slowly and softly, "In that case, why did God send so many messengers before Jesus, telling their people constantly and consistently to strive for their eternal life through keeping His commands, if He knew all along that nothing could purify them from their sin except the holy blood of His only Son Jesus?"

"I already told you before that God sent them only for the guidance of their people. But after the arrival of Jesus as the Savior of mankind, everything has changed. Now, God wants all of us to seek for our eternal life through having faith in Jesus as our only Savior and in his dying for our sin."

I was about to ask her, *why then God sent again Muhammad with His last guidebook the Quran revealing the same eternal truth of the first commandment preached and practiced by all his predecessors including Jesus, Moses and Abraham?*

But I knew it was useless, because it was not easy to discard anything to be wrong which people had believed to be absolutely true for hundreds of years. So, I thought I must tell her now about our only way to heaven as it was described in our holy scriptures-the Bible and the Quran both.

So, instead of wasting our valuable time on useless talk, I said to her politely, "Mrs. Miller, I heard what you said, but I find them inconsistent with our only way to heaven that God has shown to us in both Bible and Quran." Then I asked her pleading, "May I please share with you of what I learnt?"

"Sure. I'd love to know." Mrs. Miller agreed.

"Thanks. Please give me a moment to go to my file where I stored every piece of information and reference since I intended to write about it."

"Sure. Take your time."

"Thanks." My lap was in sleep, so it took me no longer than a few seconds to reach to my file which I named "Our Only Way to heaven."

Then I said to my guest, "Mrs. Miller, since you believe Jesus had to give his life for the sin of men which they inherited from Adam, I'd like to know what our Holy Scriptures- the Bible and the Quran have really said about it. We shall check it first in the Old Testament and then in the Quran. And, finally we shall check it in the Gospel of Jesus. I think, this comparative study will help us to know about our only way to heaven as God showed to us through all His messengers including Moses, Jesus and Muhammad, right?"

"I hope so." Mrs. Miller agreed.

The Old Testament does not blame Adam for the sin of the mankind

Though I felt tensed thinking of the outcome of our discussion, I tried to ignore it. Looking at the screen of my laptop, I said to her, "Mrs. Miller, the incident of Adam and Eve has been mentioned in the chapter

2 and 3 of Genesis-the first Book of the Old Testament. We have been told there that Adam ate the forbidden fruit from the garden of the Eden by the instigation of Satan and also by the provocation of his wife. Then, we found God made both the instigator and the instigated equally responsible for what they did and also expelled them to earth, dictating the nature of punishment to each of them separately. But nowhere in the Old Testament Adam was blamed to contaminate his children with the stain of his sin. Do you know of any such statement that somehow has escaped my notice?"

"Sorry, I can't remember right now, but I can check it later, if you want." Mrs. Miller said with a bit hesitation.

"But I don't think you will find any, because while reading the Old Testament, I came across many of its statements where I found man was made responsible for his own deeds and no one would bear the burden of others." Then I said, "Let me read to you a few of them." So saying, I started reading them one by one, slowly and also as correctly as possible.

"The fathers shall not be put to death for the children, neither shall the children be put to death for the fathers: every man shall be put to death for his own sin." (Deuteronomy 24:16)

"The soul that sinneth, it shall die. The son shall not bear the inequity of the father, neither shall the father bear the inequity of the son: the righteousness of the righteous shall be upon him, and the wickedness of the wicked shall be upon him." Ezekiel 18:20)

"When a righteous man turneth away from his righteousness, and committeth iniquity, and dieth in them; for his iniquity that he hath done shall he die. Again, when the wicked man turneth away from his wickedness that he hath committed, and doeth that which is lawful and right, he shall save his soul alive." (Ezekiel 18:26–27)

"The righteousness of the perfect shall direct his way: but the wicked shall fall by his own wickedness." (Proverbs 11:5)

"For the Lord loveth judgment, and forsaketh not his saints; they are preserved forever: but the seed of the wicked shall be cut off." (Psalm 37:28–29)

After I finished reading, I said to her, "Mrs. Miller, I think the consequence of both the righteous and the wicked people was made distinctly clear in those statements, I just read to you, right?"

Mrs. Miller did not answer.

Nowhere in the Quran Adam was held responsible for the sin of his children

In her silence, I continued, "We shall now check what the Quran has said about Adam's sin. In fact, Adam's story in the Old Testament has been told and retold in many places of the Quran but in more details and also in a more comprehensive manner. Like the Old Testament, the Quran also tells us that Adam and Eve disobeyed God and ate the forbidden fruit by the instigation of Satan. And as a punishment to their disobedience, God expelled them both from heaven, along with Satan, as an open enemy to them (Quran 7:22; 20:117). But, nowhere in the Quran Adam was held responsible for the sin of his children. Like the statements of the Old Testament, the Quran also tells us that man should bear the consequence of his own doings, as did Adam and Eve. Let me read to you the meaning of some verses of the Quran in support of that."

Then I began to read from the screen of my laptop:

"That was a nation who has already passed away. They are responsible for what they did and you are responsible for what you do, you shall not be questioned about their deeds." (2:141)

"He that seeks guidance shall be guided to his own advantage, but he that goes astray does so to his own loss. No bearer shall bear the burden of another on the Day of Judgment." (17:15)

"O mankind! Have fear of your Lord and fear that Day when no father shall avail his son nor a son his father." (31:33)

"Not equal are the blind and those who see clearly: nor are those who believe and work deeds of righteousness and those who do evil. Little do ye reflect." (40:58)

"As for those who strive for Our Cause, we will surely guide them to Our Ways; rest assured that Allah is with the righteous." (24:69)

"To those who believe and do deeds of righteousness God has promised forgiveness and a great reward." (5:10)

"And those who have done evil deeds shall be flung upon their faces in the hellfire. Should you not be rewarded according to your deeds?" (27:90)

Then I raised my head from my lap and said to her, "I think the bottom line of all those statements from both the Old Testament and the Quran is one and the same. It is, the righteous and the wicked are not equal or same in the sight of God, right?"

Repentance is required for the remission of sin

Mrs. Miller maintained her silence and I continued, "Now, I will read to you some verses from both the Old Testament and the Quran where we are told clearly and categorically that we must repent sincerely for our sin and to rectify our ways of life to obtain God's mercy and forgiveness and also to return to Him safely. But before I go into that, I'd like to mention to you one small but a very significant incident from the episode of Adam and Eve, as described in the Quran."

"The Quran tells us that both Adam and Eve became truly repentant for their disobedience to God, but as it was their first mistake, they didn't know what to do with their feeling of guilt. Then being inspired by God, they learnt how to ask for His mercy and forgiveness in that kind of slip or fall from His guidance. They begged to God pleading, *"Our Lord! We have wronged our own souls: If you do not forgive us and bestow your mercy upon us we shall certainly be the losers (7:23)."*

"Mrs. Miller, the Quran also tells us that God accepted their repentance and forgave them totally before He sent them to earth. At this point, I like to mention here that with that faith and hope, the Muslims all over the world invoke God for His mercy and forgiveness till today, using more or less the same words of Adam and Eve, at the end of their five-times-daily prayers."

I stopped here for a moment to check my emotion and then said to her, "Though the Old Testament does not mention Adam's repentance separately, it contains numerous statements which tell us clearly and consistently that sincere repentance for one's sin and mending his ways of life through keeping the commands of God, were made mandatory for all to obtain His mercy, forgiveness and also to ensure eternal life in heaven. Let me read to you some statements from the Old Testament and the Quran to justify my point.

Instances from the Old Testament

"If my people, which are called by my name, shall humble themselves, and pray, and seek my face, and turn from their wicked ways; then will I hear from heaven, and will forgive their sin, and will heal their land." (2 Chronicles 7:14)

"Let the wicked forsake his way, and the unrighteous man his thoughts: and let him return unto the Lord, and he will have mercy upon him; and to our God, for he will abundantly pardon." (Isaiah 55:7)

"… if the wicked will turn from all his sins that he hath committed, and keep all my status, and do that which is lawful and right, he shall surely live, he shall not die. All his transgressions that he hath committed, they shall not be mentioned unto him: in his righteousness that he hath done he shall live. Have I any pleasure at all that the wicked should die?

saith the Lord GOD: and not that he should return from his ways and live?(Ezekiel18:21-23)

"Therefore I will judge you, O house of Israel, everyone according to his ways, said the Lord God. Repent, and turn yourselves from all your transgressions; so inequity shall not be your ruin." (Ezekiel 18:30)

Mrs. Miller was indeed an extraordinary listener. She listened in silence until I finished and also maintained her silence after I stopped reading. So, I continued, "Similarly, Mrs. Miller, there are also numerous verses in the Quran where God commanded people through His last Prophet Muhammad to ask for His mercy and forgiveness and to turn to Him in sincere repentance and also rectifying their ways of life through keeping His commands. Let me read to you a few of them in support of that.

Instances from the Quran

"If anyone does evil or wrongs his own soul but afterwards seeks Allah's forgiveness, he will find Allah Oft-Forgiving Most Merciful." (Quran 4:110)

"Seek the forgiveness of your Lord, and turn to Him in repentance."(11:3)

"Yet your Lord is Forgiving and Merciful to those who do something wrong through ignorance, but later repent and mend their ways." (16:119)

"Your Lord knows best what is in your hearts. For if you do good deeds, certainly He is most forgiving to those who turn to Him in true repentance. (17:25)

"But the one who repents, becomes a believer, does good deeds and follows the Right Way, shall be forgiven." (20:82)

"[To Muhammad] Say: O My slaves who have transgressed against their souls, do not despair of Allah's mercy, for Allah forgives all sins. Truly, He is the Oft-Forgiving, the Most Merciful. Turn in repentance to your Lord, and submit to Him before the torment comes upon you when you will find none to help you." (39:53–55)

God's Way to Heaven Remained unchanged before and after the arrival of Jesus

After I read, I said to her, "Mrs. Miller, while describing Adam's repentance for his sin, I did not mention to you about the everlasting gift of God, which He bestowed on Adam and Eve before they were sent to earth, along with Satan as their open enemy. It was His guidance for the first couple on earth and for their progeny. God said to them, with caution and warning, *"Get down from here all of you [Adam, Eve, and Satan]; Henceforth there shall come to you guidance from Me, and those who accept and follow it shall have nothing to fear or to regret. But, those who reject and defy Our revelations will be inmates of hellfire, wherein they shall live forever (2:38–39)."*

"According to that promise, God began sending His guidance to Adam and kept on doing so through all His messengers and finally ended it with His last prophet, Muhammad. But the bottom line of all His revealed guidance has always remained the same as He commanded first to Adam. It is, whoever obeys the guidance of God, will return to Him safely, meaning have eternal life in heaven, and whoever disobeys His guidance will be doomed forever in eternal hell.

"By the phrase 'the revealed guidance of God,' we obviously mean some prescribed laws that God sent through all His messengers for the guidance of their people. Let me read to you a few of them from both the Old Testament and the Quran to check the nature of those laws that God wanted all of mankind to follow to return to Him safely and what He forbade them doing to save them from being punished in hell."

The Commands of God: Instances from the Old Testament

"Mrs. Miller, there are countless verses in Leviticus, Exodus, and Deuteronomy where we find Moses pleading with his people, until his last days, to pay heed to the commands of God so that they could possess the land flowing with milk and honey, meaning heaven, which God promised to their forefathers.

"Hear therefore, O Israel, and observe to do it; that it may be well with thee, and that ye may increase mightily, as the Lord God of thy fathers hath promised thee, in the land that floweth with milk and honey.

Hear, O Israel: The Lord our God is one Lord. And thou shalt love the Lord thy God with all thine heart, and with all thy soul, and with all thy might. But, if thine heart turn away, so that thou wilt not hear, but shall be drawn away, and worship other gods, and serve them; I denounce unto you this day, that ye shall surely perish. (Deuteronomy 6:3–5)

"Honour thy father and thy mother ... Thou shalt not kill. Thou shalt not commit adultery. Thou shalt not steal. Thou shalt not bear false witness against thy neighbor." (Exodus 20:12–17)

After I finished reading the last verse, I said, "Mrs. Miller, in this connection, I like to point out that the laws of the Ten Commandments which Moses received from God, remained almost unchanged in the teaching of all His prophets, including both Jesus and Muhammad. You may understand my point much better if I read to you some of those laws from different chapters of the Quran. Then, we shall check what the Gospel, the Book that God sent to Jesus in between Moses and Muhammad, has said about it."

Commands of God: Instances from the Quran

"O Muhammad, tell them: I am but a human being like you; the revelation is sent to me to proclaim that your God is One God; therefore,

whoever hopes to meet his Lord, let him do good deeds and join no other deity in the worship of his Lord." (18:110)

"Your Lord has decreed to you that: You shall worship none but Him, and you shall be kind to your parents; if one or both of them attain their old age in your lifetime, you shall not say to them any word of contempt nor repel them and you shall address them in kind words." (17:23)

"O believers! Stand firm for justice and bear true witness for the sake of Allah, even though it goes against yourselves, your parents or your relatives. ... If you distort your testimony or decline to give it, then you should remember that Allah is fully aware of your actions."(4:135)

"You shall not commit adultery; surely it is a shameful deed and an evil way. You shall not kill anyone whom Allah has forbidden, except for just cause." (17:32–33)

"Yea, those who commit evil and become encircled in sin are the inmates of Hellfire. As for those who believe in God and do good deeds, they will be the residents of Paradise."(2:81–82)

I looked up at Mrs. Miller from my lap and said, "I think, those verses from both the Old Testament and the Quran, have made it distinctly clear that our way to heaven through having faith in one God and through keeping His commands, have remained the same or unchanged in the teaching of all His messengers whom God sent before Jesus and also in the teaching of Muhammad, whom He sent after him, Right?"

Mrs. Miller broke her long silence with a mild protest. "But I also told you that everything has changed since Jesus was sent as the Savior of mankind."

God's way to heaven has also remained unchanged in the teaching of Jesus

"Yes, you did. But while reading the Gospel, I came across many verses which tell us clearly that Jesus was also sent following the footsteps of all his predecessors and confirming the laws of the Torah, as the Quran has said about him in 5:46. Let me read to you a few of them from Jesus' own statements in the Gospel:

"The first of all the commandments is, hear, O Israel: the Lord our God is one Lord: and thou shalt love the Lord thy God with all thy heart, and with all thy soul, and with all thy mind, and with all thy strength: this is the first commandment." (Mark 12:29–30)

"Get thee hence, Satan: for it is written, thou shalt worship the Lord thy God, and Him only shalt thou serve." (Matthew 4:10)

"Think not that I am come to destroy the law, or the prophets: I am not come to destroy, but to fulfill.

For verily I say unto you, Till heaven and earth pass, one jot or one title shall in no wise pass from the law, till all be fulfilled.

Whosoever therefore shall break one of these least commandments, and shall teach men so, he shall be called least in the kingdom of heaven: but whosoever shall do and teach them, the same shall be called great in the kingdom of heaven.

For I say unto you, That except your righteousness shall exceed the righteousness of the scribes and Pharisees, ye shall in no case enter into the kingdom of heaven." (Matthew 5:17–20)

After I finished reading, I said to her, "Mrs. Miller, I think, the message of those verses is crystal clear. First, Jesus worshipped the same one God of all his predecessors, as well as of his successor, Muhammad. Second, Jesus made it absolutely clear that he was sent to confirm the laws of the Torah. Third, Jesus was not aware of men's inborn sin and naturally he was also unaware of his giving life for their sin." Then I asked her, "Do you think, Jesus would ever tell his people to keep the commands of God or to exceed in righteousness, if he really knew all men were born sinners because of Adam and nothing could purify them or take them to heaven until or unless he atoned his life for their sin and they also believed in it?"

"Jesus said so, because he wanted us to be obedient and grateful to God through keeping His commands." Mrs. Miller tried to reason.

"But why would Jesus want that if he knew that it won't make any difference whether people obey the commands of God or disobey them?" I asked her back.

"It is to check how many of his followers sincerely love God and remain grateful to Him for making His only Son die for their sin."

"In that case, what do you think of Jesus' advice to the young man who came to him seeking for eternal life?" I asked. "Okay, let me read to you the entire conversation that took place in between Jesus and that young man."

"And, behold, one came and said unto him, Good Master, what good thing shall I do, that I may have eternal life?

And he said unto him, Why callest thou me good? There is none good but one, that is, God: but if thou wilt enter into life, keep the commandments.

He saith unto him, Which? Jesus said, thou shalt do no murder, thou shalt not commit adultery, thou shalt not steal, thou shalt not bear false witness.

Honour thy father and thy mother; and thou shalt love thy neighbour as thyself. The young man saith unto him, All these things have I kept from my youth up: what lack I yet? (Matthew 19:16–21)"

"Mrs. Miller, please notice Jesus' advice to the young man in reply to his last question. He said, *"If thou wilt be perfect, go and sell that thou hast, and give to the poor, and thou shalt have treasure in heaven: and come and follow me."*

"Now, my question is why Jesus didn't tell the man straight what exactly he needed to do for the remission of his sin or for his eternal life in heaven? Why did he tell him to do so many things which wouldn't help him a bit to attain his salvation?"

Mrs. Miller shook her head, saying, "Sorry, I have no answer for that, except telling you that God says or acts many ways, the mystery of which is beyond our knowledge."

The same old answer my missionary friends used to give when they failed to provide any acceptable explanation. But I did not expect it from an enlightened and educated teacher like her. I understood once again that our faith in God, whether it is blind or prudent, is equally strong and unshakable. But in spite of that, I felt I had to continue until I could mention to her what the Gospel has really said about Jesus' atonement.

So, keeping my frustration to myself, I said to her, choosing my words carefully, "Yes, I agree. Our intelligence is too short to comprehend the mystery in the words or in the acts of God. But Mrs. Miller, we are not talking here about the creation of the heavens or earth or how God made those celestial bodies to rotate around their orbits without making them fall or crash into one other. We are simply talking here about His way to return to our eternal home from this transitory station of our life. In that case, is not it most expected that God would always show to His people the plainest, simplest, and clearest direction, so that all of them-both wise and ordinary, could reach their Ultimate Goal safely, and without being confused or misled?"

Jesus came to give his life a ransom for many

"Sure," she agreed. "And it is what God did, because what could be easier or simpler than going to heaven through having faith in Jesus' dying for us?"

The way she said, I felt a little nervous, but I tried to overcome it, because as far as I remembered, the Gospel had no acceptable evidence in support of Jesus' atonement.

So, in reply to her argument, I tried to pull up all my strength and spirit together and then said, "Yes, you are absolutely right. Nothing could be easier than that. But the problem is I find no evidence in the Gospel in support of his atonement."

"It is not true. The Gospel contains many such statements that might have escaped your notice. Let me read to you verse 28 from Matthew 20." Mrs. Miller seemed to regain her spirit. She opened her Bible and began to read.

"Even as the Son of man came not to be ministered unto, but to minister, and to give his life a ransom for many." (Matthew 20:28)

While listening to her, I felt relaxed, because I read that verse many a time since I decided to write about Jesus' atonement.

After she finished reading, she said, "I hope now you know why we believe in Jesus' atonement, right?"

"Not completely," I replied, "can you please tell me why Jesus said he came to give his life for many, instead of saying for the entire mankind?"

After a few moments of hesitant silence, Mrs. Miller said, "Jesus said so, because he knew very well that though he was sent to save all of mankind, but except for a part of them, others would deny him as their Savior."

"In that case, how could you claim him as the Savior of the entire mankind?"

"We claim so because that is what he was sent for. I mean, the cause or the purpose of his sacrifice will always remain the same, whether others believe him or not as their Savior."

While listening to her, I remembered certain statements of the Gospel where Jesus said to his disciples clearly that he was sent for the guidance of his own people-the misguided Jews. So, I said to her, "Then let us check the truth with Jesus' own statement in the Gospel ." So saying, I went back to the file on my laptop and read to her verses 22 to 24 from Matthew 15.

"And, behold, a woman of Canaan came out of the same coasts, and cried unto him, saying, Have mercy on me. O Lord, thou son of David; my daughter is grievously vexed with a devil.

But he answered her not a word. And his disciples came and besought him, saying, Send her away; for she crieth after us.

But he answered and said, I am not sent but unto the lost sheep of the house of Israel." (Matthew 15:22–24)

After I read, I remained silent for a few moments and then said to her, "Mrs. Miller, I think, Jesus admitted here openly why he was sent for. Not only that, in the next few verses you will also find Jesus tried to prove his commitment to his assigned job by refusing to cure a sick girl who unfortunately belonged to a non-Jewish community."

I gave her few moments to read and then I said, "Now I'd like to know, if Jesus could refuse to cure a sick girl because of her non-Jewish origin, how could we expect him to give his life for the sin of mankind comprising people of so many different races, religions, customs, and cultures?"

After a few moments of silence, Mrs. Miller responded, "But how could we believe otherwise, when the Gospel tells us clearly that Jesus died on the cross for the sin of mankind?"

> None of them can by any means redeem his brother, nor give to God a ransom for him. (Psalm 49:7)

"In that case," I asked, "how would you explain Jesus' statement in Matthew 9:13, where he said he was sent to call the sinners to repentance? Okay, let me read to you the entire verse." And, I read to her,

"But go ye and learn what that meaneth, I will have mercy, and not sacrifice: for I am not come to call the righteous, but sinners to repentance."(Matthew9:13)

After I read that verse, I said, "Mrs. Miller, a sensible person would like to know why God, Who chose mercy over sacrifice, needed to sacrifice His own innocent Son in such a ghastly manner? Couldn't He show His love and mercy to all by simply forgiving them and sending them all straight to heaven?" "Besides that," I asked her again, "why did Jesus separate the righteous from the sinners, if he knew both were stained equally with the sin of Adam and needed to be purified by his holy blood, as you claim?"

A few moments passed by in silence and then she said like a fantasized school girl, "We claim so because it is what the Gospel- the Holy Book of God, has said about Jesus!"

The Gospel bears no evidence to prove Jesus died on the Cross

It was then I felt really uneasy and nervous, but thinking of my true intention behind this talk, I tried to overcome my nervousness and said to her being very cautious and polite, "Mrs. Miller, both our Holy scriptures, the Gospel and the Quran, tell us clearly that Jesus was a prophet of God, and like all his predecessors and his successor Muhammad, he also taught his people to repent for their sin sincerely, to rectify their ways and to strive for their eternal life through keeping the commands of God. Not only that, while advising the young man, Jesus also left for his followers a clear instruction of what they needed to do for their eternal life.(Matthew 19:16-21) We already talked about it, Right?"

"Yes, you did. But I don't understand why Jesus gave his life on the Cross, if it was not meant for the remission of our sin or for our eternal life in heaven? Do you have any explanation for that?"

After a few moments of disturbing silence, I said to her, "Yes, I have, but it is not in favor of Jesus' atonement but against it."

"What do you mean?" Mrs. Miller looked apprehensive.

"I mean, I can explain to you with the help of the Gospel that Jesus did not die on the cross." I said to her like a recorded tape.

"O my God! Do you mean we have believed in something for the last two thousand years that never happened?" Her soft and sweet voice faltered a bit at the end, and I wished I never chose this subject for discussion. But since I did, I felt, I had no point to return, but to proceed.

So, I said, "Mrs. Miller, only a few centuries ago, our forefathers believed the earth was flat and stationary, but now we know they were wrong, because now we have plenty of clear evidence to prove ..."

"I know what you are trying to say," she said interrupting me. "But I really don't understand what this instance has got to do with Jesus' atonement, which the same Gospel we have been reading and teaching for the last two thousand years?"

"In that case, I must believe that Jesus' early followers, the Nazarenes, had a different Gospel from yours."

"What do you mean?"

"I mean there are many old and authentic books which tell us Jesus' early followers did not believe he died on the cross. But I don't need to go into that controversy, because I will try to prove it with the same Gospel that you have been reading and teaching for the last two thousand years."

"You must be crazy," she scoffed. "Do you think anybody would believe in that?"

"It is entirely up to you whether you believe it or not. But, you have your Holy Bible right before you. If you find me misquote or misinterpret anything about this most important and essential element of your faith, you can oppose me at once and I will have a chance to know my mistake and correct it. So, what do you think? Do you want me to continue?

"Sure."

"Thanks. I hope you will stay with me until the end of our discussion. I mean, until we know for certain what the Gospel has really said about Jesus' atonement, Right?" I wanted to make sure so that she wouldn't leave me with some excuses in the middle of our discussion, as it happened before many a time with my other missionary friends.

Mrs. Miller looked at her wrist watch and then said, "It is now four forty and I've to attend a party at seven. It means it is okay if I leave by six. You certainly don't need that long to finish your talk, Right?"

"Right. But before I enter into it, I'd ask you to forgive me, if I hurt your faith or feeling anyway, though I know, I won't say anything to you besides the description of the Gospel."

"Then don't worry, I'm old and matured enough to accept the truth, if I know I am wrong."

"Thanks." I felt relaxed.

Jesus was put on the Cross by the conspiracy of the Jewish high priests

Then I said, "Let us begin with Jesus' Crucifixion. I think, as a devoted Christian and a frequent reader of the Bible, you know very well that Jesus was put on the cross by the conspiracy of the Jewish high priests and the elders of his own community, Right?"

"Yes."

"You also know that they made this conspiracy, because many of them were ignorant, arrogant, and self-serving persons. They deviated from the laws of God that Moses received from Him and began to use them to suit their own purpose. At this stage, when Jesus arrived, fulfilling their dream of the promised Messiah and also confirming the Laws of Moses, they felt themselves threatened and feared losing their place or position that they had enjoyed so long in their community. And, because of that, they had the audacity to deny Jesus as the promised Messiah of God, to misinterpret his teaching, and finally to put him on the cross by framing him with a false charge of sedition. Is that correct?"

"Yes."

"The Gospel also tells us that Jesus was betrayed by Judas, one of his close companions, and was handed over to the high priests for thirty pieces of silver. Then they made Jesus arrested by the soldiers of the governor Pilate, who found him innocent and also wanted to release him. But he could not, because when the high priests and their misguided followers heard of it, they began to shout for his crucifixion. To pacify the turbulent mob, Pilate delivered Jesus to his soldiers to carry out his persecution. But before they put him on the Cross, they began humiliating and torturing him in the most cruel and disgraceful manner. Is it true?"

"Yes."

"Now I would like to know why Jesus let himself be arrested, tortured, and humiliated on a false charge, if he knew he was sent to give his life for the sin of all human beings?"

I thought Mrs. Miller would ignore this question, but she did not. She said very politely, "There is obviously a very good reason for that. Jesus knew very well that his blood was required to make the people holy from their sin. And, he also knew that the prophecies made about him in the Scriptures would also be fulfilled. So, he endured all their taunts and tortures in silence and let his blood be shed without any protest." She stopped here for a moment and then said, "Since you read the Gospel so well, you must remember what Jesus did when the people of the high priests came to arrest him. He commanded one of his men to hold his sword which he raised to strike them. And before that, he said to his disciples that he could pray to God to save him with the help of His angels, but he did not, because he wanted his people to know how much he loved them and could suffer for them to make them free from their sin. So, it does not matter to us how he gave up his life. We simply know and believe that he gave his life for our sin and for our eternal life in heaven."

Jesus had no intention to die on the Cross

"In that case, I have to read to you some statements of the Gospel where Jesus made it absolutely clear that he had no intention to die on the Cross."

164

"Now that sounds really funny. First, you told me that Jesus did not die on the cross, and now you are telling me that he had no intention to die."

"Mrs. Miller, who am I to tell you this? I only want you to know what the Gospel tells us about it. Let me read to you Jesus' prayers to God, when he found his death on the cross was imminent." So saying, I read to her from the file of my lap.

"O my Father, if it be possible, let this cup pass from me: nevertheless not as I will, but as thou wilt." (Matthew 26:39)

"He went away again the second time, and prayed, saying, O my Father, if this cup may not pass away from me, except I drink it, thy will be done." (Matthew 26:42)

After I finished reading, I asked her politely, "Mrs. Miller, do you think the verses I just read to you, bear any indication of Jesus' willingness to die?"

When she remained silent, I said, "The answer is obviously no. They simply tell us Jesus had no intention to die. But, then he ignored his own likes and dislikes and also surrendered himself completely to the will and the command of God. In other word, Jesus was ready to accept what his Father in heaven desired for him."

In her silence, I asked her again, "Or, what do you think of Jesus' grievances in Matthew 27:46 when he felt himself being deserted of God's mercy in the last hour on the Cross? Do you think, Jesus would beg God for His mercy so desperately, if he really intended to die for the sin of mankind? Definitely not. Jesus was seen grieving to God for making him deprived from His mercy, only because he did not want to die on the Cross for a wrong cause."

"What do you mean by a wrong cause"?

"I already mentioned to you before that Jesus was put on the Cross by the Jewish high priests on a false charge of sedition and therefore he had every right to save his life from this kind of disgraceful death. But

I don't think Jesus would ever have hesitated to give his life, if he knew his blood was truly required for the sin of mankind. Did not he tell to his disciples in John 15:13, that *'Greater love has no man than this, that a man gives up his life for his friends?'*

"On the basis of that statement, we believe undoubtedly that Jesus would have given his life happily, not only once but millions of times, if his life or blood had anything to do to make the mankind free from their sin or to take them to heaven. Is not the history of mankind full of noble sacrifices made by the most common and ordinary people for the sake of their country, people or freedom? So, we don't think Jesus' status or position became any less or low because he did not want to die for a wrong cause or as a victim of an evil conspiracy."

The Quran also says that Jesus did not die on the Cross

"Mrs. Miller, I already told you before that the Quran did not mention anything about Jesus' atonement, but it has mentioned about his crucifixion. Now, let me read to you what the Quran has really said about Jesus' Crucifixion from the file of my lap."

"They [the Jews] went in their disbelief to such an extent that they uttered terrible slander against Mary.

They even said [in boast]: We have killed the Messiah Jesus, son of Mary, the Messenger of Allah. But they killed him not. Nor, they crucified him but so it was made appear to them. And those who differ therein are full of doubts with no certain knowledge. They only follow a mere conjecture, they certainly killed him not.

But Allah raised him up to Himself. And, Allah is Ever Mighty, all-Wise." (Quran 4:156–158).

After I read, I said to her, "Mrs. Miller, I think the Quran has made it distinctly clear that Jesus was raised to heaven alive before he was put on the Cross." Then looking at her impassive face, I said, "But, I know you have lots of reservations in accepting the Quran as the revealed

Book of God. So, I ask you to ignore totally what the Quran says about Jesus' Crucifixion. But I am sure you won't ignore, if I tell you that Jesus did not die on the Cross with the help of the Gospel, right?"

"Right," Mrs. Miller agreed.

"In that case, I will ask you to ponder over a few things minutely from the scene of Jesus' crucifixion. While reading the description, in the Gospel of Matthew, Mark, Luke and John, I came across with a series of occurrences which suggest strongly that Jesus did not die on the cross. Let me describe them to you, one by one.

"The Gospel tells us of a centurion who saw Jesus give up his ghost with a loud cry. But it does not tell us whether he actually knew Jesus had died or not. Same thing happened with Jesus' mother and two other women who stood afar, watching his Crucifixion. They did not know either whether Jesus died or remained unconscious after he was crucified.

"Then, two soldiers came to break Jesus' legs, but they did not, because they assumed him to be already dead. But blood and water came out rushing from Jesus' side when one of the soldiers pierced it with his spear. I really feel bad to describe this ghastly scene, but it also confirms that Jesus' body was warm until then, and the circulation of his blood did not stop.

"Finally, Joseph appeared in the scene, followed by Nicodemus—two devoted followers of Jesus. From the description in the Gospel, we came to know that Joseph managed to take Jesus' body from the governor, and Nicodemus, who joined him later with a mixture of spices to put on Jesus' body and a piece of linen to cover him, did not examine him either to see whether he died or remained unconscious before they buried him in a newly dug sepulcher."

"Do you want me to believe that they buried him alive?" asked Mrs. Miller, breaking her long silence

"Mrs. Miller, I am not asking you to believe or to disbelieve anything. I only want you to reflect on some statements of the Gospel which I think have potential elements to prove Jesus did not die on the cross and he was also buried alive."

"First, I want you to think of the circumstances when Jesus was accused, arrested, humiliated, and put on the cross."

"Second, think of Jesus' close disciples, who forsook him and fled to save themselves from the assault of his hostile persecutors".

"Third, try to visualize the whole scenario when the earthquake, eclipse, and darkness followed, immediately after Jesus' Crucifixion.

"And last of all, think about how, in the midst of all the chaos, conflict, and calamity, Jesus was buried in haste by two of his grieved disciples and also for fear of their being seen or caught by his conspirators. Taking all these occurrences into consideration, it was quite human, if the question of Jesus' still being alive, or examining him for the sign of life, escaped from their minds completely before they put him in his grave. Many such things are known to happen until this day, and I think you know that too."

On Jesus' Resurrection: Points to ponder

"In that case," Mrs. Miller asked, "how do you explain Jesus' resurrection? The Gospel tells us Jesus appeared to Mary Magdalene after he rose up from his grave and also spoke to her." (John 20:17)

"But, may I please know what makes you think that Jesus appeared to Mary after he was resurrected from his death?" I enquired. "I mean, what evidence do you have to prove that Jesus died and then he appeared to her after he became alive?"

Mrs. Miller remained awfully silent for a few seconds and then said with a touch of emotion, "You may not know it, but Jesus proved his resurrection by fulfilling his own prophecy. Let me read to you from Matthew 12:40."

Mrs. Miller opened her Bible and read, *'For as Jonah was three days and three nights in the whale's belly; so shall the Son of man be three days and three nights in the heart of the earth.'* After she finished reading, she asked me straight, "By the by madam, do you know who Jonah was and what caused him to go into the belly of the whale?"

"Yes, very well. The Muslims call him Prophet Yunus. His story has been mentioned in several places of the Quran. The reason for his going into the belly of the fish is more or less the same as it is described in the Bible. But we have learnt one thing more in the Quran. It is about a piece of brief supplication that Jonah rendered to God crying helplessly in the darkness of the whale's belly. He said, '*There is no god but You, glory be to You! Indeed I was the one who committed wrong.*' (21:87)

"Mrs. Miller, Muslims all over the world make this supplication to God till today whenever they face any kind of affliction in their lives."

"It is really impressive." Mrs. Miller said in appreciation. "Since you know about Jonah so well, you will easily understand why Jesus compared his resurrection with Jonah's coming out from the belly of the whale. By this comparison, Jesus made it absolutely clear that he came out alive from the heart of the earth, as did Jonah from the belly of the fish."

Jesus was buried alive and also came out alive by fulfilling his own prophecy

I thanked her in silence for quoting this prophecy of Jesus in support of his resurrection. If she had not, I would have done it myself, as a foolproof evidence to nullify the validity of Jesus' atonement and resurrection both.

So, in reply to her explanation, I said to her, "I think, you have quoted this prophecy in support of Jesus' resurrection without thinking of its true meaning and implication. Otherwise, you could see for yourself that this one instance was enough to nullify the validity of Jesus' atonement and resurrection both."

"May I please know what makes you think so?" she sounded tensed.

"Sure. By comparing his situation with Jonah's, Jesus made it absolutely clear that he entered in the heart of earth alive, as did Jonah in the belly of the whale. And, as Jonah remained alive inside its belly, so did Jesus inside his grave. And finally, as Jonah came out alive from the belly of the fish, so did Jesus, from the heart of earth. I think, this is a clear and a foolproof evidence from Jesus himself that he remained alive after he was crucified, that he was buried alive, that he remained alive in his grave, and that he came out alive from his grave. With this clear instance, Jesus proved undoubtedly that he did not die on the Cross and therefore the question of his atonement or resurrection for the sin of mankind does not arise at all."

"Then how could Jesus live inside his grave for three days and three nights?" Mrs. Miller asked me with a bit hesitation.

"Mrs. Miller, did you ever ask yourself, how Jonah lived in the belly of a whale, which carried him deep in the ocean, for three days and three nights?" But keeping that question to myself, I said to her casually, "Maybe, the ointment that his disciple put all over his body helped him to heal his wounds and to regain his consciousness gradually. Besides that, from the narration in the Gospel of Mark (15:42-47; 16:2-6), we also came to know that Jesus stayed in his grave only two nights and one day. May be, the air in his newly dug sepulcher was good enough to keep him alive for that period."

In her silence, I said to her again, "Besides that instance, the Gospel also contains other instances to prove Jesus did not die on the Cross. He proved it through his reappearance to his disciples from his grave. (Luke 24:36-41) I hope, you remember how they became frightened when they saw him in the middle of the room saying to them, 'Peace be upon you.' They certainly had a very good reason to be terrified, because they heard Jesus died on the cross and was laid to rest in a sepulcher about three days ago. So when they heard him greeting standing in their middle, they instantly thought they were seeing his ghost or spirit, Right?"

"Yes, naturally," she agreed.

"Jesus also understood their fear, so he tried to correct their mistake. Let me read to you from the Gospel of Luke." So saying, I read to them verses 39 to 41 from Luke 24:

"Behold my hands and my feet, that it is I myself: handle me, and see; for a spirit hath not flesh and bone, as ye see me have.

And when he had thus spoken he shewed them his hands and feet,

And while they yet believed not for joy, and wondered, he said unto them, Have ye here any meat?

And they gave him a piece of boiled fish and of a honeycomb. And he took it, and did eat before them." (Luke 24:39–41)

After I read the description, I said to her pondering, "I really have no clue how Jesus' followers could mistake him for a spirit, a ghost, or in his resurrection, after he has left for them such a vivid instance of his being alive?"

"I understand your confusion." Mrs. Miller responded, "But you will find another statement a little below in the same chapter of Luke. The number of the verse is 46 which tells us Jesus was resurrected from his death fulfilling the prophecy of the scriptures. Let me read it to you."

And, she read, *'Thus it is written, and thus it behooved Christ to suffer, and to rise from the dead the third day.'* I hope, now you understand why Jesus' followers believe in his resurrection."

"Please excuse me, if I don't understand, because I also have read that prediction, and I don't find any confusion in it. I mean, it became true in Jesus' life, just the way it was told about him."

"What do you mean?" She looked puzzled.

"Okay, let me explain to you. Jesus fulfilled the first part of the prediction by going through untold suffering in the hands of his persecutors. And, he also fulfilled the last part of the prediction by rising from the dead."

"Then how could you say that …."

"It is because," I said to her interrupting, "Jesus' rising from the dead does not mean his rising from his own death. Is not the graveyard, a place for the dead?"

Mrs. Miller remained silent. Looking at the calm and serene beauty of her face, I thought I should put an end to this endless discussion before we lose our patience or get frustrated at each other. But I could not. I still had a few things left to complete my discussion.

Jesus says, heaven is meant for the children

So, I said to her, "Mrs. Miller, I think you also have read in the Gospel that people's sins were forgiven before Jesus' alleged atonement or resurrection took place. (Mark 2:5; Luke 7:48) Besides that, Jesus was seen asking God to forgive the sin of the ignorant people (Luke 23:34) and he was also seen teaching his disciples to ask God to forgive their sin (Luke 11:2-4). Does not it tell us Jesus was unaware of man's inborn sin and therefore he was also unaware of his giving life for their sin?"

In her silence, I said to her again, "Mrs. Miller, before I finish, I would read to you another brief statement of Jesus to nullify the validity of all doctrines from original sin to his resurrection that his followers are required to believe to redeem their sin and to have eternal life in heaven."

Then, I read to her the verses 14 and 15 from the Gospel of Mark 10.

"Suffer the little children to come unto me, and forbid them not; for of such is the kingdom of God. Verily I say unto you, Whosoever shall not receive the kingdom of God as a little child, he shall not enter therein." *(Mark 10:14–15).*

After I finished reading, I asked her very politely, "Mrs. Miller, do you think, Jesus would ever tell his disciples that heaven was meant for the children, if he knew they were born with the stain of Adam's sin and nothing could make them holy or take them to heaven until he gives his life for their sin?"

In her silence, I asked her again, "Doesn't it tell us that all the doctrines related to man's original sin and Jesus' atonement for it became the integral parts of Christian faith, after he left?"

In reply to my last question, Mrs. Miller picked a bottle of water from the side table and began to sip in silence.

Jesus' followers are playing the role of 'doubting Thomas'

I also took a few sips from my water bottle and then said to her lightly, "I think Jesus' followers chose to play the role of doubting Thomas."

"May I please know what makes you compare us with him?"

"Sure. The Gospel tells us Thomas was not present when Jesus reappeared to his other apostles from his grave. But when they met Thomas later and told him that they saw their Master with their own eyes and also heard him to greet, to talk and even to eat food with them, he refused to believe them and said, "Just a moment please." I said while browsing my lap. "Let me read to you what exactly he said. You will find it in John 20:25."

I went to the file in my lap and read to her. *'But he said unto them, Except, I shall see in his hands the print of the nails, and put my finger into the print of the nails, and thrust my hand into his side, I will not believe.'*

After I finished reading, I said to her a bit seriously, "I hope, you will excuse me for comparing your present mindset with Thomas'. But I did it for a reason. Thomas had no reason to doubt his close companions' report about Jesus' reappearance, but he did. Similarly, you also have no reason to doubt those statements of the Gospel where Jesus has spelled out to you clearly what you need to do for your sin or for your eternal life in heaven, but you do."

When she remained silent as before, I said to her again, "But Thomas was very lucky, because he believed in the words of his friends completely, when he saw Jesus with his own eyes after he appeared to them again, eight days later." (John 20:26–29) I stopped here for a moment and then asked her kidding, "Do you think, you can afford to wait that long until Jesus comes back again second time to tell you that he did not really die on the Cross for your sin or for your eternal life in heaven?"

In reply to my question, Mrs. Miller asked me in pleasant surprise, "Do you believe in Jesus' Second Coming?"

"Absolutely, because the Quran has mentioned of his second coming as the sign of the Last Hour meaning the end of the world.(43:61) And, Muhammad, the Prophet of Islam has also left for us a vivid description on Jesus' second coming in a series of his predictions."

"May I please know what he said?" She asked me sweetly.

"He has mentioned the place where Jesus would descend from heaven and how he would look like at that moment."

"O my God! May I please know what else he said?"

"He also told us that Jesus would fight with the antichrist and other enemies of God and finally he would defeat them all. Then Jesus would rule the world following the laws of God and maintain peace, progress and justice for all. In other word, he will then establish on earth the promised kingdom of God which you now preach from door to door." I stopped here deliberately and did not mention of his other prophecies on Jesus' second coming.

"Do you have those books with you? Can I please borrow them?" Mrs. Miller enquired of me delightfully.

"But why do you want to know what Jesus might say or do at that time when your skulls and bones will be turned into dust?" I asked her kidding. "Is not it much better to make the best use of your time, energy and intelligence to identify the right path of God and pursue it seriously when you are still alive and are able to do it?" After a moment of silence I asked her again, "Do you think, we will be given a second chance to correct our mistake, once we cross the one way exit of death and find us there in a wrong place?"

A few moments later, she asked me very politely, "Will you mind if I leave now? It is nearly six."

"No, not at all. I hope you will not be late to attend your party, right?"

"Don't worry, I'll go in time. But I thank you a lot for your educative and informative discussion about Jesus." Then, without waiting for my reply she asked me again surprising, "By the by Madam, may I please have your telephone number and the name of your website?"

"Sure." I said trying to suppress my excitement and then gave her my ID card after I jotted down the name of my website on its back.

"Thanks." She said while getting up from the couch with her bag and the Bible.

"You are most welcome."

When I opened the door for her, she asked me again startling, "Madam, would you mind, if I come again soon with some of my seniors?"

"Of course not," I said enthusiastically. "I think that would be wonderful".

"Thanks. I will call you before I come," she said. "Until then stay happy and safe."

Reverend,

That was seven years ago, and another five years have passed since then, I am still waiting for her call.

> No compulsion in religion! Truth stands clear from error, and he who rejects false deities and believes in God, has grasped a firm handhold that never breaks. And God hears and knows all things.
>
> God is the Protecting Friend of those who have faith. From the depth of darkness, He will bring them into light. .....(Quran 2: 256-257)

AFTERWORD

AN UNEXPECTED DISRUPTION

Reverend Franklin Graham:

One morning, about a week or so after my last conversation with Mrs. Miller, when I was busy editing my last letter to you, I had a phone call from my old friend Ruby, who had settled in Houston long before I came here. I felt her voice choked with a kind of strange and unexplained emotion as she asked, "Are you watching TV?"

"No. Why?"

"Turn it on and watch."

"Which channel?" I asked.

"Any channel," she said, and then hung up her telephone, putting me in a pool of worries and apprehension.

The Most Foolish Act in the Name of God and His Religion Islam

After I turned my TV on with my remote, I felt myself pinned to the ground as I watched in the CNN a replay of what had happened a few moments before. First, I thought it was an unfortunate accident as I watched a plane crash into the high tower in New York City, followed by another almost simultaneously. But soon I understood my mistake and I only wished I never saw or heard any of it. My heart completely broke as if, by a sudden blow of shock, shame, and utter disbelief, as I came to know gradually that it was a horrendous suicidal attack, launched by a group of zealots, claiming proudly they did it for the sake of God and for His religion, Islam. Their foolish act, followed by their false claim made me feel so ashamed, low, and humiliated that I wished nobody knew here I was a Muslim. I think Muslims all over the world felt the same as I did at that moment.

Anti-Islamic propaganda began in the Western Media

Reverend, in that situation, the Western Media added fuel to the fire by playing a vindictive role against Islam, with the help of well-reputed evangelists like you and others. They seemed to compete with each other to prove who could denounce Islam the most through their frequent appearance in the public TV. If some of them blamed Islam as a religion of evil, others claimed its adherents being arrogant, hostile and fond of killing or taking revenge. If someone called Muhammad-the Prophet of Islam, a terrorist, the next one denounced the Quran as a book teaching violence and hatred among his followers. Some of them even ridiculed the name of Allah, whom the Muslims call or invoke in Arabic in place of His English name God. They found the God of the Christians bigger and more real than the god of the Muslims. Others said the god of the Muslims asked them to sacrifice their lives for him or to go to heaven, when the God of the Christians sacrificed His only Son to make them holy and take them to heaven.

They continued this nonstop anti-Islamic propaganda against a religion of the one-fourth population of the world, because a fraction of the fractions of its adherents did some cruelest and most foolish act in the name of their religion. While listening to those accusations from so many scholars and religious gurus of the Western world, I could hardly expect Mrs. Miller to visit me again or ever. Neither did I expect any devoted follower of Jesus Christ to visit my website where I posted twelve letters in reply to your comment about the 'god of Islam' being different from the 'God of the Judeo-Christian faith.' So, I abandoned my idea of bringing the name of my website to the notice of the public through some AD or publicity.

Curiosity for Islam seemed to grow in people's minds

As days passed into months and months to years, I noticed the national TV channels eventually got tired of playing a one-sided game on attacking Islam. They started inviting some Muslim scholars to talk about various sides of Islam. Then I felt amazed to know that some kind of curiosity toward Islam creeping slowly but steadily into the minds of many western people. Some of them started reading books on Islam written by the open-minded Western scholars. The sale of the meaning of the Quran, life of Muhammad and even interest in learning the language and the culture of Arab countries, went on increasing among the people of the western world.

Then one day while watching CNN, I saw you in the inset of TV screen taking questions from John King, one of its chief correspondents. He asked you for your reflection on your previous comments about Islam being a very evil and wicked religion and the Muslim worshipping a 'different god' from the God of the Jews and the Christians. I waited excitedly for your answer. You looked a little hesitant, and as far as I remember, you didn't answer the first part of his question. But in reply to the second part, you said the God of the Christians had a Son whom He sent to sacrifice for their sin, but the god of the Muslims had no son and He sent none to redeem their sin or to give them eternal life in heaven. To admit here frankly, I am not sure whether you said this last part or not, though the meaning or the implication has remained the same.

Another day, I also saw you taking questions from Paula Zahn, the young and beautiful news staff of CNN. In reply to her question about your reflection on Islam, you said to her promptly that it was a very complicated religion. Then she asked you sweetly whether you had ever studied Islam to which you admitted honestly that you did not. But Paula was too good to ask you again how did you find Islam was a complicated religion without knowing anything about it?

Reverend, I would like to thank you again most gratefully, because your brief reflection upon the God of the Muslims and their religion

Islam, steered me up once again to bring my website to the notice of the public, especially the common Christians and thus giving me a chance to fulfill the purpose of my writing which is to help them know about the God Islam and also about Jesus in the light of our Holy Scriptures –the Bible and the Quran both.

In return to that, I sincerely wish you, your family and friends a long meaningful life with full of spirit, strength, health, happiness and above all, with patience and perseverance to seek for the truth, following the advice of Jesus in John 8:32, where he said:

"And ye shall know the truth, and the truth shall make you free."

BIBLIOGRAPHY

1. *King James Versions (KJV),* Thomas Nelson Publishers, Nashville, 1977

2. *New Revised Standard Versions (NRSV),* The Harper Collins Study Bible, HarperSanFrancisco,

3. *The New International Versions(NIV),* New World Translations of the Bible,

4. *The Dictionary of the Bible,* By John Mckenzie,

5. *The Holy Quran with Arabic Text, & English Translation* By Muhammad M. Pickthal, Kutubkhana Ishayat-ul-Islam, Delhi

6. *The Holy Quran Text, Translation and Commentary* By A. Yusuf Ali, Amana Corp, Brentwood, Maryland 20722, 1983

7. *Interpretation of the Meanings of the Noble Quran in English* By Dr. Muhammad Taqi-ud-Din Al-Hilali And Dr. Muhammad Muhsin Khan, Maktaba Dar-us-Salam, Riyadh 11475, Saudi Arabia, 1993

8. *English Translation of the meaning of Al-Quran* By Muhammad Farooq-i-Azam Malik, The Institute od Islamic Knowledge, Houston, Texas, 1998

9. *Merriam-Webster's Encyclopedia of World Religions,* Springfield, MA 01102, 1999.

10. *The Concise Encyclopedia of Islam,* By Cyril Glasse, Harper Collins, New York, NY 10022

11. *Muhammad in the Veda and the Puranas,* Translated in English by Muhammad Alamgir, from its Bengali Version by Prof. Ashitkumar Bandopaddhaya; from its original Hindi transcript by Dr.Ved Prakash Upapaddhaya, a great research scholar of Sanskrit Prayag University in India.

12. *What Is His Name?* By Ahmed Deedat, IPCI, Durban 4000, RSA, 1997.

13. *Al-Quran-the Miracles of Miracles* By Ahmed Deedat, IPCI, Durban 4001, South Africa

14. *Muhammad (pbuh) the Greatest,* By Ahmed Deedat, IPCI, Durban 4001, South Africa

15. *The Choice: Islam and Christianity* By Ahmed Deedat, IPCI, Durban 4001, South Africa

16. *Jesus a Prophet of Islam* By Muhammad Ataur Rahim, Millat Book Center, Delhi 110053, India

17. *What did Jesus really say?* By Misha'l Ibn Abdullah, Islamic Assembly of North America, Ann Arbor, MI 48105, 1996.

18. *The Bible's Last Prophet By Faisal Siddiqui* Al Saadawi Publications Alexandria VA 22303, 1995

19. *Muhammad: His life based on the earlier sources* by Martin Lings, George Allen & Unwin, UK, 1983.

20. *The Vision of Islam* by Sachico Murata and William C. Chittic, Lahore, Pakistan, 1998.

21. *Trialogue of The Abrahamic Faith,* By Ismail Raji, Amana Publications, Beltsville, MD 20705, 1995

22. *Is Jesus God? The Bible Says No* By Shabir Ally, Al-Attique International Islamic Publications, Toronto, Canada, 1998

23. *Follow Jesus or Follow Paul* By Dr. Roshan Enam, Al-Attique International Islamic Publications, Toronto, Canada, 1997

24. *The Bible led me to Islam* By Abdul-Malik Leblank, Dar Al Hadyan, Riyadh, Saudi Arabia, 1997

25. *What Christians and Muslims should know about themselves* By Robert W. Mond, The Forum For Islamic Work, Flushing, New York, 11355

26. *Christ in Islam* By Robson Rev. James, 1929

27. *The Christianity of Jesus* By Backwell, R.H., 1972

28. *A History of the Corruption of Christianity,* By Priestly, Joseph, 1871

29. *The God of the Early Christians,* By MacGiffert, 1924

30. *Christianity on Trial,* By Chapman, Colin, 1974

31. *Council of Nicaea and St. Athanasius,* By Corelli, Marie, 1898

32. *The Dead Sea Scrolls, The Gospel of Barnabas and The New Testament,* By M.A Yusseff, American Trust Publications, Indianapolis, Indiana 46231, 1994

33. *What the Bible Says About Muhammad (pbuh)* By Ahmed Deedat, IPCI, Durban 4001, South Africa, 1998

34. *The Life and Work of Muhammad, By Yahiya Emerick, Alpha Books, Indianapolis, IN 46240, Published By Marie Butler-Knight*

35. *What Was the Signs of Jonah?* By Ahmed Deedat, IPCI, Durban 4001, South Africa

36. *Who Moved the Stone?* By Ahmed Deedat, IPCI, Durban 4001, South Africa

37. *Crucifixion or Cruci-Fiction* By Ahmed Deedat, IPCI, Durban 4001, South Africa, 1998

38. *Jesus will Return* By Harun Yahya, Ta-Ha Publications, London, SW9, OBB, 2006

39. Riyad-us-Saliheen, Vol Two, (# 1808) By Al-Imam Abu Zakariya Yahya bin Sharif An-Nawawi Ad-Dimashqi, translated by Dr. Muhammad Amin Abu Usamah Al Arabi bin Razduk, Darussalam, Riyadh 11416, Saudi Arabia, 1999

40. *Remembering God: Reflections On Islam*, By Charles Le Gai Eaton, ABC International Group, Inc, Chicago, IL60618

41. *Izhar-Ul-Haq (Truth Revealed) part 1-4,* By Maulana M.Rahamatullah Kairanvi, Ta-Ha Publishers, London, Sw9 OBB, UK, 1992

ABOUT THE AUTHOR

Dil. R. Banu, 73, a Muslim by birth and practice, a retired lecturer of a prestigious school & college of her homeland Bangladesh, settled in America about twenty three years ago. She got a job of a substitute teacher for the local elementary schools soon after she came here, but she gave it up one year later to start a family day care in her rented apartment where all her neighbors were Christians.

This job made a turning point of her life because it was then she came to know the followers of Jesus Christ closely while living with them in the same place for more than a decade. Besides them, she also met with many Christian Missionaries both men and women who used to visit her off and on mostly in a group. The purpose of their visit was to tell her about Jesus and how could she attain her salvation through having faith in him as her Savior Lord. As a Muslim she believes Jesus as a mighty Messenger of God and what was revealed to him for the guidance of his people. She also has learnt from both Quran and Bible that Jesus never taught those doctrines which his followers believe undoubtedly as their only way to heaven; rather he always asked them to strive for their eternal life through keeping the commands of God as did all his predecessors before him and as did Muhammad who was sent after him as the last Prophet of God.

She thinks our faith in God and in His guidance should be prudent and reflective instead of being blind or self-made. As our life is most uncertain and there is no chance to correct our mistakes once we cross the one way exit of death, she believes the sooner we identify the true path of God and follow it, the better for us.

ABOUT THE BOOK

Utilizing the Holy Scriptures-the Bible and the Quran to reinstate One God for all, this book presents a series of letters written to the well-known evangelist Franklin Graham opposing his comment, 'The god of Islam being different from the God of the Christian or the Judeo-Christian faith.'

On the basis of abundant evidence from the Bible and the Quran both, the author, who is a Muslim by birth and practice, makes it distinctly clear that it is not the Muslims, as the evangelist has said, it is in fact, the Christians who worship 'a different god' from the God of the Judeo-Christian Faith. They do so by making Jesus as an object of worship along with One True God or as one of the Gods in the Trinity, which is a clear deviation from the eternal truth of the first commandment of God that Jesus preached and practiced himself following the footsteps of all his predecessors who were sent before him for the guidance of their people.

She did not write this book to prove the Christians wrong or to sell her faith to them. What is there to prove or sell which they already have with them right from the beginning?

ABOUT REVEREND FRANKLIN GRAHAM

William Franklin Graham, known to all as Franklin Graham, is an American Christian evangelist and a dedicated missionary. He was born in July 14, 1952 in Asheville, North Carolina and his father is a well reputed and much respected evangelist Billy Graham.

Rev. Franklin Graham had his education in the Stony Brook School, Appalachian State University and Le Tourneau University. He married Jane Austin Cunningham in 1974 and had four children through this marriage.

He is the founder of Samaritan's Purse-a world relief fund for the poor and needy. He is also the president and CEO of Billy Graham Evangelist Association. He has become an international Christian for his relief and missionary work throughout the world.

In spite of his busy missionary life, he also wrote some books especially for the children. .

Some of them are: Kids praying For Kids, Operation Christmas Child and Miracles in a shoebox.

Rev. Franklin Graham has made himself a controversial religious personality through many of his abrupt and demeaning comments against Islam-the latest and the fastest growing religion of nearly one-fourth population of the world.

Printed in the United States
By Bookmasters